David Brainerd, Jonathan Edwards

An Account of the Life of the Reverend David Brainerd

Minister of the Gospel, missionary to the Indians from the Honourable Society in Scotland for the Propagation of Christian Knowledge

David Brainerd, Jonathan Edwards

An Account of the Life of the Reverend David Brainerd
Minister of the Gospel, missionary to the Indians from the Honourable Society in Scotland for the Propagation of Christian Knowledge

ISBN/EAN: 9783337191351

Printed in Europe, USA, Canada, Australia, Japan

Cover: Foto ©Lupo / pixelio.de

More available books at **www.hansebooks.com**

LIFE

OF THE REVEREND

DAVID BRAINERD,

MINISTER OF THE GOSPEL; MISSIONARY TO THE INDIANS FROM THE HONOURABLE SOCIETY, IN SCOTLAND, FOR THE PROPAGATION OF CHRISTIAN KNOWLEDGE; AND PASTOR OF A CHURCH OF CHRISTIAN INDIANS IN NEW-JERSEY.

Who died at NORTHAMPTON, in New-England, October 9th, 1747, in the 30th year of his age.

CHIEFLY TAKEN FROM HIS OWN DIARY, AND OTHER PRIVATE WRITINGS, WRITTEN FOR HIS OWN USE.

By JONATHAN EDWARDS, A. M.
LATE PRESIDENT OF THE COLLEGE IN NEW-JERSEY.

TO WHICH ARE ADDED

EXTRACTS from Mr. BRAINERD's JOURNAL,

COMPRISING THE MOST MATERIAL THINGS IN THAT PUBLICATION.

PRINTED AT WORCESTER, MASSACHUSETTS,
By LEONARD WORCESTER,
MDCCXCIII.

THE EDITOR's PREFACE.

It is acknowledged on all hands that one method of conveying religious and moral instruction is by example. This is a medium of disseminating truth, and extending the influence of virtue, which is accommodated to every capacity, and adapted in a peculiar manner to meet the feelings of mankind. Examples, drawn justly, exhibit the deformity of vice, and the beauty of virtue; not with the languor of mere speculation, but with the energy of striking fact, in which the legitimate effect of sentiment is seen. The example furnished in the following pages is that of strict and almost unvarying piety. The christian life of Mr. Brainerd, though short, was lovely. It was such as has strikingly adorned the doctrine of God our Saviour, and, as delineated in this volume, presents the most salutary instruction to all descriptions of men. It is removed from ostentatious seeming zeal on the one hand, and a stupid inaction on the other; from enthusiasm, and formality. Here we may see the leading sentiments of the gospel, having their genuine influence on the heart, and

reduced

reduced to a uniform practice; the real spirit of christianity, stripped of all disguise, and forming an obvious contrast to the barren indevout lives of thousands of professors. Mr. Brainerd was a christian, not in name only; but in reality, in life, in the progressive ardour of true godliness. His religion was supernatural, and experimental; founded in holy love, constituting a bond of union to God, embracing all the interests of his government, and resembling his pure nature. It was not the mere decency of a reformed life, the popular goodness of the present day. It reached the heart, and formed the character of the whole man. It did not consist in a being proselyted to one party or the other, but in a cordial, unconditional, persevering devotedness to God through the grace which is by Jesus Christ. Since instances of equal piety are rare, especially at the present day, it is happy for the cause of religion that such a life has been preserved from oblivion, and that, through the medium of the press, it may be spread abroad, as an object of refreshing contemplation to God's people, and as a source of restraint and conviction to sinners. The Life of Mr. Brainerd, presented to the publick by President Edwards, of which the following, excepting some few retrenchments, is an exact copy, has always been read with pleasure and improvement by the friends of pure christianity. And the editor cannot but flatter himself, that, under the blessing of God, the present edition may have its utility, in the security of the same great objects, the conviction of sinners, and the edification and consolation of some, at least, of the children of Zion

PREFACE.

Zion. The authenticity of what is exhibited in the Life and Journal of Mr. Brainerd, can admit of no doubt; since the former was published by a gentleman whose reputation for learning, integrity, and universal piety, is established even beyond the cavils of impiety itself, and was compiled by him chiefly from Mr. Brainerd's own Diary; and since the latter was written by Mr. Brainerd's own hand, was attested by several reputable ministers of the gospel, and was published under the sanction and patronage of the Society for propagating Christian Knowledge in Scotland. With respect to the retrenchments which have been made, the editor has exercised his best judgment. Nothing, in fact, has been suppressed which was of importance to an impartial display of Mr. Brainerd's character; nothing but what had either been repeatedly said before, or was local, or referred to circumstances in which the reader cannot be interested. The object of the retrenchments was merely to exclude what was superfluous, without concealing a single trait of character, or a single sentiment; to reduce, in short, all that was considerably valuable within a smaller compass. Whatever opinion the critical reader may have of this alteration; whether he may think it an amendment or disservice, the editor is confident, that the volume, as it is now presented, will be deemed by all the friends of experimental religion as a valuable possession. If we have a taste for moral beauty, if we love what constitutes the glory of God himself, we shall find satisfaction in perusing the following pages. May we find spiritual improvement also. May *we be prompted, in imitation of this eminent servant of God, to gird up the loins of our minds, to make an habitual consecration of ourselves to the will and service of God, and like him find, in our own progressive experience, that* the ways of wisdom are ways of pleasantness, and that all her paths are peace. *The serious reader will unavoidably make an estimate of his own spiritual state, in a comparison with what Mr. Brainerd appears to have experienced, and the manner in which he lived. The trial will be severe; but if made judiciously it can have no ill effect. As, however, some of God's people, who are rather prone to view things on the dark side, may be in danger of miscalculating, it cannot be improper to observe, that a man may be a real christian, though he be not of the stature of Mr. Brainerd. His life is not exhibited to the publick view as a standard, to the complete measure of which every one must come or not be saved. It is believed that the spirit of vital christianity is in its nature every where the same, and that, in the general, the same things in kind must be experienced, the same affections exercised, and the same holy conversation maintained: But of true christians there are undoubtedly some of a larger, and some of a smaller growth. If we have the distinguishing evidences of a state of grace, though not with the same indubitable clearness with which Mr. Brainerd seems to have been favoured, we are allowed to entertain hope towards God, and should do wrong to reject the consolations which infinite mercy may present us. The strong ought to bear the infirmities of the weak; and the weak, instead*

PREFACE.

stead of sinking into a dejected unprofitable despondency, ought to press forward to perfection.

It is manifest that Mr Brainerd was, from his constitutional habit, inclined to melancholy. His bodily health was generally low. And the peculiar circumstances into which he was thrown in the prosecution of his publick duty, conspired with his natural infirmities to plunge him often into extreme dejection. This dejection the careless reader may impute to his particular views of christianity. But they ought not to be confounded. This dejection formed no part of his religion. It was merely animal. His religion, in fact, was his only relief from his depressions. That the reader may be exempted from that unhappy portion of his experience and enjoy the infinitely precious part, the divine consolations with which he was favoured, is the fervent prayer of his friend and servant in Jesus Christ,

SAMUEL AUSTIN.

WORCESTER, May 29th, 1793.

ADVERTISEMENT.

ADVERTISEMENT.

IN the subscription papers the publick had a partial encouragement that should the subscribers be numerous, there would be a diminution of the price. The expectations of the Editor are not fully answered in this respect. But had they been answered, the addition of more than fifty pages to the number mentioned in the conditions will be considered as an ample equivalent to such a benefit, and be a security from all possible imputation.

THE
LIFE
OF THE REVEREND
DAVID BRAINERD.

PART I.

From his BIRTH, *to the time when he began to devote himself to the* STUDY *of* DIVINITY, *in order to his being fitted for the Work of the* MINISTRY.

MR. David Brainerd was born April 20, 1718, at Haddam, a town belonging to the county of Middlesex, in the state of Connecticut, New-England. His father, who died when this his son was about nine years of age, was the Worshipful Hezekiah Brainerd, Esq; an assistant, or one of his Majesty's Council for the then colony, and the son of Daniel Brainerd, Esq; a justice of the peace, and a deacon of the church of Christ in Haddam. His mother was Mrs. Dorothy Hobart, daughter to the Rev. Mr. Jeremiah Hobart, who preached a while at Topsfield, and then removed to Hempstead on Long-Island, and afterwards removed from Hempstead (by reason of numbers turning Quakers, and many others being so irreligious, that they would do nothing towards the support of the ministry) and came and settled in the work of the ministry at Haddam: Where he died in the 85th year of his age: Of whom it is remarkable, that he went to the publick

lick worship in the forenoon, and died in his chair between meetings. And this Rev. gentleman was son of the Rev. Mr. Peter Hobart, who was first minister of the gospel at Hingham, in the county of Norfolk in England, and by reason of the persecution of the puritans, removed with his family to New-England, and was settled in the ministry at Hingham, in Massachusetts. The mother of Mrs. Dorothy Hobart (who was afterwards Brainerd) was daughter to the Rev. Mr. Samuel Whiting, minister of the gospel, first at Boston in Lincolnshire, and afterwards at Lynn in Massachusetts, New-England: He had three sons that were ministers of the gospel.

Mr. David Brainerd was the third son of his parents. They had five sons and four daughters. Their eldest son was Hezekiah Brainerd, Esq; a justice of the peace, and for several years a representative of the town of Haddam, in the General Assembly of Connecticut. The second was the Rev. Mr. Nehemiah Brainerd, a worthy minister at Eastbury in Connecticut, who died of a consumption, November 10, 1742. The fourth was Mr. John Brainerd, who succeeded his brother David, as missionary to the Indians, and pastor of the same church of christian Indians in New-Jersey: And the fifth was Israel, student at Yale-College in New-Haven, who died soon after his brother David. Mrs. Dorothy Brainerd having lived several years a widow, died when her son, (whose life I am about to give an account of,) was about fourteen years of age: So that in his youth he was left both fatherless and motherless. What account he has given of himself, and his own life, may be seen in what follows.]

I WAS, I think, from my youth, something sober, and inclined rather to melancholy, than the contrary extreme; but do not remember any thing of conviction of sin, worthy of remark, until I was, I believe,

about

about seven or eight years of age; when I became something concerned for my soul, and terrified at the thoughts of death, and was driven to the performance of duties*. But it appeared a melancholy business, and destroyed my eagerness for play. And alas! this religious concern was but shortlived. However, I sometimes attended secret prayer; and thus lived at *ease in Zion, without God in the world,* and without much concern, as I remember, until I was above thirteen years of age. But some time in the winter, 1732, I was something roused out of carnal security, by I scarce knew what means at first; but was much excited by the prevailing of a mortal sickness in Haddam. I was frequent, constant, and something fervent in duties, and took delight in reading, especially Mr. Janeway's Token for Children; I felt sometimes much melted in duties, and took great delight in the performance of them: And I sometimes hoped that I was converted, or at least in a good and hopeful way for heaven and happiness, not knowing what conversion was. The Spirit of God at this time proceeded far with me; I was remarkably dead to the world, and my thoughts were almost wholly employed about my soul's concerns; and I may indeed say, *almost I was persuaded to be a christian.* I was also exceedingly distressed and melancholy at the death of my mother, in March, 1732. But afterwards my religious concern began to decline, and I by degrees fell back into a considerable degree of security; though I still attended secret prayer frequently.

About the 15th of April, 1733, I removed from my father's house to East-Haddam, where I spent four years, but still *without God in the world;* though

for

---

* The reader will find from the general current of Mr. Brainerd's writings, that by the term *duty*, he doth not mean any real, genuine compliance with the law or gospel, but certain external performances, the result of conviction and concern only, and entirely compatible with reigning enmity of heart to God.

for the most part I went a round of secret duty. I was not exceedingly addicted to young company, or frolicking (as it is called.) But this I know, that when I did go into company, I never returned from a frolick in my life, with so good a conscience as I went with: It always added new guilt to me, and made me afraid to come to the throne of grace, and spoiled those good frames, I was wont sometimes to please myself with. But alas! all my good frames were but self righteousness, not bottomed on a desire for the glory of God.

About the latter end of April, 1737, being full nineteen years of age, I removed to Durham, and began to work on my farm, and so continued the year out, or near, until I was twenty years old, frequently longing, from a natural inclination, after a liberal education. When I was about twenty years of age, I applied myself to study; and some time before, was more than ordinarily excited to and in duty: But now engaged more than ever in the duties of religion. I became very strict, and watchful over my thoughts, words, and actions; and thought I must be sober indeed, because I designed to devote myself to the ministry; and imagined I did dedicate myself to the Lord.

Some time in April, 1738, I went to Mr. Fiske's, and lived with him, during his life*. And I remember, he advised me wholly to abandon young company, and associate myself with grave elderly people: Which counsel I followed; and my manner of life was now exceeding regular, and full of religion, such as it was: For I read my Bible more than twice through in less than a year, I spent much time every day in secret prayer, and other secret duties: I gave great attention to the word preached, and endeavoured to my utmost to retain it. So much concerned was

---

* Mr. Fiske was the pastor of the church in Haddam.

was I about religion, that I agreed with some young persons to meet privately on Sabbath evenings for religious exercises, and thought myself sincere in these duties; and after our meeting was ended, I used to repeat the discourses of the day to myself, and recollect what I could, though sometimes it was very late in the night. Again on Monday mornings, I used sometimes to recollect the same sermons. And I had sometimes considerable movings of affections in duties, and much pleasure, and had many thoughts of joining to the church. In short, I had a very good outside, and rested entirely on my duties, though I was not sensible of it.

After Mr. Fiske's death, I proceeded in my learning with my brother; and was still very constant in religious duties, and often wondered at the levity of professors; it was a trouble to me, that they were so careless in religious matters. Thus I proceeded a considerable length on a self righteous foundation; and should have been entirely lost and undone, had not the mere mercy of God prevented.

Some time in the beginning of winter, anno 1738, it pleased God, on one Sabbath day morning, as I was walking out for some secret duties (as I remember) to give me on a sudden such a sense of my danger and the wrath of God, that I stood amazed, and my former good frames, that I had pleased myself with, all presently vanished; and from the view, that I had of my sin and vileness, I was much distressed all that day, fearing the vengeance of God would soon overtake me; I was much dejected, and kept much alone, and sometimes begrudged the birds and beasts their happiness, because they were not exposed to eternal misery, as I evidently saw I was. And thus I lived from day to day, being frequently in great distress. Sometimes there appeared mountains before me to obstruct my hopes of mercy; and
the

the work of conversion appeared so great, I thought I should never be the subject of it: But used however, to pray and cry to God, and perform other duties with great earnestness, and hoped by some means to make the case better. And though I, hundreds of times, renounced all pretences of any worth in my duties (as I thought) even in the season of the performance of them, and often confessed to God that I deserved nothing for the very best of them, but eternal condemnation: Yet still I had a secret latent hope of recommending myself to God by my religious duties; and when I prayed affectionately, and my heart seemed in some measure to melt, I hoped God would be thereby moved to pity me; my prayers then looked with some appearance of goodness in them, and I seemed to mourn for sin; and then I could in some measure venture on the mercy of God in Christ, (as I thought;) though the preponderating thought and foundation of my hope was some imagination of goodness in my heart meltings, and flowing of affections in duty, and sometimes extraordinary enlargements therein, &c. Though at some times the gate appeared so very strait, that it looked next to impossible to enter, yet at other times I flattered myself that it was not so very difficult, and hoped I should by diligence and watchfulness soon gain the point. Sometimes after enlargement in duty and considerable affection, I hoped I had made a good step towards heaven, and imagined that God was affected as I was, and that he would hear such sincere cries, (as I called them) and so sometimes when I withdrew for secret duties in great distress, I returned something comfortable; and thus healed myself with my duties.

Some time in February, 1738,9, I set apart a day for secret fasting and prayer, and spent the day in almost incessant cries to God for mercy, that he would open my eyes to see the evil of sin, and the way of life by Jesus Christ. And God was pleased that day to make considerable discoveries of my heart to me: But still I trusted in all the duties I performed; though there was no manner of goodness in the duties I then performed, there being no manner of respect to the glory of God in them, nor any such principle in my heart: Yet God was pleased to make my endeavours that day, a means to shew me my helplessness, in some measure.

Sometimes I was greatly encouraged, and imagined that God loved me and was pleased with me, and thought I should soon be fully reconciled to God; while the whole was founded on mere presumption, arising from enlargement in duty, or flowing of affections, or some good resolutions, and the like. And when, at times, great distress began to arise, on a sight of my vileness and nakedness, and inability to deliver myself from a sovereign God, I used to put off the discovery, as what I could not bear. Once, I remember, a terrible pang of distress seized me, and the thoughts of renouncing myself, and standing naked before God, stripped of all goodness, were so dreadful to me, that I was ready to say to them as Felix to Paul, *Go thy way for this time*. Thus, though I daily longed for greater conviction of sin, supposing that I must see more of my dreadful state in order to a remedy, yet when the discoveries of my vile hellish heart were made to me, the sight was so dreadful, and shewed me so plainly my exposedness to damnation, that I could not endure it. I constantly strove after whatever qualifications, I imagined others obtained before the reception of Christ, in order to recommend me to his favour. Sometimes I felt the power of an hard heart, and supposed it must be softened before Christ would accept of me; and when I felt any meltings of heart,

I hoped now the work was almoſt done: And hence, when my diſtreſs ſtill remained, I was wont to murmur at God's dealings with me; and thought, when others felt their hearts ſoftened, God ſhewed them mercy: But my diſtreſs remained ſtill.

Sometimes I grew remiſs and ſluggiſh, without any great convictions of ſin, for a conſiderable time together; but after ſuch a ſeaſon, convictions ſometimes ſeized me more violently. One night I remember in particular, when I was walking ſolitarily abroad, I had opened to me ſuch a view of my ſin, that I feared the ground would cleave aſunder under my feet, and become my grave, and ſend my ſoul quick into hell, before I could get home. And though I was forced to go to bed, leſt my diſtreſs ſhould be diſcovered by others, which I much feared; yet I ſcarce durſt ſleep at all, for I thought it would be a great wonder if I ſhould be out of hell in the morning. And though my diſtreſs was ſometimes thus great, yet I greatly dreaded the loſs of convictions, and returning back to a ſtate of carnal ſecurity, and to my former inſenſibility of impending wrath; which made me exceeding exact in my behaviour, leſt I ſhould ſtifle the motions of God's Spirit. When at any time I took a view of my convictions of my own ſinfulneſs, and thought the degree of them to be conſiderable, I was wont to truſt in my convictions: But this confidence, and the hopes that aroſe in me from it, of ſoon making ſome notable advances towards deliverance, would eaſe my mind, and I ſoon became more ſenſeleſs and remiſs: But then again when I diſcerned my convictions to grow languid, and I thought them about to leave me, this immediately alarmed and diſtreſſed me. Sometimes I expected to take a large ſtep, and get very far towards converſion by ſome particular opportunity or means I had in view.

The

The many disappointments, and great distresses and perplexity I met with, put me into a most horrible frame of contesting with the Almighty; with an inward vehemence and virulence, finding fault with his ways of dealing with mankind. I found great fault with the imputation of Adam's sin to his posterity: And my wicked heart often wished for some other way of salvation than by Jesus Christ: And being *like the troubled sea,* and my thoughts confused, I used to contrive to escape the wrath of God by some other means, and had strange projections, full of Atheism, contriving to disappoint God's designs and decrees concerning me, or to escape God's notice, and hide myself from him: But when, upon reflection, I saw these projections were vain, and would not serve me, and that I could contrive nothing for my own relief, this would throw my mind into the most horrid frame, to wish there was no God, or to wish there were some other God that could control him, &c. These thoughts and desires were the secret inclinations of my heart, that were frequently acting before I was aware; but alas, they were mine! although I was affrighted with them, when I came to reflect on them: When I considered of it, it distressed me, to think that my heart was so full of *enmity against God ;* and it made me tremble, lest God's vengeance should suddenly fall upon me. I used before to imagine my heart was not so bad as the scriptures and some other books represented. Sometimes I used to take much pains to work it up into a good frame, a humble submissive disposition; and hoped there was then some goodness in me: But it may be on a sudden, the thoughts of the strictness of the law, or the sovereignty of God, would so irritate the corruption of my heart, that I had so watched over, and hoped I had brought to a good frame, that it would break over all bounds, and burſt forth on all ſides, like floods of waters, when they break down their dam. But being ſenſible of the neceſſity of a deep humiliation in order to a ſaving cloſe with Chriſt, I uſed to ſet myſelf to work in my own heart thoſe convictions, that were requiſite in ſuch an humiliation: As, a conviction, that God would be juſt, if he caſt me off forever; and that if ever God ſhould beſtow mercy on me, it would be mere grace, though I ſhould be in diſtreſs many years firſt, and be never ſo much engaged in duty; that God was not in the leaſt obliged to pity me the more for all paſt duties, cries, and tears, &c. Theſe things I ſtrove to my utmoſt to bring myſelf to a firm belief of, and hearty aſſent to; and hoped that now I was brought off from myſelf, and truly humbled and bowed to the divine ſovereignty; and was wont to tell God in my prayers, that now I had thoſe very diſpoſitions of ſoul that he required, and on which he ſhewed mercy to others, and thereupon to beg and plead for mercy to me: But when I found no relief, and was ſtill oppreſſed with guilt and fears of wrath, my ſoul was in a tumult, and my heart roſe againſt God, as dealing hardly with me. Yet then my conſcience flew in my face, putting me in mind of my late confeſſion to God of his juſtice in my condemnation, &c. And this, giving me a ſight of the badneſs of my heart, threw me again into diſtreſs, and I wiſhed I had watched my heart more narrowly, to keep it from breaking out againſt God's dealings with me, and I even wiſhed I had not pleaded for mercy on account of my humiliation, becauſe thereby I had loſt all my ſeeming goodneſs.

Thus, ſcores of times, I vainly imagined myſelf humbled and prepared for ſaving mercy.

While I was in this diſtreſſed, bewildered, and tumultuous ſtate of mind, the corruption of my heart

heart was especially irritated with these things following:

1. The strictness of the divine law. For I found it was impossible for me, after my utmost pains, to answer the demands of it. I often made new resolutions, and as often broke them. I imputed the whole to carelessness, and the want of being more watchful, and used to call myself a fool for my negligence: But when, upon a stronger resolution, and greater endeavours, and close application of myself to fasting and prayer, I found all attempts fail, then I quarrelled with the law of God, as unreasonably rigid. I thought, if it extended only to my outward actions and behaviour, I could bear with it: But I found it condemned me for my evil thoughts, and sins of my heart, which I could not possibly prevent. I was extremely loth to give out, and own my utter helplessness in this matter: But after repeated disappointments, thought that, rather than perish, I could do a little more still, especially if such and such circumstances might but attend my endeavours and strivings; I hoped that I should strive more earnestly than ever, if the matter came to extremity (though I never could find the time to do my utmost, in the manner I intended:) And this hope of future more favourable circumstances, and of doing something great hereafter, kept me from despair in myself, and from seeing myself fallen into the hands of a sovereign God, and dependent on nothing but free and boundless grace:

2. Another thing was, that faith alone was the condition of salvation; and that God would not come down to lower terms, that he would not promise life and salvation upon my sincere and hearty prayers and endeavours. That word, Mark xvi. 16. *He that believeth not, shall be damned*, cut off all hope there: And I found, faith was the sovereign gift of God; that I could not get it as of myself, and could

not oblige God to bestow it upon me, by any of my performances. Eph. ii. 1. 8. *This*, I was ready to say, *is a hard saying, Who can hear it?* I could not bear, that all I had done should stand for mere nothing, who had been very conscientious in duty, and had been exceeding religious a great while, and had (as I thought) done much more than many others that had obtained mercy. I confessed indeed the vileness of my duties ; but then, what made them at that time seem vile, was my wandering thoughts in them ; not because I was all over defiled like a devil, and the principle corrupt from whence they flowed, so that I could not possibly do any thing that was good. And therefore I called what I did, by the name of honest faithful endeavours ; and could not bear it, that God had made no promises of salvation to them.

3. Another thing was, that I could not find out what faith was ; or what it was to believe, and come to Christ. I read the calls of Christ, made to the weary and heavy laden ; but could find no way, that he directed them to come in. I thought, I would gladly come, if I knew how, though the path of duty directed to were never so difficult. I read Mr. Stoddard's Guide to Christ (which I trust was, in the hand of God, the happy means of my conversion) and my heart rose against the author ; for though he told me my very heart all along under convictions, and seemed to be very beneficial to me in his directions ; yet here he failed, he did not tell me any thing I could do, that would bring me to Christ, but left me as it were with a great gulf between me and Christ, without any direction to get through. For I was not yet effectually and experimentally taught, that there could be no way prescribed, whereby a natural man could, of his own strength, obtain that which is supernatural, and which the highest angel cannot give.

4. Another

4. Another thing that I found a great inward opposition to, was the sovereignty of God. I could not bear, that it should be wholly at God's pleasure, to save or damn me, just as he would. That passage, Rom. ix. 11—23. was a constant vexation to me, especially verse 21. The reading or meditating on this always destroyed my seeming good frames: When I thought I was almost humbled, and almost resigned to God's sovereignty, the reading or thinking on this passage would make my enmity against the sovereignty of God appear. And when I came to reflect on my inward enmity and blasphemy, that arose on this occasion, I was the more afraid of God, and driven further from any hopes of reconciliation with him; and it gave me such a dreadful view of myself, that I dreaded more than ever to see myself in God's hands, and at his sovereign disposal, and it made me more opposite than ever to submit to his sovereignty; for I thought God designed my damnation.

All this time the Spirit of God was powerfully at work with me; and I was inwardly pressed to relinquish all self confidence, all hopes of ever helping myself by any means whatsoever: And the conviction of my lost estate was sometimes so clear and manifest before my eyes, that it was as if it had been declared to me in so many words, "It is done, it is done, it is forever impossible to deliver yourself." For about three or four days, my soul was thus distressed, especially at some turns, when for a few moments I seemed to myself lost and undone; but then would shrink back immediately from the sight, because I dared not venture myself into the hands of God, as wholly helpless, and at the disposal of his sovereign pleasure. I dared not see that important truth concerning myself, that I was *dead in trespasses and sins*. But when I had as it were thrust away these views of myself at any time, I felt distressed to have the same discoveries of myself again ; for I greatly feared being given over of God to final stupidity. When I thought of putting it off to *a more convenient season*, the conviction was so close and powerful with regard to the present time, that it was the best time, and probably the only time, that I dared not put it off. It was the sight of truth concerning myself, truth respecting my state, as a creature fallen and alienated from God, and that consequently could make no demands on God for mercy, but must subscribe to the absolute sovereignty of the Divine Being ; the sight of the truth, I say, my soul shrank away from, and trembled to think of beholding. Thus, *he that doth evil* (as all unregenerate men continually do) *hates the light of truth*, neither cares to *come to it*, because it will *reprove his deeds*, and shew him his just deserts. (John iii. 20.) And though, some time before, I had taken much pains (as I thought) to submit to the sovereignty of God, yet I mistook the thing ; and did not once imagine, that seeing and being made experimentally sensible of this truth, which my soul now so much dreaded and trembled at a sense of, was the frame of soul that I had been so earnest in pursuit of heretofore : For I had ever hoped, that when I had attained to that humiliation, which I supposed necessary to go before faith, then it would not be fair for God to cast me off ; but now I saw it was so far from any goodness in me, to own myself spiritually dead, and destitute of all goodness, that on the contrary, my mouth would be forever stopped by it : and it looked as dreadful to me, to see myself, and the relation I stood in to God, as a sinner and a criminal, and he a great judge and sovereign, as it would be to a poor trembling creature, to venture off some high precipice. And hence I put it off for a minute or two,

and

and tried for better circumstances to do it in; either I must read a passage or two, or pray first, or something of the like nature; or else put off my submission to God's sovereignty, with an objection, that I did not know how to submit: But the truth was, I could see no safety in owning myself in the hands of a sovereign God, and that I could lay no claim to any thing better than damnation.

But after a considerable time spent in such like exercises and distresses, one morning, while I was walking in a solitary place as usual, I at once saw that all my contrivances and projections to effect or procure deliverance and salvation for myself, were utterly in vain: I was brought quite to a stand, as finding myself totally lost. I had thought many times before, that the difficulties in my way were very great: But now I saw, in another and very different light, that it was forever impossible for me to do any thing towards helping or delivering myself. I then thought of blaming myself, that I had not done more, and been more engaged, while I had opportunity (for it seemed now as if the season of doing was forever over and gone) but I instantly saw, that let me have done what I would, it would no more have tended to my helping myself, than what I had done; that I had made all the pleas I ever could have made to all eternity; and that all my pleas were vain. The tumult that had been before in my mind, was now quieted; and I was something eased of that distress, which I felt while struggling against a sight of myself, and of the divine sovereignty. I had the greatest certainty, that my state was forever miserable, for all that I could do; and wondered, and was almost astonished, that I had never been sensible of it before.

In the time while I remained in this state, my notions respecting my duties, were quite different from

from what I had ever entertained in times paſt. Before this, the more I did in duty, the more I thought God was obliged to me; or at leaſt the more hard I thought it would be for God to caſt me off; though at the ſame time I confeſſed, and thought I ſaw, that there was no goodneſs or merit in my duties: But now the more I did in prayer or any other duty, the more I ſaw I was indebted to God for allowing me to aſk for mercy; for I ſaw, it was ſelf intereſt had led me to pray, and that I had never once prayed from any reſpect to the glory of God. Now I ſaw, there was no neceſſary connection between my prayers and the beſtowment of divine mercy; that they laid not the leaſt obligation upon God to beſtow his grace upon me; and that there was no more virtue or goodneſs in them, than there would be in my paddling with my hand in the water, (which was the compariſon I had then in my mind) and this becauſe they were not performed from any love or regard to God. I ſaw that I had been heaping up my devotions before God, faſting, praying, &c. pretending, and indeed really thinking, at ſome times, that I was aiming at the glory of God; whereas I never once truly intended it, but only my own happineſs. I ſaw, that, as I had never done any thing for God, I had no claim to lay to any thing from him, but perdition, on account of my hypocriſy and mockery. O how different did my duties now appear from what they uſed to do! I uſed to charge them with ſin and imperfection; but this was only on account of the wanderings and vain thoughts attending them, and not becauſe I had no regard to God in them; for this I thought I had: But when I ſaw evidently that I had regard to nothing but ſelf intereſt, then they appeared vile mockery of God, ſelf worſhip, and a continual courſe of lies; ſo that I ſaw now, there was ſomething worſe

worſe had attended my duties, than barely a few wanderings, &c. for the whole was nothing but ſelf worſhip and an horrid abuſe of God.

I continued, as I remember, in this ſtate of mind, from Friday morning until the Sabbath evening following, July 12, 1739, when I was walking again in the ſame ſolitary place where I was brought to ſee myſelf loſt and helpleſs (as was before mentioned) and here, in a mournful melancholy ſtate, was attempting to pray; but found no heart to engage in that, or any other duty; my former concern, and exerciſe, and religious affections were now gone. I thought the Spirit of God had quite left me; but ſtill was not diſtreſſed: Yet diſconſolate, as if there was nothing in heaven or earth could make me happy. And having been thus endeavouring to pray (though being, as I thought, very ſtupid and ſenſeleſs) for near half an hour, (and by this time the ſun was about half an hour high, as I remember) then, as I was walking in a dark thick grove, unſpeakable glory ſeemed to open to the view and apprehenſion of my ſoul: I do not mean any external brightneſs, for I ſaw no ſuch thing; nor do I intend any imagination of a body of light, ſome where away in the third heavens, or any thing of that nature; but it was a new inward apprehenſion or view that I had of God, ſuch as I never had before, nor any thing which had the leaſt reſemblance of it. I ſtood ſtill, and wondered and admired! I knew that I never had ſeen before any thing comparable to it for excellency and beauty: It was widely different from all the conceptions that ever I had had of God, or things divine. I had no particular apprehenſion of any one perſon in the Trinity, either the Father, the Son, or the Holy Ghoſt; but it appeared to be divine glory that I then beheld: And my ſoul rejoiced with joy unſpeakable, to ſee ſuch a God, ſuch a glorious divine Being; and I was inwardly pleased and satisfied, that he should be God over all forever and ever. My soul was so captivated and delighted with the excellency, loveliness, greatness, and other perfections of God, that I was even swallowed up in him; at least to that degree, that I had no thought (as I remember) at first, about my own salvation, and scarce reflected there was such a creature as myself.

Thus God, I trust, brought me to a hearty disposition to exalt him, and set him on the throne, and principally and ultimately to aim at his honour and glory, as King of the Universe.

I continued in this state of inward joy and peace, yet astonishment, until near dark, without any sensible abatement; and then began to think and examine what I had seen; and felt sweetly composed in my mind all the evening following: I felt myself in a new world, and every thing about me appeared with a different aspect from what it was wont to do.

At this time, the way of salvation opened to me with such infinite wisdom, suitableness and excellency, that I wondered I should ever think of any other way of salvation; was amazed that I had not dropped my own contrivances, and complied with this lovely, blessed, and excellent way before. If I could have been saved by my own duties, or any other way that I had formerly contrived, my whole soul would now have refused. I wondered that all the world did not see and comply with this way of salvation, entirely by the righteousness of Christ.

The sweet relish of what I then felt, continued with me for several days, almost constantly, in a greater or less degree: I could not but sweetly rejoice in God, lying down and rising up. The next Lord's Day I felt something of the same kind; though not so powerful as before. But, not long after, was

again

again involved in thick darkness, and under great distress; yet not of the same kind with my distress under convictions. I was guilty, afraid and ashamed to come before God, was exceedingly pressed with a sense of guilt: But it was not long before I felt, I trust, true repentance and joy in God.

About the latter end of August, I again fell under great darkness; it seemed as if the presence of God was *clean gone forever*. Though I was not so much distressed about my spiritual state, as I was at my being shut out from God's presence, as I then sensibly was. But it pleased the Lord to return graciously to me, not long after.

In the beginning of September I went to college*, and entered there: But with some degree of reluctancy, fearing left I should not be able to lead a life of strict religion, in the midst of so many temptations. After this, in the vacancy, before I went to tarry at college, it pleased God to visit my soul with clearer manifestations of himself and his grace. I was spending some time in prayer, and self examination; and the Lord by his grace so shined into my heart, that I enjoyed full assurance of his favour for that time; and my soul was unspeakably refreshed with divine and heavenly enjoyments. At this time especially, as well as some others, sundry passages of God's word opened to my soul with divine clearness, power and sweetness, so as to appear exceeding precious, and with clear and certain evidence of its being the word of God. I enjoyed considerable sweetness in religion, all the winter following.

In January, 1739,40, the measles spread much in college; and I having taken the distemper, went home to Haddam: But some days before I was taken sick, I seemed to be greatly deserted, and my soul mourned the absence of the Comforter exceedingly:

It

---

* Yale College in New-Haven.

It seemed to me, all comfort was forever gone; I prayed and cried to God for help, yet found no present comfort or relief. But through divine goodness, a night or two before I was taken ill, while I was walking alone in a very retired place, and engaged in meditation and prayer, I enjoyed a sweet refreshing visit, as I trust, from above, so that my soul was raised far above the fears of death; indeed I rather longed for death, than feared it. O how much more refreshing this one season was, than all the pleasures and delights that earth can afford! After a day or two I was taken with the measles, and was very ill indeed, so that I almost despaired of life: But had no distressing fears of death at all. However, through divine goodness I soon recovered: Yet, by reason of hard and close studies, and being much exposed on account of my freshmanship, I had but little time for spiritual duties; my soul often mourned for want of more time and opportunity to be alone with God. In the spring and summer following I had better advantages for retirement, and enjoyed more comfort in religion: Though indeed my ambition in my studies greatly wronged the activity and vigour of my spiritual life: Yet this was usually the case with me, that *in the multitude of my thoughts within me*, *God's comforts* principally *delighted my soul*: These were my greatest consolations day by day.

One day I remember in particular (I think it was in June, 1740) I walked to a considerable distance from the college, in the fields alone at noon, and in prayer found such unspeakable sweetness and delight in God, that I thought, if I must continue still in this evil world, I wanted always to be there, to behold God's glory: My soul dearly loved all mankind, and longed exceedingly that they should enjoy what I enjoyed. It seemed to be a little resemblance of Heaven.

On Lord's Day, July 6, being facrament day, I found fome divine life and fpiritual refrefhment in that holy ordinance. When I came from the Lord's table, I wondered how my fellow ftudents could live as I was fenfible moft did. Next Lord's Day, July 13, I had fome fpecial fweetnefs in religion. Again Lord's Day, July 20, my foul was in a fweet and precious frame.

Sometime in Auguft following, I became fo weakly and difordered, by too clofe application to my ftudies, that I was advifed by my tutor, to go home, and difengage my mind from ftudy; as much as I could; for I was grown fo weak, that I began to fpit blood. I took his advice, and endeavoured to lay afide my ftudies. But being brought very low, I looked death in the face more fteadfaftly; and the Lord was pleafed to give me renewedly a fweet fenfe and relifh of divine things; and particularly in October 13, I found divine help and confolation in the precious duties of fecret prayer and felf examination; and my foul took delight in the bleffed God: So likewife on the 17th of October.

Saturday, October 18, in my morning devotions, my foul was exceedingly melted for, and bitterly mourned over my exceeding finfulnefs and vilenefs. I never before had felt fo pungent and deep a fenfe of the odious nature of fin, as at this time. My foul was then unufually carried forth in love to God, and had a lively fenfe of God's love to me. And this love and hope, at that time, caft out fear. Both morning and evening I fpent fome time in felf examination, to find the truth of grace, as alfo my fitnefs to approach to God at his table the next day; and through infinite grace, found the Holy Spirit influencing my foul with love to God, as a witnefs within myfelf.

Lord's Day, October 19, in the morning I felt my foul *hungering and thirfting after righteoufnefs.*

In the forenoon when I was looking on the sacramental elements, and thinking that *Jesus Christ* would soon be *set forth crucified before me*, my soul was filled with light and love, so that I was almost in an ecstasy; my body was so weak, I could scarcely stand. I felt at the same time an exceeding tenderness and most fervent love towards all mankind; so that my soul and all the powers of it seemed, as it were, to melt into softness and sweetness. But in the season of the communion there was some abatement of this sweet life and fervour. This love and joy cast out fear; and my soul longed for perfect grace and glory. This sweet frame continued until the evening, when my soul was sweetly spiritual in secret duties.

Monday, October 20, I again found the sweet assistance of the Holy Spirit in secret duties, both morning and evening, and life and comfort in religion through the whole day.

Tuesday, October 21, I had likewise experience of the goodness of God in *shedding abroad his love in my heart*, and giving me delight and consolation in religious duties. And all the remaining part of the week, my soul seemed to be taken up with divine things. I now so longed after God, and to be freed from sin, that when I felt myself recovering, and thought I must return to college again, which had proved so hurtful to my spiritual interest the year past, I could not but be grieved, and I thought I had much rather have died; for it distressed me to think of getting away from God. But before I went, I enjoyed several other sweet and precious seasons of communion with God, (particularly October 30, and November 4,) wherein my soul enjoyed unspeakable comfort.

I returned to college about November 6, and through the goodness of God felt the power of religion almost daily, for the space of six weeks.

November 28, in my evening devotion, I enjoyed precious discoveries of God, and was unspeakably refreshed with that passage, Heb. xii. 22, 23, 24. That my soul longed to wing away for the paradise of God; I longed to be conformed to God in all things. A day or two after, I enjoyed much of the *light of God's countenance*, most of the day; and my soul rested in God.

Tuesday, December 9, I was in a comfortable frame of soul most of the day; but especially in evening devotions, when God was pleased wonderfully to assist and strengthen me; so that I thought nothing should ever move me from the love of God in Christ Jesus my Lord. O! *one hour with God* infinitely exceeds all the pleasures and delights of this lower world.

Sometime towards the latter end of January, 1740,1, I grew more cold and dull in matters of religion, by means of my old temptation, viz. ambition in my studies. But through divine goodness, a great and general awakening spread itself over the college, about the latter end of February, in which I was much quickened, and more abundantly engaged in religion.

[This awakening here spoken of, was at the beginning of that extraordinary religious commotion through the land, which is fresh in every one's memory. This awakening was for a time very great and general at New-Haven; and the college had no small share in it: That society was greatly reformed, the students in general became serious, and many of them remarkably so, and much engaged in the concerns of their eternal salvation. And however undesirable the issue of the awakenings of that day have appeared in many others, there have been manifestly happy and abiding effects of the impressions then made on the minds of many of the members of that

that college. And by all that I can learn concerning Mr. Brainerd, there can be no reason to doubt but that he had much of God's gracious presence, and of the lively actings of true grace, at that time: But yet he was afterwards abundantly sensible, that his religious experiences and affections at that time were not free from a corrupt mixture, nor his conduct to be acquitted from many things that were imprudent and blamable; which he greatly lamented himself, and was willing that others should forget, that none might make an ill improvement of such an example. And therefore, although in the time of it, he kept a constant Diary, containing a very particular account of what passed from day to day, for the next thirteen months, from the latter end of January, 1740,1, forementioned, in two small books, which he called the two first volumes of his Diary, next following the account before given of his convictions, conversion, and consequent comforts; yet, when he lay on his death bed, he gave order (unknown to me, until after his death) that these two volumes should be destroyed, and in the beginning of the third book of his Diary, he wrote thus, (by the hand of another, he not being able to write himself)—" The two preceding volumes, immediately following the account of the author's conversion, are lost. If any are desirous to know how the author lived in general, during that space of time, let them read the first thirty pages of this volume; where they will find something of a specimen of his ordinary manner of living, through that whole space of time, which was about thirteen months; excepting that here he was more refined from some imprudencies and indecent heats, than there; but the spirit of devotion running through the whole, was the same."

It could not be otherwise than that one whose heart had been so prepared and drawn to God, as

Mr.

Mr. Brainerd's had been, should be mightily enlarged, animated and engaged, at the sight of such an alteration made in the college, the town and land, and so great an appearance of men's reforming their lives, and turning from their profaneness and immorality, to seriousness and concern for their salvation, and of religion's reviving and flourishing almost every where. But as an intemperate imprudent zeal, and a degree of enthusiasm soon crept in, and mingled itself with that revival of religion; and so great and general an awakening being quite a new thing in the land, at least as to all the living inhabitants of it; neither people nor ministers had learned thoroughly to distinguish between solid religion and its delusive counterfeits; even many ministers of the gospel, of long standing and the best reputation, were for a time overpowered with the glaring appearances of the latter: And therefore surely it was not to be wondered at, that young Brainerd, but a sophimore at college, should be so; who was not only young in years, but very young in religion and experience, and had had but little opportunity for the study of divinity, and still less for observation of the circumstances and events of such an extraordinary state of things: A man must divest himself of all reason, to make strange of it. In these disadvantageous circumstances, Brainerd had the unhappiness to have a tincture of that intemperate indiscreet zeal, which was at that time too prevalent; and was led, from his high opinion of others that he looked upon better than himself, into such errors as were really contrary to the habitual temper of his mind. One instance of his misconduct at that time, gave great offence to the rulers of the college, even to that degree that they expelled him the society; which it is necessary should here be particularly related, with its circumstances.

In the time of the awakening at college, there were several religious students that associated themselves one with another for mutual conversation and assistance in spiritual things, who were wont freely to open themselves one to another, as special and intimate friends. Brainerd was one of this company. And it once happened, that he and two or three more of these his intimate friends were in the hall together, after Mr. Whittelsey, one of the tutors, had been to prayer there with the scholars; no other person now remaining in the hall, but Brainerd and these his companions. Mr. Whittelsey having been unusually pathetical in his prayer, one of Brainerd's friends on this occasion asked him what he thought of Mr. Whittelsey; he made answer, "He has no more grace than this chair." One of the freshmen happening at that time to be near the hall (though not in the room) overheard those words of his; though he heard no name mentioned, and knew not who the person was, which was thus censured. He informed a certain woman that belonged to the town, withal telling her his own suspicion, viz. that he believed Brainerd said this of some one or other of the rulers of the college. Whereupon she went and informed the rector, who sent for this freshman and examined him; and he told the rector the words that he heard Brainerd utter, and informed him who were in the room with him at that time. Upon which the rector sent for them: They were very backward to inform against their friend, of that which they looked upon as private conversation, and especially as none but they had heard or knew of whom he had uttered those words; yet the rector compelled them to declare what he said, and of whom he said it. Brainerd looked on himself greatly abused in the management of this affair; and thought, that what he said in private, was injuriously extorted ed from his friends, and that then it was injuriously required of him (as it was wont to be of such as had been guilty of some open notorious crime) to make a publick confession, and to humble himself before the whole college in the hall, for what he had said only in private conversation. He not complying with this demand, and having gone once to the separate meeting at New-Haven, when forbidden by the rector, and also having been accused by one person of saying concerning the rector, that he wondered he did not expect to drop down dead for fining the scholars who followed Mr. Tennent to Milford, though there was no proof of it (and Mr. Brainerd ever professed that he did not remember his saying any thing to that purpose) for these things he was expelled the college.

Now, how far the circumstances and exigences of that day might justify such great severity in the governours of the college, I will not undertake to determine; it being my aim, not to bring reproach on the authority of the college, but only to do justice to the memory of a person who I think to be eminently one of those whose *memory is blessed*. The reader will see, in the sequel of the story of Mr. Brainerd's life,* what his own thoughts afterwards were of his behaviour in these things, and in how christian a manner he conducted himself, with respect to this affair; though he ever, as long as he lived, supposed himself much abused in the management of it, and in what he suffered in it.

His expulsion was in the winter anno 1741,2, while he was in his third year in college.]

* Particularly under the date, *Wednesday, September* 14, 1743.

PART II.

From about the time that he first began to devote himself more especially to the STUDY *of* DIVINITY, *until he was examined and licensed to preach, by the* ASSOCIATION *of* MINISTERS *belonging to the eastern district of the county of Fairfield in Connecticut.*

[MR. Brainerd, the spring after his expulsion, went to live with the Rev. Mr. Mills of Ripton, to follow his studies with him, in order to his being fitted for the work of the ministry; where he spent the greater part of the time until the association licensed him to preach; but frequently rode to visit the neighbouring ministers, particularly Mr. Cooke of Stratfield, Mr. Graham of Southbury, and Mr. Bellamy of Bethlehem.

Here (at Mr. Mills's) he began the third book of his Diary, in which the account he wrote of himself, is as follows.]

Thursday, April 1, 1742.—I seem to be declining with respect to my life and warmth in divine things: Had not so free access to God in prayer as usual of late. O that God would humble me deeply in the dust before him! I deserve hell every day, for not loving my Lord more, *who has* (I trust) *loved me and given himself for me;* and every time I am enabled to exercise any grace renewedly, I am renewedly indebted to the God of all grace for special assistance. *Where then is boasting?* Surely *it is excluded,* when we think how we are dependent on God for the being and every act of grace. O if ever I get to heaven, it will be because God will, and nothing else; for I ver did any thing of myself, but get away

away from God! My soul will be astonished at the unsearchable riches of divine grace, when I arrive at the mansions which the blessed Saviour is gone before to prepare.

Friday, April 2.—In the afternoon I felt something sweetly in secret prayer, much resigned, calm and serene. What are all the storms of this lower world, if Jesus by his Spirit does but come *walking upon the seas!* Some time past I had much pleasure in the prospect of the heathen's being brought home to Christ, and desired that the Lord would improve me in that work: But now my soul more frequently desires to die, *to be with Christ.* O that my soul were wrapt up in divine love, and my longing desires after God increased. In the evening, was refreshed in prayer, with the hopes of the advancement of Christ's kingdom in the world.

Saturday, April 3.—Was very much amiss this morning, and had an ill night last night. I thought, if God would take me to himself now, my soul would exceedingly rejoice. O that I may be always humble and resigned to God, and that God would cause my soul to be more fixed on himself, that I may be more fitted both for doing and suffering.

Lord's Day, April 4.—My heart was wandering and lifeless. In the evening God gave me faith in prayer, and made my soul melt in some measure, and gave me to taste a divine sweetness. O my blessed God! Let me climb up near to him, and love, and long, and plead, and wrestle, and reach, and stretch after him, and for *deliverance from the body of sin and death.* Alas, my soul mourned to think I should ever lose sight of its beloved again! O *come Lord Jesus! Amen.*

[On the evening of the next day, he complains that he seemed to be void of all relish of divine things, felt much of the prevalence of corruption, and saw in himself a disposition to all manner of sin ; which brought a very great gloom on his mind, and cast him down into the depths of melancholy ; so that he speaks of himself, as astonished, amazed, having no comfort, being filled with horror, seeing no comfort in heaven or earth.]

Tuesday, April 6.—I walked out this morning to the same place where I was last night, and felt something as I did then ; but was something relieved by reading some passages in my Diary, and seemed to feel as if I might pray to the great God again with freedom ; but was suddenly struck with a damp, from the sense I had of my own vileness. Then I cried to God to wash my soul and cleanse me from my exceeding filthiness, to give me repentance and pardon ; and it began to be something sweet to pray : And I could think of undergoing the greatest sufferings in the cause of Christ, with pleasure ; and found myself willing (if God should so order it) to suffer banishment from my native land, among the heathen, that I might do something for their souls' salvation, in distresses and deaths of any kind. Then God gave me to wrestle earnestly for others, for the kingdom of Christ in the world, and for dear christian friends. I felt weaned from the world and from my own reputation amongst men, willing to be despised, and to be a gazing stock for the world to behold. It is impossible for me to express how I then felt : I had not much joy, but some sense of the majesty of God, which made me as it were tremble. I saw myself mean and vile, which made me more willing that God should do what he would with me ; it was all infinitely reasonable.

Thursday, April 8.—Had raised hopes to day respecting the heathen. O that God would bring in great numbers of them to Jesus Christ. I cannot but hope I shall see that glorious day. Every thing in this world seems exceeding vile and little to me: I look so to myself. I had some little dawn of comfort to day in prayer: But especially to night I think I had some faith and power of intercession with God, was enabled to plead with God for the growth of grace in myself; and many of the dear children of God then lay with weight upon my soul. Blessed be the Lord. It is good to wrestle for divine blessings.

Friday, April 9.—Most of my time in morning devotion was spent without sensible sweetness; yet I had one delightful prospect of arriving at the heavenly world. I am more amazed than ever at such thoughts; for I see myself infinitely vile and unworthy. I feel very heartless and dull; and though I long for the presence of God, and seem constantly to reach towards God in desires, yet I cannot feel that divine and heavenly sweetness that I used to enjoy. No poor creature stands in need of divine grace more than I, and none abuse it more than I have done, and still do.

Saturday, April 10.—Spent much time in secret prayer this morning, and not without some comfort in divine things, and I hope had some faith in exercise: But am so low, and feel so little of the sensible presence of God, that I hardly know what to call faith, and am made to *possess the sins of my youth*, and the dreadful sin of my nature, and am all sin; I cannot think, nor act, but every motion is sin. I feel some faint hopes, that God will, of his infinite mercy, return again with showers of converting grace to poor gospel abusing sinners; and my hopes of being improved in the cause of God, which of late have been almost extinct, seem now a little revived. O that all my late distresses and awful apprehensions might prove but Christ's school, to make me fit for greater service, by learning me the great lesson of humility.

Lord's Day, April 11.—In the morning, felt but little life, excepting that my heart was something drawn out in thankfulness to God for his amazing grace and condescension to me in past influences and assistances of his Spirit. Afterwards had some sweetness in the thoughts of arriving at the heavenly world. O for the happy day! After publick worship God gave me special assistance in prayer; I wrestled with my dear Lord, with much sweetness; and intercession was made a sweet and delightful employment to me. In the evening, as I was viewing the light in the north, was delighted in contemplation on the glorious morning of the resurrection.

Monday, April 12.—This morning the Lord was pleased to *lift up the light of his countenance upon me* in secret prayer, and made the season very precious to my soul. And though I have been so depressed of late, respecting my hopes of future serviceableness in the cause of God ; yet now I had much encouragement respecting that matter. I was specially assisted to intercede and plead for poor souls, and for the enlargement of Christ's kingdom in the world, and for special grace for myself, to fit me for special services. I felt exceeding calm, and quite resigned to God, respecting my future improvement, when, and where he pleased : My faith lifed me above the world, and removed all those mountains, that I could not look over of late : I thought I wanted not the favour of man to lean upon ; for I knew Christ's favour was infinitely better, and that it was no matter when, nor where, nor how Christ should send me, nor what trials he should still exercise me with, if I might be prepared for his work and will. I now found sweetly revived in my mind the wonderful discovery of infinite wisdom in all the dispensations of God towards me, which I had a little before I met with my

great

great trial at college: Every thing appeared full of the wisdom of God.

Tuesday, April 13.—Saw myself to be very mean and vile; wondered at those that shewed me respect. Afterwards was something comforted in secret retirement, and was assisted to wrestle with God, with some power, spirituality and sweetness. Blessed be the Lord, he is never unmindful of me, but always sends me needed supplies, and, from time to time, when I am like one dead, raises me to life. O that I may never distrust infinite goodness.

Wednesday, April 14.—My soul longed for communion with Christ, and for the mortification of indwelling corruption, especially spiritual pride. O there is a sweet day coming, wherein *the weary will be at rest*. My soul has enjoyed much sweetness this day in hopes of its speedy arrival.

Thursday, April 15.—My desires apparently centered in God, and I found a sensible attraction of soul after him, sundry times to day: I know I long for God, and a conformity to his will, in inward purity and holiness, ten thousand times more than for any thing here below.

Friday and Saturday, April 16, 17.—Seldom prayed without some sensible sweetness and joy in the Lord. Sometimes I longed much *to be dissolved and to be with Christ*. O that God would enable me to *grow in grace* every day. Alas! my barrenness is such, that God might well say, *Cut it down*. I am afraid of a dead heart on the Sabbath now begun: O that God would quicken me by his grace.

Lord's Day, April 18.—Retired early this morning into the woods for prayer; had the assistance of God's Spirit, and faith in exercise, and was enabled to plead with fervency for the advancement of Christ's kingdom in the world, and to intercede for dear absent friends. At noon, God enabled me to wrestle

wrestle with him, and feel (as I trust) the power of divine love in prayer. At night, saw myself infinitely indebted to God, and had a view of my short comings: It seemed to me, that I had done as it were nothing for God, and that I never had *lived to him* but a few hours of my life.

Monday, April 19.—I set apart this day for fasting and prayer to God for his grace, especially to prepare me for the work of the ministry, to give me divine aid and direction in my preparations for that great work, and in his own time to *send me into his harvest.* Accordingly, in the morning, endeavoured to plead for the divine presence for the day, and not without some life. In the forenoon, I felt a power of intercession for precious immortal souls, for the advancement of the kingdom of my dear Lord and Saviour in the world; and withal, a most sweet resignation, and even consolation and joy in the thoughts of suffering hardships, distresses, and even death itself, in the promotion of it; and had special enlargement in pleading for the enlightening and conversion of the poor heathen. In the afternoon, God *was with me of a truth.* O it was blessed company indeed! God enabled me so to agonize in prayer, that I was quite wet with sweat, though in the shade, and the wind cool. My soul was drawn out very much from the world; I grasped for multitudes of souls. I think I had more enlargement for sinners, than for the children of God; though I felt as if I could spend my life in cries for both. I enjoyed great sweetness in communion with my dear Saviour. I think I never in my life felt such an entire weanedness from this world, and so much resigned to God in every thing. O that I may always live to and upon my blessed God. Amen, Amen.

Tuesday, April 20.—This day I am twenty four years of age. O how much mercy have I received the

year

year paſt! How often has *God cauſed his goodneſs to paſs before me!* And how poorly have I anſwered the vows I made this time twelve months, to be wholly the Lord's, to be forever devoted to his ſervice! The Lord help me to live more to his glory for time to come. This has been a ſweet, a happy day, to me: Bleſſed be God. I think my ſoul was never ſo drawn out in interceſſion for others, as it has been this night. Had a moſt fervent wreſtle with the Lord to night for my enemies; and I hardly ever ſo longed to live to God, and to be altogether devoted to him; I wanted to wear out my life in his ſervice and for his glory.

Wedneſday, April 21.—Felt much calmneſs and reſignation, and God again enabled me to wreſtle for numbers of ſouls, and had much fervency in the ſweet duty of interceſſion. I enjoy of late more ſweetneſs in interceſſion for others, than in any other part of prayer. My bleſſed Lord really let me *come near to him, and plead with him.*

[The frame of mind, and exerciſes of ſoul, that he expreſſes the three days next following, Thurſday, Friday, and Saturday, are much of the ſame kind with thoſe expreſſed the two days paſt.]

Lord's Day, April 25.—This morning ſpent about two hours in ſecret duties, and was enabled more than ordinarily to agonize for immortal ſouls; though it was early in the morning, and the ſun ſcarcely ſhined at all, yet my body was quite wet with ſweat. Felt much preſſed now, as frequently of late, to plead for the meekneſs and calmneſs of *the Lamb of God* in my ſoul: Through divine goodneſs felt much of it this morning. O it is a ſweet dispoſition, heartily to forgive all injuries done to us; to wiſh our greateſt enemies as well as we do our own ſouls! Bleſſed Jeſus, may I daily be more and more conformed to thee. At night was exceedingly melted with

with divine love, and had some feeling sense of the blessedness of the upper world. Those words hung upon me, with much divine sweetness, Psal. lxxxiv. 7. *They go from strength to strength, every one of them in Zion appeareth before God.* O the near access that God sometimes gives us in our addresses to him! This may well be termed *appearing before God:* It is so indeed in the true spiritual sense, and in the sweetest sense. I think I have not had such power of intercession, these many months, both for God's children, and for dead sinners, as I have had this evening. I wished and longed for *the coming of my dear Lord:* I longed to join the angelick hosts in praises, wholly free from imperfection. O the blessed moment hastens! All I want is to be more holy, more like my dear Lord. O for sanctification! My very soul pants for the complete restoration of the blessed image of my sweet Saviour; that I may be fit for the blessed enjoyments and employments of the heavenly world.

> Farewell, vain world; my soul can bid adieu :
> My Saviour's taught me to abandon you.
> Your charms may gratify a sensual mind ;
> Not please a soul wholly for God design'd.
> Forbear t' entice, cease then my soul to call :
> 'Tis fix'd, through grace ; my God shall be my *all.*
> While he thus lets me heavenly glories view,
> Your beauties fade, my heart's no room for you.

The Lord refreshed my soul with many sweet passages of his word. O the *New Jerusalem!* my soul longed for it. O the *song of Moses and the Lamb!* And that blessed song, that no man can learn, but they that are *redeemed from the earth!* And the glorious *white robes,* that were given to *the souls under the altar!*

> Lord, I'm a stranger here alone;
> Earth no true comforts can afford :
> Yet, absent from my dearest one,
> My soul delights to cry, My Lord !

Jesus

Jesus, my Lord, my only love,
Possess my soul, nor thence depart:
Grant me kind visits, heavenly dove;
My God shall then have all my heart.

Monday, April 26.—Continued in a sweet frame of mind; but in the afternoon felt something of spiritual pride stirring. God was pleased to make it a humbling season at first; though afterwards he gave me sweetness. O, my soul exceedingly longs for that blessed state of perfection of deliverance from all sin! At night, God enabled me to give my soul up to him, to cast myself upon him, to be ordered and disposed of according to his sovereign pleasure; and I enjoyed great peace and consolation in so doing. My soul took sweet delight in God to night: My thoughts freely and sweetly centered in him. O that I could spend every moment of my life to his glory.

Tuesday, April 27.—Retired pretty early for secret devotions; and in prayer God was pleased to pour such ineffable comforts into my soul, that I could do nothing for some time but say over and over, O my sweet Saviour! O my sweet Saviour! *Whom have I in heaven, but thee? and there is none upon earth, that I desire beside thee.* If I had had a thousand lives, my soul would gladly have laid them all down at once, to have been with Christ. My soul never enjoyed so much of heaven before; it was the most refined and most spiritual season of communion with God I ever yet felt: I never felt so great a degree of resignation in my life: I felt very sweetly all the forenoon. In the afternoon I withdrew to meet with my God, but found myself much declined, and God made it a humbling season to my soul: I mourned over *the body of death*, that is in me: It grieved me exceedingly, that I could not pray to and praise God with my heart full of divine heavenly love. O that my soul might never offer any dead cold services to my God.

In the evening had not so much sweet divine love as in the morning; but had a sweet season of fervent intercession.

Wednesday, April 28.—Withdrew to my usual place of retirement in great peace and tranquillity, and spent about two hours in secret duties. I felt much as I did yesterday morning, only weaker and more overcome. I seemed to hang and depend wholly on my dear Lord; wholly weaned from all other dependences. I knew not what to say to my God, but only *lean on his bosom*, as it were, and breath out my desires after a perfect conformity to him in all things. Thirsting desires and insatiable longings possessed my soul, after perfect holiness: God was so precious to my soul, that the world with all its enjoyments was infinitely vile: I had no more value for the favour of men, than for pebbles: The Lord was my all; and he overruled all; which greatly delighted me. I think my faith and dependence on God scarce ever rose so high. I saw him such a fountain of goodness, that it seemed impossible I should distrust him again, or be any way anxious about any thing that should happen to me. I now enjoyed great sweetness in praying for absent friends, and for the enlargement of Christ's kingdom in the world. Much of the power of these divine enjoyments remained with me through the day. In the evening my heart seemed sweetly to melt, and, I trust, was really humbled for indwelling corruption, and I *mourned like a dove*. I felt that all my unhappiness arose from my being a sinner; for with resignation I could bid welcome all other trials; but sin hung heavy upon me; for God discovered to me the corruption of my heart: So that I went to bed with a heavy heart, because I was a sinner; though I did not in the least doubt of God's love. O that God would *purge away my dross, and take away my tin*, and make me seven times refined.

Thursday,

Thursday, April 29.—Was kept off at a distance from God; but had some enlargement in intercession for precious souls.

Friday, April 30.—Was something dejected in spirit: Nothing grieves me so much, as that I cannot live constantly to God's glory. I could bear any desertion or spiritual conflicts, if I could but have *my heart* all the while *burning within me* with love to God and desires of his glory: But this is impossible; for when I feel these, I cannot be dejected in my soul, but only rejoice in my Saviour, who has delivered me from the reigning power, and will shortly deliver me from the indwelling of sin.

Saturday, May 1.—Was enabled to cry to God with fervency for ministerial qualifications, and that God would appear for the advancement of his own kingdom, and that he would bring in the heathen world, &c. Had much assistance in my studies. This has been a profitable week to me; I have enjoyed many communications of the blessed Spirit in my soul.

Lord's Day, May 2.—God was pleased this morning to give me such a sight of myself, as made me appear very vile in my own eyes: I felt corruption stirring in my heart, which I could by no means suppress; felt more and more deserted; was exceeding weak, and almost sick with my inward trials.

Monday, May 3.—Had a sense of vile ingratitude. In the morning I withdrew to my usual place of retirement, and mourned for my abuse of my dear Lord: Spent the day in fasting and prayer: God gave me much power of wrestling for his cause and kingdom: And it was a happy day to my soul. God was with me all the day, and I was more above the world than ever in my life.

[Through the remaining part of this week, he complains almost every day of desertion and inward trials and conflicts, attended with dejection of spirit;
but

but yet speaks of times of relief and sweetness, and daily refreshing visits of the Divine Spirit, affording special assistance and comfort, and enabling, at some times, to much fervency and enlargement in religious duties.]

Lord's Day, May 9.—I think I never felt so much of the cursed pride of my heart, as well as the stubbornness of my will before. O dreadful! what a vile wretch I am! I could not submit to be nothing, and to lie down in the dust! O that God would humble me in the dust. I felt myself such a sinner, all day, that I had scarce any comfort. Oh, when shall I be *delivered from the body of this death!* I greatly feared, lest through stupidity and carelessness I should lose the benefit of these trials. O that they might be sanctified to my soul. Nothing seemed to touch me but only this, that I was a sinner. Had fervency and refreshment in social prayer in the evening.

Monday, May 10.—Rode to New-Haven; saw some christian friends there; had comfort in joining in prayer with them, and hearing of the goodness of God to them since I last saw them.

Tuesday, May 11.—Rode from New-Haven to Weathersfield; was very dull most of the day; had little spirituality in this journey, though I often longed to be alone with God; was much perplexed with vile thoughts; was sometimes afraid of every thing: But God was my helper. Catched a little time for retirement in the evening, to my comfort and rejoicing. Alas, I cannot live in the midst of a tumult! I long to enjoy God alone.

Wednesday, May 12.—Had a distressing view of the pride and enmity and vileness of my heart. Afterwards had sweet refreshment in conversing, and worshipping God, with christian friends.

Thursday, May 13.—Saw so much of the wickedness of my heart, that I longed to get away from myself.

myself. I never before thought, there was so much spiritual pride in my soul: I felt almost pressed to death with my own vileness. O, what *a body of death* is there in me! *Lord, deliver my soul.* I could not find any convenient place for retirement, and was greatly exercised. Rode to Hartford in the afternoon: Had some refreshment and comfort in religious exercises with christian friends; but longed for more retirement. O the closest walk with God is the sweetest heaven, that can be enjoyed on earth!

Friday, May 14.—Waited on a council of ministers convened at Hartford, and spread before them the treatment I had met with from the rector and tutors of Yale College; who thought it advisable to intercede for me with the rector and trustees, and to entreat them to restore me to my former privileges in college*. After this, spent some time in religious exercises with christian friends.

Saturday, May 15.—Rode from Hartford to Hebron; was something dejected on the road; appeared exceeding vile in my own eyes; saw much pride and stubbornness in my heart. Indeed I never saw such a week before, as this; for I have been almost ready to die with the view of the wickedness of my heart. I could not have thought I had such *a body of death* in me. O that God would *deliver my soul.*

[The three next days, which he spent at Hebron, Lebanon, and Norwich, he complains still of dulness and desertion, and expresses a sense of his vileness, and longing to hide himself in some cave or den of the earth: But yet speaks of some intervals of comfort and soul refreshment each day.]

Wednesday, May 19.—[At Millington] I was so amazingly deserted this morning, that I seemed to feel a sort of horror in my soul. Alas, when God withdraws, what is there that can afford any comfort to the soul!

[Through

* The application which was then made on his behalf, had not the desired success.

[Through the eight days next following, he expresses more calmness and comfort, and considerable life, fervency and sweetness in religion.]

Friday, May 28.—[At New-Haven] I think, I scarce ever felt so calm in my life; I rejoiced in resignation, and giving myself up to God, to be wholly and entirely devoted to him forever.

[On the three following days, there was, by the account he gives, a continuance of the same excellent frame of mind, last expressed: But it seems not to be altogether to so great a degree.]

Tuesday, June 1.—Had much of the presence of God in family prayer, and had some comfort in secret. I was greatly refreshed from the word of God this morning, which appeared exceeding sweet to me: Some things that appeared mysterious, were opened to me. O that the kingdom of the dear Saviour might come with power, and the healing *waters of the sanctuary* spread far and wide for *the healing of the nations.* Came to Ripton; but was very weak: However, being visited by a number of young people in the evening, I prayed with them.

[The remaining part of this week, he speaks of being much diverted and hindered in the business of religion, by great weakness of body, and necessary affairs, that he had to attend, and complains of having but little power in religion; but signifies, that God hereby shewed him, he was like a helpless infant cast out in the open field.]

Lord's day, June 6.—I feel much deserted: But all this teaches me my nothingness and vileness more than ever.

Monday, June 7.—Felt still powerless in secret prayer. Afterwards I prayed, and conversed, with some little life. God feeds me with crumbs: Blessed be his name for any thing. I felt a great desire, that all God's people might know how mean and little

and

and vile I am; that they might see I am nothing, that so they may pray for me aright, and not have the least dependence upon me.

Tuesday, June 8.—I enjoyed one sweet and precious season this day: I never felt it so sweet to be nothing, and less than nothing, and to be accounted nothing.

[The three next days he complains of desertion, and want of fervency in religion; but yet his Diary shews that every day his heart was engaged in religion, as his great and as it were only business.]

Saturday, June 12.—Spent much time in prayer, this morning, and enjoyed much sweetness: Felt insatiable longings after God, much of the day: I wondered how poor souls do to live, that have no God. The world, with all its enjoyments, quite vanished. I see myself very helpless: But I have a blessed God to go to. I longed exceedingly *to be dissolved, and to be with Christ*, to *behold his glory*. O, my weak weary soul longs to arrive at *my Father's house*.

Lord's Day, June 13.—Felt something calm and resigned in the publick worship: At the sacrament saw myself very vile and worthless. O that I may always lie low in the dust. My soul seemed steadily to go forth after God, in longing desires to live upon him.

Monday, June 14.—Felt something of the sweetness of communion with God, and the constraining force of his love: How admirably it captivates the soul, and makes all the desires and affections to center in God! I set apart this day for secret fasting and prayer, to entreat God to direct and bless me with regard to the great work I have in view, of preaching the gospel; and that the Lord would return to me and *shew me the light of his countenance*. Had little life and power in the forenoon: Near the middle of the afternoon, God enabled me to wrestle ardently in intercession for absent friends: But just at night, the Lord visited me marvellously in prayer; I think my soul never was in such an agony before : I felt no restraint; for the treasures of divine grace were opened to me. I wrestled for absent friends, for the ingathering of souls, for multitudes of poor souls, and for many that I thought were the children of God, personally, in many distant places. I was in such an agony, from sun half an hour high, until near dark, that I was all over wet with sweat; but yet it seemed to me that I had wasted away the day, and had done nothing. O, my dear Jesus did *sweat blood* for poor souls! I long for more compassion towards them. Felt still in a sweet frame, under a sense of divine love and grace; and went to bed in such a frame, with my heart set on God.

Tuesday, June 15.—Had the most ardent longings after God, that ever I felt in my life : At noon, in my secret retirement, I could do nothing but tell my dear Lord, in a sweet calm, that he knew I longed for nothing but himself, nothing but holiness; that he had given me these desires, and he only could give me the thing desired. I never seemed to be so unhinged from myself, and to be so wholly devoted to God. My heart was swallowed up in God, most of the day. In the evening I had such a view of the soul's being as it were enlarged, to contain more holiness, that my soul seemed ready to separate from my body and stretch to obtain it. I then wrestled in an agony for divine blessings; had my heart drawn out in prayer for some christian friends, beyond what I ever had before. I feel differently now from what ever I did under any sweet enjoyments before, more engaged to live to God forever, and less pleased with my own frames : I am not satisfied with my frames, nor feel at all more easy after such sweet strugglings than before; for it seems far too little, if I could always be so. O, how short do I fall of my duty in my sweetest moments !

[In

[In his Diary for the two next days, he expresses something of the same frame, but in a far less degree*.]

Friday, June 18.—Considering my great unfitness for the work of the ministry, my present deadness, and total inability to do any thing for the glory of God that way, feeling myself very helpless, and at a great loss *what the Lord would have me to do*, I set apart this day for prayer to God, and spent most of the day in that duty; but amazingly deserted, most of the day: Yet I found God graciously near, once in particular, while I was pleading for more compassion for immortal souls; my heart seemed to be opened at once, and I was enabled to cry with great ardency, for a few minutes. O, I was distressed, to think, that I should offer such dead cold services to the *living God!* My soul seemed to breathe after holiness, a life of constant devotedness to God. But I am almost lost sometimes in the pursuit of this blessedness, and ready to sink, because I continually fall short and miss of my desire. O that the Lord would help me to hold out, yet a little while, until the happy hour of deliverance comes.

Lord's Day, June 20.—Spent much time alone. My soul longed to be holy, and reached after God; but seemed not to obtain my desire: I hungered and thirsted; but was not sweetly refreshed and satisfied. My soul hung on God, as my only portion. O that I could *grow in grace* more abundantly every day.

[The next day he speaks of his having assistance in his studies, and power, fervency and comfort in prayer.]

Tuesday, June 22.—In the morning, spent about two hours in prayer and meditation, with considerable delight. Towards night, felt my soul go out in longing

---

* Here end the 30 first pages of the third volume of his Diary, which he speaks of in the beginning of this volume (as was observed before) as containing a specimen of his ordinary manner of living, through the whole space of time, from the beginning of those two volumes that were destroyed.

ing defires after God, in fecret retirement. In the evening, was fweetly compofed and refigned to God's will; was enabled to leave myfelf and all my concerns with him, and to have my whole dependence upon him: My fecret retirement was very refrefhing to my foul: It appeared fuch a happinefs to have God for my portion, that I had rather be any other creature in this lower creation, than not come to the enjoyment of God: I had rather be a beaft, than a man, without God, if I were to live here to eternity. Lord, endear thyfelf more to me.

[In his Diary for the next feven days, he exprefies a variety of exercifes of mind: He fpeaks of great longings after God and holinefs, and earneft defires for the converfion of others, of fervency in prayer, and power to wreftle with God, and of compofure, comfort and fweetnefs, from time to time; but exprefies a fenfe of the vile abomination of his heart, and bitterly complains of his barrennefs, and the prefling *body of death* ; and fays, he faw clearly that whatever he enjoyed better than hell, was free grace.]

Wednefday, June 30.—Spent this day alone in the woods, in fafting and prayer; underwent the moft dreadful conflicts in my foul, that ever I felt, in fome refpects: I faw myfelf fo vile, that I was ready to fay, *I fhall now perifh by the hand of Saul*. I thought, and almoft concluded, I had no power to ftand for the caufe of God, but was almoft *afraid of the fhaking of a leaf*. Spent almoft the whole day in prayer, inceffantly. I could not bear to think of chriftians' fhewing me any refpect. I almoft defpaired of doing any fervice in the world. I could not feel any hope or comfort refpecting the heathen, which ufed to afford me fome refrefhment in the darkeft hours of this nature. I fpent away the day in the *bitternefs of my foul*. Near night I felt a little better, and afterwards enjoyed fome fweetnefs in fecret prayer.

Thurfday,

Thursday, July 1.—Had some sweetness in prayer this morning. Felt exceeding sweetly in secret prayer to night, and desired nothing so ardently as that God should do with me just as he pleased.

Friday, July 2.—Felt composed in secret prayer, in the morning. My desires sweetly ascended to God this day, as I was travelling: And was comfortable in the evening. Blessed be God for all my consolations.

Lord's Day, July 4.—Had considerable assistance. In the evening, I withdrew and enjoyed a happy season in secret prayer: God was pleased to give me the exercise of faith, and thereby brought the invisible and eternal world near to my soul; which appeared sweetly to me. I hoped, that my weary *pilgrimage* in the world would be short, and that it would not be long before I was brought to my heavenly home and Father's house: I was sweetly resigned to God's will, to tarry his time, to do his work, and suffer his pleasure. I felt thankfulness to God for all my pressing desertions of late; for I am persuaded they have been made a means of making me more humble, and much more resigned. I felt pleased, to be little, to be nothing, and to *lie in the dust*. I enjoyed life and sweet consolation in pleading for the dear children of God, and the kingdom of Christ in the world: And my soul earnestly breathed after holiness and the enjoyment of God. O, *come Lord Jesus! come quickly. Amen.*

[By his Diary for the remaining days of this week, it appears that he enjoyed considerable composure and tranquillity, and had sweetness and fervency of spirit in prayer, from day to day.]

[The eight next days, he expresses considerable comfort and fervency of spirit in christian conversation and religious exercises.]

Monday, July 19.—My desires seem especially to be carried out after weanedness from the world, perfect deadness to it, and to be even crucified to all its allurements. My soul longs to feel itself more of a pilgrim and stranger here below; that nothing may divert me from pressing through the lonely desert, until I arrive at my Father's house.

Tuesday, July 20.—It was sweet, to give away myself to God, to be disposed of at his pleasure; and had some feeling sense of the sweetness of being a pilgrim on earth.

[The next day, he expresses himself as determined to be wholly devoted to God; and it appears by his Diary, that he spent the whole day in a most diligent exercise of religion, and exceeding comfortably.]

Thursday, July 22.—Journeying from Southbury to Ripton, called at a house by the way, where being very kindly entertained and refreshed, I was filled with amazement and shame, that God should stir up the hearts of any to shew so much kindness to such a *dead dog* as I; was made sensible, in some measure, how exceeding vile it is, not to be wholly devoted to God. I wondered that God would suffer any of his creatures to feed and sustain me, from time to time.

[In his Diary for the six next days, are expressed various exercises and experiences, such as sweet composure and fervency of spirit in meditation and prayer, weanedness from the world, being sensibly a pilgrim and stranger on the earth, engagedness of mind to spend every inch of time for God, &c.]

Thursday, July 29.—Was examined by the association met at Danbury, as to my learning, and also my experiences in religion, and received a licence from them to preach the gospel of Christ. Afterwards felt much devoted to God; joined in prayer with one of the ministers, my peculiar friend, in a convenient place; went to bed resolving to live devoted to God all my days.

PART

Mr. DAVID BRAINERD.

PART III.

From the time of his being licensed to preach, by the Association, until he was examined in Newyork, by the Correspondents or Commissioners of the Society in Scotland for propagating Christian Knowledge, and approved and appointed as their MISSIONARY *to the* INDIANS.

FRIDAY, *July* 30, 1742.—Rode from Danbury to Southbury; preached there from 1 Pet. iv. 8. Had much of the comfortable presence of God in the exercise: I seemed to have power with God in prayer, and power to get hold of the hearts of the people in preaching.

Saturday, July 31.—Exceeding calm and composed, and was greatly refreshed and encouraged.

[It appears by his Diary, that he continued in this sweetness and tranquillity, almost through the whole of the next week.]

Lord's Day, August 8.—In the morning felt comfortably in secret prayer; my soul was refreshed with the hopes of the heathen's coming home to Christ; was much resigned to God; I thought it was no matter what became of me. Preached both parts of the day at Bethlehem, from Job xiv. 14. It was sweet to me to meditate on death. In the evening, felt very comfortably, and cried to God fervently, in secret prayer.

Thursday, August 12.—This morning and last night was exercised with sore inward trials: I had no power to pray; but seemed shut out from God. I had in a great measure lost my hopes of God's sending me among the heathen afar off, and of seeing them
flock

flock home to Christ. I saw so much of my hellish vileness, that I appeared worse to myself, than any devil : I wondered that God would let me live, and wondered that people did not stone me, much more, that they would ever hear me preach ! It seemed as though I never could nor should preach any more ; yet about nine or ten o'clock, the people came over, and I was forced to preach : And blessed be God, he gave me his presence and spirit in prayer and preaching : So that I was much assisted, and spake with power from Job xiv. 14. Some Indians cried out in great distress*, and all appeared greatly concerned. After we had prayed and exhorted them to seek the Lord with constancy, and hired an English woman to keep a kind of school among them, we came away about one o'clock, and came to Judea, about fifteen or sixteen miles. There God was pleased to visit my soul with much comfort. Blessed be the Lord for all things I meet with.

[It appears, that the two next days he had much comfort, and had his heart much engaged in religion.]

Lord's Day, August 13.—Felt much comfort and devotedness to God this day. At night, it was refreshing, to get alone with God and *pour out my soul*. O who can conceive of the sweetness of communion with the blessed God, but those that have experience of it ! Glory to God forever, that I may taste heaven below.

Monday, August 16.—Had some comfort in secret prayer, in the morning. Felt sweetly sundry times in prayer this day : But was much perplexed in the evening with vain conversation.

Tuesday, August 17.—Exceedingly depressed in spirit. It cuts and wounds my heart, to think how much self exaltation, spiritual pride, and warmth of
temper,

---

* It was in a place near Kent, in the western borders of Connecticut, where there was a number of Indians.

temper, I have formerly had intermingled with my endeavours to promote God's work: And sometimes I long to lie down at the feet of oppofers, and confefs what a poor imperfect creature I have been and ftill am. O, the Lord forgive me, and make me for the future *wife as a ferpent, and harmlefs as a dove.* Afterwards enjoyed confiderable comfort and delight of foul.

Wednefday, Auguft 18.—Spent moft of this day in prayer and reading. I fee fo much of my own extreme vilenefs, that I feel afhamed and guilty before God and man: I look to myfelf, like the vileft fellow in the land: I wonder, that God ftirs up his people to be fo kind to me.

Thurfday, Auguft 19.—This day, being about to go from Mr. Bellamy's at Bethlehem, where I had refided fome time, prayed with him, and two or three other chriftian friends, and gave ourfelves to God with all our hearts, to be his forever. Eternity looked very near to me, while I was praying. If I never fhould fee thefe chriftians again in this world it feemed but a few moments before I fhould meet them in another world. Parted with them fweetly.

Friday, Auguft 20.—I appeared fo vile to myfelf, that I hardly dared to think of being feen, efpecially on account of fpiritual pride. However, tonight, I enjoyed a fweet hour alone with God [at Ripton.] I was lifted above the frowns and flatteries of this lower world, had a fweet relifh of heavenly joys, and my foul did as it were get into the eternal world, and really tafte of heaven. I had a fweet feafon of interceffion for dear friends in Chrift; and God helped me to cry fervently for Zion. Bleffed be God for this feafon.

Monday, Auguft 23.—Had a fweet feafon in fecret prayer: The Lord drew near to my foul, and filled me with peace and divine confolation. O, my foul tafted tasted the sweetness of the upper world; and was sweetly drawn out in prayer for the world, that it might come home to Christ! Had much comfort in the thoughts and hopes of the ingathering of the heathen; and was greatly assisted in intercession for christian friends.

[He continued still in the same frame of mind the next day, but in a lesser degree.]

Wednesday, August 25.—In family prayer, God helped me to climb up near him, so that I scarce ever got nearer.

Monday, August 30.—Felt something comfortably in the morning; conversed sweetly with some friends; was in a serious composed frame; prayed at a certain house with some degree of sweetness. Afterwards, at another house, prayed privately with a dear christian friend or two; and I think I scarce ever launched so far into the eternal world, asthen; I got so far out on the broad ocean, that my soul with joy triumphed over all the evils on the shores of mortality. I think time and all its gay amusements and cruel disappointments, never appeared so inconsiderable to me before: I was in a sweet frame; I saw myself nothing, and my soul reached after God with intense desire. O! I saw what I owed to God, in such a manner, as I scarce ever did: I knew, I had never lived a moment to him, as I should do: Indeed it appeared to me, I had never done any thing in christianity: My soul longed with a vehement desire to live to God. In the evening, sung and prayed with a number of christians: Felt *the powers of the world to come*, in my soul, in prayer. Afterwards prayed again privately, with a dear christian or two, and found the presence of God; was something humbled in my secret retirement; felt my ingratitude, because I was not wholly swallowed up in God.

[He was in a sweet frame great part of the next day.]

Wednesday,

Wednesday, September 1.—Went to Judea, to the ordination of Mr. Judd. Dear Mr. Bellamy preached from Matth. xxiv. 46. *Blessed is that servant, &c.* I felt very solemn, and very sweetly, most of the time; had my thoughts much on that time when *our Lord will come;* that time refreshed my soul much; only I was afraid, I should not be found faithful, because I have so vile a heart. My thoughts were much in eternity, where I love to dwell. Blessed be God for this solemn season. Rode home to night with Mr. Bellamy; felt something sweetly on the road; conversed with some friends until it was very late, and then retired to rest in a comfortable frame.

Thursday, September 2.—About two in the afternoon, I preached from Joh. vi. 67. and God assisted me in some comfortable degree; but more especially in my first prayer; my soul seemed then to launch quite into the eternal world, and to be as it were separated from this lower world. Afterwards preached again from Isa. v. 4. God gave me some assistance; but I saw myself a poor worm.

[On Friday, September 3, he complains of having but little life in the things of God, the former part of the day, but afterwards speaks of sweetness and enlargement.]

Saturday, September 4.—Much out of health, and exceedingly depressed in my soul, and was at an awful distance from God. Towards night spent some time in profitable thoughts on Rom. viii. 2. Near night, had a very sweet season in prayer; God enabled me to wrestle ardently for the advancement of the Redeemer's kingdom; pleaded earnestly for my own dear brother John, that God would make him more of a pilgrim and stranger on the earth, and fit him for singular serviceableness in the world; and my heart sweetly exulted in the Lord, in the thoughts of any diftreffes that might alight on him or me, in the advancement of Chrift's kingdom. It was a fweet and comfortable hour unto my foul, while I was indulged freedom to plead, not only for myfelf, but for many other fouls.

Lord's Day, September 5.—Preached all day ; was fomething ftrengthened and affifted in the afternoon ; more efpecially in the evening : Had a fenfe of my unfpeakable fhort comings in all my duties. I found, alas ! that I had never lived to God in my life.

Monday, September 6.—Was informed that they only waited for an opportunity to apprehend me for preaching at New-Haven lately, that fo they might imprifon me : This made me more folemn and ferious, and to quit all hopes of the world's friendfhip : It brought me to a further fenfe of my vilenefs, and juft defert of this, and much more, from the hand of God, though not from the hand of man : Retired into a convenient place in the woods, and fpread the matter before God.

[*Tuefday, September* 7.—This day he rode to New-Haven, but was obliged to fecrete himfelf among private friends.]

Wednefday, September 8.—Felt very fweetly, when I firft rofe in the morning. In family prayer, had fome enlargement, but not much fpirituality, until eternity came up before me and looked near : I found fome fweetnefs in the thoughts of bidding a dying farewell to this tirefome world. Though fometime ago I reckoned upon feeing my dear friends at commencement, yet being now denied the opportunity, for fear of imprifonment, I felt totally refigned, and as contented to fpend this day alone in the woods, as I could have done, if I had been allowed to go to town. Felt exceedingly weaned from the world to day. In the afternoon difcourfed fomething on fome divine things with a dear chriftian friend,

friend, whereby we were both refreshed. Then I prayed, with a sweet sense of the blessedness of communion with God: I think I scarce ever enjoyed more of God in any one prayer. O it was a blessed season indeed to my soul! I knew not that ever I saw so much of my own nothingness in my life; never wondered so, that God allowed me to preach his word; never was so astonished as now. This has been a sweet and comfortable day to my soul: Blessed be God. Prayed again with my dear friend, with something of the divine presence. I long to be wholly conformed to God, and transformed into his image.

Thursday, September 9.—Spent much of the day alone: Enjoyed the presence of God in some comfortable degree: Was visited by some dear friends, and prayed with them: Wrote sundry letters to friends; felt religion in my soul while writing: Enjoyed some sweet meditations on some scriptures. In the evening, went very privately into town, from the place of my residence at the farms, and conversed with some dear friends; felt sweetly in singing hymns with them; and made my escape to the farms again, without being discovered by my enemies, as I knew of. Thus the Lord preserves me continually.

Friday, September 10.—Longed with intense desire after God: My whole soul seemed impatient to be conformed to him, and to become *holy, as he is holy*. In the afternoon, prayed with a dear friend privately, and had the presence of God with us; our souls united together to reach after a blessed immortality, to be unclothed of *the body of sin and death*, and to enter the blessed world, where *no unclean thing enters*. O, with what intense desire did our souls long for that blessed day, that we might be freed from sin, and forever live to and in our God! In the evening, took leave of that house; but first kneeled down and
prayed;

prayed ; *the Lord was of a truth in the midst of us ;* it was a sweet parting season; felt in myself much sweetness and affection in the things of God. Blessed be God for every such divine gale of his Spirit, to speed me in my way to the New Jerusalem ! Felt some sweetness afterwards, and spent the evening in conversation with friends, and prayed with some life, and retired to rest very late.

[The five next days, he appears to have been in an exceeding comfortable, sweet frame of mind, for the most part, and to have been the subject of the like heavenly exercises as are often expressed in preceding passages of his Diary.]

Thursday, September 16.—At night, felt exceeding sweetly : Enjoyed much of God in secret prayer : Felt an uncommon resignation, to be and do what God pleased. Some days past, I felt great perplexity on account of my past conduct : My bitterness, and want of christian kindness and love, has been very distressing to my soul. The Lord forgive me my unchristian warmth, and want of a spirit of meekness.

[The next day, he speaks of much resignation, calmness and peace of mind, and near views of the eternal world.]

Saturday, September 18.—Felt some compassion for souls, and mourned I had no more. I feel much more kindness, meekness, gentleness and love towards all mankind, than ever. I long to be at the feet of my enemies and persecutors. Enjoyed some sweetness, in feeling my soul conformed to Christ Jesus, and given away to him forever, in prayer to day.

[The next ten days, he appears to have been for the most part under great degrees of melancholy, exceedingly dejected and discouraged ; speaks of his being ready to give up all for gone respecting the

cause

cause of Christ, and exceedingly longing to die: Yet had some sweet seasons and intervals of comfort, and special assistance and enlargement in the duties of religion, and in performing publick services, and considerable success in them.]

Thursday, September 30.—Still very low in spirits, and did not know how to engage in any work or business, especially to correct some disorders among christians; felt as though I had no power to be faithful in that regard. However, towards noon, preached from Deut. viii. 2. and was enabled with freedom to reprove some things in christians' conduct, that I thought very unsuitable and irregular; insisted near two hours on this subject.

[Through this and the two following weeks, he passed through a variety of exercises: He was frequently dejected, and felt inward distresses; and sometimes sunk into the depths of melancholy: At which turns, he was not exercised about the state of his soul, with regard to the favour of God and his interest in Christ, but about his own sinful infirmities, and unfitness for God's service. His mind appears sometimes extremely depressed and sunk with a sense of inexpressible vileness. But in the mean time, he speaks of many seasons of comfort and spiritual refreshment, wherein his heart was encouraged and strengthened in God, and sweetly resigned to his will, and of some seasons of very high degrees of spiritual consolation,—and of his great longings after holiness and conformity to God, of his great fear of offending God, of his heart's being sweetly melted in religious duties, of his longing for the advancement of Christ's kingdom, and of his having at some times much assistance in preaching, and of remarkable effects on the auditory.]

Lord's Day, October 17.—Had a considerable sense of my helplessness and inability; saw that I must be
dependent

dependent on God for all I want; and especially when I went to the place of publick worship: I found I could not speak a word for God without his special help and assistance: I went into the assembly trembling, as I frequently do, under a sense of my insufficiency to do any thing in the cause of God, as I ought to do. But it pleased God to afford me much assistance, and there seemed to be a considerable effect on the hearers. In the evening, I felt a disposition to praise God for his goodness to me, in special, that he had enabled me in some measure to be faithful; and my soul rejoiced to think, that I had thus performed the work of one day more, and was one day nearer my eternal, and (I trust) my heavenly home. O that I might be *faithful to the death, fulfilling as an hireling my day*, until the shades of the evening of life shall free my soul from the toils of the day! This evening, in secret prayer, I felt exceeding solemn, and such longing desires after deliverance from sin, and after conformity to God, as melted my heart. O, I longed to be *delivered from this body of death!* I felt inward pleasing pain, that I could not be conformed to God entirely, fully and forever. I scarce ever preach without being first visited with inward conflicts and sore trials. Blessed be the Lord for these trials and distresses, as they are blessed for my humbling.

Monday, October 18.—In the morning, felt some sweetness, but still pressed through some trials of soul. My life is a constant mixture of consolations and conflicts, and will be so until I arrive at the world of spirits.

Tuesday, October 19.—This morning and last night, felt a sweet longing in my soul after holiness: My soul seemed so to reach and stretch towards the mark of perfect sanctity, that it was ready to break with longings.

Thursday,

Thursday, October 21.—Had a very deep sense of the vanity of the world, most of the day; had little more regard to it, than if I had been to go into eternity the next hour. Through divine goodness I felt very serious and solemn. O, I love to live on the brink of eternity, in my views and meditations! This gives me a sweet, awful and reverential sense and apprehension of God and divine things, when I see myself as it were *standing before the judgment seat of Christ*.

Friday, October 22.—Uncommonly weaned from the world to day: My soul delighted to be a *stranger and pilgrim on the earth*: I felt a disposition in me never to have any thing to do with this world: The character given of some of the ancient people of God, in Heb. xi. 13. was very pleasing to me, *They confessed that they were pilgrims and strangers on the earth*, by their daily practice; and O that I could always do so! Spent some considerable time, in a pleasant grove, in prayer and meditation. O it is sweet, to be thus weaned from friends, and from myself, and dead to the present world, that so I may live wholly to and upon the blessed God. Saw myself little, low, and vile in myself. In the afternoon, preached at Bethlehem, from Deut. viii. 2. and felt sweetly both in prayer and preaching: God helped me to speak to the hearts of dear christians. Blessed be the Lord for this season: I trust, they and I shall rejoice on this account to all eternity. Dear Mr. Bellamy came in, while I was making the first prayer (being returned home from a journey) and after meeting, we walked away together, and spent the evening in sweetly conversing on divine things, and praying together, with sweet and tender love to each other, and retired to rest with our hearts in a serious spiritual frame.

Monday, October 25.—[At Turkey-Hills.] In the evening enjoyed the divine presence in secret prayer:

It was a sweet and comfortable season to me: *My soul longed for God, for the living God:* Enjoyed a sweet solemnity of spirit, and longing desire after the recovery of the divine image in my soul: *Then shall I be satisfied, when I shall awake in God's likeness,* and never before.

Tuesday, October 26.—[At West-Suffield.] Underwent the most dreadful distresses, under a sense of my own unworthiness: It seemed to me, I deserved rather to be driven out of the place, than to have any body treat me with any kindness, or come to hear me preach. And verily my spirits were so depressed at this time, as well as at many others, that it was impossible I should treat immortal souls with faithfulness: I could not deal closely and faithfully with them, I felt so infinitely vile in myself. O, what *dust and ashes* I am, to think of preaching the gospel to others! Indeed, I never can be faithful for one moment, but shall certainly *daub with untempered mortar,* if God does not grant me special help. In the evening, I went to the meeting house, and it looked to me near as easy for one to rise out of the grave and preach, as for me. However, God afforded me some life and power, both in prayer and sermon: God was pleased to lift me up, and shew me that he could enable me to preach. O the wonderful goodness of God to so vile a sinner! Returned to my quarters; and enjoyed some sweetness in prayer alone, and mourned that I could not live more to God.

Wednesday, October 27.—Spent the forenoon in prayer and meditation: Was not a little concerned about preaching in the afternoon: Felt exceedingly without strength, and very helpless indeed: Went into the meeting house, ashamed to see any come to hear such an unspeakably worthless wretch. However, God enabled me to speak with clearness, power, and pungency: But there was some noise and tumult

mult in the affembly, that I did not well like, and endeavoured to bear publick teftimony againft, with moderation and mildnefs, through the current of my difcourfe. In the evening, was enabled to be in fome meafure thankful and devoted to God.

[The frames and exercifes of his mind, during the four next days, were moftly very fimilar to thofe of the two days paft; excepting intervals of confiderable degrees of divine peace and confolation.]

[Within this time he rode from Suffield to Eaftbury, Hebron, and Lebanon.]

Thurfday, November 4.—[At Lebanon.] Saw much of my nothingnefs, moft of this day; but felt concerned that I had no more fenfe of my infufficiency and unworthinefs. O it is fweet *lying in the duft!* but it is diftreffing, to feel in my foul that hell of corruption, which ftill remains in me. In the afternoon, had a fenfe of the fweetnefs of a ftrict, clofe and conftant devotednefs to God, and my foul was comforted with the confolations of God; my foul felt a pleafing, yet painful concern, left I fhould fpend fome moments *without* God. O may I always *live to God.* In the evening, was vifited by fome friends, and fpent the time in prayer and fuch converfation as tended to our edification. It was a comfortable feafon to my foul: I felt an intenfe defire to fpend every moment for God. God is unfpeakably gracious to me continually: In times paft, he has given me inexpreffible fweetnefs in the performance of duty: Frequently my foul has enjoyed much of God; but has been ready to fay, *Lord it is good to be here;* and fo to indulge floth, while I have lived on the fweetnefs of my feelings. But of late, God has been pleafed to keep my foul hungry, almoft continually; fo that I have been filled with a kind of a pleafing pain: When I really enjoy God, I feel my defires of him the more infatiable, and my thirftings after holinefs the more unquenchable ; and the Lord will not allow me to feel as though I were fully supplied and fatisfied, but keeps me ftill reaching forward ; and I feel barren and empty, as though I could not live, without more of God in me ; I feel afhamed and guilty before God. O, I fee, *the law is fpiritual, but I am carnal!* I do not, I cannot live to God. O for holinefs ! O for more of God in my foul ! O this pleafing pain ! It makes my foul prefs after God; the language of it is, *Then shall I be fatisfied, when I awake in God's likenefs*, Pfal. xvii. ult. but never, never before ; and confequently I am engaged to *prefs toward the mark*, day by day. O that I may feel this continual hunger, and not be retarded, but rather animated by every clufter from Canaan, to reach forward in the narrow way, for the full enjoyment and poffeffion of the heavenly inheritance. O that I may never loiter in my heavenly journey.

[Thefe infatiable defires after God and holinefs, continued the two next days, with a great fenfe of his own exceeding unworthinefs, and the nothingnefs of the things of this world.]

Lord's Day, November 7.—[At Millington.] It feemed as if fuch an unholy wretch as I never could arrive at that bleffednefs, to be *holy, as God is holy*. At noon, I longed for fanctification, and conformity to God. O, that is the all, the all ! The Lord help me to prefs after God forever.

Monday, November 8.—Towards night, enjoyed much fweetnefs in fecret prayer, fo that my foul longed for an arrival in the heavenly country, the bleffed paradife of God. Through divine goodnefs, I have fcarce feen the day, for two months, but death has looked fo pleafant to me at one time or other of the day, that I could have rejoiced the prefent fhould be my laft, notwithftanding my preffing inward trials and conflicts : And I truft, the Lord will finally ly-make me a *conqueror, and more than so;* that I shall be able to ufe that triumphant language, *O death, where is thy fling!* And, *O grave, where is thy victory!*

[Within the next ten days, the following things are expreffed: Longing and wreftling to be holy and to live to God; a defire that every fingle thought might be for God; feeling guilty, that his thoughts were no more fwallowed up in God; fweet folemnity and calmnefs of mind, fubmiffion and refignation to God, great weanednefs from the world, abafement in the duft, grief at fome vain converfation that was obferved, fweetnefs from time to time in fecret prayer, and in converfing and praying with chriftian friends. And every day he appears to have been greatly engaged in the great bufinefs of religion and living to God, without interruption.]

Friday, November 19.—[At New-Haven.] Received a letter from the reverend Mr. Pemberton, of New-York, defiring me fpeedily to go down thither, and confult about the Indian affairs in thofe parts, and to meet certain gentlemen there, that were entrufted with thofe affairs: My mind was inftantly feized with concern; fo I retired with two or three chriftian friends and prayed; and indeed it was a fweet time with me; I was enabled to leave myfelf and all my concerns with God; and taking leave of friends, I rode to Ripton, and was comforted in an opportunity to fee and converfe with dear Mr. Mills.

[In the four next following days, he was fometimes oppreffed with the weight of that great affair, about which Mr. Pemberton had written to him; but was enabled from time to time to *caft his burden on the Lord,* and to commit himfelf and all his concerns to him: And he continued ftill in a fenfe of the excellency of holinefs, and longings after it, and earneft defires of the advancement of Chrift's kingdom

dom in the world; and had from time to time sweet comfort in meditation and prayer.]

Wednesday, November 24.—Came to New-York; felt still much concerned about the importance of my business; put up many earnest requests to God for his help and direction; was confused with the noise and tumult of the city; enjoyed but little time alone with God; but my soul longed after him.

Thursday, November 25.—Spent much time in prayer and supplication: Was examined by some gentlemen, of my christian experiences, and my acquaintance with divinity, and some other studies, in order to my improvement in that important affair of gospellizing the heathen*: Was made sensible of my great ignorance and unfitness for publick service: I had the most abasing thoughts of myself, I think, that ever I had; I thought myself the worst wretch that ever lived: It hurt me and pained my very heart, that any body should shew me any respect: Alas! me thought, how sadly they are deceived in me; how miserably would they be disappointed, if they knew my inside! O my heart! And in this depressed condition, I was forced to go and preach to a considerable assembly, before some grave and learned ministers; but felt such a pressure from a sense of my vileness, ignorance, and unfitness to appear in publick, that I was almost overcome with it; my soul was grieved for the congregation, that they should sit there to hear such a *dead dog* as I preach; I thought myself infinitely indebted to the people, and longed that God would reward them with the rewards of his grace. I spent much of the evening alone.

* These gentlemen that examined Mr. Brainerd, were the Correspondents in New-York, New-Jersey, and Pennsylvania, of the honourable Society in Scotland for propagating Christian Knowledge; to whom was committed the management of their affairs in those parts, and who were now met at New-York.

PART

PART IV.

From the time of his examination by the Correspondents of the Society for propagating Christian Knowledge, and being appointed their MISSIONARY, *to his first entrance on the business of his mission among the Indians at Kaunaumeek.*

FRIDAY, *November* 26.—Had still a sense of my great vileness, and endeavoured as much as I could to keep alone. O, what a nothing, what dust and ashes am I! Enjoyed some peace and comfort in spreading my complaints before the God of all grace.

Saturday, November 27.—Committed my soul to God with some degree of comfort; left New-York about nine in the morning; came away with a distressing sense still of my unspeakable unworthiness. Surely I may well love all my brethren; for none of them all is so vile as I; whatever they do outwardly, yet it seems to me none is conscious of so much guilt before God. O my leanness, my barrenness, my carnality, and past bitterness, and want of a gospel temper! These things oppress my soul. Rode from New-York, thirty miles, to White Plains, and most of the way continued lifting up my heart to God for mercy and purifying grace; and spent the evening much dejected in spirit.

[The three next days, he continued in this frame, in a great sense of his own vileness, with an evident mixture of melancholy, in no small degree; but had some intervals of comfort and God's sensible presence with him.]

Wednesday, December 1.—My soul breathed after God, in sweet spiritual and longing desires of conformity

formity to him; my soul was brought to rest itself and all on his rich grace, and felt strength and encouragement to do or suffer any thing that divine Providence should allot me. Rode about twenty miles, from Stratfield to Newton.

[Within the space of the next nine days, he went a journey from Newton to Haddam, his native town; and after staying there some days, returned again into the western part of Connecticut, and came to Southbury. In his account of the frames and exercises of his mind, during this space of time, are such things as these: Frequent turns of dejection, a sense of his vileness, emptiness, and unfathomable abyss of desperate wickedness in his heart, attended with a conviction that he had never seen but little of it; bitterly mourning over his barrenness, being greatly grieved that he could not live to God, to whom he owed his all ten thousand times; crying out, My leanness, my leanness! a sense of the meetness and suitableness of his lying in the dust beneath God's feet; fervency and ardour in prayer; longing to live to God, and being afflicted with some impertinent trifling conversation that he heard, but enjoying sweetness in christian conversation.]

Saturday, December 11.—Conversed with a dear friend, to whom I had thought of giving a liberal education, and being at the whole charge of it, that he might be fitted for the gospel ministry*. I acquainted him with my thoughts in that matter, and
so

---

* Mr. Brainerd having now undertaken the business of a Missionary to the Indians, and expecting in a little time to leave his native country, to go among the Savages, into the wilderness, far distant, and spend the remainder of his life among them, and having some estate left him by his father, and thinking he should have no occasion for it among them, (though afterwards he told me he found himself mistaken) he set himself to think which way he might spend it most to the glory of God; and no way presenting to his thoughts, wherein he could do more good with it, than by being at the charge of educating some young person for the ministry, that appeared to be of good abilities and well disposed, he pitched upon this person here spoken of, to this end: Who accordingly was soon put to learning; and Mr. Brainerd continued to be at the charge of his education from year to year so long as he (Mr. Brainerd) lived, which was until this young man was carried through his third year in college.

so left him to consider of it, until I should see him again. Then I rode to Bethlehem, and so came to Mr. Bellamy's lodgings ; spent the evening with him in sweet conversation and prayer : We recommended the important concern before mentioned (of sending my friend to college) unto the God of all grace. Blessed be the Lord for this evening's opportunity together.

Lord's Day, December 12.—I felt, in the morning, as if I had little or no power either to pray or preach, and felt a distressing need of divine help : I went to meeting trembling : But it pleased God to assist me in prayer and sermon : I think my soul scarce ever penetrated so far into the immaterial world, in any one prayer that ever I made, nor were my devotions ever so much refined, and free from gross conceptions, and imaginations framed from beholding material objects. I preached with some sweetness, from Matth. vi. 33. *But seek ye first*, &c. And in the afternoon from Rom. xv. 30. *And now I beseech you, brethren*, &c. There was much affection in the assembly. This has been a sweet Sabbath to me : And blessed be God, I have reason to think that my religion has become more refined and spiritual, by means of my late inward conflicts. Amen ! May I always be willing that God should use his own methods with me.

Monday, December 13.—Joined in prayer with Mr. Bellamy ; and found sweetness and composure in parting with him, who went a journey. Enjoyed some sweetness through the day, and just at night rode down to Woodbury.

Tuesday, December 14.—Some perplexity hung on my mind : Was distressed last night and this morning for the interest of Zion, especially on account of the false appearances of religion, that do but rather breed confusion, especially in some places. I cried

cried to God for help, to enable me to bear teſtimony againſt thoſe things, which inſtead of promoting, do but hinder the progreſs of vital piety. In the afternoon, rode down to Southbury, and converſed again with my friend about the important affair of his following the work of the miniſtry; and he appeared much inclined to devote himſelf to that work, if God ſhould ſucceed his attempts to qualify himſelf for ſo great a work. In the evening, I preached from 1 Theſſ. iv. 8. and endeavoured, though with tenderneſs, to undermine falſe religion. The Lord gave me ſome aſſiſtance; but, however, I ſeemed ſo vile, I was aſhamed to be ſeen when I came out of the meeting houſe.

Wedneſday, December 15.—Enjoyed ſomething of God to day, both in ſecret and ſocial prayer; but was ſenſible of much barrenneſs, and defect in duty, as well as my inability to help myſelf for the time to come, or to perform the work and buſineſs I have to do. Afterwards, felt much of the ſweetneſs of religion, and the tenderneſs of the goſpel temper; was far from bitterneſs, and found a dear love to all mankind, and was afraid of ſcarcely any thing ſo much as leſt ſome motion of anger or reſentment ſhould ſome time or other creep into my heart. Had ſome comforting ſoul refreſhing diſcourſe with ſome dear friends, juſt as we took our leave of each other, and ſuppoſed it might be likely we ſhould not meet again until we came to the eternal world*. But I doubt not, through grace, but that ſome of us ſhall have a happy meeting there, and bleſs God for this ſeaſon, as well as many others. Amen.

Thurſday,

---

* It had been determined by the Commiſſioners, who employed Mr. Brainerd as a Miſſionary, that he ſhould go as ſoon as might be conveniently, to the Indians living near the Forks of Delaware river in Penſylvania, and the Indians on Suſquehannah river; which being far off, where he would be expoſed to many hardſhips and dangers; this was the occaſion of his taking leave of his friends in this manner.

Thursday, December 16.—Rode down to Derby; had some sweet thoughts on the road: My thoughts were very clear, especially on the essence of our salvation by Christ, from those words, *Thou shalt call his name Jesus*, &c.

Friday, December 17.—Spent much time in sweet conversation on spiritual things with dear Mr. Humphreys. Rode to Ripton; spent some time in prayer with dear christian friends.

Saturday, December 18.—Spent much time in prayer in the woods: Seemed raised above the things of the world: My soul was strong in the Lord of hosts: But was sensible of great barrenness.

Lord's Day, December 19.—At the sacrament of the Lord's supper, seemed strong in the Lord; and the world with all its frowns and flatteries in a great measure disappeared, so that my soul had nothing to do with them; and I felt a disposition to be wholly and forever the Lord's. In the evening, enjoyed something of the divine presence; had a humbling sense of my vileness, barrenness and sinfulness. O, it wounded me, to think of the misimprovement of time! *God be merciful to me a sinner.*

Monday, December 20.—Spent this day in prayer, reading, and writing; and enjoyed some assistance, especially in correcting some thoughts on a certain subject; but had a mournful sense of my barrenness.

Tuesday, December 21.—Had a sense of my insufficiency for any publick work and business, as well as to live to God. I rode over to Derby, and preached there: It pleased God to give me very sweet assistance and enlargement, and to enable me to speak with a soft and tender power and energy. We had afterwards a comfortable evening in singing and prayer: God enabled me to pray with as much spirituality and sweetness as I have done for some time: My mind seemed to be unclothed of sense and imagination,

tion, and was in a meafure let into the immaterial world of fpirits. This day and evening was, I truft, through infinite goodnefs, made very profitable to a number of us, to advance our fouls in holinefs and conformity to God: The glory be to him forever. Amen. How bleffed it is to grow more and more like God!

Wednefday, December 22.—Enjoyed fome affiftance in preaching at Ripton; but my foul mourned within me for my barrennefs.

Thurfday, December 23.—Enjoyed, I truft, fomething of God this morning in fecret. O how divinely fweet it is to come into the fecret of his prefence, and abide in his pavillion! Took an affectionate leave of friends, not expecting to fee them again for a very confiderable time, if ever in this world. Rode with Mr. Humphreys to his houfe at Derby; fpent the time in fweet converfation; my foul was refrefhed and fweetly melted with divine things. O that I was always confecrated to God. Near night, I rode to New-Haven, and there enjoyed fome fweetnefs in prayer and converfation, with fome dear chriftian friends: My mind was fweetly ferious and compofed: But alas, I too much loft the fenfe of divine things!

[He continued much in the fame frame of mind, and in like exercifes, the two following days.]

Lord's Day, December 26.—Felt much fweetnefs and tendernefs in prayer; efpecially my whole foul feemed to love my worft enemies, and was enabled to pray for thofe that are ftrangers and enemies to God with a great degree of foftnefs and pathetick fervour. In the evening, rode from New-Haven to Branford, after I had kneeled down and prayed with a number of dear chriftian friends in a very retired place in the woods, and fo parted.

Monday, December 27.—Enjoyed a precious feafon indeed; had a fweet melting fenfe of divine things, of the pure spirituality of the religion of Christ Jesus. In the evening, I preached from Matth. vi. 33. with much freedom, and sweet power and pungency: The presence of God attended our meeting. O the sweetness, the tenderness I felt in my soul! If ever I felt the temper of Christ, I had some sense of it now. Blessed be my God, I have seldom enjoyed a more comfortable and profitable day than this. O that I could spend all my time for God.

Tuesday, December 28.—Rode from Branford to Haddam. In the morning, my clearness and sweetness in divine things continued; but afterwards my spiritual life sensibly declined.

[The next twelve days, he was for the most part extremely dejected, discouraged and distressed, and was evidently very much under the power of melancholy; and there are from day to day most bitter complaints of exceeding vileness, ignorance, corruption, an amazing Load of guilt, unworthiness to creep on God's earth, everlasting uselessness, fitness for nothing, &c. and sometimes expressions even of horror at the thoughts of ever preaching again. But yet in this time of great dejection, he speaks of several intervals of divine help and comfort.]

[The three next days, which were spent at Hebron and the Crank (a parish in Lebanon) he had relief, and enjoyed considerable comfort.]

Friday, January 14, 1742,3.—My spiritual conflicts to day were unspeakably dreadful, heavier than the mountains and overflowing floods: I seemed inclosed, as it were in hell itself! I was deprived of all sense of God, even of the being of a God; and that was my misery! I had no awful apprehensions of God as angry. This was distress, the nearest akin to the damned's torments, that I ever endured: Their torment, I am sure, will consist much in a privation of God, and consequently of all good. This taught me the abfolute dependence of a creature upon God the Creator, for every crumb of happinefs it enjoys. O! I feel that if there is no God, though I might live forever here, and enjoy not only this, but all other worlds, I fhould be ten thoufand times more miferable than a toad! My foul was in fuch anguifh I could not eat, but felt as I fuppofed a poor wretch would that is juft going to the place of execution. I was almoft fwallowed up with anguifh, when I faw people gathering together to hear me preach. However, I went in that diftrefs to the houfe of God, and found not much relief in the firft prayer: It feemed as if God would let loofe the people upon me, nor were the thoughts of death diftreffing to me, like my own vilenefs. But afterwards, in my difcourfe from Deut. viii. 2. God was pleafed to give me fome freedom and enlargement, fome power and fpirituality; and I fpent the evening fomething comfortably.

[The two next days, his comfort continues, and he feems to enjoy an almoft continual fweetnefs of foul in the duties and exercifes of religion and chriftian converfation. On Monday was a return of the gloom he had been under the Friday before. He rode to Coventry this day, and the latter part of the day, had more freedom. On Tuefday he rode to Canterbury, and continued more comfortable.]

Wednefday, January 19.—[At Canterbury.] In the afternoon preached the lecture at the meeting houfe: Felt fome tendernefs, and fomething of the gofpel temper: Exhorted the people to love one another, and not fet up their own frames as a ftandard to try all their brethren by. But was much preffed, moft of the day, with a fenfe of my own badnefs, inward impurity, and unfpeakable corruption. Spent the evening in loving chriftian converfation.

Thurfday, January 20.—Rode to my brother's houfe between Norwich and Lebanon; and preached in
the

the evening to a number of people: Enjoyed neither freedom nor spirituality; but saw myself exceeding unworthy.

Friday, January 21.—Had great inward conflicts; enjoyed but little comfort. Went to see Mr. Williams of Lebanon, and spent several hours with him; and was greatly delighted with his serious, deliberate and impartial way of discourse about religion.

[The next day, he was much dejected.]

Lord's Day, January 23.—Scarce ever felt myself so unfit to exist, as now: I saw, I was not worthy of a place among the Indians, where I am going, if God permit: I thought I should be ashamed to look them in the face, and much more to have any respect shewn me there. Indeed I felt myself banished from the earth, as if all places were too good for such a wretch as I: I thought I should be ashamed to go among the very savages of Africa: I appeared to myself a creature fit for nothing, neither heaven nor earth. None knows, but those that feel it, what the soul endures that is sensibly shut out from the presence of God: Alas, it is more bitter than death!

[On Monday he rode to Stoningtown, Mr. Fish's parish. On Tuesday he expresses considerable degrees of spiritual comfort and refreshment.]

Wednesday, January 26.—Preached to a pretty large assembly at Mr. Fish's meeting house: Insisted on humility, and steadfastness in keeping God's commands, and that through humility we should prefer one another in love, and not make our own frames the rule by which we judge others. I felt sweetly calm, and full of brotherly love; and never more free from party spirit. I hope some good will follow, that christians will be freed from false joy, and party zeal, and censuring one another.

[On Thursday, after considerable time spent in prayer and christian conversation, he rode to New-London.]

Friday, January 28.—Here I found some fallen into some extravagances, too much carried away with a false zeal, and bitterness. O, the want of a gospel temper is greatly to be lamented. Spent the evening in conversing with some about some points of conduct in both ministers and private christians; but did not agree with them; God had not *taught them with briers and thorns* to be of a kind disposition toward mankind.

[On Saturday, he rode to East-Haddam, and spent the three following days there; and in that space of time he speaks of his feeling weanedness from the world, a sense of the nearness of eternity, special assistance in praying for the enlargement of Christ's kingdom, times of spiritual comfort, &c.]

Wednesday, February 2.—Preached my farewell sermon, last night, at the house of an aged man, who had been unable to attend on the publick worship for some time; and this morning, spent the time in prayer, almost wherever I went; and having taken leave of friends, I set out on my journey towards the Indians; though by the way I was to spend some time at East-Hampton on Long-Island, by the leave of the commissioners who employed me in the Indian affair*; and being accompanied by a messenger from East-Hampton, we travelled to Lyme. On the road I felt an uncommon pressure of mind: I seemed to struggle hard for some pleasure in something here below, and seemed loth to give up all for gone; but then saw myself evidently throwing myself into all hardships and distresses in my present undertaking; I thought it would be less difficult to lie down in the grave: But yet I chose to go, rather than stay. Came to Lyme that night.

[He

---

* The reason why the Commissioners or Correspondents did not order Mr. Brainerd to go immediately to the Indians, and enter on his business as a Missionary to them, was that the winter was not judged to be a convenient season for him first to go out into the wilderness, and enter on the difficulties and hardships he must there be exposed to.

[He waited the two next days for a passage over the sound, and spent much of the time in inward conflicts and dejection, but had some comfort.]

[On Saturday, he crossed the sound, landed at Oyster-Ponds on Long-Island, and travelled from thence to East-Hampton. And the seven following days he spent there, for the most part, under extreme dejection and gloominess of mind, with great complaints of darkness, ignorance, &c. Yet his heart appears to have been constantly engaged in the great business of religion, much concerned for the interest of religion in East-Hampton, and praying and labouring much for it.]

Saturday, February 12.—Enjoyed a little more comfort, was enabled to meditate with some composure of mind; and especially in the evening, found my soul more refreshed in prayer, than at any time of late; my soul seemed to *take hold of God's strength*, and was comforted with his consolations. O how sweet are some glimpses of divine glory! How strengthening and quickening!

Lord's Day, February 13.—At noon, under a great degree of discouragement; knew not how it was possible for me to preach in the afternoon; was ready to give up all for gone; but God was pleased to assist me in some measure. In the evening, my heart was sweetly drawn out after God, and devoted to him.

[The next day, he had comfort and dejection intermingled.]

Tuesday, February 15.—Early in the day I felt some comfort, afterwards I walked into a neighbouring grove, and felt more as a stranger on earth, I think, than ever before; dead to any of the enjoyments of the world as if I had been dead in a natural sense. In the evening, had divine sweetness in secret duty: God was then my portion, and my soul rose above those *deep waters*, into which I have sunk so low of late: My soul then cried for Zion, and had sweetness in so doing.

[This sweet frame continued the next morning; but afterwards his inward distress returned.]

Thursday, February 17.—In the morning, found myself something comfortable, and rested on God in some measure. Preached this day at a little village belonging to East-Hampton; and God was pleased to give me his gracious presence and assistance, so that I spake with freedom, boldness and some power. In the evening, spent some time with a dear christian friend; felt sweetly serious, as on the brink of eternity; my soul enjoyed sweetness in lively apprehensions of standing before the glorious God: Prayed with my dear friend with sweetness, and discoursed with utmost solemnity. And truly it was a little emblem of heaven itself. I find my soul is more refined and weaned from a dependence on my frames and spiritual feelings.

Friday, February 18.—Felt something sweetly most of the day, and found access to the throne of grace. Blessed be the Lord for any intervals of heavenly delight and composure, while I am engaged in the field of battle. O that I might be serious, solemn, and always vigilant, while in an evil world. Had some opportunity alone to day, and found some freedom in study. O, I long to live to God.

Lord's Day, February 20.—Was something perplexed on account of my carelessness; I thought I could not be suitably concerned about the important work of the day, and so was restless with my easiness. Was exceeding infirm again to day; but the Lord strengthened me both in the outward and inward man, so that I preached with some life and spirituality, especially in the afternoon, wherein I was enabled to speak closely against selfish religion,

that

that loves Chrift for his benefits, but not for himfelf.

[During the next fortnight, it appears that he for the moft part enjoyed much fpiritual peace and comfort. In his Diary for this fpace of time, are expreffed fuch things as thefe; mourning over indwelling fin, and unprofitablenefs; deadnefs to the world; longing after God and to live to his glory; heart melting defires after his eternal home; fixed reliance on God for his help; experience of much divine affiftance both in the private and publick exercifes of religion; inward ftrength and courage in the fervice of God; very frequent refreshment, confolation and divine fweetnefs in meditation, prayer, preaching, and chriftian converfation. And it appears by his account, that this fpace of time was filled up with great diligence and earneftnefs in ferving God, in ftudy, prayer, meditation, preaching, and private inftructing and counfeling.]

Monday, March 7.—This morning when I arofe, I found my heart go forth after God in longing defires of conformity to him, and in fecret prayer found myfelf fweetly quickened and drawn out in praifes to God for all he had done to and for me, and for all my inward trials and diftreffes of late; my heart afcribed glory, glory, glory to the bleffed God! And bid welcome all inward diftrefs again, if God faw meet to exercife me with it; time appeared but an inch long, and eternity at hand; and I thought I could with patience and cheerfulnefs bear any thing for the caufe of God: For I faw that a moment would bring me to a world of peace and bleffednefs; and my foul, by the ftrength of the Lord, rofe far above this lower world, and all the vain amufements and frightful difappointments of it. Afterwards, was vifited by fome friends, but loft fome fweetnefs by the means. After that, had some sweet meditation on Gen. v. 24. *And Enoch walked with God*, &c. This was a comfortable day to my soul.

[The next day, he seems to have continued in a considerable degree of sweetness and fervency in religion.]

Wednesday, March 9.—Endeavoured to commit myself and all my concerns to God. Rode sixteen Miles to Mantauk*, and had some inward sweetness on the road ; but something of flatness and deadness after I came there and had seen the Indians : I withdrew, and endeavoured to pray, but found myself awfully deserted and left, and had an afflicting sense of my vileness and meanness. However, I went and preached from Isai. liii. 10. Had some assistance ; and, I trust, something of the divine presence was among us. In the evening, again I prayed and exhorted among them, after having had a season alone, wherein I was so pressed with the blackness of my nature, that I thought it was not fit for me to speak so much as to Indians.

[The next day, he returned to East-Hampton ; was exceeding infirm in body through the remaining part of this week ; but speaks of assistance and enlargement in study and religious exercises, and of inward sweetness and breathing after God.]

Lord's Day, March 13.—At noon, I thought it impossible for me to preach, by reason of bodily weakness and inward deadness ; and in the first prayer, was so weak that I could hardly stand ; but in sermon, God strengthened me, so that I spake near an hour and half with sweet freedom, clearness and some tender power, from Gen. v. 24. *And Enoch walked with God.* I was sweetly assisted to insist on a close *walk with God*, and to leave this as my parting

---

* Mantauk is the eastern cape or end of Long-Island, then inhabited chiefly by Indians.

ing advice to God's people here, *that they should walk with God.* May the God of all grace succeed my poor labours in this place!

Monday, March 14.—In the morning, was very busy in preparation for my journey, and was almost continually engaged in ejaculatory prayer. About ten, took leave of the dear people of East-Hampton. My heart grieved and mourned, and rejoiced at the same time; rode near fifty miles to a part of Brook-Haven, and lodged there, and had refreshing conversation with a christian friend.

[In two days more he reached New-York; but complains of much desertion and deadness on the road. He stayed one day in New-York, and on Friday went to Mr. Dickinson's at Elizabeth-Town. His complaints are the same as on the two preceding days.]

Saturday, March 19.—Was bitterly distressed under a sense of my ignorance, darkness and unworthiness; got alone, and poured out my complaint to God in the bitterness of my soul. In the afternoon, rode to Newark, and had some sweetness in conversation with Mr. Burr, and in praying together. O! blessed be God forever and ever, for any enlivening and quickening.

Lord's Day, March 20.—Preached in the forenoon: God gave me some assistance and sweetness, and enabled me to speak with real tenderness, love and impartiality. In the evening preached again; and of a truth God was pleased to assist a poor worm. Blessed be God, I was enabled to speak with life, power, and passionate desire of the edification of God's people, and with some power to sinners. In the evening, I felt something spiritual and watchful, lest my heart should by any means be drawn away from God. O, when shall I come to that blessed world, where every power of my soul will be incessantly

ceſſantly and eternally wound up, in heavenly employments and enjoyments, to the higheſt degree?

[On Monday he went to Woodbridge, where he ſpeaks of his being with a number of miniſters* ; and the remainder of this week and the greater part of the next he ſpent in a journey to Stockbridge.]

* Theſe miniſters were the Correſpondents, who now met at Woodbridge, and gave Mr. Brainerd new directions, and inſtead of ſending him to the Indians at the Forks of Delaware, as before intended, they ordered him to go to a number of Indians, at Kaunaumeek, a place in the province of New-York, in the woods between Stockbridge and Albany.

PART V.

From his first beginning to instruct the Indians at Kaunaumeek, to his Ordination.

FRIDAY, *April* 1, 1743.—I rode to Kaunaumeek, near twenty miles from Stockbridge, where the Indians live, with whom I am concerned, and there lodged on a little heap of straw: Was greatly exercised with inward trials and distresses all day; and in the evening, my heart was sunk, and I seemed to have no God to go to. O that God would help me!

[The next five days, he was for the most part in a dejected depressed state of mind, and sometimes extremely so.]

Friday, April 7.—Appeared to myself exceeding ignorant, weak, helpless, and unworthy, and altogether unequal to my work. It seemed to me, I should never do any service, or have any success among the Indians. My soul was weary of my life: I longed for death beyond measure. When I thought of any godly soul departed, my soul was ready to envy him his privilege, thinking, O when will my turn come! Must it be years first! But I know those ardent desires at this and other times, rose partly from want of resignation to God under all miseries; and so were but impatience. Towards night I had, I think, the exercise of faith in prayer, and some assistance in writing. O that God would keep me near him!

Friday, April 8.—Was exceedingly pressed under a sense of my pride, selfishness, bitterness, and party spirit in times past, while I attempted to promote the cause of God: It's vile nature and dreadful consequences appeared in such odious colours to me, that my very heart was pained: I saw how poor souls stumbled over it into everlasting destruction, that I was constrained to make that prayer in the bitterness of my soul, *O Lord, deliver me from blood guiltiness.* I saw my desert of hell on this account. My soul was full of inward anguish and shame before God, that I had spent so much time in conversation tending only to promote a party spirit. O, I saw I had not suitably prized mortification, self denial, resignation under all adversities, meekness, love, candour, and holiness of heart and life: And this day was almost wholly spent in such bitter and foul afflicting reflections on my past frames and conduct. Of late I have thought much of having the kingdom of Christ advanced in the world; but now I saw I had enough to do within myself. *The Lord be merciful to me a sinner,* and wash my soul.

Saturday, April 9.—Remained much in the same state as yesterday; excepting that the sense of my vileness was not so quick and acute.

Lord's Day, April 10.—Rose early in the morning, and walked out, and spent considerable time in the woods, in prayer and meditation. Preached to the Indians both forenoon and afternoon. They behaved soberly in general: Two or three in particular appeared under some religious concern; with whom I discoursed privately; and one told me, her heart had cried, ever since she heard me preach first.

[The two next days he complains of much desertion, and manifests a great sense of guilt and stupidity.]

Wednesday, April 13.—My heart was overwhelmed within me: I verily thought I was the meanest, vilest, most helpless, guilty, ignorant, benighted creature living. And yet I knew what God had done for my soul, at the same time. Though sometimes,

I was assaulted with damping doubts and fears, whether it was possible for such a wretch as I to be in a state of grace.

Saturday, April 16.—Still in the depths of distress. In the afternoon, preached to my people; but was more discouraged with them than before; feared that nothing would ever be done for them to any happy effect. I retired and poured out my soul to God for mercy; but without any sensible relief.— Soon after came an Irishman and a Dutchman, with a design, as they said, to hear me preach the next day; but none can tell how I felt to hear their profane talk. O, I longed that some dear christian knew my distress. I got into a kind of hovel, and there groaned out my complaint to God; and withal felt more sensible gratitude and thankfulness to God, that he had made me to differ from these men, as I knew through grace he had.

Lord's Day, April 17.—In the morning was again distressed as soon as I awaked, hearing much talk about the world and the things of it: Though I perceived the men were in some measure afraid of me; and I discoursed something about sanctifying the Sabbath, if possible, to solemnize their minds; but when they were at a little distance, they again talked freely about secular affairs. O, I thought, what a hell it would be to live with such men to eternity! The Lord gave me some assistance in preaching, all day, and some resignation, and a small degree of comfort in prayer at night.

[He continued in this disconsolate frame the next day.]

Tuesday, April 19.—In the morning, enjoyed some sweet repose and rest in God; felt some strength and confidence in God; and my soul was in some measure refreshed and comforted. Spent most of the day in writing, and had some exercise of grace sensible and comfortable;

comfortable; my soul seemed lifted above the *deep waters*, wherein it has been so long almost drowned; felt some spiritual longings and breathings of soul after God; found myself engaged for the advancement of Christ's kingdom in my own soul, more than in others, more than in the heathen world.

Wednesday, April 20.—Set apart this day for fasting and prayer, to bow my soul before God for the bestowment of divine grace; especially that all my spiritual afflictions and inward distresses might be sanctified to my soul. And endeavoured also to remember the goodness of God to me in the year past, this day being my birth day. Having obtained help of God, I have hitherto lived, and am now arrived at the age of twenty five years. My soul was pained to think of my barrenness and deadness; that I have lived so little to the glory of the eternal God. I spent the day in the woods alone, and there poured out my complaint to God. O that God would enable me to live to his glory for the future.

Thursday, April 21.—Spent the forenoon in reading and prayer, and found myself something engaged; but still much depressed in spirit under a sense of my vileness and unfitness for any publick service. In the afternoon, I visited my people, and prayed and conversed with some about their souls' concerns: And afterwards found some ardour of soul in secret prayer. O that I might grow up into the likeness of God.

Friday, April 22.—Spent the day in study, reading and prayer; and felt a little relieved of my burden, that has been so heavy of late. But still in some measure oppressed. Had a sense of barrenness. O, my leanness testifies against me! My very soul abhors itself for its unlikeness to God, its inactivity and sluggishness. When I have done all, alas, what an *unprofitable servant* am I! My soul groans, to

see

see the hours of the day roll away, because I do not fill them, in spirituality and heavenly mindedness. And yet I long they should speed their pace, to hasten me to my eternal home, where I may fill up all my moments, through eternity, for God and his glory

[For several following days he seems to have been under an increase of dejection and melancholy. On Tuesday, he expresses some relief. Wednesday he kept as a day of fasting and prayer, but in great distress. The next three days following, his melancholy continued, but in a lesser degree, and with intervals of comfort.]

Lord's Day, May 1.—Was at Stockbridge to day. In the forenoon had some relief and assistance; though not so much as usual. In the afternoon, felt poorly in body and soul; while I was preaching, seemed to be rehearsing idle tales, without the least life, fervour, sense or comfort: And especially afterwards, at the sacrament, my soul was filled with confusion, and the utmost anguish that ever I endured, under the feeling of my inexpressible vileness and meanness.

[The remaining days of this week were spent, for the most part, in inward distress and gloominess. The next Sabbath, he had encouragement, assistance and comfort; but on Monday sunk again.]

Tuesday, May 10.—Was in the same state, as to my mind, that I have been in for some time, extremely pressed with a sense of guilt, pollution, blindness: *The iniquity of my heels have compassed me about; the sins of my youth have been set in order before me; they have gone over my head, as an heavy burden, too heavy for me to bear.* Almost all the actions of my life past seem to be covered over with sin and guilt; and those of them that I performed in the most conscientious manner, now fill me with shame and confusion, that I cannot hold up my face. O! the pride, selfishness,

selfishness, hypocrisy, ignorance, bitterness, party zeal, and the want of love, candour, meekness and gentleness that have attended my attempts to promote religion and virtue; and this when I have reason to hope I had real assistance from above, and some sweet intercourse with heaven! But alas, what corrupt mixtures attended my best duties!

[The next seven days, his gloom and distress continued, for the most part; but he had some turns of relief and spiritual comfort. He gives an account of his spending part of this time in hard labour, to build himself a little cottage to live in amongst the Indians, in which he might be by himself; having (it seems) hitherto lived with a poor Scotchman; and afterwards, before his own house was habitable, lived in a wigwam among the Indians.]

Wednesday, May 18.—My circumstances are such that I have no comfort, of any kind, but what I have in God. I live in the most lonesome wilderness; have but one single person to converse with, that can speak English*: Most of the talk I hear, is either Highland-Scotch or Indian. I have no fellow christian to whom I might unbosom myself, and lay open my spiritual sorrows, and with whom I might take sweet counsel in conversation about heavenly things, and join in social prayer. I live poorly with regard to the comforts of life: Most of my diet consists of boiled corn, hasty-pudding, &c. I lodge on a bundle of straw, and my labour is hard and extremely difficult; and I have little appearance of success to comfort me. The Indians' affairs are very difficult; having no land to live on, but what

the

---

* This person was Mr. Brainerd's interpreter; who was an ingenious young Indian belonging to Stockbridge, whose name was John Wauwaumpequnnaunt, who had been instructed in the christian religion by Mr. Sergeant; and had lived with the Rev. Mr. Williams of Long-Meadow, and had been further instructed by him at the charge of Mr. Hollis of London; and understood both English and Indian very well, and wrote a good hand.

the Dutch people lay claim to, and threaten to drive them off from; they have no regard to the souls of the poor Indians; and, by what I can learn, they hate me, because I come to preach to them. But that which makes all my difficulties grievous to be borne, is, that God hides his face from me.

[The next eleven days, his burdens were for the most part alleviated; but with variety; at some times having considerable consolation, and at other times more depressed. The next day, Monday, May 30, he set out on a journey to New-Jersey, to consult the Commissioners that employed him about the affairs of his mission*: Performed his journey thither in four days; and arrived at Mr. Burr's in Newark on Thursday. In great part of his journey, he was in the depths of melancholy, under like distresses with those already mentioned. On Friday, he rode to Elizabeth-Town; and on Saturday, to New-York; and from thence on his way homewards as far as White-Plains, where he spent the Sabbath, and had considerable degrees of divine consolation and assistance in publick services. On Monday, he rode about sixty miles to New-Haven. There he attempted a reconciliation with the authority of the college; and spent this week in visiting his friends in those parts, and in his journey homewards, until Saturday, in a pretty comfortable frame of mind.— On Saturday, in his way from Stockbridge to Kaunaumeek, he was lost in the woods, and lay all night in the open air; but happily found his way in the morning, and came to his Indians on Lord's Day, June 12. And had greater assistance in preaching among them than ever before, since his first coming among them.]

[From

---

* His business with the Commissioners now, was, to obtain orders from them to set up a school among the Indians at Kaunaumeek, and that his interpreter might be appointed the schoolmaster; Which was accordingly done.

[From this time forward he was the subject of various frames and exercises of mind. How it was with him in those dark seasons, he himself further describes in his Diary for July 2, in the following manner. My soul is and has for a long time been in a piteous condition, wading through a series of sorrows, of various kinds. I have been so crushed down sometimes with a sense of my meanness and infinite unworthiness, that I have been ashamed that any even the meanest of my fellow creatures should so much as spend a thought about me, and have wished sometimes while I have travelled among the thick brakes, as one of them to drop into everlasting oblivion. Sometimes my soul has been in distress on feeling some particular corruptions rise and swell like a mighty torrent, with present violence ; having at the same time ten thousand former sins and follies presented to view, in all their blackness and aggravations. And these attended with such external circumstances as mine at present are ; destitute of most of the conveniencies of life, and I may say, of all the pleasures of it ; without a friend to communicate any of my sorrows to, and sometimes without any place of retirement, where I may unburden my soul before God, which has greatly contributed to my distress. Of late, more especially, my great difficulty has been a sort of carelessness, a kind of regardless temper of mind, whence I have been disposed to indolence and trifling : And this temper of mind has constantly been attended with guilt and shame ; so that sometimes I have been in a kind of horror, to find myself so unlike the blessed God ; and have thought I grew worse under all my trials ; and nothing has cut and wounded my soul more than this. O, if I am one of God's chosen, as I trust through infinite grace I am, I find of a truth, that *the righteous are scarcely saved!*

It

Mr. DAVID BRAINERD. 97

It is apparent, that one main occasion of that distressing gloominess of mind which he was so much exercised with at Kaunaumeek, was reflection on his past errors and misguided zeal at college, in the beginning of the late religious commotions in the land. And therefore he repeated his endeavours this year for reconciliation with the governours of the college, whom he had in that time offended. Although he had been at New-Haven, in June, this year, and had attempted a reconciliation, as has been mentioned already, yet in the beginning of July, he made another journey thither, and renewed his attempt, but still in vain.

Although he was much dejected great part of that space of time that I am now speaking of, yet there were many intermissions of his melancholy, and some seasons of comfort, sweet tranquillity and resignation of mind, and frequent special assistance in publick services, that he speaks of in his Diary. The manner of his relief from his sorrow, once in particular, is worthy to be mentioned in his own words, in his Diary, for July 25, which are as follows: Had little or no resolution for a life of holiness; was ready almost to renounce my hopes of living to God. And O how dark it looked, to think of being unholy forever! This I could not endure. The cry of my soul was that (Psal. lxv. 3,) *Iniquities prevail against me.* But was in some measure relieved by a comfortable meditation on God's eternity, that he never had a beginning, &c. whence I was led to admire his greatness and power, &c. in such a manner that I stood still and praised the Lord for his own glories and perfections; though I was (and if I should forever be) an unholy creature, my soul was comforted to apprehend an eternal, infinite, powerful, holy God.]

Saturday, July 30.—Just at night, moved into my own house, and lodged there that night; found it much

much better spending the time alone in my own house, than in the wigwam where I was before.

Lord's Day, July 31.—Felt more comfortably than some days past. Blessed be the Lord, that has now given me a place of retirement. O that I might find God in it, and that he would dwell with me forever.

Monday, August 1.—Was still busy in further labours on my house. Felt a little of the sweetness of religion, and thought it was worth the while to follow after God through a thousand snares, deserts, and death itself. O that I might always follow after holiness, that I may be fully conformed to God. Had some degree of sweetness, in secret prayer, though I had much sorrow.

Wednesday, August 3.—Spent most of the day in writing. Enjoyed some sense of religion. Through divine goodness I am now uninterruptedly alone; and find my retirement comfortable. I have enjoyed more sense of divine things within a few days last past, than for some time before. I longed after holiness, humility and meekness: O that God would enable me to *pass the time of my sojourning here in his fear*, and always live to him.

Thursday, August 4.—Was enabled to pray much through the whole day; and through divine goodness found some intenseness of soul in the duty, as I used to do, and some ability to persevere in my supplications: Had some apprehensions of divine things, that were engaging, and that gave me some courage and resolution. It is good, I find, to persevere in attempts to pray, if I cannot pray with perseverance, i. e. continue long in my addresses to the Divine Being. I have generally found that the more I do in secret prayer, the more I have delighted to do, and have enjoyed more of a spirit of prayer; and frequently have found the contrary, when, with journeying

neying or otherwise, I have been much deprived of retirement. A seasonable steady performance of secret duties in their proper hours, and a careful improvement of all time, filling up every hour with some profitable labour, either of heart, head, or hands, are excellent means of spiritual peace and boldness before God. Christ indeed is our peace, and *by him we have boldness of access to God;* but a *good conscience, void of offence,* is an excellent preparation for an approach into the divine presence. There is difference between self confidence, and a self righteous pleasing ourselves (with our own duties, attainments, and spiritual enjoyments) which godly souls sometimes are guilty of, and that holy confidence arising from the testimony of a good conscience, which good Hezekiah had when he says, *Remember, O Lord, I beseech thee, how I have walked before thee in truth, and with a perfect heart. Then* (says the holy Psalmist) *shall I not be ashamed, when I have respect to all thy commandments.* Filling up our time with and for God is the way to rise up and lie down in peace.

[The next eight days, he continued for the most part in a very comfortable frame, having his mind fixed and sweetly engaged in religion; and more than once blesses God, that he had given him a little cottage, where he might live alone, and enjoy a happy retirement, free from noise and disturbance, and could at any hour of the day lay aside all studies, and spend time in lifting up his soul to God for spiritual blessings.]

Saturday, August 13.—Was enabled in secret prayer to raise my soul to God, with desire and delight. It was indeed a blessed season to my soul: I found the comfort of being a christian: *I counted the sufferings of the present life not worthy to be compared with the glory* of divine enjoyments, even in this world. All my past sorrows seemed kindly

kindly to difappear, and I *remembered no more the for-rosw, for joy.* O, how kindly, and with what a filial tendernefs, the foul hangs on, and confides in *the Rock of ages,* at fuch a feafon, that he will *never leave it nor forfake it,* that he will caufe *all things to work together for its good,* &c. I longed that others fhould know how good a God the Lord is. My foul was full of tendernefs and love, even to the moft inveterate of my enimies: I longed they fhould fhare in the fame mercy. I loved and longed that God fhould do juft as he pleafed, with me and every thing elfe. I felt exceeding ferious, calm and peaceful, and encouraged to prefs after holinefs as long as I live, whatever difficulties and trials may be in my way. May the Lord always help me fo to do. Amen, and Amen!

Lord's Day, Auguft 14.—I had much more freedom in publick, than in private. God enabled me to fpeak with fome feeling fenfe of divine things; but perceived no confiderable effect.

Monday, Auguft 15.—Spent moft of the day in labour to procure fomething to keep my horfe on in the winter. Enjoyed not much fweetnefs in the morning: Was very weak in body, through the day, and thought this frail body would foon drop into the duft: Had fome very realizing apprehenfions of a fpeedy entrance into another world. And in this weak ftate of body, was not a little diftreffed for want of fuitable food. Had no bread, nor could I get any. I am forced to go or fend ten or fifteen miles for all the bread I eat; and fometimes it is mouldy and four, before I eat it, if I get any confiderable quantity: And then again I have none for fome days together, for want of an opportunity to fend for it, and cannot find my horfe in the woods to go myfelf; and this was my cafe now: But through divine goodnefs I had fome Indian meal, of

which

which I made little cakes and fried them. Yet felt contented with my circumstances, and sweetly resigned to God. In prayer I enjoyed great freedom; and blessed God as much for my present circumstances, as if I had been a king; and thought, I found a disposition to be contented in any circumstances: Blessed be God!

[The rest of this week, he was exceeding weak in body and much exercised with pain; and yet obliged from day to day to labour hard, to procure fodder for his horse; excepting some part of the time he was so very ill, that he was neither able to work nor study: But speaks of longings after holiness and perfect conformity to God; complains of enjoying but little of God; yet says, that little was better to him than all the world besides. In his Diary for Saturday, he says, he was something melancholy and sorrowful in mind; and adds, I never feel comfortably, but when I find my soul going forth after God: If I cannot be holy, I must necessarily be miserable forever.]

Lord's Day, August 21.—Was much straitened in the forenoon exercise: My thoughts seemed to be all scattered to the ends of the earth. At noon I fell down before the Lord, and groaned under my vileness, barrenness, deadness, and felt as if I was guilty of soul murder, in speaking to immortal souls in such a manner as I had then done. In the afternoon, God was pleased to give me some assistance, and I was enabled to set before my hearers the nature and necessity of true repentance, &c. Afterwards had some small degree of thankfulness. Was very ill and full of pain in the evening; and my soul mourned that I had spent so much time to so little profit.

Monday, August 22.—Spent most of the day in study; and found my bodily strength in a measure restored. Had some intense and passionate breathings

ings of soul after holiness, and very clear manifestations of my utter inability to procure, or work it in myself; it is wholly owing to the power of God. O, with what tenderness the love and desire of holiness fills the soul! I wanted to wing out of myself, to God; or rather to get a conformity to him: But alas, I cannot add to my stature in grace one cubit. However, my soul can never leave striving for it; or at least groaning, that it cannot strive for it, and obtain more purity of heart. At night, I spent some time in instructing my poor people: O that God would pity their souls.

Tuesday, August 23.—Studied in the forenoon, and enjoyed some freedom. In the afternoon, laboured abroad: Endeavoured to pray much; but found not much sweetness or intenseness of mind. Towards night, was very weary, and tired of this world of sorrow: The thoughts of death and immortality appeared very desirable, and even refreshed my soul. Those lines turned in my mind with pleasure.

> Come, death, shake hands; I'll kiss thy bands;
> 'Tis happiness for me to die.
> What! dost thou think, that I will shrink?
> I'll go to immortality.

In evening prayer, God was pleased to draw near my soul, though very sinful and unworthy: Was enabled to wrestle with God, and to persevere in my requests for grace: I poured out my soul for all the world, friends and enemies. My soul was concerned, not so much for souls as such, but rather for Christ's kingdom, that it might appear in the world, that God might be known to be God, in the whole earth. And O, my soul abhorred the very thought of a party in religion! Let the truth of God appear, wherever it is; and God have the glory forever. Amen. This was indeed a comfortable season: I thought I had some small taste of, and relish for the enjoyments

enjoyments and employments of the upper world. O that my soul was more attempered to it.

Wednesday, August 24.—Spent some time, in the morning, in study and prayer. Afterwards, was engaged in some necessary business abroad. Towards night, found a little time for some particular studies. I thought if God should say, Cease making any provision for this life, for you shall in a few days go out of time into eternity, my soul would leap for joy. O that I may both desire *to be dissolved to be with Christ*, and likewise *wait patiently all the days of my appointed time until my change come*. But alas, I am very unfit for the business and blessedness of heaven. O for more holiness.

Thursday, August 25.—Part of the day engaged in studies and part in labour abroad. I find it is impossible to enjoy peace and tranquillity of mind without a careful improvement of time. This is really an imitation of God and Christ Jesus: *My Father worketh hitherto, and I work*, says our Lord. But still if we would be like God, we must see that we fill up our time for him. I daily long to dwell in perfect light and love. In the mean time my soul mourns, that I make so little progress in grace and preparation for the world of blessedness: I see and know that I am a very barren tree in God's vineyard, and that he might justly say, *Cut it down*, &c. O that God would make me more lively and vigorous in grace, for his own glory! Amen.

[The two next days, he was much engaged in some necessary labours, in which he extremely spent himself. He seems, these days, to have had a great sense of the vanity of the world; and continued longings after holiness, and more fervency of spirit in the service of God.]

Lord's Day, August 28.—Was much perplexed with some irreligious Dutchmen. All their discourse turned

turned upon the things of the world; which was no small exercise to my mind. O what a hell it would be to spend an eternity with such men! Well might David say, *I beheld the transgressors and was grieved.* But adored be God, heaven is a place, *into which no unclean thing enters.* O, I long for the holiness of that world! Lord, prepare me therefor.

[The next day, he set out on a journey to New-York. Was something dejected, the two first days of his journey; but yet seems to have enjoyed some degrees of the sensible presence of God.]

Wednesday, August 31.—Rode down to Bethlehem: Was in a sweet, serious, and, I hope, christian frame, when I came there; eternal things engrossed all my thoughts; and I longed to be in the world of spirits. O how happy it is, to have all our thoughts swallowed up in that world; to feel one's self a serious considerate stranger in this world, diligently seeking a road through it, the best, the sure road to the heavenly Jerusalem.

Thursday, September 1.—Rode to Danbury. Was more dull and dejected in spirit, than yesterday. Indeed, I always feel comfortably, when God realizes death and the things of another world to my mind: Whenever my mind is taken off from the things of this world, and set on God, my soul is then at rest.

[He went forward on his journey, and came to New-York on the next Monday. And after tarrying there two or three days, set out from the city towards New-Haven, intending to be there at the commencement; and on Friday came to Horse-Neck. In the mean time, he complains much of dullness, and want of fervour in religion: But yet from time to time, speaks of his enjoying spiritual warmth and sweetness in conversation with christian friends, assistance in publick services, &c.]

Saturday,

Saturday, September 10.—Rode six miles to Stanwich, and preached to a considerable assembly of people. Had some assistance and freedom, especially towards the close. Endeavoured much afterwards, in private conversation, to establish holiness, humility, meekness, &c. as the essence of true religion; and to moderate some noisy sort of persons, that appeared to me to be acted by unseen spiritual pride. Alas, what extremes men incline to run into! Returned to Horse-Neck, and felt some seriousness and sweet solemnity in the evening.

Lord's Day, September 11.—In the afternoon, preached from Tit. iii. 8. I think God never helped me more in painting out true religion, and in detecting clearly, and tenderly discountenancing false appearances of religion, wild fire, party zeal, spiritual pride, &c. as well as a confident dogmatical spirit, and its spring, viz. ignorance of the heart. In the evening, took much pains in private conversation to suppress some confusions, that I perceived were amongst that people.

Monday, September 12.—Rode to Mr. Mills's at Ripton. Had some perplexing hours; but was some part of the day very comfortable. It is through great trials, I see, that we must enter the gates of Paradise. If my soul could but be holy, that God might not be dishonoured, methinks I could bear sorrows.

Tuesday, September 13.—Rode to New-Haven. Was sometimes dejected; not in the sweetest frame. I find it very difficult maintaining any sense of divine things, while removing from place to place, diverted with new objects, and filled with care and business. A settled steady business is best adapted to a life of strict religion.

Wednesday, September 14.—This day I ought to have taken my degree*; but God sees fit to deny it me

---

* This being Commencement day.

me. And though I was greatly afraid of being overwhelmed with perplexity and confusion, when I should see my classmates take theirs ; yet, in the very season of it, God enabled me with calmness and resignation to say, *The will of the Lord be done.* Indeed, through divine goodness, I have scarcely felt my mind so calm, sedate, and comfortable for some time. I have long feared this season, and expected my humility, meekness, patience, and resignation, would be much tried : But found much more pleasure and divine comfort, than I expected. Felt spiritually serious, tender and affectionate in private prayer with a dear christian friend to day.

Thursday, September 15.—Had some satisfaction in hearing the ministers discourse, &c. It is always a comfort to me, to hear religious and spiritual discourse. O that ministers and people were more spiritual, and devoted to God. Towards night, with the advice of christian friends, I offered the following reflections in writing, to the rector and trustees of the college (which are for substance the same that I had freely offered to the rector before, and entreated him to accept) and this I did that if possible I might cut off all occasion of stumbling and offence, from those that seek occasion. What I offered, is as follows :

" Whereas I have said before several persons, concerning Mr. Whittelsey, one of the tutors of Yale-College, that I did not believe he had any more grace than the chair I then leaned upon ; I humbly confess, that herein I have sinned against God, and acted contrary to the rules of his word, and have injured Mr. Whittelsey. I had no right to make thus free with his character ; and had no just reason to say as I did concerning him. My fault herein was the more aggravated, in that I said this concerning one that was so much my superiour, and one that I was

was obliged to treat with special respect and honour, by reason of the relation I stood in to him in the college. Such a manner of behaviour, I confess, did not become a christian; it was taking too much upon me, and did not favour of that humble respect, that I ought to have expressed towards Mr. Whittelsey. I have long since been convinced of the falseness of those apprehensions, by which I then justified such a conduct. I have often reflected on this act with grief; I hope, on account of the sin of it; and am willing to lie low, and be abased before God and man, for it: And humbly ask the forgiveness of the governours of the college, and of the whole society; but of Mr. Whittelsey in particular. And whereas I have been accused by one person of saying concerning the Rev. rector of Yale-College, that I wondered he did not expect to drop down dead for fining the scholars that followed Mr. Tennent to Milford; I seriously profess, that I do not remember my saying any thing to this purpose. But if I did, which I am not certain I did not, I utterly condemn it, and detest all such kind of behaviour; and especially in an under graduate towards the rector. And I now appear, to judge and condemn myself for going once to the separate meeting in New-Haven, a little before I was expelled, though the rector had refused to give me leave. For this I humbly ask the rector's forgiveness. And whether the governours of the college shall ever see cause to remove the academical censure I lie under, or no, or to admit me to the privileges I desire; yet I am willing to appear, if they think fit, openly to own, and to humble myself for those things I have herein confessed."

God has made me willing to do any thing, that I can do, consistent with truth, for the sake of peace, and that I might not be a stumbling block and offence to others. For this reason I can cheerfully
forego,

forego, and give up what I verily believe, after the most mature and impartial search, is my right, in some instances. God has given me that disposition, that if this were the case, that a man has done me an hundred injuries, and I (though ever so much provoked to it) have done him one, I feel disposed, and heartily willing humbly to confess my fault to him, and on my knees to ask forgiveness of him; though at the same time he should justify himself in all the injuries he has done me, and should only make use of my humble confession to blacken my character the more, and represent me as the only person guilty, &c. Yea, though he should as it were insult me, and say he knew all this before, and that I was making work for repentance, &c. Though what I said concerning Mr. Whittelsey was only spoken in private, to a friend or two; and being partly overheard, was related to the rector, and by him extorted from my friends; yet, seeing it was divulged and made publick, I was willing to confess my fault therein publickly. But I trust, God will plead my cause.

[The next day he went to Derby; then to Southbury, where he spent the Sabbath: And speaks of some spiritual comfort; but complains much of unfixedness, and wanderings of mind in religion.]

Monday, September 19.—In the afternoon, rode to Bethlehem, and there preached. Had some measure of assistance, both in prayer and preaching. I felt serious, kind and tender towards all mankind, and longed that holiness might flourish more on earth.

Tuesday, September 20.—Had thoughts of going forward on my journey to my Indians; but towards night was taken with a hard pain in my teeth, and shivering cold, and could not possibly recover a comfortable degree of warmth the whole night following. I continued very full of pain all night; and in the morning had a very hard fever, and pains almost all

over

over my whole body. I had a sense of the divine goodness in appointing this to be the place of my sickness, viz. among my friends that were very kind to me. I should probably have perished, if I had first got home to my own house in the wilderness, where I have none to converse with but the poor rude ignorant Indians. Here I saw was mercy in the midst of affliction. I continued thus, mostly confined to my bed, until Friday night; very full of pain most of the time; but through divine goodness not afraid of death. Then the extreme folly of those appeared to me, who put off their turning to God until a sick bed. Surely this is not a time proper to prepare for eternity. On Friday evening my pains went off something suddenly; and I was exceeding weak, and almost fainted; but was very comfortable the night following. Those words Psal. cxviii. 17, I frequently revolved in my mind; and thought we were to prize the continuation of life only on this account, that we may *shew forth God's goodness and works of grace.*

[From this time, he gradually recovered: And on the next Tuesday was so well as to be able to go forward on his journey homewards: But was until the Tuesday following before he reached Kaunaumeek. And seems, great part of this time, to have had a very deep and lively sense of the vanity and emptiness of all things here below, and of the reality, nearness and vast importance of eternal things.]

Tuesday, October 4.—This day rode home to my own house and people. The poor Indians appeared very glad of my return. Found my house and all things in safety. I presently fell on my knees and blessed God for my safe return, after a long and tedious journey, and a season of sickness in several places where I had been, and after I had been sick myself. God has renewed his kindness to me, in

preserving

preserving me one journey more. I have taken many considerable journeys since this time last year, and yet God has never suffered one of my bones to be broken, or any distressing calamity to befal me, excepting the ill turn I had in my last journey; though I have been often exposed to cold and hunger in the wilderness, where the comforts of life were not to be had; have frequently been lost in the woods; and sometimes obliged to ride much of the night; and once lay out in the woods all night. Blessed be God that has preserved me.

[In his Diary for the next eleven days, are great complaints of distance from God, spiritual pride, corruption, and exceeding vileness. He once says, his heart was so pressed with a sense of his pollution, that he could scarcely have the face and impudence (as it then appeared to him) to desire that God should not damn him forever. And at another time, he says he had so little sense of God, or apprehension and relish of his glory and excellency, that it made him more disposed to kindness and tenderness towards those who are blind and ignorant of God and things divine and heavenly.]

Lord's Day, October 16.—In the evening, God was pleased to give me a feeling sense of my own unworthiness; but through divine goodness such as tended to draw, rather than drive me from God: It filled me with solemnity. I retired alone (having at this time a friend with me) and poured out my soul to God with much freedom; and yet in anguish, to find myself so unspeakably sinful and unworthy before a holy God. Was now much resigned under God's dispensations towards me, though my trials had been very great. But thought whether I could be resigned, if God should let the French Indians come upon me, and deprive me of my life, or carry me away captive (though I knew of no special

cial reason then to propose this trial to myself, more than any other) and my soul seemed so far to rest and acquiesce in God, that the sting and terror of these things seemed in a great measure gone. Presently after I came to the Indians, whom I was teaching to sing psalm tunes that evening, I received the following letter from Stockbridge, by a messenger sent on the Sabbath on purpose, which made it appear of greater importance.

"*Sir*, Just now we received advices from Col. Stoddard, that there is the utmost danger of a rupture with France. He has received the same from his Excellency our Governour, ordering him to give notice to all the exposed places, that they may secure themselves the best they can against any sudden invasion. We thought best to send directly to Kaunaumeek, that you may take the prudentest measures for your safety that dwell there. I am, Sir, &c."

I thought, upon reading the contents, it came in a good season; for my heart seemed something fixed on God, and therefore I was not much surprised: But this news only made me the more serious, and taught me that I must not please myself with any of the comforts of life which I had been preparing for my support. Blessed be God, that gave me any intenseness and fervency this evening.

Monday, October 17.—Had some rising hopes sometimes, that *God would arise and have mercy on Zion*, speedily. My heart is indeed refreshed, when I have any prevailing hopes of Zion's prosperity. O that I may see that glorious day, when Zion shall become the *joy of the whole earth!* Truly there is nothing that I greatly value in this lower world.

[On Tuesday, he rode to Stockbridge; complains of being much diverted, and having but little life. On Wednesday, he expresses some solemn sense of divine things, and a longing to be always doing for God with a godly frame of spirit.]

Saturday,

Saturday, October 22.—Had but little senfible communion with God. This world is a dark cloudy manfion. O, when will the *Sun of righteousness* shine on my foul without ceffation or intermiffion.

Lord's Day, October 23.—In the morning, had a little dawn of comfort arifing from hopes of feeing glorious days in the church of God: Was enabled to pray for fuch a glorious day with fome courage, and ftrength of hope. In the forenoon, treated on the glories of heaven, &c. In the afternoon, on the miferies of hell, and the danger of going there. Had fome freedom and warmth, both parts of the day. And my people were very attentive. In the evening, two or three came to me under concern for their fouls; to whom I was enabled to difcourfe clofely, and with fome earneftnefs and defire. O that God would be merciful to their poor fouls.

[He feems, through the whole of this week, to have been greatly engaged to fill up every inch of time in the fervice of God, and to have been moft diligently employed in ftudy, prayer, and inftructing the Indians; and from time to time expreffes longings of foul after God, and the advancement of his kingdom, and fpiritual comfort and refrefhment.]

Lord's Day, October 30.—In the morning enjoyed fome fixednefs of foul in prayer, which was indeed fweet and defirable: Was enabled to leave myfelf with God, and to acquiefce in him. At noon, my foul was refrefhed with reading Rev. iii. more efpecially the 11th and 12th verfes. O my foul longed for that bleffed day, when I fhould *dwell in the temple of God*, and *go no more out* of his immediate prefence!

Monday, October 31.—Rode to Kinderhook, about fifteen miles from my place. While riding, I felt fome divine fweetnefs in the thoughts of being a *pillar in the temple of God* in the upper world, and being no more deprived of his blessed presence and the sense of his favour, which is *better than life*. My soul was so lifted up to God, that I could pour out my desires to him, for more grace and further degrees of sanctification, with abundant freedom. O, I longed to be more abundantly prepared for that blessedness, with which I was then in some measure refreshed ! Returned home in the evening ; but took an extremely bad cold by riding in the night.

Tuesday, November 1.—Was very much disordered in body, and sometimes full of pain in my face and teeth : Was not able to study much, and had not much spiritual comfort. Alas, when God is withdrawn, all is gone ! Had some sweet thoughts which I could not but write down, on the design, nature, and end of christianity.

Thursday, November 3.—Spent this day in secret fasting and prayer from morning until night. Early in the morning, had (I think) some small degree of assistance in prayer. Afterwards, read the story of Elijah the prophet, 1 Kings, xvii. xviii. and xix. chapters, and also, 2 Kings ii. and iv. chapters. My soul was much moved, observing the faith, zeal and power of that holy man ; how he wrestled with God in prayer, &c. My soul then cried with Elisha, *Where is the Lord God of Elijah ?* O, I longed for more faith ! My soul breathed after God, and pleaded with him, that a *double portion of that spirit*, which was given to Elijah, might rest on me. And that which was divinely refreshing and strengthening to my soul, was, I saw that God is the same that he was in the days of Elijah. Was enabled to wrestle with God by prayer, in a more affectionate, fervent, humble, intense and importunate manner, than I have for many months past. Nothing seemed too hard for God to perform ; nothing too great for me to hope for from him. I had for many months en-

H   tirely

tirely loft all hopes of being made inftrumental of doing any fpecial fervice for God in the world: It has appeared entirely impoffible, that one fo black and vile fhould be thus improved for God: But at this time God was pleafed to revive this hope. Afterwards read the iii. chap. of Exod. and on to the xx. and faw more of the glory and majefty of God difcovered in thofe chapters, than ever I had feen before; frequently in the mean time falling on my knees and crying to God for the faith of Mofes, and for a manifeftation of the divine glory. Efpecially the iii. and iv. and part of the xiv. and xv. chapters, were unfpeakably fweet to my foul: My foul bleffed God, that he had fhewn himfelf fo gracious to his fervants of old. The xv. chapter feemed to be the very language which my foul uttered to God in the feafon of my firft fpiritual comfort, when I had juft got through the red fea, by a way that I had no expectation of. O how my foul then *rejoiced in God!* And now thofe things came frefh and lively to my mind; now my foul bleffed God afrefh, that he had opened that unthought of way to deliver me from the fear of the Egyptians, when I almoft defpaired of life. Afterwards read the ftory of Abraham's pilgrimage in the land of Canaan: My foul was melted, in obferving his faith, how he leaned on God; how he communed with God, and what a ftranger he was here in the world. After that, read the ftory of Jofeph's fufferings, and God's goodnefs to him: Bleffed God for thefe examples of faith and patience. My foul was ardent in prayer, was enabled to wreftle ardently for myfelf, for chriftian friends, and for the church of God. And felt more defire to fee the power of God in the converfion of fouls, than I have done for a long feafon. Bleffed be God for this feafon of fafting and prayer. May his goodnefs always abide with me, and draw my foul to him.

Monday,

Monday, November 7.—This morning, the Lord afforded me some special assistance in prayer: My mind was solemn, fixed, affectionate, and ardent in desires after holiness; and felt full of tenderness and love; and my affections seemed to be dissolved into kindness and softness. In the evening, enjoyed the same comfortable assistance in prayer, as in the morning: My soul longed after God, and cried to him with a filial freedom, reverence and boldness. O that I might be entirely consecrated and devoted to God.

[The two next days, he complains of bodily illness and pain; but much more of spiritual barrenness and unprofitableness.]

Thursday, November 10.—Spent this day in fasting and prayer alone. In the morning, was very dull and lifeless; was something melancholy and discouraged. But after some time, reading 2 Kings xix. chapter, my soul was moved and affected; especially reading verse 14. and onward. I saw there was no other way for the afflicted children of God to take, but to go to God with all their sorrows. Hezekiah, in his great distress, went and spread his complaint before the Lord. I was then enabled to see the mighty power of God, and my extreme need of that power: Was enabled to cry to God affectionately and ardently for his divine power and grace to be exercised towards me. Afterwards, read the story of David's trials, and observed the course he took under them, how he strengthened his hands in God; whereby my soul was carried out after God, enabled to cry to him and rely upon him, and felt *strong in the Lord*. Was afterwards refreshed, observing the blessed temper that was wrought in David by his trials: All bitterness and desire of revenge seemed wholly taken away; so that he mourned for the death of his enemies; 2 Sam. i. 17. and iv. 9. ad fin.

Was enabled to blefs God, that he had given me something of this divine temper, that my foul freely forgives, and heartily loves my enemies.

[It appears by his Diary for the remaining part of this week, and for the two following weeks, that great part of the time he was very ill and full of pain; and yet obliged through his circumftances, in this ill ftate of body, to be at great fatigues, in labour, and travelling day and night, and to expofe himfelf, in ftormy and fevere feafons. He, from time to time, within this fpace, fpeaks of outgoings of foul after God; his heart ftrengthened in God; feafons of divine fweetnefs and comfort; his heart affected with gratitude for mercies, &c. And yet there are many complaints of lifeleffnefs, weaknefs of grace, diftance from God, and great unprofitablenefs. But ftill there appears a conftant care, from day to day, not to lofe time, but to improve it all for God.]

Lord's Day, November 27.—In the evening, was greatly affected in reading an account of the very joyful death of a pious gentleman; which feemed to invigorate my foul in God's ways: I felt courageoufly engaged to purfue a life of holinefs and felf denial as long as I live; and poured out my foul to God for his help and affiftance in order thereto. Eternity then feemed near, and my foul rejoiced, and longed to meet it. O, I truft, that will be a bleffed day, that finifhes my toil here!

Monday, November 28.—In the evening, was obliged to fpend time in company and converfation that was unprofitable. Nothing lies heavier upon me, than the mifimprovement of time.

Tuefday, November 29.—Began to ftudy the Indian tongue, with Mr Sargeant, at Stockbridge*. Was perplexed

---

*.The Commiffioners that employed him, had directed him to fpend much time this winter with Mr. Sargeant, to learn the language of the Indians; which neceffitated him very often to ride, backwards and forwards, 20 miles through the uninhabited woods between Stockbridge and Kaunaumeek; which many times expofed him to extreme hardfhip in the fevere feafons of the winter, perplexed for want of more retirement. I love to live alone in my own little cottage, where I can spend much time in prayer, &c.

Wednesday, November 30.—Pursued my study of Indian: But was very weak and disordered in body, and was troubled in mind at the barrenness of the day, that I had done so little for God. I had some enlargement in prayer at night. O, a barn, or stable, hedge or any other place, is truly desirable, if God is there! Sometimes, of late, my hopes of Zion's prosperity are more raised, than they were in the summer past. My soul seems to confide in God, that he will yet *shew forth his salvation* to his people, and make *Zion the joy of the whole earth. O how excellent is the loving kindness of the Lord!* My soul sometimes inwardly exults at the lively thoughts of what God has already done for his church, and what mine *eyes have seen of the salvation of God.* It is sweet, to hear nothing but spiritual discourse from God's children; and sinners *inquiring the way to Zion,* saying, *What shall we do, &c.?* O that I may see more of this blessed work!

Thursday, December 1.—Both morning and evening, I enjoyed some intenseness of soul in prayer, and longed for the enlargement of Christ's kingdom in the world. My soul seems of late, to wait on God for his blessing on Zion. O that religion might powerfully revive!

Friday, December 2.—Enjoyed not so much health of body, or fervour of mind as yesterday. If the chariot wheels move with ease and speed at any time, for a short space; yet by and by they drive heavily again. *O that I had the wings of a dove, that I might fly away* from sin and corruption, *and be at rest* in God!

Saturday, December 3.—Rode home, to my house and people. Suffered much with the extreme cold.

I truſt, I ſhall, before long, arrive ſafe at my journey's end, where my toils ſhall ceaſe.

Lord's Day, December 4.—Had but little ſenſe of divine and heavenly things. My ſoul mourns over my barrenneſs. O how ſad is ſpiritual deadneſs!

Tueſday, December 6.—Was perplexed to ſee the vanity and levity of profeſſed chriſtians. Spent the evening with a chriſtian friend, that was able in ſome meaſure to ſympathize with me in my ſpiritual conflicts. Was a little refreſhed to find one with whom I could converſe of inward trials, &c.

Wedneſday, December 7.—Spent the evening in perplexity, with a kind of guilty indolence. When I have no heart or reſolution for God and the duties incumbent on me, I feel guilty of negligence and miſimprovement of time. Certainly I ought to be engaged in my work and buſineſs, to the utmoſt extent of my ſtrength and ability.

Thurſday, December 8.—My mind was much diſtracted with different affections. Seemed to be at an amazing diſtance from God: And looking round in the world, to ſee if there was not ſome happineſs to be derived from it, God, and ſome certain objects in the world, ſeemed each to invite my heart and affections; and my ſoul ſeemed to be diſtracted between them. I have not been ſo much beſet with the world for a long time; and that with relation to ſome particular objects which I thought myſelf moſt dead to. But even while I was deſiring to pleaſe myſelf with any thing below, guilt, ſorrow and perplexity attended the firſt motions of deſire. Indeed I cannot ſee the appearance of pleaſure and happineſs in the world, as I uſed to do: And bleſſed be God for any habitual deadneſs to the world. I found no peace, or deliverance from this diſtraction and perplexity of mind, until I found acceſs to the throne of grace: And as ſoon as I had any ſenſe of

God

God and things divine, the allurements of the world vanished, and my heart was determined for God. But my soul mourned over my folly, that I should defire any pleasure, but only in God. God forgive my spiritual idolatry.

Saturday, December 24.—Had some assistance, and longing defires after sanctification, in prayer, this day; especially in the evening: Was sensible of my own weakness and spiritual impotency: Saw plainly, I should fall into sin, if God of his abundant mercy did not *uphold my soul, and withhold me from evil.* O that God would *uphold me by his free spirit, and save me from the hour of temptation.*

Lord's Day, December 25.—Prayed much, in the morning, with a feeling sense of my own spiritual weakness and insufficiency for any duty. God gave me some assistance in preaching to the Indians; and especially in the afternoon, when I was enabled to speak with uncommon plainness, freedom, and earnestness. Blessed be God for any assistance granted to one so unworthy. Afterwards felt some thankfulness; but still sensible of barrenness. Spent some time in the evening, with one or two persons under spiritual concern, and exhorting others to their duty, &c.

Monday, December 26.—Rode down to Stockbridge. Was very much fatigued with my journey, wherein I underwent great hardship: Was much exposed and very wet by falling into a river. Spent the day and evening without much sense of divine and heavenly things; but felt guilty, grieved, and perplexed with wandering careless thoughts.

Tuesday, December 27.—Had a small degree of warmth in secret prayer, in the evening: But, alas, had but little spiritual life, and consequently but little comfort! O, the pressure of a *body of death!*

Wednesday, December 28.—Rode about six miles, to the ordination of Mr. Hopkins. In the season of the solemnity was somewhat affected with a sense of the greatness and importance of the work of a minister of Christ. Afterwards was grieved to see the vanity of the multitude. In the evening, spent a little time with some christian friends, with some degree of satisfaction; but most of the time had rather have been alone.

Thursday, December 29.—Spent the day mainly in conversing with friends; yet enjoyed little satisfaction, because I could find but few disposed to converse of divine and heavenly things. Alas, what are things of this world, to afford satisfaction to the soul! Near night, returned to Stockbridge; in secret blessed God for retirement, and that I be not always exposed to the company and conversation of the world. O that I could live *in the secret of God's presence!*

Friday, December 30.—Was in a solemn devout frame in the evening. Wondered that earth with all its charms, should ever allure me in the least degree. O that I could always realize the being and holiness of God.

Saturday, December 31.—Rode from Stockbridge, home to my house: The air was clear and calm, but as cold as ever I felt it in the world, or near. I was in great danger of perishing by the extremity of the season. Was enabled to meditate much on the road.

Lord's Day, January 1, 1743,4.—In the morning, had some small degree of assistance in prayer. Saw myself so vile and unworthy, that I could not look my people in the face, when I came to preach. O, my meanness, folly, ignorance, and inward pollution! In the evening, had a little assistance in prayer, so that the duty was delightsome, rather than burdensome.

densome. Reflected on the goodness of God to me in the past year, &c. Blessed be the Lord, that has carried me through all the toils, fatigues, and hardships of the year past, as well as the spiritual sorrows and conflicts that have attended it. O that I could begin this year with God, and spend the whole of it to his glory, either in life or death.

Monday, January 2.—Had some affecting sense of my own impotency and spiritual weakness. It is nothing but the power of God that keeps me from all manner of wickedness. I see I am nothing, and can do nothing without help from above. O, for divine grace! In the evening, had some ardour of soul in prayer, and longing desires to have God for my guide and safeguard at all times.

Wednesday, January 4.—Was in a resigned and mortified temper of mind, much of the day. Time appeared a moment, life a vapour, and all its enjoyments as empty bubbles, and fleeting blasts of wind.

Thursday, January 5.—Had a humbling and pressing sense of my unworthiness. My sense of the badness of my own heart filled my soul with bitterness and anguish; which was ready to sink, as under the weight of a heavy burden. And thus spent the evening, until late. Was somewhat intense and ardent in prayer.

Friday, January 6.—Feeling and considering my extreme weakness, and want of grace, the pollution of my soul, and danger of temptations on every side, I set apart this day for fasting and prayer, neither eating nor drinking from evening to evening, beseeching God to have mercy on me. And my soul intensely longed, that the dreadful spots and stains of sin might be washed away from it. Saw something of the power and all sufficiency of God. My soul seemed to rest on his power and grace; longed for resignation to his will, and mortification to all things

here

here below. My mind was greatly fixed on divine things: My refolutions for a life of mortification, continual watchfulnefs, felf denial, ferioufnefs, and devotion to God, were ftrong and fixed; my defires ardent and intenfe; my confcience tender, and afraid of every appearance of evil. My foul grieved with the reflection on paft levity, and want of refolution for God. I folemnly renewed my dedication of myfelf to God, and longed for grace to enable me always to keep covenant with him. Time appeared very fhort, eternity near; and a great name, either in or after life, together with all earthly pleafures and profits, but an empty bubble, a deluding dream.

Saturday, January 7.—Spent this day in ferioufnefs, with ftedfaft refolutions for God and a life of mortification. Studied clofely, until I felt my bodily ftrength fail. Felt fome degree of refignation to God, with an acquiefcence in his difpenfations. Was grieved, that I could do fo little for God before my bodily ftrength failed. In the evening, though tired, yet was enabled to continue inftant in prayer for fome time. Spent the time in reading, meditation, and prayer, until the evening was far fpent: Was grieved, to think that I could not *watch unto prayer* the whole night. But bleffed be God, heaven is a place of continual and inceffant devotion, though earth is dull.

[The fix days following, he continued in the fame happy frame of mind; enjoyed the fame compofure, calmnefs, refignation, ardent defire and fweet fervency of fpirit, in a high degree, every day, not one excepted. Thurfday, this week, he kept as a day of fecret fafting and prayer.]

Saturday, January 14.—This morning, enjoyed a moft folemn feafon in prayer: My foul feemed enlarged and affifted to pour out itfelf to God for grace, and for every bleffing I wanted, for myfelf, my dear chriftian christian friends, and for the Church of God; and was so enabled to *see him who is invisible*, that my soul rested upon him for the performance of every thing I asked agreeable to his will. It was then my happiness to continue instant in prayer, and was enabled to continue in it for near an hour. My soul was then *strong in the Lord and in the power of his might*: Longed exceedingly for angelick holiness and purity, and to have all my thoughts, at all times, employed in divine and heavenly things. O how blessed is an heavenly temper! O how unspeakably blessed it is, to feel a measure of that rectitude, in which we were at first created! Felt the same divine assistance in prayer sundry times in the day. My soul confided in God for myself, and for his Zion; trusted in divine power and grace, that he would do glorious things in his church, on earth, for his own glory.

Monday, January 23.—[At Salisbury] I think I never felt more resigned to God, nor so much dead to the world, in every respect, as now: Was dead to all desire of reputation and greatness, either in life or after death: All I longed for, was to be holy, humble, crucified to the world, &c.

Tuesday, January 24.—Near noon, rode over to Canaan. In the evening, was unexpectedly visited by a considerable number of people, with whom I was enabled to converse profitably of divine things: Took pains to describe the difference between a regular and irregular self love: The one consisting with a supreme love to God, but the other not; the former uniting God's glory and the soul's happiness, that they become one common interest, but the latter disjoining and separating God's glory and the man's happiness, seeking the latter with a neglect of the former. Illustrated this by that genuine love that is found between the sexes; which is diverse from that which

is

is wrought up towards a person only by rational arguments, or hope of self interest. Love is a pleasing passion, it affords pleasure to the mind where it is; but yet true genuine love is not nor can be placed upon any object with that design of pleasing itself with the feeling of it in a man's own breast.

[On Wednesday, he rode to Sheffield; the next day, to Stockbridge; and on Saturday, home to Kaunaumeek, though the season was cold and stormy: Which journey was followed with illness and pain. It appears by his Diary, that he spent the time, while riding, in profitable meditations, and in lifting up his heart to God; and he speaks of assistance, comfort, and refreshment; but still complains of barrenness, &c. His Diary for the five next days is full of the most heavy bitter complaints; and he expresses himself as full of shame and self loathing for his lifeless temper of mind and sluggishness of spirit.]

Thursday, February 2.—Spent this day in fasting and prayer, seeking the presence and assistance of God, that he would enable me to overcome all my corruptions and spiritual enemies.

Friday, February 3.—Enjoyed more freedom and comfort than of late; was intensely engaged in meditation upon the different whispers of the various powers and affections of a pious mind, exercised with a great variety of dispensations: And could not but write as well as meditate on so entertaining a subject. I hope the Lord gave me some true sense of divine things this day: But alas, how great and pressing are the remains of indwelling corruption! I am now more sensible than ever, that God alone, is *the author and finisher of our faith*, i. e. that the whole and every part of sanctification, and every good word, work, or thought, that is found in me, is the effect of his power and grace; that *without him*

I can do nothing, in the strictest sense; and that *he works in us to will and to do of his own good pleasure*, and from no other motive. O, how amazing it is that people can talk so much about men's power and goodness; when, if God did not hold us back every moment, we should be devils incarnate! This my bitter experience, for several days last past, has abundantly taught me concerning myself.

Saturday, February 4.—Enjoyed some degree of freedom and spiritual refreshment; was enabled to pray with some fervency, and longing desires of Zion's prosperity; and my faith and hope seemed to *take hold of God*, for the performance of what I was enabled to plead for. Sanctification in myself, and the ingathering of God's elect, was all my desire; and the hope of its accomplishment, all my joy.

Lord's Day, February 5.—Was enabled in some measure to rest and confide in God, and to prize his presence and some glimpses of the light of his countenance, above my necessary food. Thought myself, after the season of weakness, temptation, and desertion I endured the last week, to be somewhat like Sampson when his locks began to grow again. Was enabled to preach to my people with more life and warmth, than I have for some weeks past.

Monday, February 6.—This morning my soul again was strengthened in God, and found some sweet repose in him in prayer: Longing especially for the complete mortification of sensuality and pride, and for resignation to God's dispensations, at all times, as through grace I felt it at this time. I did not desire deliverance from any difficulty, that attends my circumstances, unless God was willing. O how comfortable is this temper! Spent most of the day in reading God's word, in writing and prayer. Enjoyed repeated and frequent comfort, and intenseness of soul in prayer through the day. In the evening, spent some hours in private conversation with my people: And afterwards, felt some warmth in secret prayer.

Tuesday, February 7.—Was much engaged in some sweet meditations on the powers and affections of the godly soul in their pursuit of their beloved object: Wrote something of the native language of spiritual sensation, in its soft and tender whispers; declaring, that it now feels and *tastes that the Lord is gracious*; that he is the supreme good, the only soul satisfying happiness; that he is a complete, sufficient, and almighty portion; saying, " *Whom have I in heaven but thee? And there is none upon earth that I desire,* besides this blessed portion. O, I feel it is heaven to please him, and to be just what he would have me to be! O that my soul were *holy, as he is holy!* O that it were *pure even as Christ is pure;* and *perfect as my Father in heaven is perfect!* These, I feel, are the sweetest commands in God's book, comprising all others. And shall I break them! Must I break them! Am I under a necessity of it as long as I live in the world! O my soul, wo, wo is me that I am a sinner, because I now necessarily grieve and offend this blessed God, who is infinite in goodness and grace! O, methinks, if he would punish me for my sins, it would not wound my heart so deep to offend him: But though I sin continually, yet he continually repeats his kindness to me! O methinks I could bear any suffering; but how can I bear to grieve and dishonour this blessed God! How shall I yield ten thousand times more honour to him? What shall I do to glorify and worship this best of beings? O that I could consecrate myself, soul and body, to his service forever. O that I could give up myself to him so as never more to attempt to be my own, or to have any will or affections that are not perfectly conformed to him. But alas, alas, I find I cannot be thus entirely devoted to God:

I cannot live and not sin. O ye angels, do ye glorify him inceffantly; and if poffible, proftrate yourfelves lower before the bleffed king of heaven. I long to bear a part with you; and, if it were poffible, to help you. O when we have done all that we can to all etetnity, we fhall not be able to offer the ten thoufandth part of the homage that the glorious God deferves!"

Felt fomething fpiritual, devout, refigned and mortified to the world, much of the day; and efpecially towards and in the evening. Bleffed be God, that he enables me to love him for himfelf.

Wednefday, February 8.—Was in a comfortable frame of foul moft of the day; though fenfible of and reftlefs under fpiritual barrennefs. I find that both mind and body are quickly tired with intenfenefs and fervour in the things of God. O that I could be as inceffant as angels in devotion and fpiritual fervour.

[The following day he fpent as a day of fafting and prayer; and the two next he appears to have been under fome depreffion.]

Lord's Day, February 12.—My foul feemed to confide in God, and to repofe itfelf on him; and had outgoings of foul after God in prayer. Enjoyed fome divine affiftance, in the forenoon, in preaching; but in the afternoon, was more perplexed with fhame, &c. Afterwards, found fome relief in prayer: Loved, as a feeble, afflicted, defpifed creature, to caft myfelf on a God of infinite grace and goodnefs, hoping for no happinefs but from him.

Monday, February 13.—Was calm and fedate in morning devotions; and my foul feemed to rely on God. Rode to Stockbridge, and enjoyed fome comfortable meditations by the way: Had a more refrefhing tafte and relifh of heavenly bleffednefs, than I have enjoyed for many months paft. I have many times of late, felt as ardent defires of holinefs as ever: But not fo much fenfe of the fweetnefs and unfpeakable pleafure of the enjoyments and employments of heaven. My foul longed to leave earth, and bear a part with angels in their celeftial employments. My foul faid, *Lord, it is good to be here;* and it appeared to me better to die, than to lofe the relifh of thefe heavenly delights.

[A fenfe of divine things feemed to continue with him, in a leffer degree, through the next day. On Wednefday he was, by fome difcourfe that he heard, caft into a melancholy gloom, that operated much in the fame manner as his melancholy had formerly done, when he came firft to Kaunaumeek; the effects of which feemed to continue in fome degree the fix following days.]

Wednefday, February 22.—In the morning, had as clear a fenfe of the exceeding pollution of my nature, as ever I remember to have had in my life. I then appeared to myfelf inexpreffibly loathfome, and defiled: Sins of childhood, of early youth, and fuch follies as I had not thought of for years together, (as I remember) came now frefh to my view, as if committed but yefterday, and appeared in the moft odious colours: They appeared more in number than the hairs of my head: Yea, they *went over my head as an heavy burden*. In the evening, the hand of faith feemed to be ftrengthened in God: My foul feemed to reft and acquiefce in him: Was fupported under my burdens, reading the cxxv. Pfalm: Found that it was fweet and comfortable to lean on God.

Friday, February 24.—Was exceeding reftlefs and perplexed under a fenfe of the mifimprovement of time; mourned to fee time pafs away; felt in the greateft hurry; feemed to have every thing to do: Yet could do nothing, but only grieve and groan under my ignorance, unprofitablenefs, meannefs, the

foolifhnefs

foolishness of my actions and thoughts, the pride and bitterness of my past frames (at some times, at least) all which at this time appeared to me in lively colours, and filled me with shame. I could not compose my mind to any profitable studies, by reason of this pressure.

[He continued in much the same frame of uneasiness at the misimprovement of time, and pressure of spirit under a sense of vileness, unprofitableness, &c. for the six next following days; excepting some intervals of calmness and composure, in resignation to and confidence in God.]

Friday, March 2.—Was most of the day employed in writing on a divine subject. Was frequent in prayer, and enjoyed some small degree of assistance. But in the evening, God was pleased to grant me a divine sweetness in prayer; especially in the duty of intercession. I think I never felt so much kindness and love to those who I have reason to think are my enemies, (though at that time I found such a disposition to think the best of all, that I scarce knew how to think that any such thing as enmity and hatred lodged in any soul; it seemed as if all the world must needs be friends) and never prayed with more freedom and delight, for myself, or dearest friend, than I did now for my enemies.

Saturday, March 3.—In the morning spent, I believe, an hour in prayer, with great intenseness and freedom, and with the most soft and tender affection towards mankind. I longed that those who I have reason to think owe me ill will, might be eternally happy: It seemed refreshing, to think of meeting them in heaven, how much soever they had injured me on earth: Had no disposition to insist upon any confession from them, in order to reconciliation and the exercise of love and kindness to them. O it is an emblem of heaven itself, to love all the world

world with a love of kindnefs, forgivenefs, and benevolence. Prayer was fo fweet an exercife to me, that I knew not how to ceafe, left I fhould lofe the fpirit of prayer. Felt no difpofition to eat or drink for the fake of the pleafure of it, but only to fupport my nature, and fit me for divine fervice.

Lord's Day, March 4.—In the morning enjoyed the fame intenfenefs in prayer as yefterday morning; though not in fo great a degree: Felt the fame fpirit of love, univerfal benevolence, forgivenefs, humility, refignation, mortification to the world, and compofure of mind, as then. *My foul refted in God*; and I found I wanted no other refuge or friend.—While my foul thus trufts in God, all things feem to be at peace with me, even the ftones of the earth: But when I cannot apprehend and confide in God, all things appear with a different afpect.

[Through the four next days he complains of barrennefs, want of holy confidence in God, ftupidity, wanderings of mind, &c. and fpeaks of oppreffion of mind under a fenfe of exceeding meannefs, paft follies, as well as prefent workings of corruption. On Friday, he feems to have been reftored to a confiderable degree of the fame excellent frame that he enjoyed the Saturday before.]

Saturday, March 10.—In the morning, felt exceeding dead to the world and all its enjoyments: I thought I was ready and willing to give up life and all its comforts, as foon as called to it: And yet then had as much comfort of life as almoft ever I had. Life itfelf now appeared but an empty bubble: The riches, honours, and common enjoyments of life appeared extremely taftelefs. I longed to be perpetually and entirely *crucified* to all things here below, by the *crofs of Chrift*. My foul was fweetly refigned to God's difpofal of me, in every regard; and I faw,

there

there had nothing happened to me but what was best for me. I confided in God, that he would *never leave me*, though I should *walk through the valley of the shadow of death*. It was then *my meat and drink* to be holy, to *live to the Lord*, and *die to the Lord:* And I thought that I then enjoyed such a heaven as far exceeded the most sublime conceptions of an unregenerate soul; and even unspeakably beyond what I myself could conceive of at another time. I did not wonder that Peter said, *Lord, it is good to be here*, when thus refreshed with divine glories. My soul was full of love and tenderness in the duty of intercession; especially felt a most sweet affection to some precious godly ministers, of my acquaintance. Prayed earnestly for dear christians, and for those I have reason to fear are my enemies: And could not have spoken a word of bitterness, or entertained a bitter thought against the vilest man living. Had a sense of my own great unworthiness. My soul seemed to breathe forth love and praise to God afresh, when I thought he would let his children love and receive me as one of their brethren and fellow citizens: And when I thought of their treating me in that manner, I longed to lie at their feet; and could think of no way to express the sincerity and simplicity of my love and esteem of them, as being much better than myself.

Lord's Day, March 11.—My soul was in some measure *strengthened in God*, in morning devotion; so that I was released from trembling, fear and distress. Preached to my people from the parable of the sower, Matth. xiii. And enjoyed some assistance, both parts of the day: Had some freedom, affection, and fervency in addressing my poor people; longed that God should take hold of their hearts, and make them spiritually alive. And indeed I had so much to say to them that I knew not how to leave off speaking*.

Monday, March 12.—In the morning was in a devout, tender, and loving frame of mind; and was enabled to cry to God, I hope, with a child like spirit, with importunity, and resignation, and composure of mind. My spirit was full of quietness, and love to mankind; and longed that peace should reign on the earth: Was grieved at the very thoughts of a fiery, angry and intemperate zeal in religion; mourned over past follies in that regard; and my soul confided in God for strength and grace sufficient for my future work and trials. Spent the day mainly in hard labour, making preparation for my intended journey.

Tuesday, March 13.—Felt my soul going forth after God sometimes; but not with such ardency as I longed for. In the evening, was enabled to continue instant in prayer, for some considerable time together; and especially had respect to the journey I designed to enter upon, with the leave of Divine Providence, on the morrow. Enjoyed some freedom and fervency, entreating that the divine presence might attend me in every place where my business might lead me; and had a particular reference to the trials and temptations that I apprehended I might be more eminently exposed to in particular places. Was strengthened and comforted; although I was before very weary. Truly the *joy of the Lord* is *strength* and *life*.

Wednesday, March 14.—Enjoyed some intenseness of soul in prayer, repeating my petitions for God's presence in every place where I expected to be in my journey. Besought the Lord that I might not be

---

* This was the last Sabbath that ever he performed publick service at Kaunaumeek, and these the last sermons that ever he preached there. It appears by his Diary, that while he continued with these Indians, he took great pains with them, and did it with much discretion; but the particular manner how, has been omitted for brevity's sake.

be too much pleased and amused with dear friends and acquaintance, in one place and another. Near ten set out on my journey, and near night came to Stockbridge.

Thursday, March 15.—Rode down to Sheffield. Here I met a messenger from East-Hampton, on Long-Island; who, by the unanimous vote of that large town, was sent to invite me thither, in order to settle with that people, where I had been before frequently invited. Seemed more at a loss what was my duty than before. When I heard of the great difficulties of that place, I was much concerned and grieved, and felt some desires to comply with their request; but knew not what to do: Endeavoured to commit the case to God.

Lord's Day, March 18.—[At Salisbury.] Was exceeding weak and faint, so that I could scarce walk: But God was pleased to afford me much freedom, clearness and fervency in preaching: I have not had the like assistance in preaching to sinners for many months past. Here another messenger met me, and informed me of the vote of another congregation, to give me an invitation to come among them upon probation for settlement*. Was something exercised in mind with a weight and burden of care. O that God would *send forth faithful labourers into his harvest.*

[After this, he went forward on his journey towards New-York and New-Jersey: In which he proceeded slowly; performing his journey under great degrees of bodily indisposition. However, he preached several times by the way, being urged by friends; in which he had considerable assistance. He speaks of comfort in conversation with christian friends from time to time, and of various things in

---

* This congregation was that at Millington, near Haddam. They were very earnestly desirous of his coming among them.

the exercises and frames of his heart, that shew much of a divine influence on his mind in this journey.]

Thursday, April 5.—Was again much exercised with weakness, and with pain in my head. Attended on the commissioners in their meeting*. Resolved to go on still with the Indian affair, if Divine Providence permitted; although I had before felt some inclination to go to East-Hampton, where I was solicited to go.

[After this he continued two or three days in the Jerseys, very ill; and then returned to New-York; and from thence into New-England; and went to his native town of Haddam: Where he arrived on Saturday, April 14. And he continues still his bitter complaints of want of retirement. While he was in New-York, he says thus, O, it is not the pleasures of the world can comfort me! If God deny his presence, what are the pleasures of the city to me? One hour of sweet retirement where God is, is better than the whole world. And he continues to cry out of his ignorance, meanness, and unworthiness. However, he speaks of some seasons of special assistance and divine sweetness. He spent some days among his friends at East-Hampton, and Millington.]

Tuesday, April 17.—Rode to Millington again; and felt perplexed when I set out; was feeble in body, and weak in faith. I was going to preach a lecture; and feared I should never have assistance enough to get through. But contriving to ride alone at a distance from the company that was going, I spent

---

* The Indians at Kaunaumeek being but few in number, and Mr. Brainerd having now been labouring among them about a year, and having prevailed upon them to be willing to leave Kaunaumeek, and remove to Stockbridge, to live constantly under Mr. Sargeant's ministry; he thought he might now do more service for Christ among the Indians elsewhere: And therefore went this journey to New-Jersey to lay the matter before the commissioners; who met at Elizabeth-Town, on this occasion, and determined that he should forthwith leave Kaunaumeek, and go to the Delaware Indians.

spent the time in lifting up my heart to God : Had not gone far before my foul was abundantly ftrengthened with thofe words, *If God be for us, who can be againft us?* I went on, confiding in God; and fearing nothing fo much as felf confidence. In this frame I went to the houfe of God, and enjoyed fome affiftance. Afterwards felt the fpirit of love and meeknefs in converfation with fome friends. Then rode home to my brother's : And in the evening, finging hymns with friends, my foul feemed to melt: And in prayer afterwards, enjoyed the exercife of faith, and was enabled to be fervent in fpirit : Found more of God's prefence, than I have done any time in my late wearifome journey. Eternity appeared very near : My nature was very weak, and feemed ready to be diffolved : The fun declining, and the fhadows of the evening drawing on apace. O I longed to fill up the remaining moments all for God! Though my body was fo feeble, and wearied with preaching, and much private converfation, yet I wanted to fit up all night to do fomething for God. To God, the giver of thefe refrefhments, be glory forever and ever : Amen.

[After this, he vifited feveral minifters in Connecticut; and then travelled towards Kaunaumeek, and came to Mr. Sargeant's at Stockbridge, Thurfday, April 26. He performed this journey in a very weak ftate of body.]

Friday, and Saturday, April 27, *and* 28.—Spent fome time in vifiting friends, and difcourfing with my people (who were now moved down from their own place to Mr. Sargeant's) and found them very glad to fee me returned. Was exercifed in my mind with a fenfe of my own unworthinefs.

Lord's Day, April 29.—Preached for Mr. Sargeant, both parts of the day, from Rev. xiv. 4.

Monday,

Monday, April 30.—Rode to Kaunaumeek, but was extremely ill: Did not enjoy the comfort I hoped for in my own house.

Tuesday, May 1.—Having received new orders to go to a number of Indians on Delaware river in Pennsylvania, and my people here being mostly removed to Mr. Sargeant's, I this day took all my clothes, books, &c. and disposed of them, and set out for Delaware river; but made it my way to return to Mr. Sargeant's: Which I did this day, just at night. Rode several hours in the rain through the howling wilderness, although I was so disordered in body, that little or nothing but blood came from me.

[He continued at Stockbridge, the next day; and on Thursday rode a little way, to Sheffield, under a great degree of illness; but with encouragement and cheerfulness of mind under his fatigues. On Friday, he rode to Salisbury, and continued there until after the Sabbath. On Monday, he rode to Sharon; and speaks of himself as distressed at the consideration of the misimprovement of time.]

Tuesday, May 8.—Set out from Sharon in Connecticut, and travelled about forty five miles to a place called the Fish-Kill, and lodged there. Spent much of my time, while riding, in prayer, that God would go with me to Delaware. My heart sometimes was ready to sink with the thoughts of my work, and going alone in the wilderness, I knew not where: But still it was comfortable, to think, that others of God's children had *wandered about in caves and dens of the earth;* and Abraham, when he was called to go forth, *went out not knowing whither he went.* O that I might follow after God.

[The next day, he went forward on his journey; crossed Hudson's river, and went to Goshen in the highlands; and so travelled across the woods, from Hudson's river to Delaware, about an hundred miles,
through

through a desolate and hideous country, above New Jersey; where were very few settlements: In which journey he suffered much fatigue and hardship. He visited some Indians in the way, and discoursed with them concerning christianity. Was considerably melancholy and disconsolate, being alone in a strange wilderness. On Saturday, he came to a settlement of Irish and Dutch people, about twelve miles above the Forks of Delaware.]

Lord's Day, May 13.—Rose early: Felt very poorly after my long journey, and after being wet and fatigued. Was very melancholy; have scrace ever seen such a gloomy morning in my life; there appeared to be no Sabbath; the children were all at play; I a stranger in the wilderness, and knew not where to go; and all circumstances seemed to conspire to render my affairs dark and discouraging. Was disappointed respecting an interpreter, and heard that the Indians were much scattered, &c. O I mourned after the presence of God, and seemed like a creature banished from his sight: Yet he was pleased to support my sinking soul, amidst all my sorrows; so that I never entertained any thought of quitting my business among the poor Indians, but was comforted, to think, that death would before long set me free from these distresses. Rode about three or four miles to the Irish people, where I found some that appeared sober and concerned about religion. My heart then began to be a little encouraged: Went and preached, first to the Irish, and then to the Indians: And in the evening, was a little comforted; my soul seemed to rest on God, and take courage. O that the Lord would be my support and comforter in an evil world.

Monday, May 14.—Was very busy in some necessary studies. Felt myself very loose from all the world: All appeared *vanity and vexation of spirit*. Seemed something

something lonesome and disconsolate, as if I was banished from all mankind, and bereaved of all that is called pleasure in the world: But appeared to myself so vile and unworthy, it seemed fitter for me to be here than any where.

[He continued much in the same frame the three next days.]

Friday, *May* 18.—Felt again something of the sweet spirit of religion; and my soul seemed to confide in God, that he would never leave me. But oftentimes saw myself so mean a creature, that I knew not how to think of preaching. O that I could always live to and upon God!

Saturday, *May* 19.—Was, some part of the time, greatly oppressed with the weight and burden of my work: It seemed impossible for me ever to go through with the business I had undertaken. Towards night, was very calm and comfortable; and I think my soul trusted in God for help.

Lord's Day, *May* 20.—Preached twice to the poor Indians, and enjoyed some freedom in speaking, while I attempted to remove their prejudices against christianity. My soul longed for assistance from above, all the while; for I saw I had no strength sufficient for that work. Afterwards, preached to the Irish people: Was much assisted in the first prayer, and something in sermon. Several persons seemed much concerned for their souls, with whom I discoursed afterwards with much freedom and some power. Blessed be God for any assistance afforded to an unworthy worm. O that I could live to him!

[Through the rest of this week, he was sometimes ready to sink with a sense of his unworthiness and unfitness for the work of the ministry; and sometimes encouraged and lifted above his fears and sorrows, and was enabled confidently to rely on God; and especially on Saturday, towards night, he enjoyed

joyed calmnefs and compofure, and affiftance in prayer to God. He rejoiced (as he fays) *that God remains unchangeably powerful and faithful, a fure and fufficient portion, and the dwelling place of his children in all generations.*]

Lord's Day, May 27.—Vifited my Indians in the morning, and attended upon a funeral among them: Was affected to fee their heathenifh practices. O that they might be *turned from darknefs to light.* Afterwards, got a confiderable number of them together, and preached to them; and obferved them very attentive. After this, preached to the white people from Heb. ii. 3. Was enabled to fpeak with fome freedom and power: Several people feemed much concerned for their fouls; efpecially one who had been educated a Roman Catholick. Bleffed be the Lord for any help.

Monday, May 28.—Set out from the Indians above the Forks of Delaware, on a journey towards Newark in New-Jerfey, according to my orders. Rode through the wildernefs; was much fatigued with the heat; lodged at a place called Black-River; was exceedingly tired and worn out.

[On Tuefday, he came to Newark: The next day, went to Elizabeth-Town: On Thurfday, he went to New-York; and on Friday returned to Elizabeth-Town. Thefe days were fpent in fome perplexity of mind. He continued at Elizabeth-Town until Friday in the week following. Was enlivened, refrefhed, and ftrengthened on the Sabbath at the Lord's table. The enfuing days of the week were fpent chiefly in ftudies preparatory to his ordination; and on fome of them he feemed to have much of God's gracious prefence, and of the fweet influences of his fpirit; but was in a very weak ftate of body. On Saturday, he rode to Newark.]

Lord's Day, June 10.—[At Newark.] In the morning, was much concerned how I fhould perform the

work

work of the day; and trembled at the thoughts of being left to myself. Enjoyed very considerable assistance in all parts of the publick service. Had an opportunity again to attend on the ordinance of the Lord's supper, and through divine goodness was refreshed in it: My soul was full of love and tenderness towards the children of God, and towards all men: Felt a certain sweetness of disposition towards every creature. At night, I enjoyed more spirituality, and sweet desire of holiness, than I have felt for some time: Was afraid of every thought and every motion, lest thereby my heart should be drawn away from God. O that I might never leave the blessed God! Lord, *in thy presence is fulness of joy.* O the blessedness of living to God!

Monday, June 11.—This day the Presbytery met together at Newark, in order to my ordination. Was very weak and disordered in body; yet endeavoured to repose my confidence in God. Spent most of the day alone; especially the forenoon. At three in the afternoon preached my probation sermon, from Acts xxvi. 17. 18. being a text given me for that end. Felt not well, either in body or mind; however, God carried me through comfortably. Afterwards, passed an examination before the Presbytery. Was much tired, and my mind burdened with the greatness of that charge I was in the most solemn manner about to take upon me: My mind was so pressed with the weight of the work incumbent upon me, that I could not sleep this night, though very weary and in great need of rest.

Tuesday, June 12.—Was this morning further examined, respecting my experimental acquaintance with christianity*. At ten o'clock my ordination was

---

* Mr. Pemberton, in a letter to the Honourable Society in Scotland that employed Mr. Brainerd, which he wrote concerning him, (published in Scotland, in the *Christian monthly History*) writes thus, "We can with pleasure say, that Mr. Brainerd passed through his ordination trials, to the universal approbation of the Presbytery, and appeared

was attended: The sermon preached by the Rev. Mr. Pemberton. At this time I was affected with a sense of the important trust committed to me; yet was composed, and solemn, without distraction: And I hope, I then (as many times before) gave myself up to God, to be for him, and not for another. O that I might always be engaged in the service of God, and duly remember the solemn charge I have received, in the presence of God, angels and men; Amen! May I be assisted of God for this purpose. Towards night, rode to Elizabeth-Town.

appeared uncommonly qualified for the work of the ministry. He seems to be armed with a great deal of self denial, and animated with a noble zeal to propagate the gospel among those barbarous nations, who have long dwelt in the darkness of heathenism."

PART

PART VI.

From his ORDINATION *until he first began to preach to the* INDIANS *at* CROSWEEKSUNG, *among whom he had his most remarkable success.*

WEDNESDAY, *June* 13.—Spent some considerable time in writing an account of the Indian affairs to go to Scotland; spent some time in conversation with friends; but enjoyed not much sweetness and satisfaction.

Thursday, June 14.—Received some particular kindness from friends; and wondered that God should open the hearts of any to treat me with kindness: Saw myself to be unworthy of any favour from God, or any of my fellow men. Was much exercised with pain in my head; however determined to set out on my journey towards Delaware in the afternoon: But in the afternoon my pain increased exceedingly; so that I was obliged to betake myself to the bed; and the night following, was greatly distressed with pain and sickness: Was sometimes almost bereaved of the exercise of reason by the extremity of pain. Continued much distressed until Saturday; when I was something relieved by an emetick: But was unable to walk abroad until the Monday following, in the afternoon; and still remained very feeble. I often admired the goodness of God, that he did not suffer me to proceed on my journey from this place, where I was so tenderly used, and to be sick by the way among strangers. God is very gracious to me, both in health and sickness, and intermingles much mercy with all my afflictions and toils.

toils. Enjoyed some sweetness in things divine, in the midst of my pain and weakness. O, that I could praise the Lord!

[On Tuesday, June 19, he set out on his journey home, and in three days reached his place, near the Forks of Delaware. Performed the journey under much weakness of body; but had comfort in his soul, from day to day: And both his weakness of body, and consolation of mind, continued through the week.]

Lord's Day, June 24.—Extremely feeble; scarce able to walk: However, visited my Indians, and took much pains to instruct them: Laboured with some that were much disaffected to christianity. My mind was much burdened with the weight and difficulty of my work. My whole dependence and hope of success seemed to be on God; who alone, I saw, could make them willing to receive instruction. My heart was much engaged in prayer, sending up silent requests to God, even while I was speaking to them. O that I could always go in the strength of the Lord!

Monday, June 25.—Was something better in health than of late: Was able to spend a considerable part of the day in prayer and close studies. Had more freedom and fervency in prayer than usual of late.

Tuesday, June 26.—In the morning, my desires seemed to rise, and ascend up freely to God. Was busy most of the day in translating prayers into the language of the Delaware Indians: Met with great difficulty by reason that my interpreter was altogether unacquainted with the business. But though I was much discouraged with the extreme difficulty of that work, yet God supported me; and especially in the evening, gave me sweet refreshment: In prayer my soul was enlarged, and my faith drawn into sensible exercise; was enabled to cry to God
for

for my poor Indians; and though the work of their converfion appeared *impoffible with man, yet with God* I faw *all things were poffible*. My faith was much ftrengthened, by obferving the wonderful affiftance God afforded his fervants Nehemiah and Ezra, in reforming his people, and reeftablifhing his ancient church. I was much affifted in prayer for dear chriftian friends, and for others that I apprehended to be chriftlefs; but was more efpecially concerned for the poor heathen, and thofe of my own charge: Was enabled to be inftant in prayer for them; and hoped that God would bow the heavens and come down for their falvation. It feemed to me, there could be no impediment fufficient to obftruct that glorious work, feeing the living God, as I ftrongly hoped, was engaged for it. I continued in a folemn frame, lifting up my heart to God for affiftance, and grace, that I might be more mortified to this prefent world, that my whole foul might be taken up continually in concern for the advancement of Chrift's kingdom: Longed that God would purge me more, that I might be as a chofen veffel to bear his name among the heathen. Continued in this frame until I dropped afleep.

Wednefday, June 27.—Felt fomething of the fame folemn concern, and fpirit of prayer, that I enjoyed laft night, foon after I rofe in the morning. In the afternoon, rode feveral miles to fee if I could procure any lands for the poor Indians, that they might live together, and be under better advantages for inftruction.

Thurfday, June 28.—Spent the morning, in reading feveral parts of the holy fcripture, and in fervent prayer for my Indians; that God would fet up his kingdom among them, and bring them into his church. About nine, I withdrew to my ufual place of retirement in the woods; and there again

enjoyed

enjoyed some assistance in prayer. My great concern was for the conversion of the heathen to God; and the Lord helped me to plead with him for it. Towards noon, rode up to the Indians, in order to preach to them; and while going my heart went up to God in prayer for them; could freely tell God, he knew that the cause was not mine, which I was engaged in; but it was his own cause, and it would be for his own glory to convert the poor Indians: And blessed be God, I felt no desire of their conversion, that I might receive honour from the world, as being the instrument of it. Had some freedom in speaking to the Indians.

[The two next days he speaks of some serious concern for the kingdom of the blessed Redeemer; and confidence in God, that he would advance it; but complains much of barrenness, wanderings, inactivity, &c.]

Lord's Day, July 1.—In the morning, was perplexed with wandering vain thoughts: Was much grieved, judged and condemned myself before God. And O, how miserable did I feel, because I could not live to God. At ten, rode away with a heavy heart to preach to my Indians. Upon the road, I attempted to lift up my heart to God; but was infested with an unsettled wandering frame of mind; and was exceeding restless and perplexed, and filled with shame and confusion before God. I seemed to myself to be *more brutish than any man*; and thought, none deserved to be *cast out of God's presence* so much as I. If I attempted to lift up my heart to God, as I frequently did by the way, on a sudden before I was aware, my thoughts were wandering *to the ends of the earth*: And my soul was filled with surprise and anxiety, to find it thus. Thus also after I came to the Indians, my mind was confused; and I felt nothing sensibly of that sweet reliance on God,

God, that my soul has been comforted with in days past. Spent the forenoon in this posture of mind, and preached to the Indians without any heart. In the afternoon, I felt still barren, when I began to preach; and after about half an hour, I seemed to myself to know nothing, and to have nothing to say to the Indians; but soon after, I found in myself a spirit of love, and warmth, and power to address the poor Indians; and God helped me to plead with them to *turn from all the vanities of the heathen, to the living God:* And I am persuaded the Lord touched their consciences; for I never saw such attention raised in them before. And when I came away from them, I spent the whole time while I was riding to my lodgings, three miles distant, in prayer and praise to God. And after I had rode more than two miles, it came into my mind to dedicate myself to God again; which I did with great solemnity, and unspeakable satisfaction; especially gave up myself to him renewedly in the work of the ministry. And this I did by divine grace, I hope, without any exception or reserve; not in the least shrinking back from any difficulties, that might attend this great and blessed work. I seemed to be most free, cheerful, and full in this dedication of myself: My whole soul cried, "Lord, to thee I dedicate myself: O accept of me, and let me be thine forever. Lord, I desire nothing else; I desire nothing more. O come, come, Lord accept a poor worm. *Whom have I in heaven, but thee; and there is none upon earth, that I desire beside thee.*" After this, was enabled to praise God with my whole soul, that he had enabled me to devote and consecrate all my powers to him in this solemn manner. My heart rejoiced in my particular work as a missionary; rejoiced in my necessity of self denial in many respects; and still continued to give up myself to God,

and

and implore mercy of him; praying inceffantly every moment, with fweet fervency. My nature being very weak of late, and much fpent, was now confiderably overcome: My fingers grew very feeble and fomewhat numb; fo that I could fcarcely ftretch them out ftraight: And when I lighted from my horfe, could hardly walk: My joints feemed all to be loofed. But I felt abundant *ftrength in the inner man*. Preached to the white people: God helped me much, efpecially in prayer. Sundry of my poor Indians were fo moved as to come to meeting alfo; and one appeared much concerned.

Monday, July 2.—Had fome relifh of the divine comforts of yefterday; but could not get that warmth and exercife of faith, that I defired. Had fometimes a diftreffing fenfe of my paft follies, and prefent ignorance and barrennefs: And efpecially in the afternoon, was funk down under a load of fin and guilt, in that I had lived fo little to God, after his abundant goodnefs to me yefterday. In the evening, though very weak, was enabled to pray with fervency, and to continue inftant in prayer, near an hour. My foul mourned over the power of its corruption, and longed exceedingly to be *wafhed*, and *purged as with hyffop*. Was enabled to pray for my dear abfent friends, Chrift's minifters, and his church; and enjoyed much freedom and fervency, but not fo much comfort, by reafon of guilt and fhame before God. Judged and condemned myfelf for the follies of the day.

[The two next days he feems to have had fpecial affiftance and fervency moft of the time. Thurfday was fpent in great bodily weaknefs; and in great bitternefs of fpirit by reafon of his vilenefs and corruption; he fays thus, I thought there was not one creature living fo vile as I. O, my inward pollution! O, my guilt and fhame before God! I know not what to do. O, I longed ardently to be cleansed and washed from the stains of inward pollution ! O, to be made like God, or rather to be made fit for God to own !

Friday, July 6.—Awoke this morning in the fear of God : Soon called to mind my sadness in the evening past ; and spent my first waking minutes in prayer for sanctification, that my soul might be washed from its exceeding pollution and defilement. After I arose, I spent some time in reading God's word and prayer. I cried to God under a sense of my great indigency. I am, of late, most of all concerned for ministerial qualifications, and the conversion of the heathen : Last year, I longed to be prepared for a world of glory, and speedily to depart out of this world ; but of late all my concern almost is for the conversion of the heathen ; and for that end, I long to live. But blessed be God, I have less desire to live for any of the pleasures of the world, than ever I had : I long and love to be a pilgrim ; and want grace to imitate the life, labours and sufferings of St. Paul among the heathen. And when I long for holiness now, it is not so much for myself as formerly ; but rather that thereby I may become an able minister of the New Testament, especially to the heathen. Spent about two hours this morning, in reading and prayer, by turns ; and was in a watchful tender frame, afraid of every thing that might cool my affections, and draw away my heart from God. Was something strengthened in my studies ; but near night was very weak and weary.

Saturday, July 7.—Was very much disordered this morning, and my vigour all spent and exhausted : But was affected, and refreshed in reading the sweet story of Elijah's translation, and enjoyed some affection and fervency in prayer ; longed much for ministerial

isterial gifts and graces, that I might do something in the cause of God.

Lord's Day, July 8.—Was ill last night, not able to rest quietly. Had some small degree of assistance in preaching to the Indians; and afterwards was enabled to preach to the white people, with some power, especially in the close of my discourse, from Jer. iii. 23. The Lord also assisted me in some measure in the first prayer: Blessed be his name. Near night, though very weary, was enabled to read God's word with some sweet relish of it, and to pray with affection, fervency, and (I trust) faith: My soul was more sensibly dependent on God, than usual. Was watchful, tender, and jealous of my own heart, lest I should admit carelessness and vain thoughts, and grieve the blessed Spirit, so that he should withdraw his sweet, kind, and tender influences. Longed to *depart and be with Christ*, more than at any time of late. My soul was exceedingly united to the saints of ancient times, as well as those now living; especially my soul melted for the society of Elijah and Elisha. Was enabled to cry to God with a child like spirit, and to continue instant in prayer for some time. Was much enlarged in the sweet duty of intercession.

Tuesday, July 10.—Was very ill and full of pain, and very dull and spiritless. In the evening, had an affecting sense of my ignorance, &c. and of my need of God at all times, to do every thing for me; and my soul was humbled before God.

Wednesday, July 11.—Was still exercised with illness and pain. Had some degree of affection and warmth in prayer and reading God's word: Longed for Abraham's faith and fellowship with God; and felt some resolution to spend all my time for God, and to exert myself with more fervency in his service; but found my body weak and feeble. In the afternoon, though very ill, was enabled to spend some considerable time in prayer; spent indeed most of the day in that exercise; and my soul was diffident, watchful and tender, lest I should offend my blessed friend, in thought or behaviour. I am persuaded my soul confided in, and leaned upon the blessed God. O what need did I see myself to stand in of God at all times, to assist me and lead me! Found a great want of strength and vigour, both in the outward and inner man.

[The exercises and experiences, that he speaks of in the next nine days, are very similar to those of the preceding days of this and the foregoing week.]

Saturday, July 21.—This morning, was greatly oppressed with guilt and shame, from a sense of inward vileness and pollution. Towards night my burden respecting my work among the Indians began to increase much; and was aggravated by hearing sundry things that looked very discouraging, in particular that they intended to meet together the next day for an idolatrous feast and dance. Then I began to be in anguish: I thought I must in conscience go and endeavour to break them up; and knew not how to attempt such a thing. However, I withdrew for prayer, hoping for strength from above. And in prayer I was exceedingly enlarged, and my soul was as much drawn out as ever I remember it to have been in my life, or near. So, as far as I could judge, I was wholly free from selfish ends in my fervent supplications for the poor Indians. I knew, they were met together to worship devils, and not God; and this made me cry earnestly, that God would now appear, and help me in my attempts to break up this idolatrous meeting. My soul pleaded long; and I thought God would hear, and would go with me to vindicate his own cause: I seemed to confide in God for his presence and assistance. And
thus

thus I spent the evening, praying inceffantly for divine affiftance, and that I might not be felf dependent, but ftill have my whole dependence upon God. What I paffed through was remarkable, and indeed inexpreffible. I exceedingly longed, that God would *get to himfelf a name among the heathen* : And I appealed to him with the greateft freedom, that he knew I preferred him above my chief joy. Indeed, I had no notion of joy from this world : I cared not where or how I lived, or what hardfhips I went through ; fo that I could but gain fouls to Chrift. I continued in this frame all the evening and night. While I was afleep, I dreamed of thefe things ; and when I awaked (as I frequently did) the firft thing I thought of was this great work of pleading for God againft Satan.

Lord's Day, July 22.—When I waked, my foul was burdened with what feemed to be before me : I cried to God, before I could get out of my bed : And as foon as I was dreffed, I withdrew into the woods, to pour out my burdened foul to God, efpecially for affiftance in my great work ; for I could fcarcely think of any thing elfe : And enjoyed the fame freedom and fervency as the laft evening ; and did with unfpeakable freedom give up myfelf afrefh to God for life or death, for all hardfhips he fhould call me to among the heathen ; and felt as if nothing could difcourage me from this bleffed work. I had a ftrong hope, that God would *bow the heavens and come down*, and do fome marvellous work among the heathen. And when I was riding to the Indians, three miles, my heart was continually going up to God for his prefence and affiftance ; and hoping, and almoft expecting, that God would make this *the day of his power and grace* amongft the poor Indians. When I came to them, I found them engaged in their frolick ; but through divine goodnefs I

K 4 got

them to break up, and attend to my preaching : Yet still there appeared nothing of the special power of God among them. Preached again to them in the afternoon; and observed the Indians were more sober than before : But still saw nothing special among them ; from whence Satan took occasion to tempt and buffet me with these cursed suggestions, *There is no God,* or if there be, he is not able to convert the Indians, before they have more knowledge, &c. I was very weak and weary, and my soul borne down with perplexity : But was mortified to all the world, and was determined still to wait upon God for the conversion of the heathen, though the devil tempted me to the contrary.

Monday, July 23.—Retained still a deep and pressing sense of what lay with so much weight upon me yesterday : But was more calm and quiet ; enjoyed freedom and composure, after the temptations of the last evening : Had sweet resignation to the divine will ; and desired nothing so much as the conversion of the heathen to God, and that his kingdom might come in my own heart, and the hearts of others. Rode to a settlement of Irish people, about fifteen miles southwestward ; spent my time in prayer and meditation by the way. Near night, preached from Matth. v. 3. God was pleased to afford me some degree of freedom and fervency. Blessed be God for any measure of assistance.

Tuesday, July 24.—Rode about seventeen miles westward, over a hideous mountain, to a number of Indians. Got together near thirty of them : Preached to them in the evening, and lodged among them. Was weak, and felt something disconsolate.

[The next day, he preached to these Indians again ; and then returned to the Irish settlement, and there preached to a numerous congregation : There was a considerable appearance of awakening in the congregation.

gation. Thursday, he returned home, exceedingly fatigued and spent; still in the same frame of mortification to the world, and solicitous for the advancement of Christ's kingdom: And on this day he says thus, " I have felt, this week, more of the spirit of a *pilgrim on earth*, than perhaps ever before; and yet so desirous to see Zion's prosperity, that I was not so willing to leave this scene of sorrow as I used to be." The two remaining days of the week, he was very ill, and cries out of wanderings, dulness, and want of spiritual fervency and sweetness. On the Sabbath, he was confined by illness, not able to go out to preach. After this, his illness increased upon him, and he continued very ill all the week. Concerning the next five days he writes thus: " On Lord's Day, August 5, was still very poor. But though very weak, I visited and preached to the poor Indians twice, and was strengthened vastly beyond my expectations. And indeed, the Lord gave me some freedom and fervency in addressing them; though I had not strength enough to stand, but was obliged to sit down the whole time; towards night, was extremely weak, faint, sick, and full of pain. And thus I have continued much in the same state that I was in last week, through the most of this (it being now Friday;) unable to engage in any business; frequently unable to pray in the family. I am obliged to let all my thoughts and concerns run at random; for I have neither strength to read, meditate, or pray: And this naturally perplexes my mind. I seem to myself like a man that has all his estate embarked in one small boat, unhappily going adrift, down a swift torrent. The poor owner stands on the shore, and looks, and laments his loss."

[The next three weeks after this, his illness was not so extreme: He was in some degree capable of business, both publick and private; (although he

had

had some turns wherein his indisposition prevailed to a great degree:) He also in this space had, for the most part, much more inward assistance, and strength of mind: He often expresses great longings for the enlargement of Christ's kingdom; especially by the conversion of the heathen to God: He speaks of his hope of this as all his delight and joy. He continues still to express his usual longings after holiness and living to God, and his sense of his own unworthiness: He several times speaks of his appearing to himself the vilest creature on earth; and once says, that he verily thought there were none of God's children who fell so far short of that holiness, and perfection in their obedience, which God requires, as he. He speaks of his feeling more dead than ever to the enjoyments of the world. He sometimes mentions special assistance that he had in this space of time, in preaching to the Indians, and of appearances of religious concern among them. He speaks also of assistance in prayer for absent friends, and especially ministers and candidates for the ministry; and of much comfort he enjoyed in the company of some ministers that came to visit him.]

Saturday, September 1.—Was so far strengthened, after a season of great weakness, that I was able to spend two or three hours in writing on a divine subject. Enjoyed some comfort and sweetness in things divine and sacred: And as my bodily strength was in some measure restored, so my soul seemed to be somewhat vigorous, and engaged in the things of God.

Lord's Day, September 2.—Was enabled to speak to my poor Indians with much concern and fervency; and I am persuaded, God enabled me to exercise faith in him, while I was speaking to them. I perceived, that some of them were afraid to hearken to, and embrace christianity, lest they should be enchanted

chanted and poisoned by some of the powows: But I was enabled to plead with them not to fear these; and confiding in God for safety and deliverance, I bid a challenge to all these *powers of darkness*, to do their worst upon me first. Afterwards I found my soul rejoice in God for his assisting grace.

[After this he went a journey into New-England, and was absent from the place of his abode, at the Forks of Delaware, about three weeks. He was in a feeble state the greater part of the time. But in the latter part of the journey, he found he gained much in health and strength. And as to the state of his mind, and his religious and spiritual exercises, it was much with him as had been before usual in journeys; excepting that the frame of his mind seemed more generally to be comfortable.]

Wednesday, September 26.—Rode home to the Forks of Delaware. What reason have I to bless God, who has preserved me in riding more than four hundred and twenty miles, and has *kept all my bones that not one of them has been broken!* My health likewise is greatly recovered. O that I could dedicate my all to God: This is all the return I can make to him.

Thursday, September 27.—Was something melancholy: Had not much freedom and comfort in prayer: My soul is disconsolate when God is withdrawn.

[The three next days he speaks of the same longings for the advancement of Christ's kingdom, and the conversion of the Indians; but complains greatly of the ill effects of the diversions of his late journey, as unfixing his mind from that degree of engagedness, fervency, watchfulness, &c. which he enjoyed before.]

Monday, October 1.—Was engaged this day in making preparation for my intended journey to Susquehannah:

quehannah : Withdrew several times to the woods for secret duties, and endeavoured to plead for the divine presence to go with me to the poor pagans, to whom I was going to preach the gospel. Towards night rode about four miles, and met brother Byram*; who was come, at my desire, to be my companion in travel to the Indians. I rejoiced to see him; and, I trust, God made his conversation profitable to me. I saw him, as I thought, more dead to the world, its anxious cares, and alluring objects, than I was: And this made me look within myself, and gave me a greater sense of my guilt, ingratitude, and misery.

Tuesday, October 2.—Set out on my journey, in company with dear brother Byram, and my interpreter, and two chief Indians from the Forks of Delaware. Travelled about twenty five miles, and lodged in one of the last houses on our road; after which there was nothing but a hideous and howling wilderness.

Wednesday, October 3.—We went on our way into the wilderness, and found the most difficult and dangerous travelling, by far, that ever any of us had seen; we had scarce any thing else but lofty mountains, deep valleys, and hideous rocks, to make our way through. However, I felt some sweetness in divine things, part of the day, and had my mind intensely engaged in meditation on a divine subject. Near night, my beast that I rode upon, hung one of her legs in the rocks, and fell down under me; but, through divine goodness, I was not hurt. However, she broke her leg; and being in such a hideous place, and near thirty miles from any house, I saw nothing that could be done to preserve her life, and so was obliged to kill her, and to prosecute my journey on foot.

---

* Minister at a place called Rockciticus, about forty miles from Mr. Brainerd's lodgings.

foot. This accident made me admire the divine goodnefs to me, that my bones were not broken, and the mulitude of them filled with ftrong pain. Juft at dark we kindled a fire, cut up a few bufhes, and made a fhelter over our heads to fave us from the froft, which was very hard that night; and committing ourfelves to God by prayer, we lay down on the ground and flept quietly.

[The next day they went forward on their journey, and at night took up their lodging in the woods in like manner.]

Friday, October 5.—We arrived at Sufquehannah River, at a place called Opeholhaupung : Found there twelve Indian houfes. After I had faluted the king in a friendly manner, I told him my bufinefs, and that my defire was to teach them chriftianity. After fome confultation, the Indians gathered, and I preached to them. And when I had done, I afked if they would hear me again. They replied, that they would confider of it; and foon after fent me word, that they would immediately attend if I would preach: Which I did, with freedom, both times. When I afked them again whether they would hear me further, they replied, they would the next day. I was exceeding fenfible of the impoffibility of doing any thing for the poor heathen, without fpecial affiftance from above : And my foul feemed to reft on God, and leave it to him to do as he pleafed in that which I faw was his own caufe : And indeed, through divine goodnefs, I had felt fomething of this frame moft of the time while I was travelling thither; and in fome meafure before I fet out.

Saturday, October 6.—Rofe early and befought the Lord for help in my great work. Near noon preached again to the Indians : And in the afternoon, vif-, ited them from houfe to houfe, and invited them to
come

come and hear me again the next day, and put off their hunting design, which they were just entering upon, until Monday. This night, I trust, the Lord stood by me to encourage and strengthen my soul: I spent more than an hour in secret retirement; was enabled to pour out my heart before God, for the increase of grace in my soul, for ministerial endowments, for success among the poor Indians, for God's ministers and people, and for dear friends vastly distant, &c. Blessed be God.

[The next day he complains of great want of fixedness and intenseness in religion, so that he could not keep any spiritual thought one minute without distraction; which occasioned anguish of spirit.— He felt, he says, amazingly guilty, and extremely miserable; and cries out, O my soul, what death it is, to have the affections unable to center in God, by reason of darkness, and consequently roving after that satisfaction elsewhere, that is only to be found here! However, he preached twice to the Indians with some freedom and power: But was afterwards damped by the objections they made against christianity. In the evening, in a sense of his great defects in preaching, he entreated God not to impute to him blood guiltiness; but yet was at the same time enabled to *rejoice in God*.]

Monday, October 8.—Visited the Indians with a design to take my leave of them, supposing they would this morning go out to hunting early; but beyond my expectation and hope, they desired to hear me preach again. I gladly complied with their request, and afterwards endeavoured to answer their objections against christianity. Then they went away; and we spent the rest of the afternoon in reading and prayer, intending to go homeward very early the next day. My soul was in some measure refreshed in secret prayer and meditation. Blessed be the Lord for all his goodness.

Tuesday,

Tuesday, October 9.—We rose about four in the morning, and, commending ourselves to God by prayer, and asking his special protection, we set out on our journey homewards about five, and travelled with great steadiness until past six at night. And then made us a fire, and a shelter of barks, and so rested. I had some clear and comfortable thoughts on a divine subject, by the way, towards night. In the night, the wolves howled around us; but God preserved us.

[The next day they rose early, and set forward, and travelled that day until they came to an Irish settlement, where Mr. Brainerd was acquainted, and lodged there.]

Friday, October 12.—Rode home to my lodging; where I poured out my soul to God in secret prayer, and endeavoured to bless him for his abundant goodness to me in my late journey. I scarce ever enjoyed more health, at least of later years; and God marvellously, and almost miraculously, supported me under the fatigues of the way, and travelling on foot. Blessed be the Lord, that continually preserves me in all my ways.

[On Saturday he went again to the Irish settlement, to spend the Sabbath there, his Indians being gone.]

Lord's Day, October 14.—Was much confused and perplexed in my thoughts; could not pray; and was almost discouraged, thinking I should never be able to preach any more. But afterwards God was pleased to give me some relief from these confusions: But still I was afraid, and even trembled before God. I went to the place of publick worship, lifting up my heart to God for assistance and grace, in my great work: And God was gracious to me, and helped me to plead with him for holiness, and to use the strongest arguments with him, drawn from the incarnation and sufferings of Christ for this very end, that men might be made holy. Afterwards, I was much affifted in preaching. I know not that ever God helped me to preach in a more clofe and diftinguifhing manner for the trial of men's ftate. Through the infinite goodnefs of God, I felt what I fpake; and God enabled me to treat on divine truth with uncommon clearnefs: And yet I was fo fenfible of my defects in preaching, that I could not be proud of my performance, as at fome times; and bleffed be the Lord for this mercy. In the evening, I longed to be entirely alone, to blefs God for help in a time of extremity; and longed for great degrees of holinefs, that I might fhew my gratitude to God.

[The next morning he fpent fome time before funrife in prayer, in the fame fweet and grateful frame of mind, that he had been in the evening before: And afterwards went to his Indians, and fpent fome time in teaching and exhorting them.]

Tuefday, October 16.—Felt a fpirit of folemnity and watchfulnefs; was afraid I fhould not live to and upon God: Longed for more intenfenefs and fpirituality. Spent the day in writing; frequently lifting up my heart to God for more heavenly mindednefs. In the evening enjoyed fweet affiftance in prayer, and thirfted and pleaded to be as holy as the bleffed angels: Longed for minifterial gifts and graces, and fuccefs in my work: Was fweetly affifted in the duty of interceffion, and enabled to remember, and plead for numbers of dear friends, and Chrift's minifters.

[He feemed to have much of the fame frame of mind, the two next days.]

Friday, October 19.—My foul enjoyed a fweet feafon of bitter repentance and forrow, that I had wronged that bleffed God, who, I was perfuaded, was reconciled to me in his dear Son. My foul was
now

now tender, devout, and solemn. And I was afraid of nothing, but sin; and afraid of that in every action and thought.

[The four following days, were manifestly spent in a most constant tenderness, watchfulness, diligence and self diffidence. But he complains of wanderings of mind, languor of affections, &c.]

Wednesday, October 24.—Near noon, rode to my people; spent some time, and prayed with them: Felt the frame of a pilgrim on earth; longed much to leave this gloomy mansion; but yet found the exercise of patience and resignation. And as I returned home from the Indians, spent the whole time in lifting up my heart to God. In the evening, enjoyed a blessed season alone in prayer; was enabled to cry to God with a child like spirit, for the space of near an hour: Enjoyed a sweet freedom in supplicating for myself, for dear friends, ministers, and some who are preparing for that work, and for the church of God; and longed to be as lively myself in God's service as the angels.

Friday, October 26.—In the morning my soul was melted with a sense of divine goodness and mercy to such a vile unworthy worm as I: Delighted to lean upon God, and place my whole trust in him. My soul was exceedingly grieved for sin, and prized and longed after holiness; it wounded my heart deeply, yet sweetly, to think how I had abused a kind God. I longed to be perfectly holy, that I might not grieve a gracious God; who will continue to love, notwithstanding his love is abused: I longed for holiness more for this end, than I did for my own happiness sake. And yet this was my greatest happiness, never more to dishonour, but always to glorify the blessed God. Afterwards rode up to the Indians, in the afternoon, &c.

[The four next days he was exercised with much disorder and pain of body, with a degree of melancholy and gloominess of mind, bitterly complaining of deadness and unprofitableness, yet mourning and longing after God.]

Wednesday, October 31.—Was sensible of my barrenness, and decay, in the things of God: My soul failed, when I remembered the fervency I had enjoyed at the throne of grace. O, I thought, if I could but be spiritual, warm, heavenly minded, and affectionately breathing after God, this would be better than life to me! My soul longed exceedingly for death, to be loosed from this dulness and barrenness, and made forever active in the service of God. I seemed to live for nothing, and to do no good: And O, the burden of such a life! O, Death, Death, my kind friend, hasten and deliver me from dull mortality, and make me spiritual and vigorous to eternity.

Friday, November 2.—Was filled with sorrow and confusion, in the morning, and could enjoy no sweet sense of divine things, nor get any relief in prayer. Saw I deserved that every one of God's creatures should be let loose upon me to be the executioners of his wrath against me: And yet therein I saw I deserved what I did not fear as my portion. About noon rode up to the Indians; and while going, could feel no desires for them, and even dreaded to say any thing to them; but God was pleased to give me some freedom and enlargement, and made the season comfortable to me. In the evening had enlargement in prayer.

Saturday, November 3.—I read the life and trials of a godly man, and was much warmed by it: I wondered at my past deadness; and was more convinced of it than ever. Was enabled to confess and bewail my sin before God, with self abhorrence.

Lord's

Lord's Day, November 4.—Had, I think, some exercise of faith in prayer in the morning: Longed to be spiritual. Had considerable help in preaching to my poor Indians: Was encouraged with them, and hoped that God designed mercy for them.

[The next day he set out on a journey to New-York, to the meeting of the presbytery there; and was gone from home more than a fortnight. He seemed to enter on this journey with great reluctance; fearing that the diversions of it would prove a means of cooling his religious affections, as he had found in other journeys. But yet in this journey he had some special seasons wherein he enjoyed extraordinary evidences and fruits of God's gracious presence. He was greatly fatigued and exposed in this journey by cold and storms: And when he returned from New-York to New-Jersey, on Friday, was taken very ill, and was detained by his illness some time.]

Wednesday, November 21.—Rode from Newark to Rockciticus in the cold, and was almost overcome with it. Enjoyed some sweetness in conversation with dear Mr. Jones, while I dined with him: My soul loves the people of God, and especially the ministers of Jesus Christ, who feel the same trials that I do.

Thursday, November 22.—Came on my way from Rockciticus to Delaware river. Was very much disordered with a cold and pain in my head. About six at night, I lost my way in the wilderness, and wandered over rocks and mountains, down hideous steeps, through swamps, and most dreadful and dangerous places: And the night being dark, so that few stars could be seen, I was greatly exposed: Was much pinched with cold, and distressed with an extreme pain in my head, attended with sickness at my stomach; so that every step I took was distressing to me. I had but little hope for several hours together, but that I must lie out in the woods all night in this distressed case. But, about nine o'clock, I found a house, through the abundant goodness of God, and was kindly entertained. Thus I have frequently been exposed, and sometimes lain out the whole night: But God has hitherto preserved me; and blessed be his name. Such fatigues and hardships as these, serve to wean me more from the earth; and, I trust, will make heaven the sweeter. Formerly, when I was thus exposed to cold, rain, &c. I was ready to please myself with the thoughts of enjoying a comfortable house, a warm fire, and other outward comforts; but now these have less place in my heart, through the grace of God, and my eye is more to God for comfort.

Friday, November 23.—Visited a sick man; discoursed and prayed with him. Then visited another house, where was one dead and laid out; looked on the corpse and longed that my time might come to *depart*, that I might be *with Christ*. Then went home to my lodgings, about one o'clock. Felt poorly; but was able to read most of the afternoon.

[Within the space of the next twelve days, he passed under many changes in the frames and exercises of his mind. He had many seasons of the special influence of God's Spirit, animating, invigorating, and comforting him in the ways of God and duties of religion; but had some turns of great dejection and melancholy. He spent much time, within this space, in hard labour, with others, to make for himself a little cottage or hut, to live in by himself through the winter.

Thursday, December 6.—Having now a happy opportunity of being retired in a house of my own, which I have lately procured and moved into, and considering that it is now a long time since I have been

been able, either on account of bodily weakness, or for want of retirement, or some other difficulty, to spend any time in secret fasting and prayer; considering also the greatness of my work, and the extreme difficulties that attend it; and that my poor Indians are now worshiping devils, notwithstanding all the pains I have taken with them, which almost overwhelms my spirit: Moreover, considering my extreme barrenness, spiritual deadness, and dejection, of late; as also the power of some particular corruptions; I sat apart this day for secret prayer and fasting, to implore the blessing of God on myself, on my poor people, on my friends, and on the church of God. At first, I felt a great backwardness to the duties of the day, on account of the seeming impossibility of performing them: But the Lord helped me to break through this difficulty. I enjoyed much more intenseness, fervency, and spirituality, than I expected; God was better to me than my fears. And, towards night, I felt my soul rejoice, that God is unchangeably happy and glorious; that he will be glorified, whatever becomes of his creatures. I was enabled to persevere in prayer until some time in the evening; at which time I saw so much need of divine help, in every respect, that I knew not how to leave off, and had forgot that I needed food. This evening I was much assisted in meditating on Isai. lii. 3. Blessed be the Lord for any help in the past day.

Friday, December 7.—Spent some time in prayer, in the morning; enjoyed some freedom and affection in the duty, and had longing desires of being made *faithful to the death.* Spent a little time in writing on a divine subject: Then visited the Indians, and preached to them: But under inexpressible dejection. I had no heart to speak to them, and could not do it, but as I forced myself: I knew they must

must hate to hear me, as having but just got home from their idolatrous feast and devil worship. In the evening had some freedom in prayer and meditation.

Saturday, December 8.—Have been uncommonly free this day from dejection, and from that distressing apprehension that I could do nothing : Was enabled to pray and study with some comfort ; and especially was assisted in writing on a divine subject. In the evening my soul rejoiced in God ; and I blessed his name for shining on my soul. O the sweet and blessed change I then felt, when God *brought me out of darkness into his marvellous light.*

Lord's Day, December 9.—Preached both parts of the day at a place called Greenwich, in New-Jersey, about ten miles from my own house. In the first discourse I had scarce any warmth or affectionate longing for souls. In the intermission season I got alone among the bushes, and cried to God for pardon of my deadness ; and was in anguish and bitterness, that I could not address souls with more compassion and tender affection : Judged and condemned myself for want of this divine temper : Though I saw I could not get it as of myself any more than I could make a world. In the latter exercise, blessed be the Lord, I had some fervency, both in prayer and preaching ; and especially in the application of my discourse was enabled to address precious souls with affection, concern, tenderness and importunity. The Spirit of God, I think, was there ; as the effects were apparent, tears running down many cheeks.

Wednesday, December 12.—Was very weak ; but somewhat assisted in secret prayer, and enabled with pleasure and sweetness to cry, *Come, Lord Jesus! Come, Lord Jesus; come quickly.* My soul *longed for God, for the living God.* O how delightful it is, to

pray

pray under such sweet influences! O how much better is this than one's necessary food! I had at this time no disposition to eat, though late in the morning; for earthly food appeared wholly tasteless. O how much *better is thy love than wine*, than the sweetest wine! I visited and preached to the Indians in the afternoon; but under much dejection. Found my interpreter under some concern for his soul; which was some comfort to me; and yet filled me with new care. I longed greatly for his conversion; lifted up my heart to God for it while I was talking to him: Came home and poured out my soul to God for him: Enjoyed some freedom in prayer, and was enabled, I think, to leave all with God.

Thursday, December 13.—Endeavoured to spend the day in fasting and prayer, to implore the divine blessing, more especially on my poor people; and in particular, I sought for converting grace for my interpreter, and three or four more under some concern for their souls. I was much disordered in the morning when I arose; but having determined to spend the day in this manner, I attempted it. Some freedom I had in pleading for these poor concerned souls, several times; and when interceding for them, I enjoyed greater freedom from wandering and distracting thoughts, than in any part of my supplications: But in the general was greatly exercised with wanderings; so that in the evening it seemed as if I had need to pray for nothing so much as for the pardon of sins committed in the day past, and the vileness I then found in myself. The sins I had most sense of were pride, and wandering thoughts, whereby I mocked God. The former of these cursed iniquities excited me to think of writing, or preaching, or converting heathen, or performing some other great work, that my name might live when I should be dead. My soul was in anguish, and ready to drop into despair, to find so much of that cursed temper. With this and the other evil I laboured under, viz. wandering thoughts, I was almost overwhelmed, and even ready to give over striving after a spirit of devotion; and oftentimes sunk into a considerable degree of despondency, and thought I was *more brutish than any man*. Yet after all my sorrows, I trust, through grace, this day and the exercises of it have been for my good, and taught me more of my corruption, and weakness without Christ, than I knew before.

Monday, December 17.—Was something comfortable in mind, most of the day; and was enabled to pray with some freedom, cheerfulness, composure, and devotion; had also some assistance in writing on a divine subject.

Tuesday, December 18.—Went to the Indians, and discoursed to them near an hour, without any power to come close to their hearts. But at last, I felt some fervency, and God helped me to speak with warmth. My interpreter also was amazingly assisted; and I doubt not but *the Spirit of God was upon him* (though I had no reason to think he had any true and saving grace, but was only under conviction of his lost state;) and presently upon this most of the grown persons were much affected, and the tears ran down their checks; and one old man (I suppose, an hundred years old) was so affected, that he wept, and seemed convinced of the importance of what I taught them. I stayed with them a considerable time, exhorting and directing them; and came away, lifting up my heart to God in prayer and praise, and encouraged and exhorted my interpreter to *strive to enter in at the strait gate*. Came home, and spent most of the evening in prayer and thanksgiving; and found myself much enlarged and quickened. Was greatly concerned, that the Lord's work, which
seemed

seemed to be begun, might be carried on with power, to the conversion of poor souls, and the glory of divine grace.

Wednesday, December 19.—Spent a great part of the day in prayer to God for the *out pouring of his spirit* on my poor people; as also to bless his name for awakening my interpreter, and some others, and giving us some tokens of his presence yesterday. And blessed be God, I had much freedom, five or six times in the day, in prayer and praise, and felt a weighty concern upon my spirit for the salvation of those precious souls, and the enlargement of the Redeemer's kingdom among them. My soul hoped in God for some success in my ministry: And blessed be his name for so much hope.

Friday, December 21.—Was enabled again to pray with freedom, cheerfulness, and hope. God was pleased to make the duty comfortable and pleasant to me; so that I delighted to persevere, and repeatedly to engage in it. Towards noon, visited my people, and spent the whole time in the way to them in prayer, longing to see the *power of God* among them, as there appeared something of it the last Tuesday; and I found it sweet to rest and hope in God. Preached to them twice, and at two distinct places: Had considerable freedom, each time, and so had my interpreter. Several of them followed me from one place to the other: And I thought, there were some divine influences discernible amongst them. In the evening, was assisted in prayer again. Blessed, blessed be the Lord.

Lord's Day, December 30.—Discoursed, both parts of the day, from Mark viii. 34. *Whosoever will come after me,* &c. God gave me very great freedom and clearness, and in the afternoon especially, considerable warmth and fervency. In the evening also, had very great clearness while conversing with friends

friends on divine things : I do not remember ever to have had more clear apprehensions of religion in my life : But found a struggle, in the evening, with spiritual pride.

[On Monday he preached again in the same place with freedom, and fervency ; and rode home to his lodging ; and arrived in the evening, under a considerable degree of bodily illness, which continued the two next days. And he complains much of spiritual emptiness and barrenness on those days.]

Thursday, January 3, 1744,5.—Being sensible of the great want of divine influences, and the out pouring of God's spirit, I spent this day in fasting and prayer, to seek so great a mercy for myself, and my poor people in particular, and for the church of God in general. In the morning, was very lifeless in prayer, and could get scarce any sense of God. Near noon, enjoyed some sweet freedom to pray that the *will of God* might in every respect become mine : And I am persuaded, it was so at that time in some good degree. In the afternoon, I was exceeding weak, and could not enjoy much fervency in prayer, but felt a great degree of dejection ; which, I believe, was very much owing to my bodily weakness and disorder.

Lord's Day, January 6.—Was still distressed with vapoury disorders. Preached to my poor Indians ; but had little heart or life. Towards night, my soul was pressed under a sense of my unfaithfulness. O the joy and peace that arises from a sense of *having obtained mercy of God to be faithful !* And O, the misery and anguish that spring from an apprehension of the contrary !

[His dejection continued the two next days ; but not to so great a degree on Tuesday, when he enjoyed some freedom and fervency in preaching to the Indians.]

Wednesday,

Wednesday, January 9.—In the morning, God was pleased to remove that gloom which has of late oppressed my mind, and gave me freedom and sweetness in prayer, I was encouraged and strengthened, and enabled to plead for grace for myself, and mercy for my poor Indians; and was sweetly assisted in my intercessions with God for others. Blessed be his holy name forever and ever: Amen, and Amen. Those things that of late have appeared most difficult and almost impossible, now appeared not only possible, but easy. My soul so much delighted to continue instant in prayer, at this blessed season, that I had no desire for my necessary food; even dreaded leaving off praying at all, left I should lose this spirituality, and this blessed thankfulness to God which I then felt. I felt now quite willing to live, and undergo all trials that might remain for me in a world of sorrow; but still longed for heaven, that I might glorify God in a perfect manner. O *come, Lord Jesus, come quickly.* Spent the day in reading a little; and in some diversions, which I was necessitated to take by reason of much weakness and disorder. In the evening, enjoyed some freedom and intenseness in prayer.

[The three remaining days of the week, he was very low and feeble in body; but nevertheless continued constantly in the same comfortable sweet frame of mind, as is expressed on Wednesday. On the Sabbath, this sweetness and spiritual alacrity began to abate: But still he enjoyed some degree of comfort, and had assistance in preaching to the Indians. On Monday and Tuesday he was in a state of depression.]

Wednesday, and Thursday, January 16, *and* 17.—I spent most of the time in writing on a sweet divine subject, and enjoyed some freedom and assistance. Was likewise enabled to pray more frequently and fervently

fervently than usual; and my soul, I think, rejoiced in God; especially on the evening of the last of these days: Praise then seemed comely, and I delighted to bless the Lord. O what reason have I to be thankful, that God ever helps me to labour and study for him! He does but receive his own, when I am enabled in any measure to praise him, labour for him, and live to him. O, how comfortable and sweet it is, to feel the assistance of divine grace in the performance of the duties God has enjoined us! *Bless the Lord, O my soul.*

[The same enlargement of heart and joyful frame of soul continued through the next day. But on the day following it began to decline; which decay seems to have continued the whole of the next week; which seems to have continued the week following with an increase of dejection and melancholy. Yet he enjoyed some seasons of special and sweet assistance.]

Lord's Day, February 3.—In the morning, I was somewhat relieved of that gloom and confusion, that my mind has of late been greatly exercised with: Was enabled to pray with some composure, and comfort. But however, went to my Indians trembling; for my soul remembered *the wormwood and the gall* (I might almost say the hell) of Friday last; and I was greatly afraid I should be obliged again to drink of that *cup of trembling*, which was inconceivably more bitter than death, and made me long for the grave more, unspeakably more, than for hid treasures, yea, inconceivably more than the men of this world long for such treasures. But God was pleased to hear my cries, and to afford me great assistance; so that I felt peace in my own soul; and was satisfied that if not one of the Indians should be profited by my preaching, but should all be damned, yet I should be accepted and rewarded as faithful;

for I am persuaded, God enabled me to be so. Had some good degree of help afterwards, at another place; and much longed for the conversion of the poor Indians. Was somewhat refreshed, and comfortable, towards night, and in the evening. O that my soul might praise the Lord for his goodness. Enjoyed some freedom, in the evening, in meditation on Luke xiii. 24.

[In the three next days, he was the subject of much dejection: But the three remaining days of the week seem to have been spent with much composure and comfort. On the next Sabbath, he preached at Greenwich, in New-Jersey. In the evening, he rode eight miles to visit a sick man at the point of death, and found him speechless and senseless.]

Monday, February 11.—About break of day, the sick man died. I was affected at the sight: Spent the morning with the mourners; and after prayer, and some discourse with them, I returned to Greenwich, and preached again from Psal. lxxxix. 15. And the Lord gave me assistance: I felt a sweet love to souls, and to the kingdom of Chrst; and longed that poor sinners might know *the joyful sound*. Several persons were much affected. And after meeting, I was enabled to discourse, with freedom and concern, to some persons that applied to me under spiritual trouble. Left the place sweetly composed, and rode home to my house about eight miles distant. Discoursed to friends, and inculcated divine truths upon some. In the evening, was in the most solemn frame that almost ever I remember to have experienced: I know not that ever death appeared more real to me, or that ever I saw myself in the condition of a dead corpse, laid out, and dressed for a lodging in the silent grave, so evidently as at this time. And yet I felt exceeding comfortably: My
mind

mind was composed and calm, and death appeared without a sting. I think I never felt such an universal mortification to all created objects as now. O how great and solemn a thing it appeared to die! O how it lays the greatest honour in the dust! And O, how vain and trifling did the riches, honours, and pleasures of the world appear! I could not, I dare not, so much as think of any of them; for death, death, solemn (though not frightful) death appeared at the door. O, I could see myself dead, and laid out, and inclosed in my coffin, and put down into the cold grave, with greatest solemnity, but without terror! I spent most of the evening, in conversing with a dear christian friend: And, blessed be God, it was a comfortable evening to us both. What are friends? What are comforts? What are sorrows? What are distresses? *The time is short: It remains, that they which weep, be as though they wept not; and they which rejoice, as though they rejoiced not; for the fashion of this world passeth away.* O come, Lord Jesus, come quickly: Amen. Blessed be God for the comforts of the past day.

Tuesday, February 12.—Was exceeding weak; but in a sweet resigned, composed frame, most of the day: Felt my heart freely go forth after God in prayer.

Wednesday, February 13.—Was much exercised with vapoury disorders; but still enabled to maintain solemnity, and I think spirituality.

Thursday, February 14.—Spent the day in writing on a divine subject: Enjoyed health, and freedom in my work: Had a solemn sense of death; as I have indeed had every day this week, in some measure: What I felt on Monday last, has been abiding, in some considerable degree, ever since.

Friday, February 15.—Was engaged in writing again almost the whole day. In the evening, was
much

much assisted in meditating on that precious text, Joh. vii. 37. *Jesus stood and cried*, &c. I had then a sweet sense of the free grace of the gospel: My soul was encouraged, warmed and quickened, and my desires drawn out after God in prayer: My soul was watchful, and afraid of losing so sweet a guest as I then entertained. I continued long in prayer, and meditation, intermixing one with the other; and was unwilling to be diverted by any thing at all from so sweet an exercise. I longed to proclaim the grace I then meditated upon, to the world of sinners. O how quick and powerful is the word of the blessed God.

[The next day, he complains of great conflicts with corruption, and much discomposure of mind.]

Lord's Day, February 17.—Preached to the white people (my interpreter being absent) in the wilderness, upon the sunny side of a hill. Had a considerable assembly, consisting of people that lived (at least many of them) not less than thirty miles asunder; some of them came near twenty miles. I discoursed to them, all day, from Joh. vii. 37. *Jesus stood and cried, saying, If any man thirst*, &c. In the afternoon, it pleased God to grant me great freedom and fervency in my discourse; and I was enabled to imitate the example of Christ in the text, who *stood and cried*. I think I was scarce ever enabled to offer the free grace of God to perishing sinners with more freedom and plainness in my life. And afterwards, I was enabled earnestly to invite the children of God to come renewedly, and drink of this fountain of water of life, from whence they have heretofore derived unspeakable satisfaction. It was a very comfortable time to me: There were many tears in the assembly; and I doubt not but that the Spirit of God was there, convincing poor sinners of their need of Christ. In the evening, I felt composed, and comfortable,

fortable, though much tired: I had some sweet sense of the excellency and glory of God; and my soul rejoiced, that he was *God over all blessed forever;* but was too much crowded with company and conversation, and longed to be more alone with God. O that I could forever bless God for the mercy of this day, who *answered me in the joy of my heart.*

[The rest of this week seems to have been spent under a decay of this life and joy, and in distressing conflicts with corruption; but not without some seasons of refreshment and comfort.]

Lord's Day, February 24.—In the morning, was much perplexed: My interpreter being absent, I knew not how to perform my work among the Indians. However, I rode to the Indians, got a Dutchman to interpret for me, though he was but poorly qualified for the business. Afterwards, I came and preached to a few white people from Joh. vi. 67. Here the Lord seemed to unburden me in some measure; especially towards the close of my discourse: I felt freedom to open the *love of Christ* to his own dear disciples: When the rest of the world forsakes him, and are forsaken by him, that he calls them no more, he then turns to his own, and says, *Will ye also go away?* I had a sense of the free grace of Christ to his own people, in such seasons of general apostasy, and when they themselves in some measure backslide with the world. O the free grace of Christ, that he seasonably minds his people of their danger of backsliding, and invites them to persevere in their adherence to himself! I saw that backsliding souls, who seemed to be about to go away with the world, might return, and welcome, to him immediately; without any thing to recommend them; notwithstanding all their former backslidings. And thus my discourse was suited to my own soul's case: For, of late, I have found a great want of this sense and apprehension apprehenfion of divine grace; and have often been greatly diftreffed in my own foul, becaufe I did not fuitably apprehend this *fountain opened to purge away sin*; and fo have been too much labouring for fpiritual life, peace of confcience, and progreffive holinefs, in my own ftrength: But now God fhewed me, in fome meafure, the arm of all ftrength, and the fountain of all grace. In the evening, I felt folemn, devout, and fweet, refting on free grace for affiftance, acceptance, and peace of confcience.

[Within the fpace of the next nine days, he had frequent refrefhing, invigorating influences of God's fpirit; attended with complaint of dulnefs, and with longings after fpiritual life and holy fervency.]

Wednefday, March 6.—Spent moft of the day in preparing for a journey to New-England. Spent fome time in prayer, with a fpecial reference to my intended journey. Was afraid I fhould forfake the *fountain of living waters*, and attempt to derive fatisfaction from *broken cifterns*, my dear friends and acquaintance, with whom I might meet in my journey. I looked to God to keep me from this vanity in fpecial, as well as others. Towards night, and in the evening, was vifited by fome friends, fome of whom, I truft, were real chriftians; who difcovered an affectionate regard to me, and feemed grieved that I was about to leave them; efpecially feeing I did not expect to make any confiderable ftay among them, if I fhould live to return from New-England*. O how kind has God been to me! How has he raifed up friends in every place, where his providence has called me! Friends are a great comfort; and it is God that gives them; it is he makes them friendly to me. *Blefs the Lord, O my foul, and forget not all his benefits.*

M [The

---

* It feems he had a defign, by what afterwords appears, to remove and live among the Indians at Sufquehannah river.

[The next day, he set out on his journey; and it was about five weeks before he returned. The special design of this journey, he himself declares afterwards, in his Diary for March 21. Where, speaking of his conversing with a certain minister in New-England, he says thus, Contrived with him how to raise some money among christian friends, in order to support a colleague with me in the wilderness, (I having now spent two years in a very solitary manner) that we might be together; as Christ sent out his disciples, two and two: And as this was the principal concern I had in view, in taking this journey, so I took pains in it, and hope God will succeed it if for his glory. He first went into various parts of New-Jersey, and visited several ministers there: And then went to New-York; and from thence into New-England, going to various parts of Connecticut: And then returned into New-Jersey. He met a number of ministers at Woodbridge, who (he says) met there to consult about the affairs of Christ's kingdom, in some important articles. He seems, for the most part, to have been free from melancholy in this journey; and many times to have had extraordinary assistance in publick ministrations, and his preaching sometimes attended with very hopeful appearances of a good effect on the auditory. He also had many seasons of special comfort and spiritual refreshment, in conversation with ministers and other christian friends, and also in meditation and prayer by himself alone.]

Saturday, April 13.—Rode home to my own house at the Forks of Delaware: Was enabled to remember the goodness of the Lord, who has now preserved me while riding full six hundred miles in this journey; has kept me that none of my bones have been broken. Blessed be the Lord, who has preserved me in this tedious journey, and returned me in safety to my my own houfe. Verily it is God that has upheld me, and guarded my goings.

Lord's Day, April 14.—Was difordered in body with the fatigues of my late journey; but was enabled however to preach to a confiderable affembly of white people, gathered from all parts round about, with fome freedom, from Ezek. xxxiii. 11. *As I live, faith the Lord God,* &c. had much more affiftance than I expected.

[This week, he went a journey to Philadelphia, in order to engage the governour there to ufe his intereft with the chief man of the Six Nations, (with whom he maintained a ftrict friendfhip) that he would give him leave to live at Sufquehannah, and inftruct the Indians that are within their territories. In his way to and from thence, he lodged with Mr. Beaty, a young Prefbyterian minifter. He fpeaks of feafons of fweet fpiritual refrefhment, that he enjoyed at his lodgings.]

Saturday, April 20.—Rode with Mr. Beaty to Abington, to attend Mr. Treat's adminiftration of the facrament, according to the method of the church of Scotland. When we arrived, we found Mr. Treat preaching: Afterwards I preached a fermon from Matth. v. 3. *Bleffed are the poor in fpirit,* &c. God was pleafed to give me great freedom and tendernefs, both in prayer and fermon: The affembly was fweetly melted, and fcores were all in tears. It was, as I then hoped and was afterwards abundantly fatisfied by converfing with them, a *word fpoken in feafon, to many weary fouls.* I was extremely tired, and my fpirits much exhaufted, fo that I could fcarcely fpeak loud; yet I could not help rejoicing in God.

Lord's Day, April 21.—In the morning, was calm and compofed, and had fome outgoings of foul after God in fecret duties, and longing defires of his prefence in the fanctuary and at his table; that his prefence might be in the assembly; and that his children might be entertained with a *feast of fat things*. In the forenoon, Mr. Treat preached. I felt some affection and tenderness in the season of the administration of the ordinance. Mr. Beaty preached to the multitude abroad, who could not half have crowded into the meeting house. In the season of the communion, I had comfortable and sweet apprehensions of the blissful communion of God's people, when they shall meet at their father's table in his kingdom, in a state of perfection. In the afternoon, I preached abroad to the whole assembly, from Rev. xiv. 4. *These are they that follow the Lamb*, &c. God was pleased again to give me very great freedom and clearness, but not so much warmth as before. However, there was a most amazing attention in the whole assembly; and, as I was informed afterwards, this was a sweet season to many.

Monday, April 22.—I enjoyed some sweetness in retirement, in the morning. At eleven o'clock Mr. Beaty preached, with freedom and life. Then I preached from Joh. vii. 37. and concluded the solemnity. Had some freedom; but not equal to what I had enjoyed before: Yet in the prayer, the Lord enabled me to cry (I hope) with a child like temper, with tenderness, and brokenness of heart. Came home with Mr. Beaty to his lodgings; and spent the time, while riding, and afterwards, very agreeably on divine things.

Tuesday, April 23.—Left Mr. Beaty's, and returned home to the Forks of Delaware: Enjoyed some sweet meditations, on the road, and was enabled to lift up my heart to God in prayer and praise.

[The two next days, he speaks of much bodily disorder, but of some degrees of spiritual assistance and freedom.]

Friday,

Friday, April 26.—Conversed with a christian friend with some warmth; and felt a spirit of mortification to the world, in a very great degree. Afterwards, was enabled to pray fervently and to rely on God sweetly, for all things *pertaining to life and godliness*. Just in the evening, was visited by a dear christian friend, with whom I spent an hour or two in conversation, on the very soul of religion. There are many with whom I can talk about religion: But alas, I find few with whom I can talk religion itself: But, blessed be the Lord, there are some that love to feed on the kernel, rather than the shell.

[The next day he went to the Irish settlement, often before mentioned, about fifteen miles distant; where he spent the Sabbath, and preached with some considerable assistance. On Monday, he returned, in a very weak state, to his own lodgings.]

Tuesday, April 30.—Was scarce able to walk about, and was obliged to betake myself to the bed, much of the day; and spent away the time in a very solitary manner; being neither able to read, meditate, nor pray, and had none to converse with in that wilderness. O, how heavily does time pass away, when I can do nothing to any good purpose; but seem obliged to trifle away precious time! But of late, I have seen it my duty to divert myself by all lawful means, that I may be fit, at least some small part of my time, to labour for God. And here is the difference between my present diversions, and those I once pursued, when in a natural state. Then I made a god of diversions, delighted in them with a neglect of God, and drew my highest satisfaction from them: Now I use them as means to help me in living to God; fixedly delighting in him, and not in them, drawing my highest satisfaction from him. Then they were my all; now they are only means leading to my all. And those things that are the greatest diversion, when pursued with this view, do not tend to hinder, but promote my spirituality; and I see now, more than ever, that they are absolutely necessary.

Wednesday, May 1.—Was not able to sit up more than half the day; and yet had such recruits of strength sometimes, that I was able to write a little on a divine subject. Was grieved that I could no more live to God. In the evening, had some sweetness and intenseness in secret prayer.

Thursday, May 2.—In the evening, being a little better in health, I walked into the woods, and enjoyed a sweet season of meditation and prayer. My thoughts run upon Psal. xvii. 15. *I shall be satisfied, when I awake with thy likeness.* And it was indeed a precious text to me. I longed to preach to the whole world: And it seemed to me, they must needs all be melted in hearing such precious divine truths, as I had then a view and relish of. My thoughts were exceeding clear, and my soul was refreshed. Blessed be the Lord, that in my late and present weakness, now for many days together, my mind is not gloomy, as at some other times.

Friday, May 3.—Felt a little vigour of body and mind, in the morning: Had some freedom, strength, and sweetness in prayer. Rode to and spent some time with my Indians. In the evening, again retiring into the woods, I enjoyed some sweet meditations on Isai. liii. 10. *Yet it pleased the Lord to bruise him,* &c.

[The three next days were spent in much weakness of body: But yet he enjoyed some assistance in publick and private duties: And seems to have remained free from melancholy.]

Tuesday, May 7.—Spent the day mainly in making preparation for a journey into the wilderness. Was still weak, and concerned how I should perform so difficult a journey. Spent some time in prayer for the divine blessing, direction and protection in my intended journey; but wanted bodily strength to spend the day in fasting and prayer.

[The next day, he set out on his journey to Susquehannah, with his interpreter. He endured great hardships and fatigues in his way thither through a hideous wilderness; where, after having lodged one night in the open woods, he was overtaken with a northeasterly storm, in which he was almost ready to perish. Having no manner of shelter, and not being able to make a fire in so great a rain, he could have no comfort if he stopped; therefore determined to go forward, in hopes of meeting with some shelter, without which he thought it impossible he should live the night through: But their horses happening to have eat poison for want of other food, at a place where they lodged the night before, were so sick that they could neither ride nor lead them, but were obliged to drive them before them, and travel on foot; until, through the mercy of God, just at dusk, they came to a bark hut, where they lodged that night. After he came to Susquehannah, he travelled about the length of an hundred miles on the river, and visited many towns and settlements of the Indians; saw some of seven or eight distinct tribes; and preached to different nations, by different interpreters. He was sometimes much discouraged, and sunk in his spirits, through the opposition that appeared in the Indians to christianity. At other times, he was encouraged by the disposition that some of these people manifested to hear, and willingness to be instructed. He here met with some that had formerly been his hearers at Kaunaumeek, and had removed hither; who saw and heard him again with great joy. He spent a fortnight among the Indians on this river; and passed through considerable labours

bours and hardships, frequently lodging on the ground, and sometimes in the open air; and at length he fell extremely ill, as he was riding in the wilderness, being seized with an ague, followed with a burning fever, and extreme pains in his head and bowels, attended with a great evacuation of blood ; so that he thought he must have perished in the wilderness : But at last coming to an Indian trader's hut, he got leave to stay there ; and though without physick or food proper for him, it pleased God, after about a week's distress, to relieve him so far that he was able to ride. He returned homewards from Juncauta, an Island far down the river ; where was a considerable number of Indians, who appeared more free from prejudices against christianity than most of the other Indians. He arrived at the Forks of Delaware on Thursday, May 30, after having rode in this journey about three hundred and forty miles. He came home in a very weak state, and under dejection of mind ; which was a great hindrance to him in religious exercises.— However, on the Sabbath, after having preached to the Indians, he preached to the white people; with some success, from Isai. liii. 10. *Yet it pleased the Lord to bruise him*, &c. some being awakened by his preaching. The next day, he was much exercised for want of spiritual life and fervency.]

Tuesday, June 4.—Towards evening was in distress for God's presence and a sense of divine things : Withdrew myself to the woods, and spent near an hour in prayer and meditation ; and I think the Lord had compassion on me, and gave me some sense of divine things ; which was indeed refreshing and quickening to me : My soul enjoyed intenseness and freedom in prayer, so that it grieved me to leave the place.

Wednesday,

Wednesday, June 5.—Felt thirsting desires after God, in the morning. In the evening enjoyed a precious season of retirement: Was favoured with some clear and sweet meditations upon a sacred text: Divine things opened with clearness and certainty, and had a divine stamp upon them. My soul was also enlarged and refreshed in prayer; and I delighted to continue in the duty; and was sweetly assisted in praying for fellow christians, and my dear brethren in the ministry. Blessed be the dear Lord for such enjoyments. O how sweet and precious it is, to have a clear apprehension and tender sense of the *mystery of godliness*, of true holiness, and likeness to the best of beings! O what a blessedness it is, to be as much like God as it is possible for a creature to be like his great Creator! Lord give me more of *thy likeness:* I shall be *satisfied, when I awake with it.*

Thursday, June 6.—Was engaged a considerable part of the day, in meditation and study on divine subjects. Enjoyed some special freedom, clearness, and sweetness in meditation. O how refreshing it is, to be enabled to improve time well!

[The next day he went a journey of near fifty miles, to Neshaming, to assist at a sacramental occasion, to be attended at Mr. Beaty's meeting house; being invited thither by him and his people.]

Saturday, June 8.—Was exceeding weak and fatigued with riding in the heat yesterday: But being desired, I preached in the afternoon, to a crowded audience, from Isai. xl. 1. *Comfort ye, comfort ye my people, saith your God.* God was pleased to give me great freedom, in opening the sorrows of God's people, and in setting before them comforting considerations. And blessed be the Lord, it was a sweet melting season in the assembly.

Lord's Day, June 9.—Felt some longing desires of the presence of God to be with his people on the solemn occasion of the day. In the forenoon Mr. Beaty preached; and there appeared some warmth in the assembly. Afterwards I assisted in the administration of the Lord's Supper: And towards the close of it, I discoursed to the multitude extempore, with some reference to that sacred passage, Isai. liii. 10. *Yet it pleased the Lord to bruise him.* Here God gave me great assistance in addressing sinners: And the word was attended with amazing power; many scores, if not hundreds, in that great assembly, consisting of three or four thousand, were much affected; so that there was a *very great mourning, like the mourning of Hadadrimmon.* In the evening I could hardly look any body in the face, because of the imperfections I saw in my performances in the day past.

Monday, June 10.—Preached with a good degree of clearness and with some sweet warmth, from Psal. xvii. 15. *I shall be satisfied, when I awake with thy likeness.* And blessed be God, there was a great solemnity and attention in the assembly, and sweet refreshment among God's people; as was evident then and afterwards.

Tuesday, June 11.—Spent the day mainly in conversation with dear christian friends; and enjoyed some sweet sense of divine things. O how desirable it is, to keep company with God's dear children! These are the *excellent ones of the earth, in whom,* I can truly say, *is all my delight.* O what delight will it afford, to meet them all in a state of perfection! Lord, prepare me for that state.

[The next day he left Mr. Beaty's, and went to Maidenhead in New-Jersey; and spent the next seven days in a comfortable state of mind, visiting several ministers in those parts.]

Tuesday,

Tuesday, June 18.—Set out from New-Brunswick with a design to visit some Indians at a place called Crosweeksung in New-Jersey, towards the sea. In the afternoon, came to a place called Cranberry, and meeting with a serious minister, Mr. M'Night, I lodged there with him. Had some enlargement and freedom in prayer with a number of people.

PART VII.

From his first beginning to preach to the Indians at CROSWEEKSUNG, *until he returned from his last journey to* SUSQUEHANNAH *ill with the consumption, whereof he died.*

[WE are now come to that part of Mr Brainerd's life wherein he had his greatest success, in his labours for the good of souls, and in his particular business as a Missionary to the Indians. An account of which, if here published, would doubtless be very entertaining to the reader, after he has seen by the preceding parts of this account of his life, how great and long continued his desires for the spiritual good of this sort of people were, how he prayed, laboured and wrestled, and how much he denied himself and suffered, to this end. After all Mr. Brainerd's agonizing in prayer, and travelling in birth, for the conversion of Indians, and all the interchanges of his raised hopes and expectations, and then disappointments and discouragements; and after waiting in a way of persevering prayer, labour and suffering, as it were through a long night, at length the day dawns : *Weeping continues for a night, but joy comes in the morning.* He *went forth weeping, bearing precious seed,* and now he *comes with rejoicing, bringing his sheaves with him.* The desired event is brought to pass at last ; but at a time, in a place, and upon subjects, that scarce ever entered into his heart. An account of the whole scene the reader will find in the annexed journal.]

Wednesday,

Wednesday, June 19, 1745.—Rode to the Indians at Crofweekfung: Found few at home; difcourfed to them however; and obferved them very ferious and attentive. At night I was extremely worn out, and fcarce able to walk or fit up. O how tirefome is earth! How dull the body!

Friday, June 21.—Rode to Freehold, to fee Mr. William Tennent; and fpent the day comfortably with him. My finking fpirits were a little raifed and encouraged; and I felt my foul breathing after God, in the midft of chriftian converfation. And in the evening was refrefhed in fecret prayer: Saw myfelf a poor worthlefs creature, without wifdom to direct or ftrength to help myfelf. O bleffed be God, that lays me under a happy, a bleffed neceffity of living upon himfelf!

[In the five next days is nothing remarkable in his diary, but what is in his publick journal.]

Thurfday, June 27.—My foul rejoiced to find that God enabled me to be faithful, and that he was pleafed to awaken thefe poor Indians by my means. O how heart reviving, and foul refrefhing is it to me to fee the fruit of my labours!

Friday, June 28.—In the evening my foul was revived and my heart lifted up to God in prayer, for my poor Indians, myfelf and friends, and the dear church of God. And O how refrefhing, how fweet was this! Blefs the Lord, O my foul, and forget not his goodnefs and tender mercy.

Saturday, June 29.—Preached twice to the Indians; and could not but wonder at their ferioufnefs, and the ftrictnefs of their attention. Bleffed be God that has inclined their hearts to hear. And O how refrefhing it is to me, to fee them attend with fuch uncommon diligence and affection, with tears in their eyes, and concern in their hearts! In the evening could not but lift up my heart to God in prayer,
while

while riding to my lodgings : And blessed be his name, had assistance and freedom. O how much better than life is the presence of God!

[His Diary gives an account of nothing remarkable on the two next days, besides what is in his publick journal; excepting his heart's being lifted up with thankfulness, rejoicing in God, &c.]

Tuesday, July 2.—Rode from the Indians to Brunswick, near forty miles, and lodged there. Felt my heart drawn out after God in prayer, almost all the forenoon; especially while riding. And in the evening could not help crying to God for those poor Indians; and after I went to bed, my heart continued to go out to God for them, until I dropped asleep. O blessed be God that I may pray!

[He was so beat out by constant preaching to these Indians, yielding to their earnest and importunate desires, that he found it necessary to give himself some relaxation. He spent, therefore, about a week in New-Jersey, after he left these Indians, visiting several ministers, and performing some necessary business, before he went to the Forks of Delaware. And though he was very weak in body, yet he seems to have been strong in spirit. On Friday, July 12, he arrived at his own house in the Forks of Delaware; continuing still free from melancholy; from day to day, enjoying freedom, assistance and refreshment in the inner man. But on Wednesday, the next week, he seems to have had some melancholy thoughts about his doing so little for God; being so much hindered by weakness of body.]

Thursday, July 18.—Longed to spend the little inch of time I have in the world more for God. Felt a spirit of seriousness, tenderness, sweetness, and devotion, and wished to spend the whole night in prayer and communion with God.

Friday,

Friday, July 19.—In the evening, walked abroad for prayer and meditation, and enjoyed compofure and freedom in thefe fweet exercifes ; efpecially in meditation on Rev. iii. 12. *Him that overcometh, will I make a pillar in the temple of my God,* &c. This was then a delightful theme to me, and it refrefhed my foul to dwell upon it. O, when fhall I *go no more out* from the fervice and enjoyment of the dear Lord ? Lord, haften the bleffed day.

[Within the fpace of the next fix days, he fpeaks of much inward refrefhment and enlargement from time to time.]

Friday, July 26.—In the evening, God was pleafed to help me in prayer, beyond what I have experienced for fome time ; efpecially my foul was drawn out for the enlargement of Chrift's kingdom, and for the converfion of my poor people ; and my foul relied on God for the accomplifhment of that great work. O, how fweet were the thoughts of death to me at this time ! O, how I longed to be with Chrift, to be employed in the glorious work of angels, and with an angel's freedom, vigour and delight ! And yet how willing was I to ftay a while on earth, that I might do fomething, if the Lord pleafed, for his intereft in the world ! My foul, my very foul, longed for the ingathering of the poor heathen ; and I cried to God for them moft willingly and heartily ; and yet becaufe I could not but cry. This was a fweet feafon ; for I had fome lively tafte of heaven, and a temper of mind fuited in fome meafure to the employments and entertainments of it. My foul was grieved to leave the place ; but my body was weak and worn out, and it was near nine o'clock. O, I longed that the remaining part of my life might be filled up with more fervency and activity in the things of God ! O, the inward peace, compofure, and God like ferenity of fuch a frame !

Heaven

Heaven muft needs differ from this only in degree, and not in kind. *Lord ever give me this bread of life.*

[Much of this frame feemed to continue the next day.]

Lord's Day, July 28.—In the evening my foul was melted, and my heart broken, with a fenfe of paft barrennefs and deadnefs : And O, how I then longed to live to God, and bring forth much fruit to his glory !

Monday, July 29.—Was much exercifed with a fenfe of vilenefs, with guilt and fhame before God.

[On Wednefday, July 31, he fet out on his return to Crofweekfung, and arrived there the next day. In his way thither, he had longing defires that he might come to the Indians there, *in the fulnefs of the bleffing of the gofpel of Chrift*; attended with a fenfe of his own great weaknefs, dependence and worthleffnefs.]

Friday, Auguft 2.—In the evening I retired, and my foul was drawn out in prayer to God ; efpecially for my poor people, to whom I had fent word that they might gather together, that I might preach to them the next day. I was much enlarged in praying for their faving converfion ; and fcarce ever found my defires of any thing of this nature fo fenfibly and clearly (to my own fatisfaction) difinterefted, and free from felfifh views. It feemed to me, I had no care, or hardly any defire to be the inftrument of fo glorious a work, as I wifhed and prayed for among the Indians : If the bleffed work might be accomplifhed to the honour of God, and the enlargement of the dear Redeemer's kingdom, this was all my defire and care ; and for this mercy I hoped, but with trembling ; for I felt what Job expreffes, chapter ix. 16. My rifing hopes, refpecting the converfion of the Indians, have been fo often dafhed, that my fpirit is as it were broken, and courage wafted, and I hardly dare hope.

[Concerning

[Concerning his labours and marvellous succefs amongft the Indians, for the following fixteen days, let the reader fee his Journal. The things worthy of note in his Diary, not there publifhed, are his earneft and importunate prayers for the Indians, and the *travail of his foul* for them from day to day; and his great refrefhment and joy in beholding the wonderful mercy of God, and the glorious manifeftations of his power and grace in his work among them; and his ardent thankfgivings to God; his heart's rejoicing in Chrift, as king of his church, and king of his foul, in particular at the facrament of the Lord's fupper, at Mr. M'Night's meeting houfe; a fenfe of his own exceeding unworthinefs; which fometimes was attended with dejection and melancholy.]

Monday, Auguft 19.—Near noon I rode to Freehold and preached to a confiderable affembly, from Matth. v. 3. It pleafed God to leave me to be very dry and barren; fo that I do not remember to have been fo ftraitened for a whole twelve month paft. God is juft, and he has made my foul acquiefce in his will in this regard. It is contrary to *flefh and blood* to be cut off from all freedom, in a large auditory, where their expectations are much raifed; but fo it was with me: And God helped me to fay Amen to it; *Good is the will of the Lord.* In the evening I felt quiet and compofed, and had freedom and comfort in fecret prayer.

Tuefday, Auguft 20.—Was compofed and comfortable, ftill in a refigned frame. Travelled from Mr. Tennent's in Freehold, to Elizabeth-Town. Was refrefhed to fee friends, and relate to them what God had done, and was ftill doing among my poor people.

Wednefday, Auguft 21.—Spent the forenoon in converfation with Mr. Dickinfon, contriving fomething for the fettlement of the Indians together in a body,

body, that they might be under better advantages for inftruction. In the afternoon, fpent time agreeably with other friends; wrote to my brother at college: But was grieved that time flid away, while I did fo little for God.

Friday, Auguft 23.—In the morning was very weak; but favoured with fome freedom and fweetnefs in prayer: Was compofed and comfortable in mind. After noon rode to Crofweekfung to my poor people.

Saturday, Auguft 24.—Had compofure and peace, while riding from the Indians to my lodgings: Was enabled to pour out my foul to God for dear friends in New-England. Felt a fweet tender frame of fpirit: My foul was compofed and refrefhed in God. Had likewife freedom and earneftnefs in praying for my dear people: Bleffed be God. *O the peace of God that paffeth all underftanding.* It is impoffible to defcribe the fweet peace of confcience, and tendernefs of foul, I then enjoyed. O the bleffed foretaftes of heaven !

Lord's Day, Auguft 25.—I rode to my lodgings in the evening, bleffing the Lord for his gracious vifitation of the Indians, and the foul refrefhing things I had feen the day paft amongft them, and praying that God would ftill carry on his divine work among them.

Monday, Auguft 26.—I went from the Indians to my lodgings, rejoicing for the goodnefs of God to my poor people; and enjoyed freedom of foul in prayer, and other duties, in the evening. Blefs the Lord, O my foul.

[The next day he fet out on a journey towards the Forks of Delaware, defigning to go from thence to Sufquehannah, before he returned to Crofweekfung. It was five days from his departure from Crofweekfung before he reached the Forks, going round by the way of Philadelphia, and waiting on the governour

our of Pennsylvania, to get a recommendation from him to the chiefs of the Indians; which he obtained. He speaks of much comfort and spiritual refreshment in this journey; and also a sense of his exceeding unworthiness, thinking himself the meanest creature that ever lived.]

Lord's Day, September 1.—[At the Forks of Delaware.] God gave me the spirit of prayer, and it was a blessed season in that respect. My soul cried to God for mercy, in an affectionate manner. In the evening also my soul rejoiced in God.

[His private Diary has nothing remarkable, for the two next days, but what is in his Journal.]

Wednesday, September 4.—Rode fifteen miles to an Irish settlement, and preached there from Luke xiv. 22. *And yet there is room*. God was pleased to afford me some tenderness and enlargement in the first prayer, and much freedom, as well as warmth, in sermon. There were many tears in the assembly: The people of God seemed to melt, and others to be in some measure awakened. Blessed be the Lord, that lets me see his work going on in one place and another.

Lord's Day, September 8.—In the evening God was pleased to enlarge me in prayer, and give me freedom at the throne of grace: I cried to God for the enlargement of his kingdom in the world, and in particular among my dear people; was also enabled to pray for many dear ministers of my acquaintance, both in these parts, and in New-England; and also for other dear friends in New-England. And my soul was so engaged and enlarged in that sweet exercise, that I spent near an hour in it, and knew not how to leave the mercy seat. O, how I delighted to pray and cry to God! I saw God was both able and willing to do all that I desired, for myself and friends, and his church in general. I was likewise much enlarged and assisted in family prayer;

And afterwards, when I was juſt going to bed, God helped me to renew my petitions with ardency and freedom. O, it was to me a bleſſed evening of prayer. Bleſs the Lord, O my ſoul.

[The next day he ſet out from the Forks of Delaware to go to Suſquehannah. And on the fifth day of his journey, he arrived at Shaumoking, a large Indian town on Suſquehannah river. He performed the journey under a conſiderable degree of melancholy, occaſioned at firſt by his hearing that the Moravians were gone before him to the Suſquehannah Indians.]

Saturday, September 14.—[At Shaumoking.] In the evening my ſoul was enlarged and ſweetly engaged in prayer; eſpecially that God would ſet up his kingdom in this place, where the devil now reigns in the moſt eminent manner. And I was enabled to aſk this for God, for his glory, and becauſe I longed for the enlargement of his kingdom, to the honour of his dear name. I could appeal to God with the greateſt freedom, that he knew it was his dear cauſe, and not my own, that engaged my heart: And my ſoul cried, Lord, ſet up thy kingdom, for thine own glory. Glorify thyſelf; and I ſhall rejoice. Get honour to thy bleſſed name; and this is all I deſire. Do with me juſt what thou wilt. Bleſſed be thy name forever, that thou art God, and that thou wilt glorify thyſelf. O that the whole world might glorify thee. O let theſe poor people be brought to know thee, and love thee, for the glory of thy dear ever bleſſed name. I could not but hope that God would bring in theſe miſerable wicked Indians; though there appeared little human probability of it, for they were then dancing and revelling, as if poſſeſſed by the devil. But yet I hoped, though againſt hope, that God would be glorified, and that God's name would be glorified by theſe poor Indians.

ans. I continued long in prayer and praise to God; and had great freedom, enlargement and sweetness, remembering dear friends in New-England, as well as the people of my charge. Was entirely free from that dejection of spirit, with which I am frequently exercised: Blessed be God.

[His Diary, from this time through several days, is not legible, by reason of the badness of the ink.]

Wednesday, September 25.—Rode still homeward. In the forenoon enjoyed freedom and intenseness of mind in meditation on Job xlii. 5. 6. *I have heard of thee by the hearing of the ear; but now mine eye seeth thee: Wherefore I abhor myself, and repent in dust and ashes.* The Lord gave me clearness to penetrate into the sweet truths contained in that text. It was a comfortable and sweet season to me.

Friday, September 27.—Spent considerable time, in the morning, in prayer and praise to God. My mind was somewhat intense in the duty; and my heart in some degree warmed with a sense of divine things. My soul was melted, to think, that *God had accounted me faithful, putting me into the ministry*, notwithstanding all my barrenness and deadness. My soul was also in some measure enlarged in prayer for the dear people of my charge, as well as for other dear friends. In the afternoon visited some christian friends, and spent the time, I think, profitably: My heart was warmed, and more engaged in the things of God. In the evening I enjoyed enlargement, warmth, and comfort in prayer: My soul relied on God for assistance and grace to enable me to do something in his cause: My heart was drawn out in thankfulness to God for what he had done for his own glory among my poor people of late: And I felt encouraged to proceed in his work, being persuaded of his power, and hoping *his arm* might be further *revealed*, for the enlargement of his dear kingdom : And my foul *rejoiced in hope of the glory of God*, in hope of the advancement of his declarative glory in the world, as well as of enjoying him in a world of glory. O, bleſſed be God, the living God, forever!

[He continued in this comfortable ſweet frame of mind the two next days. On the day following he went to his own houſe, in the Forks of Delaware, and continued ſtill in the ſame frame. The next day, which was Tueſday, he viſited his Indians. Wedneſday he ſpent moſtly in writing the meditations he had had in his late journey to Suſquehannah. On Thurſday he left the Forks of Delaware, and travelled towards Croſweekſung, where he arrived on Saturday (October 5) and continued from day to day in a comfortable ſtate of mind. There is nothing material in his Diary for this day and the next, but what is in his Journal.]

Monday, October 7.—Being called by the church and people of Eaſt-Hampton, on Long-Iſland, as a member of a council, to aſſiſt and adviſe in affairs of difficulty in that church, I ſet out on my journey this morning, before it was well light, and travelled to Elizabeth-Town, and there lodged. Enjoyed ſome comfort on the road, in converſation with Mr. William Tennent, who was ſent for on the ſame buſineſs.

[He proſecuted his journey with the other miniſters that were ſent for; and did not return until October 24. While he was at Eaſt-Hampton, the importance of the buſineſs that the council were come upon, lay with ſuch weight on his mind, and he was ſo concerned for the intereſt of religion in that place, that he ſlept but little for ſeveral nights ſucceſſively. In his way to and from Eaſt-Hampton, he had ſeveral ſeaſons of ſweet refreſhment, wherein his ſoul was enlarged and comforted with divine conſolations,

in

in secret retirement; and he had special assistance in publick ministerial performances in the house of God; and yet, at the same time, a sense of extreme vileness and unprofitableness.]

Monday, October 28.—Had an evening of sweet refreshing; my thoughts were raised to a blessed eternity; my soul was melted with desires of perfect holiness, and perfectly glorifying God.

Tuesday, October 29.—About noon rode and viewed the Indian lands at Cranberry : Was much dejected, and greatly perplexed in mind : Knew not how to see any body again, my soul was so sunk within me. O that these trials might make me more humble and holy. O that God would keep me from giving way to sinful dejection, which may hinder my usefulness.

Wednesday, October 30.—My soul was refreshed with a view of the continuance of God's blessed work among the Indians.

Thursday, October 31.—Spent most of the day in writing: Enjoyed not much spiritual comfort; but was not so much sunk with melancholy as at some other times.

[*November* 1, 2, 3, *and* 4.—See the Journal.]

[Tuesday, November 5, he left the Indians, and spent the remaining part of this week in travelling to various parts of New-Jersey, in order to get a collection for the use of the Indians, and to obtain a schoolmaster to instruct them. And in the mean time, he speaks of very sweet refreshment and entertainment with christian friends, and of his being sweetly employed, while riding, in meditation on divine subjects; his heart's being enlarged, his mind clear, his spirit refreshed with divine truths, and his *heart's burning within him, while he went by the way, and the Lord opened to him the scriptures.*]

Lord's Day, November 10.—[At Elizabeth-Town.] Was comfortable in the morning, both in body and mind; preached in the forenoon from 2 Cor. v. 20. God was pleased to give me freedom and fervency in my discourse; and the presence of God seemed to be in the assembly: Numbers were affected, and there were many tears among them. In the afternoon, preached from Luke xiv. 22. *And yet there is room.* Was favoured with divine assistance in the first prayer, and poured out my soul to God with a filial temper of mind; the living God also assisted me in sermon.

[The next day, he went to New-Town, on Long-Island, to a meeting of the Presbytery. He speaks of some sweet meditations he had while there, on *Christ's delivering up the kingdom to the Father*, and of his soul's being much refreshed and warmed with the consideration of that blissful day.]

Friday, November 15.—Could not cross the ferry by reason of the violence of the wind; nor could I enjoy any place of retirement at the ferry house: So that I was in perplexity. Yet God gave me some satisfaction and sweetness in meditation, and lifting up my heart to God in the midst of company. And although some were drinking and talking profanely, which was indeed a grief to me, yet my mind was calm and composed. And I could not but bless God, that I was not like to spend an eternity in such company. In the evening, I sat down and wrote with composure and freedom; and can say through pure grace it was a comfortable evening to my soul, an evening I was enabled to spend in the service of God.

Saturday, November 16.—Crossed the ferry about ten o'clock; arrived at Elizabeth-Town near night. Was in a calm composed frame of mind, and felt an entire resignation with respect to a loss I had lately

ly sustained, in having my horse stolen from me the last Wednesday night, at New-Town. Had some longings of soul for the dear people of Elizabeth-Town, that God would pour out his spirit upon them, and revive his work amongst them.

[He spent the four next days at Elizabeth-Town; for the most part, in a free and comfortable state of mind, intensely engaged in the service of God, and enjoying at some times, the special assistances of his Spirit. On Thursday, this week, he rode to Freehold, and spent the day under considerable dejection.]

Friday, November 22.—Rode to Mr. Tennent's, and from thence to Crosweeksung. Had little freedom in meditation, while riding; which was a grief and burden to my soul. O that I could fill up all my time, whether in the house or by the way, for God! I was enabled, I think, this day, to give up my soul to God, and put over all my concerns into his hands; and found some real consolation in the thought of being entirely at the divine disposal, and having no will or interest of my own.

[There is nothing very material in his Diary for the five next days, but what is also in his Journal.]

Thursday, November 28.—I enjoyed some divine comfort, and fervency in the publick exercise, and afterwards. And while riding to my lodgings, was favoured with some sweet meditations on Luke ix. 31. *Who appeared in glory, and spake of his decease, which he should accomplish at Jerusalem.* My thoughts ran with freedom, and I saw and felt what a glorious subject the death of Christ is for glorified souls to dwell upon in their conversation. O, the death of Christ! How infinitely precious.

[For the three next days, see the Journal.]

Monday, December 2.—Was much affected with grief, that I had not lived more to God; and felt
strong

strong resolutions to double my diligence in my Master's service.

[After this, he went to a meeting of the Presbytery, at a place in New-Jersey, called Connecticut-Farms; which occasioned his absence from his people the rest of this week. He speaks of some seasons of sweetness, solemnity, and spiritual affection, in his absence.]

[For the most of the following week he was employed in providing to live in a house by himself.]

Saturday, December 14.—Rose early, and wrote by candle light some considerable time; spent most of the day in writing: But was somewhat dejected. In the evening, was exercised with a pain in my head.

[For the three next days, see his Journal. The remainder of this week he spent chiefly in writing: Some part of the time under a degree of melancholy; but some part of it with a sweet ardency in religion.]

Monday, and Tuesday, December 23, *and* 24.—Spent these days in writing, with the utmost diligence. Felt in the main a sweet mortification to the world, and a desire to live and labour only for God; but wanted more warmth and spirituality, a more sensible and affectionate regard to the glory of God.

Thursday, and Friday, December 26, *and* 27.—Laboured in my studies, to the utmost of my strength: And though I felt a steady disposition of mind to live to God, and that I had nothing in this world to live for; yet I did not find that sensible affection in the service of God that I wanted to have; my heart seemed barren, though my head and hands were full of labour.

[For the four next days, see his Journal.]

Wednesday, January 1, 1745,6.—I am this day beginning a new year; and God has carried me through
numerous

numerous trials and labours in the paſt. He has amazingly ſupported my feeble frame; for *having obtained help of God, I continue to this day*. O that I might live nearer to God, this year, than I did the laſt. The buſineſs I have been called to, and enabled to go through, I know, has been as great as nature could bear up under, and what would have ſunk and overcome me quite, without ſpecial ſupport. But alas, alas! though I have done the labours, and endured the trials, with what ſpirit have I done the one, and borne the other? How cold has been the frame of my heart oftentimes! And how little have I ſenſibly eyed the glory of God, in all my doings and ſufferings! I have found, that I could have no peace without filling up all my time with labours; and thus neceſſity has been laid upon me; yea, in that reſpect, I have loved to labour: But the miſery is, I could not ſenſibly labour for God, as I would have done. May I for the future be enabled more ſenſibly to make the glory of God my all.

[For the ſpace from this time until the next Monday, ſee the Journal.]

Monday, January 6.—Being very weak in body, I rode for my health. While riding, my thoughts were ſweetly engaged, for a time, upon *the ſtone cut out of the mountain without hands, which brake in pieces* all before it, *and waxed great, and became a great mountain, and filled the whole earth*: And I longed that Jeſus ſhould *take to himſelf his great power, and reign to the ends of the earth*. And O, how ſweet were the moments, wherein I felt my ſoul warm with hopes of the enlargement of the Redeemer's kingdom! I wanted nothing elſe but that Chriſt ſhould reign, to the glory of his bleſſed name.

[The next day he complains of want of fervency.]

Wedneſday, January 8.—In the evening, my heart was drawn out after God in ſecret: My ſoul was refreſhed

freshed and quickened; and I trust, faith was in exercise. I had great hopes of the ingathering of precious souls to Christ; not only among my own people, but others also. I was sweetly resigned and composed under my bodily weakness; and was willing to live or die, and desirous to labour for God to the utmost of my strength.

Friday, January 10.—My soul was in a sweet, calm, composed frame, and my heart filled with love to all the world; and christian simplicity and tenderness seemed then to prevail and reign within me. Near night, visited a serious baptist minister, and had some agreeable conversation with him; and found that I could taste God in friends.

[For the seven next days nothing very remarkable appears but what is to be found in the Journal.]

[The next day, he set out on a journey to Elizabeth-Town, to confer with the correspondents at their meeting there; and enjoyed much spiritual refreshment from day to day, through this week. The things expressed in this space of time, are such as these; serenity, composure, sweetness, and tenderness of soul, thanksgiving to God for his success among the Indians, delight in prayer and praise, sweet and profitable meditations on various divine subjects, longing for more love, for more vigour to live to God, for a life more entirely devoted to God, that he might spend all his time profitably for God, and in his cause; conversing on spiritual subjects with affection; and lamentation for unprofitableness.]

Lord's Day, January 26.—[At Connecticut-Farms.] Was calm and composed. Was made sensible of my utter inability to preach, without divine help; and was in some good measure willing to leave it with God, to give or withhold assistance, as he saw would be most for his own glory. Was favoured with a considerable degree of assistance in my
publick

publick work. After publick worship, I was in a sweet and solemn frame of mind, thankful to God that he had made me in some measure faithful in addressing precious souls, but grieved that I had been no more fervent in my work; and was tenderly affected towards all the world, longing that every sinner might be saved; and could not have entertained any bitterness towards the worst enemy living. In the evening, rode to Elizabeth-Town: While riding, was almost constantly engaged in lifting up my heart to God, lest I should lose that sweet heavenly solemnity and composure of soul I then enjoyed. Afterwards, was pleased, to think that God reigneth; and thought I could never be uneasy with any of his dispensations; but must be entirely satisfied, whatever trials he should cause me or his church to encounter. Never felt more sedateness, divine serenity and composure of mind: Could freely have left the dearest earthly friend, for the society of *angels and spirits of just men made perfect*. My affections soared aloft to the blessed Author of every dear enjoyment: I viewed the emptiness and unsatisfactory nature of the most desirable earthly objects, any further than God is seen in them: And longed for a life of spirituality and inward purity; without which, I saw there could be no true pleasure.

[He retained a great degree of this excellent frame of mind, the four next days.]

Saturday, February 1.—Towards night, enjoyed some of the clearest thoughts on a divine subject, viz. that treated of 1 Cor. xv. 13.—16. that ever I remember to have had upon any subject whatsoever; and spent two or three hours in writing them. I was refreshed with this intenseness: My mind was so engaged in these meditations, I could scarcely turn it to any thing else; and indeed I could not be willing to part with so sweet an entertainment.

Lord's Day, February 2.—After publick worship, my bodily strength being much spent, my spirits sunk amazingly; and especially on hearing that I was so generally taken to be a Roman Catholick, sent by the Papists to draw the Indians into an insurrection against the English, that some were in fear of me, and others were for having me taken up by authority and punished. Alas, what will not the devil do to bring a slur and disgrace on the work of God! O, how holy and circumspect had I need to be!

Monday, February 3.—My spirits were still much sunk with what I heard the day before, of my being suspected to be engaged in the pretender's interest: It grieved me, that after there had been so much evidence of a glorious work of grace among these poor Indians, as that the most carnal men could not but take notice of the great change made among them, so many poor souls should still suspect the whole to be only a popish plot, and so cast an awful reproach on this blessed work of the divine Spirit; and at the same time wholly exclude themselves from receiving any benefit by this divine influence. This put me upon searching whether I had ever dropped any thing inadvertently, that might give occasion to any to suspect that I was stirring up the Indians against the English: And could think of nothing, unless it was my attempting sometimes to vindicate the rights of the Indians, and complaining of the horrid practice of making the Indians drunk, and then cheating them out of their lands and other properties: And once I remembered I had done this with too much warmth of spirit. And this much distressed me; thinking that this might possibly prejudice them against this work of grace, to their everlasting destruction. God, I believe, did me good by this trial; which served to humble me, and shew me the necessity

necessity of watchfulness, and of being *wise as a serpent*, as well as *harmless as a dove*. This exercise led me often to the throne of grace; and there I found some support: Though I could not get the burden wholly removed. Was assisted in prayer, especially in the evening.

[He remained still under a degree of exercise of mind about this affair; which continued to have the same effect upon him, to cause him to reflect upon, and humble himself, and frequent the throne of grace: But soon found himself much more relieved and supported. He was, this week, in an extremely weak state, and obliged (as he expresses it) to consume considerable time in diversions for his health.

The Monday after, he set out on a journey to the Forks of Delaware, to visit the Indians there. The things appertaining to his inward frames and exercises, expressed within this week, are sweet composure of mind, thankfulness to God for his mercies to him and others, resignation to the divine will, comfort in prayer and religious conversation, his heart drawn out after God, and affected with a sense of his own barrenness, as well as the fulness and freeness of divine grace.]

Lord's Day, February 16.—In the evening, was in a sweet composed frame of mind. It was exceeding refreshing and comfortable, to think that God had been with me, affording me some good measure of assistance. I then found freedom and sweetness in prayer and thanksgiving to God; and found my soul sweetly engaged and enlarged in prayer for dear friends and acquaintance. Blessed be the name of the Lord, that ever I am enabled to do any thing for his dear interest and kingdom. Blessed be God, who enables me to be faithful. Enjoyed more resolution and courage for God, and more refreshment of spirit, than I have been favoured with for many weeks past.

Monday,

Monday, February 17.—I was refreshed and encouraged: Found a spirit of prayer, in the evening, and earnest longings for the illumination and conversion of these poor Indians.

Thursday, February 20.—God was pleased to support and refresh my spirits, by affording me assistance, this day, and so hopeful a prospect of success; and I returned home rejoicing, and blessing the name of the Lord; and found freedom and sweetness afterwards in secret prayer, and had my soul drawn out for dear friends. O, how blessed a thing is it, to labour for God faithfully, and with encouragement of success! Blessed be the Lord forever and ever, for the assistance and comfort granted this day.

Friday, February 21.—My soul was refreshed and comforted, and I could not but bless God, who had enabled me in some good measure to be faithful in the day past. O how sweet it is to be spent and worn out for God!

Saturday, February 22.—My spirits were much supported, though my bodily strength was much wasted. O that God would be gracious to the souls of these poor Indians.

God has been very gracious to me this week: He has enabled me to preach every day; and has given me some assistance, and encouraging prospects of success, in almost every sermon. Blessed be his name. Divers of the white people have been awakened this week, and sundry of the Indians much cured of the prejudices and jealousies they had conceived against christianity, and some seem to be really awakened.

[The next day he left the Forks of Delaware, to return to Crosweeksung; and spent the whole week until Saturday, before he arrived there; but preached by the way every day, excepting one; and was several times greatly assisted; and had much inward comfort,

comfort, and earnest longings to fill up all his time with the service of God. He utters such expressions as these, after preaching : O that I may be enabled to plead the cause of God faithfully, to my dying moment. O how sweet it would be to spend myself wholly for God, and in his cause, and to be freed from selfish motives in my labours !]

[For Saturday and Lord's Day, March 1, and 2, see the Journal. The four next days were spent in great bodily weakness; but he speaks of some seasons of considerable inward comfort.]

Thursday, March 6.—I walked alone in the evening, and enjoyed sweetness and comfort in prayer, beyond what I have of late enjoyed: My soul rejoiced in my pilgrimage state, and I was delighted with the thoughts of labouring and enduring hardness for God: Felt some longing desires to preach the gospel to dear immortal souls; and confided in God, that he would be with me in my work, and that he *never would leave nor forsake me*, to the end of my race. O, may I obtain mercy of God to be faithful, to my dying moment!

[For the following Lord's Day, see the Journal.]

Monday, March 10.—My soul was refreshed with freedom and enlargement, and I hope the lively exercise of faith, in secret prayer, this night: My will was sweetly resigned to the divine will, and my hopes respecting the enlargement of the dear kingdom of Christ somewhat raised, and could commit Zion's cause to God as his own.

[In his Diary for several following days it appears that he was ill in body, and dejected in mind under an apprehension that his usefulness was about to terminate.]

Monday, March 24.—After the Indians were gone to their work, to clear their lands, I got alone, and poured out my soul to God, that he would smile upon

upon these feeble beginnings, and that he would settle an Indian town, that might be a *mountain of holiness*; and found my soul much refreshed in these petitions, and much enlarged for Zion's interest, and for numbers of dear friends in particular. My sinking spirits were revived and raised, and I felt animated in the service God has called me to. This was the dearest hour I have enjoyed for many days, if not weeks. I found an encouraging hope, that something would be done for God, and that God would use and help me in his work. And O, how sweet were the thoughts of labouring for God, when I felt my spirit and courage, and had any hope that ever I should be succeeded!

[The next day, his schoolmaster was taken sick with a pleurisy; and he spent great part of the remainder of this week in tending him: Which in his weak state was almost an overbearing burden to him; he being obliged constantly to wait upon him all day, from day to day, and to lie on the floor at night. His spirits sunk in a considerable degree, with his bodily strength, under this burden.]

Monday, March 31.—Towards night, enjoyed some sweet meditations on those words, *It is good for me to draw near to God*. My soul, I think, had some sweet sense of what is intended in those words.

Wednesday, April 2.—Was somewhat exercised with a spiritless frame of mind. Was a little relieved and refreshed in the evening, with meditation alone in the woods. But alas, my days pass away as the chaff. It is but little I do, or can do, that turns to my account; and it is my constant misery and burden, that I am so fruitless in the vineyard of the Lord. O that I were spirit, that I might be active for God. This, I think, more than any thing else, makes me long, that *this corruptible* might *put on incorruption,* and *this mortal put on immortality.*

God

God deliver me from clogs, fetters, and a *body of death*, that impede my service for him.

[The next day, he complains bitterly of some exercises by corruption he found in his own heart.]

Friday, April 4.—Spent most of the day in writing on Rev. xxii. 17. *And whosoever will*, &c. Enjoyed some freedom and encouragement in my work; and found some comfort and composure in prayer.

Saturday, April 5.—After publick worship, a number of my dear christian Indians came to my house; with whom I felt a sweet union of soul: My heart was knit to them; and I cannot say, I have felt such a sweet and fervent love to the brethren, for some time past: And I saw in them appearances of the same love. This gave me something of a view of the heavenly state; and particularly that part of the happiness of heaven, which consists in the communion of saints; and this was affecting to me.

[The following week was spent in a journey to Elizabeth-Town and Staten-Island, at which last place he preached on the Sabbath to an assembly of Dutch and English.]

Monday, April 14.—My spirits this day were raised and refreshed, and my mind composed, so that I was in a comfortable frame of soul, most of the day. In the evening, my head was clear, my mind serene; I enjoyed sweetness in secret prayer, and meditation on Psal. lxxiii. 28. O, how free, how comfortable, cheerful, and yet solemn do I feel when I am in a good measure freed from those damps and melancholy glooms, that I often labour under! And blessed be the Lord, I find myself relieved in this respect.

Tuesday, April 15.—My soul longed for more spirituality; and it was my burden, that I could do no more for God. O, my barrenness is my daily affliction

affliction and heavy load! O, how precious is time; and how it pains me, to see it slide away, while I do so very little to any good purpose! O that God would make me more fruitful and spiritual.

[The next day he speaks of his being almost overwhelmed with vapoury disorders; but yet not so as wholly to destroy the composure of his mind.]

Thursday, April 17.—Enjoyed some comfort in prayer, some freedom in meditation, and composure in my studies. Spent some time in writing, in the forenoon. In the afternoon, spent some time in conversation with several dear ministers. In the evening, preached from Psal. lxxiii. 28. *But it is good for me to draw near to God.* God helped me to feel the truth of my text, both in the first prayer and in sermon. I was enabled to pour out my soul to God, with great freedom, fervency, and affection: And, blessed be the Lord, it was a comfortable season to me. I was enabled to speak with tenderness, and yet with faithfulness: And divine truths seemed to fall with weight and influence upon the hearers. My heart was melted for the dear assembly, and I loved every body in it; and scarce ever felt more love to immortal souls in my life; my soul cried, O that the dear creatures might be saved! O that God would have mercy on them!

[He seems to have been in a very comfortable frame of mind the two next days.]

Lord's Day, April 20*.—Enjoyed some freedom, and, I hope, exercise of faith in prayer, in the morning; especially when I came to pray for Zion. I was free from that gloomy discouragement, that so often oppresses my mind; and my soul rejoiced in the hopes of Zion's prosperity, and the enlargement of the dear kingdom of the great Redeemer. O that his kingdom might come.

Tuesday,

---

* This day he entered into the 29th year of his age.

Tuesday, April 22.—My mind was remarkably free, this day, from melancholy damps and glooms, and animated in my work. I found such fresh vigour and resolution in the service of God, that the mountains seemed to become a plain before me. O blessed be God for an interval of refreshment, and fervent resolution in my Lord's work! In the evening, my soul was refreshed in secret prayer, and my heart drawn out for divine blessings; especially for the church of God, and his interest among my own people, and for dear friends in remote places. O that Zion might prosper, and precious souls be brought home to God!

[See, for about this time, the Journal.]

Saturday, May 3.—Rode from Elizabeth-Town home to my people, at or near Cranberry; whither they are now removed, and where, I hope, God will settle them as a christian congregation. Was refreshed in lifting up my heart to God, while riding; and enjoyed a thankful frame of spirit, for divine favours received the week past. Was somewhat uneasy and dejected, in the evening; having no house of my own to go into in this place; but God was my support.

Wednesday, May 7.—Spent most of the day in writing, as usual. Enjoyed some freedom in my work. Was favoured with some comfortable meditations, this day. In the evening, was in a sweet composed frame of mind: Was pleased and delighted to leave all with God, respecting myself, for time and eternity, and respecting the people of my charge, and dear friends. Had no doubt but that God would take care of me, and of his own interest among my people: And was enabled to use freedom in prayer, as a child with a tender father. O, how sweet is such a frame!

Thursday, May 8.—In the evening, was somewhat refreshed with divine things, and enjoyed a tender melting frame in secret prayer, wherein my soul was drawn out for the interest of Zion, and comforted with the lively hope of the appearing of the kingdom of the great Redeemer. These were sweet moments: I felt almost loth to go to bed, and grieved that sleep was necessary. However, I lay down with a tender reverential fear of God, sensible that *his favour is life*, and his smiles better than all that earth can boast of, infinitely better than life itself.

[*Friday, May* 9.—See the Journal.]

Saturday, May 10.—Rode to Allen's-Town, to assist in the administration of the Lord's supper. In the afternoon, preached from Tit. ii. 14. *Who gave himself for us*, &c. God was pleased to carry me through with some competency of freedom; and yet to deny me that enlargement and power I longed for. In the evening, my soul mourned, and could not but mourn, that I had treated so excellent a subject in so defective a manner; that I had borne so broken a testimony for so worthy and glorious a Redeemer. And if my discourse had met with the utmost applause from all the world (as I accidentally heard it applauded by some persons of judgment) it would not have given me any satisfaction. O, it grieved me, to think that I had had no more holy warmth and fervency, that I had been no more melted in discoursing of Christ's death, and the end and design of it! Afterwards, enjoyed some freedom and fervency in secret and family prayer, and longed much for the presence of God to attend his word and ordinances the next day.

Lord's Day, May 11.—Assisted in the administration of the Lord's supper; but enjoyed little enlargement: Was grieved and sunk with some things I thought undesirable, &c. In the afternoon, went to the house of God weak and sick in soul, as well as feeble in body: And longed, that the people might

might be entertained and edified with divine truths, and that an honest fervent testimony might be borne for God; but knew not how it was possible for me to do any thing of that kind, to any good purpose. Yet God, who is rich in mercy, was pleased to give me assistance, both in prayer and preaching. God helped me to wrestle for his presence in prayer, and to tell him, that he had promised, *Where two or three are met together in his name, there he would be in the midst of them;* and that we were, at least some of us, so met; and pleaded, that for his truth's sake he would be with us. And blessed be God, it was sweet to my soul, thus to plead, and rely on God's promises. Discoursed upon Luke ix. 30. 31. *And behold, there talked with him two men, which were Moses and Elias; who appeared in glory, and spake of his decease, which he should accomplish at Jerusalem.* Enjoyed special freedom, from the beginning to the end of my discourse, without interruption. Things pertinent to the subject were abundantly presented to my view, and such a fulness of matter, that I scarce knew how to dismiss the various heads and particulars I had occasion to touch upon. And, blessed be the Lord, I was favoured with some fervency and power, as well as freedom; so that the word of God seemed to awaken the attention of a stupid audience, to a considerable degree. I was inwardly refreshed with the consolations of God; and could with my whole heart say, *Though there be no fruit in the vine,* &c. *yet will I rejoice in the Lord.* After publick service, was refreshed with the sweet conversation of some christian friends.

[The four next days seem to have been mostly spent with spiritual comfort and profit.]

Friday, May 16.—Near night, enjoyed some agreeable and sweet conversation with a dear minister, which, I trust, was blessed to my soul: My heart was warmed, and my soul engaged to live to God; so that I longed to exert myself with more vigour, than ever I had done, in his cause.: And those words were quickening to me, *Herein is my Father glorified, that ye bring forth much fruit.* O, my soul longed, and wished, and prayed, to be enabled to live to God with utmost constancy and ardour! In the evening, God was pleased to shine upon me in secret prayer, and draw out my soul after himself; and I had freedom in supplication for myself, but much more in intercession for others: So that I was sweetly constrained to say, Lord, use me as thou wilt; do as thou wilt with me: But O, promote thine own cause. Zion is thine; O visit thine heritage; O let thy kingdom come; O let thy blessed interest be advanced in the world! When I attempted to look to God respecting my worldly circumstances, and his providential dealings with me, in regard of my settling down in my congregation, which seems to be necessary, and yet very difficult, and contrary to my fixed intention for years past, as well as my disposition, which has been, and still is, at times especially, to go forth, and spend my life in preaching the gospel from place to place, and gathering souls afar off to Jesus the great Redeemer; when I attempted to look to God with regard to these things, and his designs concerning me, I could only say, *The will of the Lord be done:* It is no matter for me. The same frame of mind I felt with respect to another important affair I have lately had some serious thoughts of: I could say, with utmost calmness and composure, Lord, if it be most for thy glory, let me proceed in it; but if thou seest that it will in any wise hinder my usefulness in thy cause, O prevent my proceeding: For all I want, respecting this world, is such circumstances as may best capacitate me to do service for God in the world. But blessed be be God, I enjoyed liberty in prayer for my dear flock, and was enabled to pour out my foul into the bofom of a tender father. My heart within me was melted, when I came to plead for my dear people, and for the kingdom of Chrift in general. O, how fweet was this evening to my foul! I knew not how to go to bed; and when got to bed, longed for fome way to improve time for God, to fome excellent purpofe. Blefs the Lord, O my foul.

Saturday, May 17.—Walked out in the morning; and felt much of the fame frame I enjoyed the evening before: Had my heart enlarged in praying for the advancement of the kingdom of Chrift, and found utmoft freedom in leaving all my concerns with God.

I find difcouragements to be an exceeding hindrance to my fpiritual fervency and affection: But when God enables me fenfibly to find that I have done fomething for him, this refrefhes and animates me, fo that I could break through all hardfhips, undergo any labours, and nothing feems too much either to do or to fuffer. But O, what a death it is, to ftrive and ftrive; to be always in a hurry, and yet do nothing, or at leaft nothing for God! Alas, alas, that time flies away, and I do fo little for God!

Lord's Day, May 18.—I felt my own utter infufficiency for my work: God made me to fee that I was a child; yea, that I was a fool. I difcourfed both parts of the day, from Rev. iii. 20. *Behold, I ftand at the door and knock.* God gave me freedom and power in the latter part of my forenoon's difcourfe; although, in the former part of it, I felt peevifh and provoked with the unmannerly behaviour of the white people, who crowded in between my people and me; which proved a great temptation to me. But bleffed be God, I got thefe fhackles off before the middle of my difcourfe, and was favoured with a fweet frame

of

of spirit in the latter part of the exercise; was full of love, warmth, and tenderness, in addressing my dear people. In the intermission season, could not but discourse to my people on the kindness and patience of Christ, in *standing* and *knocking at the door*, &c. In the evening I was grieved that I had done so little for God. O that I could be a *flame of fire* in the service of my God.

Thursday, May 22.—In the evening was in a frame somewhat remarkable: Had apprehended for several days before, that it was the design of Providence I should settle among my people here; and had in my own mind begun to make provision for it; and to contrive means to hasten it; and found my heart something engaged in it, hoping I might then enjoy more agreeable circumstances of life, in several respects: And yet was never fully determined, never quite pleased with the thoughts of being settled and confined to one place. Nevertheless, I seemed to have some freedom in that respect, because the congregation I thought of settling with, was one that God had enabled me to gather from amongst Pagans. For I never, since I began to preach, could feel any freedom to *enter into other men's labours*, and settle down in the ministry where the *gospel was preached before*; I never could make that appear to be my province. When I felt any disposition to consult my ease and worldly comfort, God has never given me any liberty in that respect, either since, or for years before I began to preach. But God having succeeded my labours, and made me instrumental of gathering a church for him among these Indians, I was ready to think it might be his design to give me a quiet settlement and a stated home of my own. And this, considering the late frequent sinking and failure of my spirits, and the need I stood in of some agreeable society, and my great desire of enjoying conveniences and opportunities

nities for profitable studies, was not altogether disagreeable to me: Although I still wanted to go about, far and wide, in order to spread the blessed gospel among benighted souls, far remote; yet I never had been so willing to settle in any one place, for more than five years past, as I was in the foregoing part of this week. But now these thoughts seemed to be wholly dashed to pieces; not by necessity, but of choice: For it appeared to me, that God's dealings towards me had fitted me for a life of solitariness and hardship: It appeared to me, I had nothing to lose, nothing to do with earth, and consequently nothing to lose by a total renunciation of it: And it appeared just right that I should be destitute of house and home, and many comforts of life, which I rejoiced to see others of God's people enjoy. And at the same time, I saw so much of the excellency of Christ's kingdom, and the infinite desirableness of its advancement in the world, that it swallowed up all my other thoughts; and made me willing, yea, even rejoice, to be made a pilgrim or hermit in the wilderness, to my dying moment, if I might thereby promote the blessed interest of the great Redeemer. And if ever my soul presented itself to God for his service, without any reserve of any kind, it did so now. The language of my thoughts and disposition (although I spake no words) now were, *Here I am, Lord, send me;* send me to *the ends of the earth;* send me to the rough, the savage Pagans of the wilderness; send me from all that is called comfort in earth, or earthly comfort; send me even to death itself, if it be but in thy service, and to promote thy kingdom. And at the same time I had as quick and lively a sense of the value of worldly comforts, as ever I had; but only saw them infinitely overmatched by the worth of Christ's kingdom, and the propagation of his blessed gospel. The quiet settlement, the certain place of abode, the tender friendship, which I thought I might be likely to enjoy in consequence of such circumstances, appeared as valuable to me, considered absolutely and in themselves, as ever before; but considered comparatively, they appeared nothing: Compared with the value and preciousness of an enlargement of Christ's kingdom, they vanished like the stars before the rising sun. And sure I am, that although the comfortable accommodations of life appeared valuable and dear to me, yet I did surrender and resign myself, soul and body, to the service of God, and promotion of Christ's kingdom; though it should be in the loss of them all. And I could not do any other, because I could not will or choose any other. I was constrained, and yet chose to say, Farewell friends and earthly comforts, the dearest of them all, the very dearest, if the Lord calls for it: Adieu, adieu; I will spend my life, to my latest moments, in caves and dens of the earth, if the kingdom of Christ may thereby be advanced. I found extraordinary freedom at this time in pouring out my soul to God, for his cause; and especially that his kingdom might be extended among the Indians, far remote; and I had a great and strong hope that God would do it. I continued wrestling with God in prayer for my dear little flock here; and more especially for the Indians elsewhere; as well as for dear friends in one place and another; until it was bed time, and I feared I should hinder the family, &c. But O, with what reluctancy did I find myself obliged to consume time in sleep! I longed to be as *a flame of fire*, continually glowing in the divine service, preaching and building up Christ's kingdom, to my latest, my dying moment.

Friday, May 23.—In the morning was in the same frame of mind, as in the evening before. The glory of Christ's kingdom so much outshone the pleasure

ure of earthly accommodations and enjoyments, that they appeared comparatively nothing, though in themselves good and desirable. My soul was melted in secret meditation and prayer, and I found myself divorced from any part in this world; so that in those affairs that seemed of the greatest importance to me, in respect of the present life, and those wherein the tender powers of the mind are most sensibly touched, I could only say, *The will of the Lord be done.* But just the same things that I felt the evening before, I felt now; and found the same freedom in prayer for the people of my charge, for the propagation of the gospel among the Indians, and for the enlargement and spiritual welfare of Zion in general, and my dear friends in particular, now, as I did then; and longed to burn out in one continued flame for God. Retained much of the same frame through the day. In the evening was visited by my brother John Brainerd: The first visit I have ever received from any near relative, since I have been a Missionary. Felt the same frame of spirit in the evening, as in the morning; and found that *it was good for me to draw near to God,* and leave all my concerns and burdens with him. Was enlarged and refreshed in pouring out my soul for the propagation of the gospel of the Redeemer among the distant tribes of Indians. Blessed be God. If ever I filled up a day with studies and devotion, I was enabled so to fill up this day.

Saturday, May 24.—Enjoyed, this day, something of the same frame of mind as I felt the day before.

Monday, June 2.—In the evening, enjoyed some freedom in secret prayer and meditation.

Tuesday, June 3.—My soul rejoiced early in the morning, to think that all things were at God's disposal. O it pleased me to leave them there. Felt afterwards much as I did on Thursday evening,

May 22 laſt; and continued in this frame for several hours. Walked out into the wilderneſs, and enjoyed freedom, fervency, and comfort in prayer: And again enjoyed the ſame in the evening.

Wedneſday, June 4.—Spent the day in writing, and enjoyed ſome comfort, ſatisfaction and freedom in my work. In the evening I was favoured with a ſweet refreſhing frame of ſoul in ſecret prayer and meditation. Prayer was now wholly turned into praiſe; and I could do little elſe but try to adore and bleſs the living God: The wonders of his grace diſplayed in gathering to himſelf a church among the poor Indians here, were the ſubject matter of my meditation, and the occaſion of exciting my ſoul to praiſe and bleſs his name. My ſoul was ſcarce ever more diſpoſed to inquire, *What I ſhould render to God for all his benefits*, than at this time. O, I was brought into a ſtrait, a ſweet and happy ſtrait, to know what to do! I longed to make ſome returns to God; but found I had nothing to return: I could only rejoice that God had done the work himſelf; and that none in heaven or earth might pretend to ſhare the honour of it with him: I could only be glad that God's declarative glory was advanced by the converſion of theſe ſouls, and that it was to the enlargement of his kingdom in the world: But ſaw I was ſo poor that I had nothing to offer to him. My ſoul and body, through grace, I could cheerfully ſurrender to him: But it appeared to me this was rather a cumber than a gift: And nothing could I do to glorify his dear and bleſſed name. Yet I was glad at heart, that he was unchangeably poſſeſſed of glory and bleſſedneſs. O that he might be adored and praiſed by all his intelligent creatures, to the utmoſt of their powers and capacities. My ſoul would have rejoiced to ſee others praiſe him, though I could do nothing towards it myſelf.

[The

[The next day he speaks of his being subject to some degree of melancholy; but of being something relieved in the evening.]

[*Friday, June* 6.—See the Journal.]

Saturday, June 7.—Rode to Freehold, to assist Mr. Tennent in the administration of the Lord's supper. In the afternnon preached from Psal. lxxiii. 28. God gave me some freedom and warmth in my discourse; and, I trust, his presence was in the assembly. Was comfortably composed, and enjoyed a thankful frame of spirit; and my soul was grieved, that I could not render something to God for his benefits bestowed. O that I could be swallowed up in his praise!

Lord's Day, June 8.—Spent much time in the morning in secret duties; but between hope and fear, respecting the enjoyment of God in the business of the day then before us. Was agreeably entertained, in the forenoon, by a discourse from Mr. Tennent, and felt somewhat melted and refreshed. In the season of communion enjoyed some comfort; and especially in serving one of the tables. Blessed be the Lord it was a time of refreshing to me, and, I trust, to many others. A number of my dear people sat down by themselves at the last table; at which time God seemed to be in the midst of them. And the thoughts of what God had done among them were refreshing and melting to me. In the afternoon God enabled me to preach with uncommon freedom, from 2 Cor. v. 20. Through the goodness of God I was favoured with a constant flow of pertinent matter, and proper expressions, from the beginning to the end of my discourse. In the evening I could not but rejoice in God, and bless him for the manifestations of his grace in the day past. O, it was a sweet and solemn day and evening! A season of comfort to the godly, and of awakening to some souls. O that I could praise the Lord.

Monday,

Monday, June 9.—Enjoyed some sweetness in secret duties. Preached the concluding sermon from Gen. v. 24. *And Enoch walked with God,* &c. God gave me enlargement and fervency in my discourse; so that I was enabled to speak with plainness and power; and God's presence seemed to be in the assembly. Praised be the Lord it was a sweet meeting, a desirable assembly. I found my strength renewed, and lengthened out even to a wonder; so that I felt much stronger at the conclusion, than in the beginning of this sacramental solemnity. I have great reason to bless God for this solemnity, wherein I have found assistance in addressing others, and sweetness in my own soul.

[On Tuesday, he found himself spent, and his spirits exhausted by his late labours; and on Wednesday complains of vapoury disorders, and dejection of spirit, and of enjoying but little comfort or spirituality.]

Thursday, June 12.—In the evening enjoyed freedom of mind, and some sweetness in secret prayer: It was a desirable season to me; my soul was enlarged in prayer for my own dear people, and for the enlargement of Christ's kingdom, and especially for the propagation of the gospel among the Indians, back in the wilderness. Was refreshed in prayer for dear friends in New-England, and elsewhere: I found it sweet to pray at this time; and could with all my heart say, *It is good for me to draw near to God.*

Friday, June 13.—I came away from the meeting of the Indians, this day, rejoicing and blessing God for his grace manifested at this season.

Saturday, June 14.—Rode to Kingston, to assist the Rev. Mr. Wales in the administration of the Lord's supper. In the afternoon preached; but almost fainted in the pulpit:. Yet God strengthened me me when I was just gone, and enabled me to speak his word with freedom, fervency, and application to the conscience. And praised be the Lord, *out of weakness I was made strong.* I enjoyed some sweetness, in and after publick worship; but was extremely tired. O, how many are the mercies of the Lord! *To them that have no might, he increaseth strength.*

Lord's Day, June 15.—Was in a dejected spiritless frame, that I could not hold up my head, nor look any body in the face. Administered the Lord's supper at Mr. Wales's desire: And found myself in a good measure unburdened and relieved of my pressing load, when I came to ask a blessing on the elements: Here God gave me enlargement, and a tender affectionate sense of spiritual things; so that it was a season of comfort, in some measure, to me, and, I trust, more so to others. In the afternoon, preached to a vast multitude, from Rev. xxii. 17. *And whosoever will,* &c. God helped me to offer a testimony for himself, and to leave sinners inexcusable in neglecting his grace. I was enabled to speak with such freedom, fluency and clearness, as commanded the attention of the great. Was extremely tired in the evening, but enjoyed composure and sweetness.

Monday, June 16.—Preached again, and God helped me amazingly, so that this was a sweet refreshing season to my soul and others. O, forever blessed be God for help afforded at this time, when my body was so weak, and while there was so large an assembly to hear. Spent the afternoon in a comfortable agreeable manner.

[The next day was spent comfortably.

On Wednesday he went to a meeting of ministers at Hopewell.]

[*Thursday, June* 19.—See his Journal.]

[On Friday and Saturday he was very much amiss; but yet preached to his people on Saturday. His
P   illness

illness continued on the Sabbath; but he preached, notwithstanding, to his people, both parts of the day: And after the publick worship was ended, he endeavoured to apply divine truths to the consciences of some, and addressed them personally for that end: Several were in tears, and some appeared much affected. But he was extremely wearied with the services of the day, and was so ill at night, that he could have no bodily rest; but remarks that *God was his support*, and that he was not left destitute of comfort in him. On Monday he continued very ill, but speaks of his mind's being calm and composed, resigned to the divine dispensations, and content with his feeble state. And by the account he gives of himself, the remaining part of this week, he continued very feeble, and for the most part dejected in mind, and enjoyed no great freedom nor sweetness in spiritual things; excepting that for some very short spaces of time he had refreshment and encouragement, which engaged his heart on divine things; and sometimes his heart was melted with spiritual affection.]

Lord's Day, June 29.—Preached both parts of the day, from John xiv. 19. *Yet a little while, and the world seeth me no more,* &c. God was pleased to assist me, to afford me both freedom and power; especially towards the close of my discourses, both forenoon and afternoon. God's power appeared in the assembly, in both exercises. Numbers of God's people were refreshed and melted with divine things; one or two comforted who had been long under distress: Convictions, in divers instances, powerfully revived; and one man in years much awakened, who had not long frequented our meeting, and appeared before as stupid as a stock. God amazingly renewed and lengthened out my strength. I was so spent at noon, that I could scarce walk, and all my joints trembled;

trembled; so that I could not sit nor so much as hold my hand still: And yet God strengthened me to preach with power in the afternoon; although I had given out word to my people, that I did not expect to be able to do it. Spent some time afterwards in conversing, particularly, with several persons, about their spiritual state; and had some satisfaction concerning one or two. Prayed afterwards with a sick child, and gave a word of exhortation. Was assisted in all my work. Blessed be God. Returned home with more health than I went out with; although my linen was wringing wet upon me, from a little after ten in the morning, until past five in the afternoon. My spirits also were considerably refreshed; and my soul rejoiced in hope, that I had through grace done something for God. In the evening, walked out, and enjoyed a sweet season in secret prayer and praise. But O, I found the truth of the Psalmist's words, *My goodness extendeth not to thee!* I could not make any returns to God: I longed to live only to him, and to be in tune for his praise and service forever. O, for spirituality and holy fervency, that I might *spend and be spent* for God, to my latest moment!

Monday, June 30.—Spent the day in writing; but under much weakness and disorder. Felt the labours of the preceding day; although my spirits were so refreshed the evening before, that I was not then sensible of my being spent.

Tuesday, July 1.—In the afternoon visited and preached to my people, from Heb. ix. 27. on occasion of some persons' lying at the point of death, in my congregation. God gave me some assistance; and his word made some impressions on the audience, in general. This was an agreeable and comfortable evening to my soul: My spirits were somewhat refreshed with a small degree of freedom and help enjoyed in my work.

[On Wednesday he went to Newark, to a meeting of the Presbytery: Complains of lowness of spirits; and greatly laments his spending his time so unfruitfully. The remaining part of the week he spent there, and at Elizabeth-Town; and speaks of comfort and divine assistance from day to day: But yet greatly complains for want of more spirituality.]

Lord's Day, July 6.—[At Elizabeth-Town.] Enjoyed some composure and serenity of mind, in the morning: Heard Mr. Dickinson preach in the forenoon, and was refreshed with his discourse; was in a melting frame, some part of the time of sermon: Partook of the Lord's supper, and enjoyed some sense of divine things in that ordinance. In the afternoon I preached from Ezek. xxxiii. 11. *As I live, saith the Lord God,* &c. God favoured me with freedom and fervency; and helped me to plead his cause, beyond my own power.

Monday, July 7.—My spirits were considerably refreshed and raised, in the morning. There is no comfort, I find, in any enjoyment, without enjoying God, and being engaged in his service. In the evening had the most agreeable conversation that ever I remember in all my life, upon God's being *all in all,* and all enjoyments being just that to us which God makes them, and no more. It is good to begin and end with God. O, how does a sweet solemnity lay a foundation for true pleasure and happiness!

Tuesday, July 8.—Rode home, and enjoyed some agreeable meditations by the way.

Wednesday, July 9.—Spent the day in writing. Enjoyed some comfort and refreshment of spirit in my evening retirement.

Thursday, July 10.—Spent most of the day in writing. Towards night rode to Mr. Tennent's; enjoyed some agreeable conversation: Went home in the evening, in a solemn sweet frame of mind;
was

was refreshed in secret duties, longed to live wholly and only for God, and saw plainly there was nothing in the world worthy of my affection; so that my heart was dead to all below; yet not through dejection as at some times, but from views of a better inheritance.

Friday, July 11.—Was in a calm composed frame in the morning, especially in the season of my secret retirement: I think I was well pleased with the will of God, whatever it was, or should be, in all respects I had then any thought of. Intending to administer the Lord's supper the next Lord's Day, I looked to God for his presence and assistance upon that occasion; but felt a disposition to say, *The will of the Lord be done,* whether it be to give me assistance or not. Spent some little time in writing: Visited the Indians, and spent some time in serious conversation with them; thinking it not best to preach, by reason that many of them were absent.

Saturday, July 12.—This day was spent in fasting and prayer by my congregation, as preparatory to the sacrament. I discoursed, both parts of the day, from Rom. iv. 25. *Who was delivered for our offences,* &c. God gave me some assistance in my discourses, and something of divine power attended the word; so that this was an agreeable season. Afterwards led them to a solemn renewal of their covenant, and fresh dedication of themselves to God. This was a season both of solemnity and sweetness, and God seemed to be *in the midst of us.* Returned to my lodgings, in the evening, in a comfortable frame of mind.

Lord's Day, July 13.—In the forenoon discoursed on the *bread of life,* from John vi. 35. God gave me some assistance, in part of my discourse especially; and there appeared some tender affection in the assembly under divine truths; my soul also was somewhat refreshed. Administered the sacrament of the Lord's supper to thirty one persons of the Indians. God seemed to be present in this ordinance; the communicants were sweetly melted and refreshed, most of them. O, how they melted, even when the elements were first uncovered! There was scarcely a dry eye amongst them, when I took off the linen, and shewed them the symbols of *Christ's broken body*. Having rested a little, after the administration of the sacrament, I visited the communicants, and found them generally in a sweet loving frame; not unlike what appeared among them on the former sacramental occasion, on April 27. In the afternoon discoursed upon *coming to Christ*, and the sanctification of those who do so, from the same verse I insisted on in the forenoon. This was likewise an agreeable season, a season of much tenderness, affection and enlargement in divine service: And God, I am persuaded, crowned our assembly with his divine presence. I returned home much spent, yet rejoicing in the goodness of God.

Monday, July 14.—Went to my people and discoursed to them from Psal. cxix. 106. *I have sworn and I will perform it*, &c. Observed, 1. That all God's judgments or commandments are righteous. 2. That God's people have sworn to keep them; and this they do especially at the Lord's table. There appeared to be a powerful divine influence on the assembly, and considerable melting under the word. Afterwards, I led them to a renewal of their covenant before God (that they would watch over themselves and one another, lest they should fall into sin, and dishonour the name of Christ) just as I did on Monday, April 28. This transaction was attended with great solemnity: And God seemed to own it by exciting in them a fear and jealousy of themselves, lest they should sin against God; so that the presence of God

seemed

seemed to be amongst us in this conclusion of the sacramental solemnity.

[The next day he set out on a journey towards Philadelphia; from whence he did not return until Saturday. He went this journey, and spent the week, under a great degree of illness of body, and dejection of mind.]

Lord's Day, July 20.—Preached twice to my people from John xvii. 24. *Father, I will that they also whom thou hast given me, be with me, where I am, that they may behold my glory, which thou hast given me.* Was helped to discourse with great clearness and plainness in the forenoon. In the afternoon, enjoyed some tenderness, and spake with some influence. Divers were in tears; and some, to appearance, in distress.

Monday, July 21.—Preached to the Indians, chiefly for the sake of some strangers. Then proposed my design of taking a journey speedily to Susquehannah: Exhorted my people to pray for me, that God would be with me in that journey, &c. Then chose divers persons of the congregation to travel with me. Afterwards, spent time in discoursing to the strangers, and was somewhat encouraged with them. Took care of my people's secular business, and was not a little exercised with it. Had some degree of composure and comfort in secret retirement.

Tuesday, July 22.—Was in a dejected frame, most of the day: Wanted to wear out life and have it at an end; but had some desires of living to God, and wearing out life for him. O that I could indeed do so!

[The next day he went to Elizabeth-Town, to a meeting of the Presbytery.]

Lord's Day, July 27.—Discoursed to my people, in the forenoon, from Luke xii. 37. on the duty and benefit of watching. God helped me in the latter part of my difcourfe, and the power of God appeared in the affembly. In the afternoon, difcourfed from Luke xiii. 25.; Here alfo I enjoyed fome affiftance, and the Spirit of God feemed to attend what was fpoken, fo that there was a great folemnity, and fome tears among Indians and others.

Monday, July 28.—Was very weak, and fcarce able to perform any bufinefs at all; but enjoyed fweetnefs and comfort in prayer, both morning and evening; and was compofed and comfortable through the day. My mind was intenfe, and my heart fervent, at leaft in fome degree, in fecret duties; and I longed to *fpend and be fpent for God.*

Tuefday, July 29.—My mind was cheerful, and free from thofe melancholy damps, that I am often exercifed with: Had freedom in looking up to God, at fundry times in the day. In the evening I enjoyed a comfortable feafon in fecret prayer; was helped to plead with God for my own dear people, that he would carry on his own bleffed work among them; was affifted alfo, in praying for the divine prefence to attend me in my intended journey to Sufquehannah; was alfo helped to remember dear brethren and friends in New-England; fcarce knew how to leave the throne of grace, and it grieved me that I was obliged to go to bed; I longed to do fomething for God, but knew not how. Bleffed be God for this freedom from dejection.

Wednefday, July 30.—Was uncommonly comfortable, both in body and mind; in the forenoon efpecially: My mind was folemn, I was affifted in my work, and God feemed to be near to me; fo that the day was as comfortable as moft I have enjoyed for fome time. In the evening was favoured with affiftance in fecret prayer, and felt much as I did the evening before. Bleffed be God for that freedom I then enjoyed at the throne of grace, for my-

felf,

self, my people, and my dear friends. *It is good for me to draw near to God.*

[He seems to have continued very much in the same free, comfortable state of mind the next day.]

Friday, August 1.—In the evening enjoyed a sweet season in secret prayer; clouds of darkness and perplexing care were sweetly scattered, and nothing anxious remained. O, how serene was my mind at this season! How free from that distracting concern I have often felt! *Thy will be done*, was a petition sweet to my soul; and if God had bidden me choose for myself in any affair, I should have chosen rather to have referred the choice to him; for I saw he was infinitely wise, and could not do any thing amiss, as I was in danger of doing. Was assisted in prayer, for my dear flock, that God would promote his own work among them, and that God would go with me in my intended journey to Susquehannah; was helped to remember dear friends in New-England, and my dear brethren in the ministry. I found enough in the sweet duty of prayer to have engaged me to continue in it the whole night, would my bodily state have admitted of it. O how sweet it is, to be enabled heartily to say, *Lord, not my will, but thine be done!*

Saturday, August 2.—Near night preached from Matth. xi. 29. Was considerably helped; and the presence of God seemed to be somewhat remarkably in the assembly; divine truths made powerful impressions, both upon saints and sinners. Blessed be God for such a revival among us. In the evening was very weary, but found my spirits supported and refreshed.

Lord's Day, August 3.—Discoursed to my people, in the forenoon, from Coloss. iii. 4. Observed that Christ is the believer's life. God helped me and gave me his presence in this discourse; and it was a season of considerable power in the assembly. In the afternoon preached from Luke xix. 41. 42. I enjoyed some assistance; though not so much as in the forenoon.

Monday, August 4.—Spent the day in writing; enjoyed much freedom and assistance in my work: Was in a composed and comfortable frame, most of the day; and in the evening enjoyed some sweetness in prayer. Blessed be God, my spirits were yet up, and I was free from sinking damps; as I have been in general ever since I came from Elizabeth-Town last. O what a mercy is this!

Tuesday, August 5.—Towards night, preached at the funeral of one of my christians, from Isai. lvii. 2. Was oppressed with the nervous headach, and considerably dejected: However, had a little freedom, some part of the time I was discoursing. Was extremely weary in the evening; but notwithstanding enjoyed some liberty and cheerfulness of mind in prayer; and found the dejection that I feared, much removed, and my spirits considerably refreshed.

[He continued in a very comfortable cheerful frame of mind the next day, with his heart enlarged in the service of God.]

Thursday, August 7.—Rode to my house, where I spent the last winter, in order to bring some things I needed for my Susquehannah journey: Was refreshed to see that place, which God so marvellously visited with the showers of his grace. O how amazingly did the power of God often appear there! *Bless the Lord, O my soul, and forget not all his benefits.*

[The next day, he speaks of liberty, enlargement, and sweetness of mind, in prayer and religious conversation.]

Saturday, August 9.—In the afternoon, visited my people; set their affairs in order, as much as possible,

ble, and contrived for them the management of their worldly bufinefs: Difcourfed to them in a folemn manner, and concluded with prayer. Was compofed, and comfortable in the evening, and fomewhat fervent in fecret prayer: Had fome fenfe and view of the eternal world, and found a ferenity of mind. O that I could magnify the Lord for any freedom he affords me in prayer.

Lord's Day, Auguft 10.—Difcourfed to my people, both parts of the day, from Acts iii. 19. In difcourfing of repentance, in the forenoon, God helped me, fo that my difcourfe was fearching. Some were in tears, both of the Indians and white people; and the word of God was attended with fome power. In the intermiffion feafon, I was engaged in difcourfing to fome in order to their baptifm; as well as with one who had then lately met with fome comfort, after fpiritual trouble and diftrefs. In the afternoon, was fomewhat affifted again, though weak and weary. Afterwards baptized fix perfons; three adults, and three children. Was in a comfortable frame in the evening, and enjoyed fome fatisfaction in fecret prayer. I fcarce ever in my life felt myfelf fo full of tendernefs, as this day.

Monday, Auguft 11.—Being about to fet out on a journey to Sufquehannah the next day, with leave of Providence, I fpent fome time this day in prayer with my people, that God would blefs and fucceed my intended journey, that he would fend forth his bleffed Spirit with his word, and fet up his kingdom among the poor Indians in the wildernefs. While I was opening and applying part of the cxth and iid Pfalms, the *power of God* feemed to defcend on the affembly in fome meafure; and while I was making the firft prayer, numbers were melted, and I found fome affectionate enlargement of foul myfelf. Preached from Acts iv. 31. God helped me, and my my interpreter alfo : There was a fhaking and melting among us; and divers, I doubt not, were in fome meafure *filled with the Holy Ghoſt*. Afterwards, Mr. M'Knight prayed : I then opened the two laſt ſtanzas of the lxxiid Pſal. at which time God was prefent with us; efpecially while I infiſted upon the promife of all nations' bleſſing the great Redeemer : My foul was refreſhed, to think, that this day, this bleſſed glorious feafon, fhould furely come; and I truſt, numbers of my dear people were alfo refreſhed. Afterwards prayed; had fome freedom, but was almoſt fpent: Then walked out, and left my people to carry on religious exercifes among themfelves : They prayed repeatedly, and fung, while I reſted and refreſhed myfelf. Afterwards, went to the meeting; prayed with, and difmiſſed the aſſembly.

[The next day he fet out on his journey towards Sufquehannah, and fix of his chriſtian Indians with him, whom he had chofen out of his congregation, as thofe that he judged moſt fit to aſſiſt him in the bufinefs he was going upon. He took his way through Philadelphia; intending to go to Sufquehannah river, far down along, where it is fettled by the white people, below the country inhabited by the Indians; and fo to travel up the river to the Indian habitations : For although this was much further about, yet hereby he avoided the huge mountains, and hideous wildernefs, that muſt be croſſed in the nearer way; which in time paſt he had found to be extremely difficult and fatiguing. He rode this week as far as Charleſtown, a place of that name about thirty miles weſtward of Philadelphia; where he arrived on Friday : And in his way hither, was for the moſt part in a compofed comfortable ſtate of mind.]

Saturday, Auguſt 16.—[At Charleſtown.] It being a day kept by the people of the place where I now

now was, as preparatory to the celebration of the Lord's supper, I tarried; heard Mr. Treat preach; and then preached myself. God gave me some good degree of freedom, and helped me to discourse with warmth and application to the conscience. Afterwards, I was refreshed in spirit, though much tired; and spent the evening agreeably, having some freedom in prayer, as well as christian conversation.

Lord's Day, August 17.—Enjoyed liberty, composure, and satisfaction, in the secret duties of the morning: Had my heart somewhat enlarged in prayer for dear friends, as well as for myself. In the forenoon, attended Mr. Treat's preaching, partook of the Lord's supper, five of my people also communicating in this holy ordinance: I enjoyed some enlargement and outgoing of soul in this season. In the afternoon, preached from Ezek. xxxiii. 11. Enjoyed not so much sensible assistance as the day before; however, was helped to some fervency in addressing immortal souls.

Monday, August 18.—Rode on my way towards Paxton, upon Susquehannah river. Felt my spirits sink, towards night, so that I had little comfort.

Tuesday, August 19.—Rode forward still; and at night lodged by the side of Susquehannah. Was weak and disordered, both this and the preceding day, and found my spirits considerably damped, meeting with none that I thought godly people.

Wednesday, August 20.—Having lain in a cold sweat all night, I coughed much bloody matter this morning, and was under great disorder of body, and not a little melancholy; but what gave me some encouragement, was, I had a secret hope that I might speedily get a dismission from earth and all its toils and sorrows. Rode this day to one Chambers's upon Susquehannah, and there lodged. Was much afflicted in the evening, with an ungodly crew, drinking,

ing, swearing, &c. O, what a hell it would be, to be numbered with the ungodly! Enjoyed some agreeable conversation with a traveller, who seemed to have some relish of true religion.

Thursday, August 21.—Rode up the river about fifteen miles, and there lodged, in a family that appeared quite destitute of God. Laboured to discourse with the man about the life of religion, but found him very artful in evading such conversation. O, what a death it is to some, to hear of the things of God! Was out of my element; but was not so dejected as at some times.

Friday, August 22.—Continued my course up the river; my people now being with me, who before were parted from me: Travelled above all the English settlements; at night, lodged in the open woods; and slept with more comfort, than while among an ungodly company of white people. Enjoyed some liberty in secret prayer, this evening; and was helped to remember dear friends, as well as my dear flock, and the church of God in general.

Saturday, August 23.—Arrived at the Indian town, called Shaumoking, near night. Was not so dejected as formerly; but yet somewhat exercised. Felt somewhat composed in the evening; enjoyed some freedom in leaving my all with God: Through the great goodness of God, I enjoyed some liberty of mind; was not distressed with a despondency, as frequently heretofore.

Lord's Day, August 24.—Towards noon visited some of the Delawares, and discoursed with them about christianity. In the afternoon, discoursed to the king, and others, upon divine things; who seemed disposed to hear. Spent most of the day in these exercises. In the evening, enjoyed some comfort and satisfaction; and especially had some sweetness in secret prayer: This duty was made so agreeable to to me, that I loved to walk abroad and repeatedly engage in it. O, how comfortable is a little glimpse of God!

Monday, August 25.—Spent most of the day in writing. Sent out my people that were with me, to talk with the Indians, and contract a friendship, and familiarity with them, that I might have a better opportunity of treating with them about christianity. Some good seemed to be done by their visits this day; divers appeared willing to hearken to christianity. My spirits were a little refreshed, this evening; and I found some liberty and satisfaction in prayer.

Tuesday, August 26.—About noon, discoursed to a considerable number of Indians: God helped me, I am persuaded: I was enabled to speak with much plainness, and some warmth and power. The discourse had impression upon some, and made them appear very serious. I thought, things now appeared as encouraging as they did at Crosweeksung, at the time of my first visit to those Indians. I was a little encouraged: I pressed things with all my might; and called out my people who were then present, to give in their testimony for God; which they did. Towards night, was refreshed; felt a heart to pray for the setting up of God's kingdom here; as well as for my dear congregation below, and my dear friends elsewhere.

Thursday, August 28.—In the forenoon, was under great concern of mind about my work. Was visited by some who desired to hear me preach; discoursed to them, in the afternoon, with some fervency, and laboured to persuade them to turn to God. Was full of concern for the kingdom of Christ, and found some enlargement of soul in prayer, both in secret and in my family. Scarcely ever saw more clearly, than this day, that it is God's work to convert

vert souls, and especially poor heathens: I knew, I could not touch them; I saw, I could only speak to *dry bones*, but could give them no sense of what I said. My eyes were up to God for help: I could say, the work was his; and if done, the glory would be his.

Saturday, August 30.—Spent the forenoon in visiting a trader, that came down the river sick; who appeared as ignorant as any Indian. In the afternoon, spent some time in writing, reading, and prayer.

Lord's Day, August 31.—Spent much time, in the morning, in secret duties: Found a weight upon my spirit, and could not but cry to God with concern and engagement of soul. Spent some time also in reading and expounding God's word to my dear family, that was with me, as well as in singing and prayer with them. Afterwards, spake the word of God to some few of the Susquehannah Indians. In the afternoon, felt very weak and feeble. Near night, was something refreshed in mind, with some views of things relating to my great work. O, how heavy is my work, when faith cannot take hold of an almighty arm, for the performance of it! Many times have I been ready to sink in this case. Blessed be God, that I may repair to a full fountain.

Monday, September 1.—Set out on a journey towards a place called the Great-Island, about fifty miles distant from Shaumoking, in the northwestern branch of Susquehannah. Travelled some part of the way, and at night lodged in the woods. Was exceeding feeble, this day, and sweat much the night following.

Tuesday, September 2.—Rode forward; but no faster than my people went on foot. Was very weak, on this, as well as the preceding days: Was so feeble and faint, that I feared it would kill me to lie
out

out in the open air; and some of our company being parted from us, so that we had now no axe with us, I had no way but to climb into a young pine tree, and with my knife to lop the branches, and so made a shelter from the dew. But the evening being cloudy and very likely for rain, I was still under fears of being extremely exposed: Sweat much in the night, so that my linen was almost wringing wet all night. I scarce ever was more weak and weary, than this evening, when I was able to sit up at all. This was a melancholy situation I was in; but I endeavoured to quiet myself with considerations of the possibility of my being in much worse circumstances amongst enemies, &c.

Wednesday, September 3.—Rode to the Delaware-Town; found divers drinking and drunken. Discoursed with some of the Indians about christianity; observed my interpreter much engaged and assisted in his work: Some few persons seemed to hear with great earnestness and engagement of soul. About noon, rode to a small town of Shauwaunoes, about eight miles distant; spent an hour or two there, and returned to the Delaware-Town, and lodged there. Was scarce ever more confounded with a sense of my own unfruitfulness, and unfitness for my work, than now. O, what a dead, heartless, barren, unprofitable wretch did I now see myself to be!

Thursday, September 4.—Discoursed with the Indians, in the morning, about christianity; my interpreter, afterwards, carrying on the discourse, to a considerable length: Some few appeared well disposed, and somewhat affected. Left this place, and returned towards Shaumoking; and at night lodged in the place where I lodged the Monday night before: Was in very uncomfortable circumstances in the evening, my people being belated, and not coming to me until past ten at night; so that I had no fire

fire to drefs any victuals, or to keep me warm, or keep off wild beafts; and I was fcarce ever more weak and worn out in all my life. However, I lay down and flept before my people came up, expecting nothing elfe but to fpend the whole night alone and without fire.

Friday, September 5.—Was exceeding weak, fo that I could fcarcely ride; it feemed fometimes as if I muft fall off from my horfe, and lie in the open woods: However, got to Shaumoking towards night: Felt fomething of a fpirit of thankfulnefs, that God had fo far returned me: Was refrefhed, to fee one of my chriftians, whom I left here in my late excurfion.

Saturday, September 6.—Spent the day in a very weak ftate; coughing and fpitting blood, and having little appetite to any food I had with me: Was able to do very little, except difcourfe a while of divine things to my own people, and to fome few I met with. Had, by this time, very little life or heart to fpeak for God, through feeblenefs of body, and flatnefs of fpirits.

Lord's Day, September 7.—Was much in the fame weak ftate of body, and afflicted frame of mind, as in the preceding day: My foul was grieved, and mourned, that I could do nothing for God. Read and expounded fome part of God's word to my own dear family, and fpent fome time in prayer with them; difcourfed alfo a little to the pagans: But fpent the Sabbath with little comfort.

Monday, September 8.—Spent the forenoon among the Indians; in the afternoon left Shaumoking, and returned down the river, a few miles. Had propofed to have tarried a confiderable time longer among the Indians upon Sufquehannah, but was hindered from purfuing my purpofe by the ficknefs that prevailed there, the weakly circumftances of my own people that were with me, and efpecially my own
extraordinary

extraordinary weakneſs, having been exerciſed with great nocturnal ſweats, and a coughing up of blood, in almoſt the whole of the journey ; and was a great part of the time ſo feeble and faint, that it ſeemed as though I never ſhould be able to reach home ; and at the ſame time very deſtitute of the comforts and even neceſſaries of life ; at leaſt, what was neceſſary for one in ſo weak a ſtate.

Tueſday, September 9.—Rode down the river, near thirty miles. Was extreme weak, much fatigued, and wet with a thunder ſtorm. Diſcourſed with ſome warmth and cloſeneſs to ſome poor ignorant ſouls, on the life and power of religion ; what were and what were not the evidences of it. They ſeemed much aſtoniſhed, when they ſaw my Indians aſk a bleſſing and give thanks at dinner ; concluding that a very high evidence of grace in them : But were aſtoniſhed, when I inſiſted that neither that, nor yet ſecret prayer, was any ſure evidence of grace. O the ignorance of the world ! How are ſome empty outward forms, that may all be entirely ſelfiſh, miſtaken for true religion, infallible evidences of it ! The Lord pity a deluded world.

Thurſday, September 11.—Rode homeward ; but was very weak, and ſometimes ſcarce able to ride. Had a very importunate invitation to preach at a meeting houſe I came by, the people being then gathering ; but could not by reaſon of weakneſs. Was reſigned and compoſed under my weakneſs ; but was much exerciſed with concern for my companions in travel, whom I had left with much regret, ſome lame, and ſome ſick.

Friday, September 12.—Rode about fifty miles ; and came juſt at night to a chriſtian friend's houſe, about twenty five miles weſtward from Philadelphia. Was courteouſly received, and kindly entertained,

tained, and found myself much refreshed in the midst of my weakness and fatigues.

Saturday, September 13.—Was still agreeably entertained with christian friendship, and all things necessary for my weak circumstances: In the afternoon heard Mr. Treat preach; and was refreshed in conversation with him, in the evening.

Lord's Day, September 14.—At the desire of Mr. Treat and the people, I preached both parts of the day, but short, from Luke xiv. 23. God gave me some freedom and warmth in my discourse; and I trust, helped me in some measure to labour *in singleness of heart*. Was much tired in the evening, but was comforted with the most tender treatment I ever met with in my life. My mind through the whole of this day was exceeding calm; and I could ask for nothing in prayer, with any encouragement of soul, but that the *will of God might be done*.

Monday, September 15.—Spent the whole day, in concert with Mr. Treat, in endeavours to compose a difference, subsisting between certain persons in the congregation where we now were: There seemed to be a blessing on our endeavours. In the evening, baptized a child: Was in a calm composed frame, and enjoyed, I trust, a spiritual sense of divine things, while administering the ordinance. Afterwards, spent the time in religious conversation, until late in the night. This was indeed a pleasant agreeable evening.

Friday, September 19.—Rode from Mr. Treat's to Mr. Stockton's at Prince-Town: Was extreme weak, but kindly received and entertained. Spent the evening with some degree of satisfaction.

Saturday, September 20.—Arrived among my own people, just at night: Found them praying together: Went in and gave them some account of God's dealings with me and my companions in the journey;

ncy; which feemed affecting to them. I then prayed with them, and thought the divine prefence was amongft us; divers were melted into tears, and feemed to have a fenfe of divine things. Being very weak, I was obliged foon to repair to my lodgings, and felt much worn out in the evening. Thus God has carried me through the fatigues and perils of another journey to Sufquehannah, and returned me again in fafety, though under a great degree of bodily indifpofition. O that my foul were truly thankful for renewed inftances of mercy! Many hardfhips and diftreffes I endured in this journey: But the Lord fupported me under them all.

PART VII.

After his Return from his last Journey to SUSQUE-HANNAH, *until his* DEATH.

LORD's DAY, *September* 21, 1746.—I was so weak I could not preach, nor pretend to ride over to my people in the forenoon. In the afternoon rode out; sat in my chair, and discoursed to my people from Rom. xiv. 7. 8. I was strengthened and helped in my discourse: And there appeared something agreeable in the assembly. I returned to my lodgings extremely tired; but thankful, that I had been enabled to speak a word to my poor people I had been so long absent from. Was able to sleep very little this night, through weariness and pain. O how blessed should I be, if the little I do were all done with right views! O that whether *I live I might live to the Lord*, &c.

Saturday, September 27.—Spent this day, as well as the whole week past, under a great degree of bodily weakness, exercised with a violent cough, and a considerable fever; had no appetite to any kind of food; and frequently brought up what I eat, as soon is it was down; and oftentimes had little rest in my bed, by reason of pains in my breast and back: Was able, however, to ride over to my people, about two miles, every day, and take some care of those who were then at work upon a small house for me to reside in amongst the Indians. I was sometimes scarce able to walk, and never able to sit up the whole day, through the week. Was calm and composed, and but little exercised with melancholy damps, as in
former

former seasons of weakness. Whether I should ever recover, or no, seemed very doubtful; but this was many times a comfort to me, that life and death did not depend upon my choice. I was pleased, to think that he who is infinitely wise, had the determination of this matter; and that I had no trouble, to consider and weigh things upon all sides, in order to make the choice, whether I would live or die. Thus my time was consumed; I had little strength to pray, none to write or read, and scarce any to meditate: But through divine goodness, I could with great composure look death in the face, and frequently with sensible joy. O, how blessed it is, to be habitually prepared for death! The Lord grant, that I may be actually ready also.

Lord's Day, September 28.—Rode to my people, and, though under much weakness, attempted to preach, from 2 Cor. xiii. 5. Discoursed about half an hour; at which season divine power seemed to attend the word: But being extreme weak, I was obliged to desist; and after a turn of faintness, with much difficulty, rode to my lodgings; where betaking myself to my bed, I lay in a burning fever, and almost delirious, for several hours; until towards morning, my fever went off with a violent sweat. I have often been feverish, and unable to rest quietly after preaching; but this was the most severe distressing turn, that ever preaching brought upon me. Yet I felt perfectly at rest in my own mind, because I had made my utmost attempts to speak for God, and knew I could do no more.

Tuesday, September 30.—Yesterday, and today, was in the same weak state, or rather weaker than in days past; was scarce able to sit up half the day. Was in a composed frame of mind, remarkably free from dejection and melancholy damps; as God has been pleased, in great measure, to deliver me from these unhappy glooms, in the general courſe of my preſent weakneſs hitherto, and alſo from a peeviſh froward ſpirit : And O, how great a mercy is this ! O that I might always be perfectly quiet in ſeaſons of greateſt weakneſs, although nature ſhould ſink and fail.

Saturday, October 4.—Spent the former part of this week under a great degree of infirmity and diſorder, as I had done ſeveral weeks bᶠore : Was able however, to ride a little every day, although unable to ſit up half of the day, until Thurſday. Took ſome care daily of ſome perſons at work upon my houſe. On Friday, afternoon, found myſelf wonderfully revived and ſtrengthened; and having ſome time before given notice to my people, and thoſe of them at the Forks of Delaware, in particular, that I deſigned, with the leave of Providence, to adminiſter the ſacrament of the Lord's ſupper upon the firſt Sabbath in October, the Sabbath now approaching, on Friday afternoon I preached, preparatory to the ſacrament, from 2 Cor. xiii. 5. Finiſhing what I had propoſed to offer upon the ſubject the Sabbath before. The ſermon was bleſſed of God to the ſtirring up religious affection, and a ſpirit of devotion, in the people of God ; and to the greatly affecting one who had backſlidden from God, which cauſed him to judge and condemn himſelf. This being Saturday, I diſcourſed particularly with divers of the communicants ; and this afternoon preached from Zech. xii. 10. There ſeemed to be a tender melting, and hearty mourning for ſin, in numbers in the congregation. My ſoul was in a comfortable frame, and I enjoyed freedom and aſſiſtance in publick ſervice : Was myſelf, as well as moſt of the congregation, much affected with the humble confeſſion, and apparent brokenheartedneſs of the forementioned backſlider ; and could not but rejoice, that God had

given

given him such a sense of his sin and unworthiness. Was extremely tired in the evening; but lay on my bed, and discoursed to my people.

Lord's Day, October 5.—Was still very weak; and, in the morning, considerably afraid I should not be able to go through the work of the day; having much to do, both in private and publick. Discoursed before the administration of the sacrament, from John i. 29. *Behold the Lamb of God, that taketh away the sin of the world.* Where I considered, I. In what respects Christ is called the *Lamb of God;* and observed that he is so called, 1. From the purity and innocency of his nature. 2. From his meekness and patience under sufferings. 3. From his being that atonement, which was pointed out in the sacrifice of lambs, and in particular by the paschal lamb. II. Considered how and in what sense he *takes away the sin of the world:* And observed, that the means and manner, in and by which he takes away the sins of men, was his *giving himself for them*, doing and suffering in their room and stead, &c. And he is said to take away the *sin of the world*, not because all the world shall actually be redeemed from sin by him; but because, 1. He has done and suffered sufficient to answer for the sins of the world, and so to redeem all mankind. 2. He actually does take away the sins of the elect world. And III. Considered how we are to behold him, in order to have our sins taken away. 1. Not with our bodily eyes: Nor 2. By imagining him on the cross, &c. But by a spiritual view of his glory and goodness, engaging the soul to rely on him, &c. The divine presence attended this discourse; and the assembly was considerably melted with divine truths. After sermon baptized two persons. Then administered the Lord's supper to near forty communicants, of the Indians, besides divers dear christians of the white people. It seemed ed to be a feason of divine power and grace ; and numbers seemed to rejoice in God. O, the sweet union and harmony then appearing among the religious people! My soul was refreshed, and my religious friends, of the white people, with me. After the sacrament, could scarcely get home, though it was not more than twenty rods ; but was supported and led by my friends, and laid on my bed ; where I lay in pain until some time in the evening ; and then was able to sit up and discourse with friends. O how was this day spent in prayers and praises among my dear people! One might hear them, all the morning before publick worship, and in the evening, until near midnight, praying and singing praises to God, in one or other of their houses. My soul was refreshed, though my body was weak.

[This week he went in a very low state, in two days, to Elizabeth-Town, to attend the meeting of the Synod there : But was disappointed by its removal to New-York. He continued in a very composed comfortable frame of mind.]

Saturday, October 11.—Towards night was seized with an ague, which was followed with a hard fever, and considerable pain : Was treated with great kindness, and was ashamed to see so much concern about so unworthy a creature, as I knew myself to be. Was in a comfortable frame of mind, wholly submissive, with regard to life or death. It was indeed a peculiar satisfaction to me, to think, that it was not my concern or business to determine whether I should live or die. I likewise felt peculiarly satisfied, while under this uncommon degree of disorder ; being now fully convinced of my being really weak, and unable to perform my work ; whereas at other times my mind was perplexed with fears, that I was a misimprover of time, by conceiting I was sick, when I was not in reality so. O, how precious
is

is time! And how guilty it makes me feel, when I think I have trifled away and mifimproved it, or neglected to fill up each part of it with duty, to the utmoft of my ability and capacity!

Lord's Day, October 12.—Was fcarce able to fit up, in the forenoon: In the afternoon, attended publick worfhip, and was in a compofed and comfortable frame.

[The following week, he went back to his Indians at Cranberry, to take fome care of their fpiritual and temporal concerns: And was much fpent with riding; though he rode but a little way in a day.]

Friday, October 24.—Spent the day in overfeeing and directing my people, about mending their fence, and fecuring their wheat. Found that all their concerns of a fecular nature depended upon me. Was fomewhat refrefhed in the evening, having been able to do fomething valuable in the day time. O, how it pains me, to fee time pafs away, when I can do nothing to any purpofe!

Saturday, October 25.—Vifited fome of my people; fpent fome time in writing, and felt much better in body, than ufual: When it was near night, I felt fo well, that I had thoughts of expounding: But in the evening was much difordered again, and fpent the night in coughing, and fpitting of blood.

Lord's Day, October 26.—In the morning, was exceeding weak: Spent the day, until near night, in pain to fee my poor people, wandering *as fheep not having a fhepherd*, waiting and hoping to fee me able to preach to them before night: It could not but diftrefs me, to fee them in this cafe, and to find myfelf unable to attempt any thing for their fpiritual benefit. But towards night, finding myfelf a little better, I called them together to my own houfe, and fat down and read and expounded Matth. v. 1.—16. This difcourfe, though delivered in much weaknefs,

was

was attended with power to many of the hearers; especially what was spoken upon the last of those verses; where I insisted on the infinite wrong done to religion, by having our light become darkness, instead of *shining before men*. As many in the congregation were now deeply affected with a sense of their deficiency, in regard of a spirtual conversation, that might recommend religion to others, and as a spirit of concern and watchfulness seemed to be excited in them; so there was one, in particular, that had fallen into the sin of drunkenness, some time before, who was now deeply convinced of his sin, and the great dishonour done to religion by his misconduct, and discovered a great degree of grief and concern on that account. My soul was refreshed to see this.

Monday, October 27.—Spent the day in overseeing and directing the Indians, about mending the fence round their wheat: Was able to walk with them, and contrive their business, all the forenoon. In the afternoon, was visited by two dear friends, and spent some time in conversation with them; towards night, was able to walk out, and take care of the Indians again. In the evening, enjoyed a very peaceful frame.

Tuesday, October 28.—Rode to Prince-Town, in a very weak state: Had such a violent fever, by the way, that I was forced to alight at a friend's house; and lie down for some time. Near night was visited by Mr. Treat, Mr. Beaty and his wife, and another friend. My spirits were refreshed to see them; but I was surprised, and even ashamed, that they had taken so much pains as to ride thirty or forty miles to see me! Was able to sit up most of the evening; and spent the time in a very comfortable manner with my friends.

Wednesday, October 29.—Rode about ten miles with my friends that came yesterday to see me; and
then

then parted with them, all but one, who stayed on purpose to keep me company, and cheer my spirits. Was extremely weak, and very feverish, especially towards night; but enjoyed comfort and satisfaction.

Lord's Day, November 2.—Was unable to preach, and scarcely able to sit, the whole day. Was grieved, and almost sunk, to see my poor people destitute of the means of grace; especially considering they could not read, and so were under great disadvantages for spending the Sabbath comfortably. O methought, I could be contented to be sick, if my poor flock had a faithful pastor to feed them with spiritual knowledge! A view of their want of this was more afflictive to me, than all my bodily illness.

Monday, November 3.—Being now in so weak and low a state, that I was utterly uncapable of performing my work, and having little hope of recovery, unless by much riding, I thought it my duty to take a lengthy journey into New-England, and to divert myself among my friends, whom I had not now seen for a long time. And accordingly took leave of my congregation this day. Before I left my people, I visited them all in their respective houses, and discoursed to each one, as I thought most proper and suitable for their circumstances, and found great freedom and assistance in so doing: I scarcely left one house but some were in tears; and many were not only affected with my being about to leave them, but with the solemn addresses I made them upon divine things; for I was helped to be *fervent in spirit*, while I discoursed to them. When I had thus gone through my congregation, which took me most of the day, and had taken leave of them, and of the school, I left home, and rode about two miles to the house where I lived in the summer past, and there lodged. Was refreshed, this evening, in that I had left my congregation so well disposed and affected,

and

and that I had been so much assisted in making my farewell addresses to them.

Tuesday, November 4.—Rode to Woodbridge, and lodged with Mr. Pierson; continuing still in a very weak state.

Wednesday, November 5.—Rode to Elizabeth-Town; intending, as soon as possible, to prosecute my journey into New-England. But was, in an hour or two after my arrival, taken much worse.

After this, for near a week, was confined to my chamber, and most of the time to my bed: And then so far revived as to be able to walk about the house; but was still confined within doors.

In the beginning of this extraordinary turn of disorder, after my coming to Elizabeth-Town, I was enabled, through mercy, to maintain a calm, composed, and patient spirit, as I had been before from the beginning of my weakness. After I had been in Elizabeth-Town about a fortnight, and had so far recovered that I was able to walk about house, upon a day of thanksgiving kept in this place, I was enabled to recall and recount over the mercies of God, in such a manner as greatly affected me, and filled me, I think, with thankfulness and praise to God: Especially my soul praised him for his work of grace among the Indians, and the enlargement of his dear kingdom: My soul blessed God for what he is in himself, and adored him, that he ever would display himself to creatures: I rejoiced that he was God, and longed that all should know it and feel it, and rejoice in it. *Lord, glorify thyself,* was the desire and cry of my soul. O that all people might love and praise the blessed God: That he might have all possible honour and glory from the intelligent world.

After this comfortable thanksgiving season, I frequently enjoyed freedom and enlargement, and engagedness

gagedness of soul, in prayer, and was enabled to intercede with God for my dear congregation, very often for every family, and every person, in particular; and it was often a great comfort to me, that I could pray heartily to God for those, to whom I could not speak, and whom I was not allowed to see. But at other times, my spirits were so flat and low, and my bodily vigour so much wasted, that I had scarce any affections at all.

In December I had revived so far as to be able to walk abroad, and visit friends, and seemed to be on the gaining hand with regard to my health, in the main, until Lord's Day, December 21.

After this, having perhaps taken some cold, I began to decline as to bodily health; and contiuned to do so, until the latter end of January, 1746,7.

On Lord's Day, February 1, though in a very weak and low state, I enjoyed a considerable deal of comfort and sweetness in divine things; and was enabled to plead and use arguments with God in prayer, I think, with a child like spirit. That passage of scripture occurred to my mind, and gave me great assistance, *If ye, being evil, know how to give good gifts to your children, how much more will your heavenly Father give the Holy Spirit to them that ask him?* This text I was helped to plead and insist upon; and saw the divine faithfulness engaged, for dealing with me better than any earthly parent can do with his child. This season so refreshed my soul that my body seemed also to be a gainer by it. And from this time, I began gradually to amend. And as I recovered some strength, vigour and spirit, I found at times some freedom and life in the exercises of devotion, and some longings after spirituality and a life of usefulness to the interests of the great Redeemer; although, at other times, I was awfully barren and lifeless, and out of frame for the things of God; so

that

that I was ready often to cry out, *O that it were with me as in months paſt!* O that God had taken me away in the midſt of my uſefulneſs, with a ſudden ſtroke, that I might not have been under a neceſſity of trifling away time in diverſions! O that I had never lived to ſpend ſo much precious time, in ſo poor a manner, and to ſo little purpoſe! Thus I often reflected, was grieved, aſhamed, and even confounded, ſunk and diſcouraged.

On Tueſday, February 24, I was able to ride as far as Newark, (having been confined within Elizabeth-Town almoſt four months) and the next day returned to Elizabeth-Town. My ſpirits were ſomewhat refreſhed with the ride, though my body was weary.

On Saturday, February 28, was viſited by an Indian, of my own congregation; who brought me letters, and good news of the ſober and good behaviour of my people, in general. This refreſhed my ſoul; I could not but ſoon retire, and bleſs God for his goodneſs; and found, I truſt, a truly thankful frame of ſpirit, that God ſeemed to be building up that congregation for himſelf.

On Wedneſday, March 4, I met with reproof from a friend, which, although I thought I did not deſerve it from him, yet was, I truſt, bleſſed of God to make me more tenderly afraid of ſin, more jealous over myſelf, and more concerned to keep both heart and life pure and unblamable: It likewiſe cauſed me to reflect on my paſt deadneſs, and want of ſpirituality, and to abhor myſelf, and look on myſelf moſt unworthy.

Wedneſday, March 11.—Being kept in Elizabeth-Town as a day of faſting and prayer, I was able to attend publick worſhip; which was the firſt time I was able ſo to do after December 21. O, how much weakneſs and diſtreſs did God carry me through in this space of time! *But having obtained help from him, I yet live: O that I could live more to his glory.*

Lord's Day, March 15.—Was able again to attend the publick worship, and felt some earnest desires of being restored to the ministerial work: Felt, I think, some spirit and life to speak for God.

Wednesday, March 18.—Rode out with a design to visit my people, and the next day arrived among them: Was under great dejection in my journey.

On Friday morning, I rose early, walked about among my people, and inquired into their state and concerns; and found an additional weight and burden on my spirits, upon hearing some things disagreeable. I endeavoured to go to God with my distresses, and made some kind of lamentable complaint; and in a broken manner spread my difficulties before God; but, notwithstanding, my mind continued very gloomy. About ten o'clock, I called my people together, and after having explained and sung a Psalm, I prayed with them: There was a considerable deal of affection among them; I doubt not, in some instances, that which was more than merely natural.

[This was the last interview that he ever had with his people. About eleven o'clock the same day, he left them; and the next day, came to Elizabeth-Town; his melancholy remaining still; and he continued for a considerable time under a great degree of dejection through vapoury disorders.]

Lord's Day, April 5.—It grieved me to find myself so inconceivably barren. My soul thirsted for grace: But alas, how far was I from obtaining what I saw so exceeding excellent! I was ready to despair of ever being a holy creature; and yet my soul was desirous of *following hard after God;* but never did I see myself so far from having apprehended, or being already perfect, as at this time. The Lord's supper being this day adminiſtered, I attended the ordinance: And though I ſaw in myſelf a dreadful emptineſs, and want of grace, and ſaw myſelf as it were at an infinite diſtance from that purity, which is becoming the goſpel; yet in the ſeaſon of communion, eſpecially in the time of the diſtribution of the bread, I enjoyed ſome warmth of affection, and felt a tender *love to the brethren*; and, I think, to the glorious Redeemer, the firſt-born among them. I endeavoured then to *bring forth* mine and *his enemies, and ſlay them before him*; and found great freedom in begging deliverance from this ſpiritual death, as well as in aſking divine favours for my friends, and congregation, and the church of Chriſt in general.

Friday, April 10.—Spent the forenoon in Preſbyterial buſineſs: In the afternoon rode to Elizabeth-Town; found my brother John there*: Spent ſome time in converſation with him; but was extremely weak and outdone, my ſpirits conſiderably ſunk, and my mind dejected.

Thurſday, April 16.—Was in bitter anguiſh of ſoul, in the morning, ſuch as I have ſcarce ever felt, with a ſenſe of ſin and guilt. I continued in diſtreſs the whole day, attempting to pray wherever I went; and indeed could not help ſo doing: But looked upon myſelf ſo vile, I dared not look any body in the face; and was even grieved, that anybody ſhould ſhew me any reſpect, or at leaſt, that they ſhould be ſo deceived as to think I deſerved it.

Friday, April 17.—In the evening could not but think that God helped me to draw near to the throne of grace, though moſt unworthy, and gave me a ſenſe of his favour; which gave me inexpreſſible ſupport and encouragement

---

* This brother of his had been ſent for by the Correſpondents, to take care of, and inſtruct Mr. Brainerd's congregation of Indians; he being obliged by his illneſs to be abſent from them. And he continued to take care of them until Mr. Brainerd's death: And ſince his death, was ordained his ſucceſſor in his miſſion, and to the charge of his congregation; which continued much to flouriſh under his paſtoral care.

encouragement; though I scarcely dared to hope the mercy was real, it appeared so great: Yet could not but rejoice, that ever God should discover his reconciled face to such a vile sinner. Shame and confusion, at times, covered me; and then hope and joy and admiration of divine goodness gained the ascendant. Sometimes I could not but admire the divine goodness, that the Lord had not let me fall into all the grossest vilest acts of sin and open scandal, that could be thought of; and felt myself so necessitated to praise God, that this was ready for a little while, to swallow up my shame and pressure of spirit on account of my sins.

[After this his dejection and pressure of spirit returned; and he remained under it the two next days.]

Monday, April 20.—Was in a very disordered state, and kept my bed most of the day. I enjoyed a little more comfort, than in several of the preceding days. This day I arrived at the age of twenty nine years.

Tuesday, April 21.—I set out on my journey for New-England, in order (if it might be the will of God) to recover my health by riding: Travelled to New-York, and there lodged.

[This proved his final departure from New-Jersey. He travelled slowly, and arrived among his friends, at East-Haddam, about the beginning of May. There is very little account in his Diary of the time that passed from his setting out on this journey to May 10. He speaks of his sometimes finding his heart rejoicing in the glorious perfections of God, and longing to live to him; but complains of the unfixedness of his thoughts, and their being easily diverted from divine subjects, and cries out of his leanness, as testifying against him in the loudest manner. And concerning those diversions he was obliged to use for his health, he says, that he sometimes found he could use diversions with *singleness of heart*, aiming at the glory of God; but that he also found there was a necessity of great care and watchfulness lest he should lose that spiritual temper of mind in his diversions, and left they should degenerate into what was merely selfish without any supreme aim at the glory of God in them.]

Lord's Day, May 10.—[At Had-Lime.] I could not but feel some measure of gratitude to God at this time (wherein I was much exercised) that he had always disposed me, in my ministry, to insist on the great doctrines of *regeneration, the new creature, faith in Christ, progressive sanctification, supreme love to God, living entirely to the glory of God, being not our own*, and the like. God has helped me to see in the surest manner, from time to time, that these and the like doctrines, necessarily connected with them, are the only foundation of safety and salvation for perishing sinners; and that those divine dispositions, which are consonant hereto, are that *holiness without which no man shall see the Lord:* The exercise of these godlike tempers, wherein the soul acts in a kind of concert with God, and would be and do every thing that is pleasing to God; this, I saw, would stand by the soul in a dying hour; for God must, I think, *deny himself*, if he casts away *his own image*, even the soul that is one in desires with himself.

Lord's Day, May 17.—[At Millington.] Spent the forenoon at home, being unable to attend the publick worship. At this time, God gave me some affecting sense of my own vileness, and the exceeding sinfulness of my heart; that there seemed to be nothing but sin and corruption within me. Innumerable evils compassed me about; my want of spirituality and holy living, my neglect of God, and living to myself; all the abominations of my heart and life seemed to be open to my view; and I had nothing

to

to say, but *God be merciful to me a sinner.* Towards noon, I saw, that the grace of God in Christ is infinitely free towards sinners, and such sinners as I was; I also saw, that God is the supreme good, that in his presence is life; and I began to long to die, that I might *be with him*, in a state of freedom from all sin. O, how a small glimpse of his excellency refreshed my soul! O, how worthy is the blessed God to be loved, adored, and delighted in, for himself, for his own divine excellencies.

Though I felt much dulness, and want of a spirit of prayer, this week, yet I had some glimpses of the excellency of divine things; and especially one morning, in secret meditation and prayer, the excellency and beauty of holiness, as a likeness to the glorious God, was so discovered to me, that I began to long earnestly to be in that world where holiness dwells in perfection: And I seemed to long for this perfect holiness, not so much for the sake of my own happiness (although I saw clearly that this was the greatest, yea, the only happiness of the soul) as that I might please God, live entirely to him, and glorify him to the utmost stretch of my rational powers and capacities.

[On Thursday, May 28, he came from Long-Meadow to Northampton; appearing vastly better than, by his account, he had been in the winter; indeed, so well that he was able to ride twenty five miles in a day, and to walk half a mile; and appeared cheerful, and free from melancholy: But yet, undoubtedly, at that time, in a confirmed, incurable consumption.

I had had much opportunity, before this, of particular information concerning him, from many that were well acquainted with him. But now I had opportunity for a more full acquaintance with him. I found him remarkably sociable, pleasant and entertaining in his converfation ; yet folid, favoury, fpiritual, and very profitable ; appearing meek, modeft, and humble ; far from any ftiffnefs, morofenefs, fuperftitious demurenefs, or affected fingularity in fpeech or behaviour, and feeming to naufeate all fuch things. We enjoyed not only the benefit of his converfation, but had the comfort and advantage of hearing him pray in the family, from time to time. His manner of praying was very agreeable ; moft becoming a worm of the duft, and a difciple of Chrift, addreffing an infinitely great and holy God, and Father of mercies ; not with florid expreffions, or a ftudied eloquence ; not with any intemperate vehemence, or indecent boldnefs ; at the greateft diftance from any appearance of oftentation, and from every thing that might look as though he meant to recommend himfelf to thofe that were about him, or fet himfelf off to their acceptance ; free too from vain repetitions, without impertinent excurfions, or needlefs multiplying of words. He expreffed himfelf with the ftricteft propriety, with weight, and pungency ; and yet what his lips uttered feemed to flow from the fulnefs of his heart, as deeply impreffed with a great and folemn fenfe of our neceffities, unworthinefs, and dependence, and of God's infinite greatnefs, excellency, and fufficiency, rather than merely from a warm and fruitful brain, pouring out good expreffions. And I know not, that ever I heard him fo much as afk a bleffing or return thanks at table, but there was fomething remarkable to be obferved, both in the matter and manner of performance. In his prayers he infifted much on the profperity of Zion, the advancement of Chrift's kingdom in the world, and the flourifhing and propagation of religion among the Indians. And he generally made it one petition in his prayer, that we might not outlive our ufefulnefs.]

Lord's

Lord's Day, May 31.—[At Northampton.] I had little inward sweetness in religion, for most of the week past; not realizing and beholding spiritually the glory of God, and the blessed Redeemer; from whence always arise my comforts and joys in religion, if I have any at all: And if I cannot so behold the excellencies and perfections of God, as to cause me to rejoice in him for what he is in himself, I have no solid foundation for joy. To rejoice only because I apprehend I have an interest in Christ, and shall be finally saved, is a poor mean business indeed.

[This week, he consulted doctor Mather, at my house, concerning his illness; who plainly told him, that there were great evidences of his being in a confirmed consumption, and that he could give him no encouragement, that he should ever recover. But it seemed not to occasion the least discomposure in him, nor to make any manner of alteration as to the cheerfulness and serenity of his mind, or the freedom or pleasantness of his conversation.]

Lord's Day, June 7.—My attention was greatly engaged, and my soul so drawn forth, this day, by what I heard of the exceeding preciousness of the saving grace of God's Spirit, that it almost overcame my body in my weak state: I saw that true grace is exceeding precious indeed; that it is very rare; and there is but a very small degree of it, even where the reality of it is to be found; at least, I saw this to be my case.

In the preceding week I enjoyed some comfortable seasons of meditation. One morning the cause of God appeared exceeding precious to me: The Redeemer's kingdom is all that is valuable in the earth, and I could not but long for the promotion of it in the world: I saw also that this cause is God's, that he has an infinitely greater regard and concern for it, it, than I could possibly have; that if I have any true love to this blessed interest, it is only a drop derived from that ocean. Hence, I was ready to lift up my head with joy; and conclude, well, if God's cause be so dear and precious to him, he will promote it. And thus I did as it were rest on God, that surely he would promote that which was so agreeable to his own will; though the time when must still be left to his sovereign pleasure.

[He was advised by physicians still to continue riding, as what would tend, above any other means, to prolong his life. He was at a loss for some time, which way to bend his course next; but finally determined to ride from hence to Boston; we having concluded that one of this family should go with him, and be helpful to him in his weak and low state.]

Tuesday, June 9.—I set out on a Journey from Northampton to Boston: Travelled slowly, and got some acquaintance with divers ministers on the road.

I having now continued to ride for some considerable time together, felt myself much better than I had formerly done; and I found that in proportion to the prospect I had of being restored to a state of usefulness, so I desired the continuance of life: But death appeared inconceivably more desirable to me, than a useless life; yet, blessed be God, I found my heart, at times, fully resigned and reconciled to this greatest of afflictions, if God saw fit thus to deal with me.

Friday, June 12.—I arrived in Boston this day, somewhat fatigued with my journey. Observed, that there is no rest but in God: Fatigues of body, and anxieties of mind attend us, both in town and country; no place is exempted.

Lord's Day, June 14.—I enjoyed some enlargement and sweetness in family prayer, as well as in secret

secret exercises; God appeared excellent, his ways full of pleasure and peace, and all I wanted was a spirit of holy fervency, to live to him.

Wednesday, June 17.—This and the two preceding days, I spent mainly in visiting the ministers of the town, and was treated with great respect by them.

On Thursday, June 18, I was taken exceeding ill, and brought to the gates of death, by the breaking of small ulcers in my lungs, as my physician supposed. In this extreme weak state I continued for several weeks, and was frequently reduced so low as to be utterly speechless, and not able so much as to whisper a word; and even after I had so far revived, as to walk about house, and to step out of doors, I was exercised every day with a faint turn, which continued usually four or five hours; at which times, though I was not utterly speechless, so but that I could say yes or no, yet I could not converse at all, nor speak one sentence without making stops for breath; and divers times in this season, my friends gathered round my bed, to see me breathe my last, which they looked for every moment, as I myself also did.

How I was the first day or two of my illness, with regard to the exercise of reason, I scarcely know; but I believe I was something shattered with the violence of the fever, at times: But the third day of my illness, and constantly afterwards, for four or five weeks together, I enjoyed as much serenity of mind and clearness of thought, as perhaps I ever did in my life: And I think my mind never penetrated with so much ease and freedom into divine things, as at this time; and I never felt so capable of demonstrating the truth of many important doctrines of the gospel as now. And as I saw clearly the truth of those great doctrines, which are justly stiled the DOCTRINES of GRACE; so I saw with no less clearness,

clearness, that the essence of religion consisted in the soul's conformity to God, and acting above all selfish views, for his glory, longing to be for him, to live to him, and please and honour him in all things; and this from a clear view of his infinite excellency and worthiness in himself, to be loved, adored, worshipped and served by all intelligent creatures. Thus I saw, that when a soul loves God with a supreme love, he therein acts like the blessed God himself, who most justly loves himself in that manner: So when God's interest and his are become one, and he longs that God should be glorified, and rejoices to think that he is unchangeably possessed of the highest glory and blessedness, herein also he acts in conformity to God: In like manner, when the soul is fully resigned to, and rests satisfied and contented with the divine will, here it is also conformed to God.

I saw further, that as this divine temper, whereby the soul exalts God, and treads self in the dust, is wrought in the soul by God's discovering his own glorious perfections *in the face of Jesus Christ* to it, by the special influences of the Holy Spirit, so he cannot but have regard to it, as his own work; and as it is his image in the soul, he cannot but take delight in it. Then I saw again, that if God should slight and reject his own moral image, he must needs deny himself; which he cannot do. And thus I saw the stability and infallibility of this religion, and that those who are truly possessed of it, have the most complete and satisfying evidence of their being interested in all the benefits of Christ's redemption, having their hearts *conformed to him;* and that these and these only are qualified for the employments and entertainments of God's kingdom of glory; as none but these have any relish for the business of heaven, which is to ascribe glory to God, and not to
themselves;

themselves; and that God, though I would speak it with great reverence of his name and perfections, cannot, without denying himself, finally cast such away.

The next thing I had then to do, was to inquire, whether this was my religion: And here God was pleased to help me to the most easy remembrance and critical review of what had passed in course, of a religious nature, through several of the latter years of my life: And although I could discover much corruption attending my best duties, many selfish views and carnal ends, much spiritual pride and self exaltation, and innumerable other evils which compassed me about; I say, although I now discerned the sins of my holy things, as well as other actions, yet God was pleased, as I was reviewing, quickly to put this question out of doubt, by shewing me, that I had, from time to time, acted above the utmost influence of mere self love; that I had longed to please and glorify him, as my highest happiness, &c. And this review was through grace attended with a present feeling of the same divine temper of mind; I felt now pleased to think of the glory of God, and longed for heaven as a state wherein I might glorify God perfectly, rather than a place of happiness for myself: And this feeling of the love of God in my heart, which I trust the Spirit of God excited in me afresh, was sufficient to give me full satisfaction, and make me long, as I had many times before done, to be with Christ. I did not now want any of the sudden suggestions, which many are so pleased with, that Christ and his benefits are mine, that God loves me, &c. in order to give me satisfaction about my state.

These things I saw with great clearness, when I was thought to be dying. And God gave me great concern for his church and interest in the world, at this time.

As God was pleased to afford me clearness of thought, and composure of mind, almost continually, for several weeks together, under my great weakness; so he enabled me, in some measure, to improve my time, as I hope, to valuable purposes. I was enabled to write a number of important letters to friends in remote places: And sometimes I wrote when I was speechless; i. e. unable to maintain conversation with any body; though perhaps I was able to speak a word or two so as to be heard.

[He was much visited, while in Boston, by many persons of considerable note and figure, and of the best character, and by some of the first rank: Who shewed him uncommon respect, and appeared highly pleased and entertained with his conversation. And besides his being honoured with the company and respect of ministers of the town, he was visited by several ministers from various parts of the country. And as he took all opportunities to discourse of the peculiar nature, and distinguishing characters of true spiritual and vital religion, and to bear his testimony against the various false appearances of it, consisting in, or arising from impressions on the imagination, and sudden and supposed immediate suggestions of truths, not contained in the scripture, and that faith which consists primarily in a person's believing that Christ died for him in particular, &c. So what he said was for the most part heard with uncommon attention and regard; and his discourses and reasonings appeared manifestly to have great weight and influence, with many that he conversed with, both ministers and others.

Mr. Brainerd's restoration from his extremely low state in Boston, so as to go abroad again and to travel, was very unexpected to him and his friends. My daughter, who was with him, writes thus concerning him, in a letter dated June 23. "——On Thursday, he he was very ill with a violent fever, and extreme pain in his head and breast, and, at turns, delirious. So he remained until Saturday evening, when he seemed to be in the agonies of death: The family was up with him until one or two o'clock, expecting every hour would be his last. On Sabbath day he was a little revived, his head was better, but very full of pain, and exceeding sore at his breast, much put to it for breath, &c. Yesterday he was better upon all accounts. Last night he slept but little. This morning he is much worse. Doctor Pynchon says, he has no hopes of his life; nor does he think it likely he will ever come out of the chamber; though he says he may be able to come to Northampton."

In another letter, dated June 29, she says as follows: "Mr. Brainerd has not so much pain nor fever, since I last wrote, as before: Yet he is extremely weak and low, and very faint, expecting every day will be his last. He says, it is impossible for him to live for want of life. He has hardly vigour enough to draw his breath. I went this morning into town, and when I came home, Mr. Bromfield said, he never expected I should see him alive; for he lay two hours, as they thought, dying; one could scarcely tell, whether he was alive or not; he was not able to speak, for some time: But now is much as he was before. The Doctor thinks, he will drop away in such a turn. Mr. Brainerd says, he never felt any thing so much like dissolution, as what he felt today; and says, he never had any conception of its being possible for any creature to be alive, and yet so weak as he is from day to day. Doctor Pynchon says, he should not be surprised, if he should so recover as to live half a year; nor would it surprise him, if he should die in half a day. Since I began to write, he is not so well; having had a faint turn again: Yet patient and refigned, having no diftreffing fears, but the contrary."

His phyfician, the honourable Jofeph Pynchon, Efq; when he vifited him in his extreme illnefs in Bofton, attributed his finking fo fuddenly into a ftate fo extremely low, and nigh unto death, to the breaking of ulcers, that had been long gathering in his lungs, as Mr. Brainerd himfelf intimates in a forementioned paffage in his Diary, and there difcharging and diffufing their purulent matter; which, while nature was labouring and ftruggling to throw off, that could be done no otherwife, than by gradual ftraining of it through the fmall veffels of thofe vital parts. This occafioned an high fever, and violent coughing, and threw the whole frame of nature into the utmoft diforder, and brought it near to a diffolution: But fuppofed, if the ftrength of nature held until the lungs had this way gradually cleared themfelves of this putrid matter, he might revive, and continue better, until new ulcers gathered and broke; but then would furely fink again; and that there was no hope of his recovery; but, as he expreffed himfelf to one of my neighbours, who at that time faw him in Bofton, he was as certainly a dead man, as if he was fhot through the heart.

But fo it was ordered in divine Providence, that the ftrength of nature held out through this great conflict, fo as juft to efcape the grave at that turn; and then he revived, to the aftonifhment of all that knew his cafe.

After he began to revive he was vifited by his youngeft brother, Mr. Ifrael Brainerd, a ftudent at Yale-College; who having heard of his extreme illnefs, went from thence to Bofton, in order to fee him, if he might find him alive, which he but little expected.

This vifit was attended with a mixture of joy and forrow to Mr. Brainerd. He greatly rejoiced to fee his

his brother, especially because he had desired an opportunity of some religious conversation with him before he died. But this meeting was attended with sorrow, as his brother brought to him the sorrowful tidings of his sister Spencer's death at Haddam; a sister, between whom and him had long subsisted a peculiarly dear affection, and much intimacy in spiritual matters, and whose house he used to make his home, when he went to Haddam, his native place. He had heard nothing of her sickness until this report of her death. But he had these comforts, together with the tidings, viz. a confidence of her being gone to heaven, and an expectation of his soon meeting her there. His brother continued with him until he left the town, and came with him from thence to Northampton.

Concerning the last Sabbath Mr. Brainerd spent in Boston, he writes in his Diary as follows.]

Lord's Day, July 19.—I was just able to attend publick worship, being carried to the house of God in a chaise. Heard Dr. Sewall preach, in the forenoon: Partook of the Lord's supper at this time. In this sacrament, I saw astonishing divine wisdom displayed; such wisdom as I saw required the tongues of angels and glorified saints to celebrate: It seemed to me, I never should do any thing at adoring the infinite wisdom of God discovered in the contrivance of man's redemption, until I arrived at a world of perfection; yet I could not help striving to *call upon my soul and all within me to bless the name of God.* In the afternoon, heard Mr. Prince preach. I saw more of God in the wisdom discovered in the plan of man's redemption, than I saw of any other of his perfections, through the whole day.

[He left Boston the next day. But before he came away, he had occasion to bear a very full, plain, and open testimony against that opinion, that the essence

sence of saving faith lies in believing that Christ died for me in particular, and that this is the first act of faith in a true believer's closing with Christ. He did it in a long conference he had with a gentleman, that has very publickly and strenuously appeared to defend that tenet. He had this discourse with him in the presence of a number of considerable persons, who came to visit Mr. Brainerd before he left the town, and to take their leave of him. In which debate he made this plain declaration, at the same time confirming what he said by many arguments, That the essence of saving faith was wholly left out of that definition of saving faith which that gentleman has published; and that the faith which he had defined, had nothing of God in it, nothing above nature, nor indeed above the power of the devils; and that all such as had this faith, and had no better, though they might have this to never so high a degree, would surely perish. And he declared also, that he never had greater assurance of the falseness of the principles of those that maintained such a faith, and of their dangerous and destructive tendency, or a more affecting sense of the great delusion and misery of those that depended on getting to heaven by such a faith, while they had no better, than he lately had when he was supposed to be at the point to die, and expected every minute to pass into eternity. Mr. Brainerd's discourse at this time, and the forcible reasonings by which he confirmed what he asserted, appeared to be greatly to the satisfaction of those present; as several of them took occasion expresly to manifest to him, before they took leave of him.

When this conversation was ended, having bid an affectionate farewell to his friends, he set out in the cool of the afternoon, on his journey to Northampton, attended by his brother, and my daughter

that

that went with him to Boston; and would have been accompanied out of the town by a number of gentlemen, besides that honourable person who gave him his company for some miles on that occasion, as a testimony of their esteem and respect, had not his aversion to any thing of pomp and shew prevented it.]

Saturday, July 25.—I arrived here at Northampton; having set out from Boston on Monday, about four o'clock P. M. In this journey, I rode about sixteen miles a day, one day with another. I was sometimes extremely tired and faint on the road, so that it seemed impossible for me to proceed any further: At other times I was considerably better, and felt some freedom both of body and mind.

Lord's Day, July 26.—This day I saw clearly, that I should never be happy; yea, that God himself could not make me happy, unless I could be in a capacity to please and glorify him forever: Take away this, and admit me into all the fine heavens that can be conceived of by men or angels, and I should still be miserable forever.

[Though he had so far revived, as to be able to travel thus far, yet he manifested no expectation of recovery: He supposed, as his physician did, that his being brought so near to death at Boston, was owing to the breaking of ulcers in his lungs: He told me, that he had had several such ill turns before, only not to so high a degree, but as he supposed, owing to the same cause, viz. the breaking of ulcers; and that he was brought lower and lower every time; and it appeared to him, that in his last sickness, in Boston, he was brought as low as it was possible and yet live; and that he had not the least expectation of surviving the next return of this breaking of ulcers: But still appeared perfectly calm in the prospect of death.

On Wednefday morning, the week after he came to Northampton, he took leave of his brother Ifrael, as never expecting to fee him again in this world; he now fetting out from hence on his journey to New-Haven.

When Mr. Brainerd came hither, he had fo much ftrength as to be able, from day to day, to ride out two or three miles, and to return; and fometimes to pray in the family; but from this time he gradually, but fenfibly, decayed, and became weaker and weaker.

While he was here his converfation from firft to laft was much on the fame fubjects as it had been when in Bofton: He was much in fpeaking of the nature of true religion of heart and practice, as diftinguifhed from its various counterfeits; expreffing his great concern, that the latter did fo much prevail in many places. He often manifefted his great abhorrence of all fuch doctrines and principles in religion, as in any wife favoured of, and had any though but a remote, tendency to Antinomianifm; of all fuch notions, as feemed to diminifh the neceffity of holinefs of life, or to abate men's regard to the commands of God, and a ftrict, diligent, and univerfal practice of virtue and piety, under a pretence of depreciating our works, and magnifying God's free grace. He fpake often, with much deteftation, of fuch experiences and pretended difcoveries and joys, as have nothing of the nature of fanctification in them, and do not tend to ftrictnefs, tendernefs, and diligence in religion, and meeknefs and benevolence towards mankind, and an humble behaviour: And he alfo declared, that he looked on fuch pretended humility as worthy of no regard, that was not manifefted by modefty of conduct and converfation. He fpake often, with abhorrence, of the fpirit and practice that appears among the greater part of feparatifts

at

at this day in the land, particularly those in the eastern parts of Connecticut; in their condemning and separating from the standing ministry and churches, their crying down learning, and a learned ministry, their notion of an immediate call to the work of the ministry, and the forwardness of laymen to set up themselves as publick teachers. He had been much conversant in the eastern part of Connecticut, his native place being near to it, when the same principles, notions and spirit began to operate, which have since prevailed to a greater height; and had acquaintance with some of those persons who are become heads and leaders of the separatists; he had also been conversant with persons of the same way elsewhere: And I heard him say, once and again, he knew by his acquaintance with this sort of people, that what was chiefly and most generally in repute among them as the power of godliness, was an entirely different thing from that true vital piety recommended in the scriptures, and had nothing in it of that nature. He manifested a great dislike of a disposition in persons to much noise and show in religion, and affecting to be abundant in proclaiming and publishing their own experiences: Though at the same time he did not condemn, but approved of christians' speaking of their own experiences on some occasions, and to some persons, with due modesty and discretion.

After he came hither, as long as he lived, he was much in speaking of that future prosperity of Zion, that is so often foretold and promised in the scripture: It was a theme he delighted to dwell upon; and his mind seemed to be carried forth with earnest concern about it, and intense desires, that religion might speedily and abundantly revive and flourish; though he had not the least expectation of recovery; yea, the nearer death advanced, and the more the symptoms

symptoms of its approach increased, still the more did his mind seem to be taken up with this subject. He told me, when near his end, that "he never in all his life, had his mind so led forth in desires and earnest prayers for the flourishing of Christ's kingdom on earth, as since he was brought so exceeding low at Boston." He seemed much to wonder, that there appeared no more of a disposition in ministers and people to pray for the flourishing of religion through the world; that so little a part of their prayers was generally taken up about it in their families, and elsewhere; and particularly, he several times expressed his wonder, that there appeared no more forwardness to comply with the proposal lately made, in a memorial from a number of ministers in Scotland, and sent over into America, for united extraordinary prayer, among Christ's ministers and people, for the coming of Christ's kingdom: And he sent it as his dying advice to his own congregation that they should practise agreeably to that proposal*.

Though he was constantly exceeding weak, yet there appeared in him a continual care well to improve time, and fill it up with something that might be profitable, and in some respect for the glory of God or the good of men; either profitable conversation, or writing letters to absent friends, or noting something in his Diary, or looking over his former writings, correcting them, and preparing them to be left in the hands of others at his death, or giving some directions concerning a future conducting and management of his people, or employment in secret devotions. He seemed never to be easy, however ill,

---

* His congregation, since this, have with great cheerfulness and unanimity fallen in with this advice, and have practised agreeably to the proposal from Scotland; and have at times, appeared with uncommon engagedness and fervency of spirit in their meetings and united devotions, pursuant to that proposal: Also the Presbyteries of New-York, and New-Brunswick, since this, have with one consent, fallen in with the proposal, as likewise some others of God's people in those parts.

ill, if he was not doing something for God, or in his service.

After he came hither, he wrote a preface to a Diary of the famous Mr. Shepard's, having been much urged to it by those gentlemen in Boston, who had the care of the publication : Which Diary, with his preface, has since been published,

In his Diary for Lord's Day, August 9, he speaks of longing desires after death, through a sense of the excellency of a state of perfection.

In his Diary for Lord's Day, August 16, he speaks of his having so much refreshment of soul in the house of God, that it seemed to refresh his body. And this is not only noted in his Diary, but was very observable to others; it was very apparent, not only, that his mind was exhilarated with inward consolation, but also that his animal spirits and bodily strength seemed to be remarkably restored, as though he had forgot his illness. But this was the last time that ever he attended publick worship on the Sabbath.

On Tuesday morning that week, I being absent on a journey, he prayed with my family; but not without much difficulty, for want of bodily strength : And this was the last family prayer that ever he made.

He had been wont, until now, frequently to ride out, two or three miles : But this week, on Thursday, was the last time he ever did so.]

Lord's Day, August 23.—This morning I was considerably refreshed with the thought, yea, the hope and expectation of the enlargement of Christ's kingdom; and I could not but hope, the time was at hand, when Babylon the great would fall, and rise no more : This led me to some spiritual meditations, that were very refreshing to me. I was unable to attend publick worship either part of the day;

day; but God was pleased to afford me fixedness and satisfaction in divine thoughts. Nothing so refreshes my soul, as when I can go to God, yea, to God *my exceeding joy*. When he is so, sensibly, to my soul, O, how unspeakably delightful is this!

In the week past, I had divers turns of inward refreshing; though my body was inexpressibly weak, followed continually with agues and fevers. Sometimes my soul centered in God, as my only portion; and I felt that I should be forever unhappy, if he did not reign: I saw the sweetness and happiness of being his subject, at his disposal: This made all my difficulties quickly vanish.

From this Lord's Day, viz. August 23, I was troubled very much with vapoury disorders, and could neither write nor read, and could scarcely live; although, through mercy, was not so much oppressed with heavy melancholy and gloominess, as at many other times.

[Until this week he had been wont to lodge in a room above stairs; but he now grew so weak, that he was no longer able to go up stairs and down; Friday August 28, was the last time he ever went above stairs; henceforward he betook himself to a lower room.

On Wednesday, September 2, being the day of our publick lecture, he seemed to be refreshed with seeing the neighbouring ministers that came hither to the lecture, and expressed a great desire once more to go to the house of God on that day: And accordingly rode to the meeting, and attended divine service, while the Rev. Mr. Woodbridge of Hatfield preached. He signified that he supposed it to be the last time that ever he should attend the publick worship; as it proved. And indeed it was the last time that ever he went out at our gate alive.

On the Saturday evening next following, he was unexpectedly visited by his brother, Mr. John Brainerd, who came to see him from New-Jersey. He was much refreshed by this unexpected visit, this brother being peculiarly dear to him; and he seemed to rejoice in a devout and solemn manner, to see him, and to hear the comfortable tidings he brought concerning the state of his dear congregation of Christian Indians: And a circumstance of this visit, that he was exceeding glad of, was, that his brother brought him some of his private writings from New-Jersey, and particularly his Diary that he had kept for many years past.]

Lord's Day, September 6.—I began to read some of my private writings, which my brother brought me; and was considerably refreshed, with what I met with in them.

Monday, September 7.—I proceeded farther in reading my old private writings, and found they had the same effect upon me as before: I could not but rejoice and bless God for what passed long ago, which without writing had been entirely lost.

This evening, when I was in great distress of body, my soul longed that God should be glorified: I saw there was no heaven but this. I could not but speak to the bystanders then of the only happiness, viz. pleasing God. O that I could forever live to God! The day I trust, is at hand, the perfect day: O, the day of deliverance from all sin!

Lord's Day, September 13.—I was much refreshed and engaged in meditation and writing, and found a heart to act for God. My spirits were refreshed, and my soul delighted to do something for God.

[On the evening following that Lord's Day, his feet began to appear sensibly swelled; which thenceforward swelled more and more. A symptom of his dissolution coming on.

The next day, his brother John left him, being obliged to return to New-Jerfey on fome bufinefs of great importance and neceffity; intending to return again with all poffible fpeed, hoping to fee his brother yet once more in the land of the living.

On the Thurfday of this week, September 17, was the laft time that ever he went out of his lodging room. That day, he was again vifited by his brother Ifrael, who continued with him thenceforward until his death. On that evening, he was taken with fomething of a diarrhœa; which he looked upon as another fign of his approaching death: Whereupon he expreffed himfelf thus; O, the glorious time is now coming! I have longed to ferve God perfectly: Now God will gratify thofe defires! And from time to time, at the feveral fteps and new fymptoms of the fenfible approach of his diffolution, he was fo far from being funk or damped, that he feemed to be animated, and made more cheerful; as being glad at the appearances of death's approach. He often ufed the epithet, glorious, when fpeaking of the day of his death, calling it that glorious day. And as he faw his diffolution gradually approaching, he was much in talking about it, with perfect calmnefs fpeaking of a future ftate; and alfo fettling all his affairs, very particularly and minutely giving directions concerning what he would have done in one refpect and another after he was dead. And the nearer death approached, the more defirous he feemed to be of it. He feveral times fpake of the different kinds of willingnefs to die; and fpoke of it as an ignoble, mean kind of willingnefs to die, to be willing to leave the body, only to get rid of pain; or to go to heaven only to get honour and advancement there.]

Saturday, September 19.—Near night, while I attempted to walk a little, my thoughts turned thus;

How

How infinitely sweet it is, to love God, and be all for him! Upon which it was suggested to me, You are not an angel, not lively and active. To which my whole soul immediately replied, I as sincerely desire to love and glorify God, as any angel in heaven. Upon which it was suggested again, But you are filthy, not fit for heaven. Hereupon instantly appeared the blessed robes of Christ's righteousness, which I could not but exult and triumph in; and I viewed the infinite excellency of God, and my soul even broke with longings, that God should be glorified. I thought of dignity in heaven; but instantly the thought returned, I do not go to heaven to get honour, but to give all possible glory and praise. O, how I longed that God should be glorified on earth also! O, I was made for eternity, if God might be glorified! Bodily pains I cared not for: Though I was then in extremity, I never felt easier; I felt willing to glorify God in that state of bodily distress, as long as he pleased I should continue in it. The grave appeared really sweet, and I longed to lodge my weary bones in it: But O that God might be glorified! This was the burden of all my cry. O I knew I should be active as an angel, in heaven; and that I should be stripped of my filthy garments! So that there was no objection. But O, to love and praise God more, to please him forever! This my soul panted after, and even now pants for while I write. O that God might be glorified in the whole earth. Lord, let *thy kingdom come*. I longed for a spirit of preaching to descend and rest on ministers, that they might address the consciences of men with closeness and power. I saw God had the residue of the spirit; and my soul longed it should be poured from on high. I could not but plead with God for my dear congregation, that he would preserve it, and not suffer his great name to lose its glory in
that

that work: My foul ftill longing, that God might be glorified.

[The extraordinary frame that he was in, that evening, could not be hid; *his mouth fpake out of the abundance of his heart*, expreffing in a very affecting manner much the fame things as are written in his Diary: And among very many other extraordinary expreffions, which he then uttered, were fuch as thefe; My heaven is to pleafe God, and glorify him, and give all to him, and to be wholly devoted to his glory; that is the heaven I long for; that is my religion, and that is my happinefs; and always was, ever fince I fuppofe I had any true religion; and all thofe that are of that religion, fhall meet me in heaven. I do not go to heaven to be advanced, but to give honour to God. It is no matter where I fhall be ftationed in heaven, whether I have a high or a low feat there; but to love and pleafe and glorify God is all: Had I a thoufand fouls, if they were worth any thing, I would give them all to God; but I have nothing to give, when all is done. It is impoffible for any rational creature to be happy without acting all for God: God himfelf could not make him happy any other way. I long to be in heaven, praifing and glorifying God with the holy angels: All my defire is to glorify God. My heart goes out to the burying place; it feems to me a defirable place: But O to glorify God; that is it; that is above all. It is a great comfort to me, to think that I have done a little for God in the world: O! it is but a very fmall matter; yet I have done a little; and I lament it, that I have not done more for him. There is nothing in the world worth living for, but doing good, and finifhing God's work, doing the work that Chrift did. I fee nothing elfe in the world, that can yield any fatisfaction, befides living to God, pleafing him, and doing his whole will.

My

My greateſt joy and comfort has been, to do ſomething for promoting the intereſt of religion, and the ſouls of particular perſons: And now in my illneſs, while I am full of pain and diſtreſs from day to day, all the comfort I have, is in being able to do ſome little char, or ſmall piece of work for God, either by ſomething that I ſay, or by writing, or ſome other way.

He intermingled with theſe and other like expreſſions, many pathetical counſels to thoſe that were about him; particularly to my children and ſervants. He applied himſelf to ſome of my younger children at this time; calling them to him, and ſpeaking to them one by one; ſetting before them, in a very plain manner, the nature and eſſence of true piety, and its great importance and neceſſity; earneſtly warning them not to reſt in any thing ſhort of that true and thorough change of heart, and a life devoted to God; counſelling them not to be ſlack in the great buſineſs of religion, nor in the leaſt to delay it; enforcing his counſels with this, that his words were the words of a dying man: Said he, I ſhall die here, and here I ſhall be buried, and here you will ſee my grave, and do you remember what I have ſaid to you. I am going into eternity: And it is ſweet to me to think of eternity; the endleſſneſs of it makes it ſweet: But O, what ſhall I ſay to the eternity of the wicked! I cannot mention it, nor think of it: The thought is too dreadful. When you ſee my grave, then remember what I ſaid to you while I was alive; then think with yourſelf, how that man, that lies in that grave, counſelled and warned me to prepare for death.

His body ſeemed to be marvellouſly ſtrengthened, through the inward vigour and refreſhment of his mind; ſo that, although before he was ſo weak that he could hardly utter a ſentence, yet now he continued

ued his most affecting and profitable discourse to us for more than an hour, with scarce any intermission; and said of it, when he had done, it was the last sermon that ever he should preach.

This extraordinary frame of mind continued the next day; of which he says in his Dairy as follows.]

Lord's Day, September 20.—Was still in a sweet and comfortable frame; and was again melted with desires that God might be glorified, and with longings to love and live to him. Longed for the influences of the Divine Spirit to descend on ministers, in a special manner. And O, I longed to be with God, to behold his glory, and to bow in his presence.

[It appears by what is noted in his Diary, both of this day, and the evening preceding, that his mind at this time was much impressed with a sense of the importance of the work of the ministry, and the need of the grace of God, and his special spiritual assistance in this work: And it also appeared in what he expressed in conversation; particularly in his discourse to his brother Israel, who was then a member of Yale-College at New-Haven, and had been prosecuting his studies and academical exercises there, to that end, that he might be fitted for the work of the ministry, and was now with him*. He now, and from time to time, in this his dying state, recommended to his brother, a life of self denial, of weanedness from the world, and devotedness to God, and an earnest endeavour to obtain much of the grace of God's Spirit, and God's gracious influences on his heart; representing the great need which ministers stand in of them, and the unspeakable benefit of them from his own experience. Among many

---

* This young gentleman was an ingenious, serious, studious, and hopefully truly pious person: There appeared in him many qualities giving hope of his being a great blessing in his day. But it has pleased God, since the death of his brother, to take him away also. He died that winter, at New-Haven, on Jan. 6, 1747-8. of a nervous fever, after about a fortnight's illness.

ny other expreſſions, he ſaid thus; When miniſters feel theſe ſpecial gracious influences on their hearts, it wonderfully aſſiſts them to come at the conſciences of men, and as it were to handle them with hands; whereas, without them, whatever reaſon and oratory we make uſe of, we do but make uſe of ſtumps, inſtead of hands."

Monday, September 21.—I began to correct a little volume of my private writings: God, I believe, remarkably helped me in it; my ſtrength was ſurpriſingly lengthened out, and my thoughts quick and lively, and my ſoul refreſhed, hoping it might be a work for God. O, how good, how ſweet it is, to labour for God!

Tueſday, September 22.—Was again employed in reading and correcting, and had the ſame ſucceſs, as the day before. I was exceeding weak; but it ſeemed to refreſh my ſoul, thus to ſpend time.

Wedneſday, September 23.—I finiſhed my corrections of the little piece forementioned, and felt uncommonly peaceful: It ſeemed as if I had now done all my work in this world, and ſtood ready for my call to a better. As long as I ſee any thing to be done for God, life is worth having: But O, how vain and unworthy it is, to live for any lower end! This day I indited a letter, I think, of great importance, to the Rev. Mr. Byram in New-Jerſey: O that God would bleſs and ſucceed that letter, which was written for the benefit of his church*! O that God would *purify the ſons of Levi,* that his glory may be advanced! This night, I endured a dreadful turn, wherein my life was expected ſcarce an hour or minute together. But bleſſed be God, I have enjoyed conſiderable ſweetneſs in divine things, this week, both by night and day.

Thurſday,

---

* It was concerning the qualifications of miniſters, and the examination and licenſing of candidates for the work of the miniſtry.

Thursday, September 24.—My strength began to fail exceedingly; which looked further as if I had done all my work: However, I had strength to fold and superscribe my letter. About two I went to bed, being weak and much disordered, and lay in a burning fever until night, without any proper rest. In the evening I got up, having lain down in some of my clothes; but was in the greatest distress, that ever I endured, having an uncommon kind of hiccough; which either strangled me, or threw me into a straining to vomit; and at the same time was distressed with griping pains. O, the distress of this evening! I had little expectation of my living the night through, nor indeed had any about me: And I longed for the finishing moment! I was obliged to repair to bed by six o'clock; and through mercy enjoyed some rest; but was grievously distressed at turns with the hiccough. My soul breathed after God, while the watcher was with me: When shall I come to God, even to God, my exceeding joy? O for this blessed likeness!

Friday, September 25.—This day, I was unspeakably weak, and little better than speechless all the day: However, I was able to write a little, and felt comfortably in some part of the day. O, it refreshed my soul, to think of former things, of desires to glorify God, of the pleasures of living to him! O my dear God, I am speedily coming to thee, I hope! Hasten the day, O Lord, if it be thy blessed will: O come, Lord Jesus, come quickly. Amen.*

Saturday, September 26.—I felt the sweetness of divine things, this forenoon; and had the consolation of a consciousness that I was doing something for God.

Lord's

---

* This was the last that ever he wrote in his Diary with his own hand: Though it is continued a little farther, in a broken manner; written by his brother Israel, but indited by his mouth in this his weak and dying state.

Lord's Day, September 27.—This was a very comfortable day to my foul; I think, I awoke with God. I was enabled to lift up my foul to God, early this morning; and while I had little bodily ftrength, I found freedom to lift up my heart to God for myfelf and others. Afterwards, was pleafed with the thoughts of fpeedily entering into the unfeen world.

[Early this morning, as one of the family came into the room, he expreffed himfelf thus: I have had more pleafure this morning, than all the drunkards in the world enjoy; if it were all extracted! So much did he efteem the joy of faith above the pleafures of fin.

He felt, that morning, an ufual appetite to food, with which his mind feemed to be exhilarated, as looking on it a fign of the very near approach of death; and faid upon it, I was born on a Sabbath day; and I have reafon to think I was new born on a Sabbath day; and I hope I fhall die on this Sabbath day: I fhould look upon it as a favour, if it may be the will of God that it fhould be fo: I long for the time. O, *why is his chariot fo long in coming? Why tarry the wheels of his chariots?* I am very willing to part with all: I am willing to part with my dear brother John, and never to fee him again, to go to be forever with the Lord*. O, when I go there, how will God's dear church on earth be upon my mind!

Afterwards, the fame morning, being afked how he did, he anfwered, I am almoft in eternity; I long to be there. My work is done; I have done with all my friends; all the world is nothing to me; I
long

---

* He had, before this, expreffed a defire, if it might be the will of God, to live until his brother returned from New-Jerfey: Who, when he went away, intended, if poffible, to perform his journey and return in a fortnight; hoping once more to meet his brother in the land of the living. The fortnight was now near expired, it ended the next day.

long to be in heaven, praising and glorifying God with the holy angels: All my desire is to glorify God. During the whole of these last two weeks of his life he seemed to continue in this frame of heart, loose from all the world, as having done his work, and done with all things here below, having nothing to do but to die, and abiding in an earnest desire and expectation of the happy moment, when his soul should take its flight, and go to a state of perfection of holiness, and perfect glorifying and enjoying God, manifested in a variety of expressions. He said, that the consideration of the day of death, and the day of judgment, had a long time been peculiarly sweet to him. He from time to time spake of his being willing to leave the body and the world immediately, that day, that night, and that moment, if it was the will of God. He also was much in expressing his longings that the church of Christ on earth might flourish, and Christ's kingdom here might be advanced, notwithstanding he was about to leave the earth, and should not with his eyes behold the desirable event, nor be instrumental in promoting it. He said to me, one morning as I came into the room, my thoughts have been employed on the old dear theme, the prosperity of God's church on earth. As I waked out of sleep, I was led to cry for the pouring out of God's spirit, and the advancement of Christ's kingdom, which the dear Redeemer did and suffered so much for. It is this that especially makes me long for it. He expressed much hope that a glorious advancement of Christ's kingdom was near at hand.

He once told me, that he had formerly longed for the outpouring of the spirit of God, and the glorious times of the church, and hoped they were coming; and should have been willing to have lived to promote religion at that time, if that had been the
will

will of God; but, fays he, I am willing it fhould be as it is; I would not have the choice to make for myfelf for ten thoufand worlds. He expreffed, on his death bed, a full perfuafion, that he fhould in heaven fee the profperity of the church on earth, and fhould rejoice with Chrift therein; and the confideration of it feemed to be highly pleafing and fatisfying to his mind.

He alfo ftill dwelt much on the great importance of the work of minifters of the gofpel; and expreffed his longings, that they might be filled with the fpirit of God; and manifefted much defire to fee fome of the neighbouring minifters, whom he had fome acquaintance with, and whofe fincere friendfhip he was confident of, that he might converfe freely with them on that fubject, before he died. And it fo happened, that he had opportunity with fome of them according to his defire.

Another thing that lay much on his heart, and that he fpake of, from time to time, in thefe near approaches of death, was the fpiritual profperity of his own congregation of chriftian Indians in New-Jerfey: And when he fpake of them, it was with peculiar tendernefs; fo that his fpeech would be prefently interrupted and drowned with tears.

He alfo expreffed much fatisfaction in the difpofals of Providence, with regard to the circumftances of his death; particularly that God had before his death given him the opportunity he had had in Bofton, with fo many confiderable perfons, minifters and others, to give in his teftimony for God, and againft falfe religion, and many miftakes that lead to it and promote it; and there to lay before pious and charitable gentlemen, the ftate of the Indians and their neceffities, to fo good effect; and that God had fince given him opportunity to write to them further concerning thefe affairs; and to write other letters

letters of importance, that he hoped might be of good influence with regard to the state of religion among the Indians, and elsewhere, after his death. He expressed great thankfulness to God for his mercy in these things. He also mentioned it as what he accounted a merciful circumstance of his death, that he should die here. And speaking of these things, he said, God had granted him all his desire; and signified, that now he could with the greater alacrity leave the world.]

Monday, September 28.—I was able to read, and make some few corrections in my private writings; but found I could not write, as I had done; I found myself sensibly declined in all respects. It has been only from a little while before noon, until about one or two o'clock, that I have been able to do any thing, for some time past: Yet this refreshed my heart, that I could do any thing, either publick or private, that I hoped was for God.

[This evening he was supposed to be dying: He thought so himself, and was thought so by those who were about him. He seemed glad at the appearance of the near approach of death. He was almost speechless, but his lips appeared to move; and one that sat very near him, heard him utter such expressions as these, *Come, Lord Jesus, come quickly. O, why is his chariot so long in coming!* After he revived, he blamed himself for having been too eager to be gone. And in expressing what he found in the frame of his mind at that time, he said, he then found an inexpressibly sweet love to those that he looked upon as belonging to Christ, beyond almost all that ever he felt before; so that it seemed, to use his own words, like a little piece of heaven to have one of them near him. And being asked whether he heard the prayer that was, at his desire, made with him; he said, yes, he heard every word,
and

and had an uncommon sense of the things that were uttered in that prayer, and that every word reached his heart.

On the evening of the next day, viz. Tuesday, September 29, as he lay in his bed, he seemed to be in an extraordinary frame; his mind greatly engaged in sweet meditations concerning the prosperity of Zion: There being present here at that time two young gentlemen of his acquaintance, that were candidates for the ministry, he desired us all to unite in singing a Psalm on that subject, even Zion's prosperity. And on his desire we sung a part of the ciid Psalm. This seemed much to refresh and revive him, and gave him new strength; so that, though before he could scarcely speak at all, now he proceeded, with some freedom of speech, to give his dying counsels to those two young gentlemen forementioned, relating to their preparation for, and prosecution of that great work of the ministry they were designed for; and in particular, earnestly recommending to them frequent secret fasting and prayer: And enforced his counsel with regard to this, from his own experience of the great comfort and benefit of it; which, said he, I should not mention, were it not that I am a dying person. And after he had finished his counsel, he made a prayer, in the audience of us all; wherein, besides praying for this family, for his brethren, and those candidates for the ministry, and for his own congregation, he earnestly prayed for the reviving and flourishing of religion in the world.

Until now he had every day sat up part of the day; but after this he never rose from his bed.]

Wednesday, September 30.—I was obliged to keep my bed the whole day, through weakness. However, redeemed a little time, and with the help of my brother, read and corrected about a dozen pages in my M.S. giving an account of my conversion.

Thursday,

Thursday, October 1.—I endeavoured again to do something by way of writing, but soon found my powers of body and mind utterly fail. Felt not so sweetly as when I was able to do something that I hoped would do some good. In the evening, was discomposed and wholly delirious; but it was not long before God was pleased to give me some sleep, and fully composed my mind*. O, blessed be God for his great goodness to me, since I was so low at Mr. Bromfield's, on Thursday, June 18 last past. He has, except those few minutes, given me the clear exercise of my reason, and enabled me to labour much for him, in things both of a publick and private nature; and, perhaps, to do more good than I should have done if I had been well; besides the comfortable influences of his blessed Spirit, with which he has been pleased to refresh my soul. May his name have all the glory forever and ever. Amen.

Friday, October 2.—My soul was this day, at turns, sweetly set on God: I longed to be with him, that I might behold his glory. I felt sweetly disposed to commit all to him, even my dearest friends, my dearest flock, and my absent brother, and all my concerns for time and eternity. O that his kingdom might come in the world; that they might all love and glorify him, for what he is in himself; and that the blessed Redeemer might *see of the travail of his soul and be satisfied*. O, come, Lord Jesus, come quickly. Amen†.

[The next evening we very much expected his brother John from New-Jersey; it being about a week after the time that he proposed for his return, when he went away. And though our expectations were

---

* From this time forward, he had the free use of his reason until the day before his death; excepting that at some times he appeared a little lost for a moment, at first waking out of sleep.

† Here ends his Diary: These are the last words that are written in it, either by his own hand, or by any other from his mouth.

were still disappointed, yet Mr. Brainerd seemed to continue unmoved, in the same calm and peaceful frame, that he had before manifested; as having resigned all to God, and having done with his friends, and with all things below.

On the morning of the next day, being Lord's Day, October 4, as my daughter Jerusha, who chiefly tended him, came into the room, he looked on her very pleasantly, and said, Dear Jerusha, are you willing to part with me? I am quite willing to part with you: I am willing to part with all my friends: I am willing to part with my dear brother John, although I love him the best of any creature living: I have committed him and all my friends to God, and can leave them with God. Though if I thought I should not see you, and be happy with you in another world, I could not bear to part with you. But we shall spend an happy eternity together!

In the evening, as one came into the room with a Bible in her hand, he expressed himself thus; O, that dear book! that lovely book! I shall soon see it opened! The mysteries that are in it, and the mysteries of God's providence, will be all unfolded!

His distemper now very apparently preyed on his vitals in an extraordinary manner: Not by a sudden breaking of ulcers in his lungs, as at Boston, but by a constant discharge of purulent matter, in great quantities: So that what he brought up by expectoration, seemed to be as it were mouthfuls of almost clear pus; which was attended with very great inward pain and distress.

On Tuesday, October 6, he lay for a considerable time, as if he were dying. At which time, he was heard to utter, in broken whispers, such expressions as these: He will come, he will not tarry. I shall soon be in glory. I shall soon glorify God with the angels. But after some time he revived.

The next day, viz. Wednesday, October 7, his brother John arrived, being returned from New-Jersey; where he had been detained much longer than he intended, by a mortal sickness prevailing among the christian Indians, and by some other things in their circumstances that made his stay with them necessary. Mr. Brainerd was affected and refreshed with seeing him, and appeared fully satisfied with the reasons of his delay; seeing the interest of religion and of the souls of his people required it.

The next day, Thursday, October 8, he was in great distress and agonies of body; and for the bigger part of the day, was much disordered as to the exercise of his reason. In the evening he was more composed, and had the use of his reason well; but the pain of his body continued and increased. He told me it was impossible for any to conceive of the distress he felt in his breast. He manifested much concern lest he should dishonour God, by impatience under his extreme agony; which was such, that he said, the thought of enduring it one minute longer was almost insupportable. He desired that others would be much in lifting up their hearts continually to God for him, that God would support him, and give him patience. He signified that he expected to die that night; but seemed to fear a longer delay: And the disposition of his mind with regard to death appeared still the same that it had been all along. And notwithstanding his bodily agonies, yet the interest of Zion lay still with great weight on his mind; as appeared by some considerable discourse he had that evening with the Rev. Mr. Billing, one of the neighbouring ministers, who was then present, concerning the great importance of the work of the ministry, &c. And afterwards, when it was very late in the night, he had much

very

very proper and profitable difcourfe with his brother John, concerning his congregation in New-Jerfey, and the intereft of religion among the Indians. In the latter part of the night, his bodily diftrefs feemed to rife to a greater height than ever; and he faid to thofe then about him, that it was another thing to die, than people imagined; explaining himfelf to mean that they were not aware what bodily pain and anguifh is undergone before death. Towards day, his eyes fixed; and he continued lying immoveable, until about fix o'clock in the morning, and then expired, on Friday, October 9, 1747, when his foul, as we may well conclude, was received by his dear Lord and Mafter, as an eminently faithful fervant, into that ftate of perfection of holinefs, and fruition of God, which he had fo often and fo ardently longed for; and was welcomed by the glorious affembly of the upper world, as one peculiarly fitted to join them in their bleffed employments and enjoyments.

Much refpect was fhewn to his memory at his funeral; which was on the Monday following, after a fermon preached the fame day, on that folemn occafion. His funeral was attended by eight of the neighbouring minifters, and feventeen other gentlemen of liberal education, and a great concourfe of people.]

Some further REMAINS *of the Rev. Mr.* DAVID BRAINERD.

Some SIGNS *of* GODLINESS.

The distinguishing Marks of a TRUE CHRISTIAN, *taken from one of my old Manuscripts; where I wrote as I felt and experienced, and not from any considerable degree of doctrinal knowledge or acquaintance with the sentiments of others in this point.*

1. HE has a true knowledge of the glory and excellency of God, that he is most worthy to be loved and praised for his own divine perfections. Psal. cxlv. 3.

2. God is his portion. Psal. lxxiii. 25. And God's glory, his great concern. Matth. vi. 22.

3. Holiness is his delight; nothing he so much longs for, as to be holy, as God is holy. Phil. iii. 9—12.

4. Sin is his greatest enemy. This he hates for its own nature, for what it is in itself, being contrary to a holy God. Jer. ii. 1. And consequently he hates all sin. Rom. vii. 24. 1 John iii. 9.

5. The laws of God also are his delight. Psal. cxix. 97. Rom. vii. 22. These he observes, not out of constraint, from a servile fear of hell; but they are his choice. Psal. cxix. 30. The strict observance of them is not his bondage, but his greatest liberty. Verse 45.

LETTERS,

LETTERS, *written by Mr.* BRAINERD *to his* FRIENDS.

To his Brother JOHN, *at Yale-College in New-Haven.*

KAUNAUMEEK, December 27, 1743.

DEAR BROTHER,

I LONG to fee you, and know how you fare in your journey through a world of inexpreffible forrow, where we are compaffed about with vanity, confufion and *vexation of fpirit*. I am more weary of life, I think, than ever I was. The whole world appears to me like a huge vacuum, a vaft empty fpace, whence nothing defirable, or at leaft fatisfactory, can poffibly be derived ; and I long daily to die more and more to it ; even though I obtain not that comfort from fpiritual things, which I earneftly defire. Worldly pleafures, fuch as flow from greatnefs, riches, honours, and fenfual gratifications, are infinitely worfe than none. May the Lord deliver us more and more from thefe vanities. I have fpent moft of the fall and winter hitherto in a very weak ftate of body ; and fometimes under preffing inward trials and fpiritual conflicts : But *having obtained help from God, I continue to this day ;* and am now fomething better in health, than I was fometime ago. I find nothing more conducive to a life of chriftianity, than a diligent, induftrious, and faithful improvement of precious time. Let us then faithfully perform that bufinefs, which is allotted to us by Divine Providence, to the utmoft of our bodily ftrength, and mental vigour. Why fhould we fink, and grow difcouraged, with any particular trials, and perplexities, we are called to encounter in the world ? Death and eternity are juft before us ; a

few

few tossing billows more will waft us into the world of spirits, and, we hope, through infinite grace, into endless pleasures, and uninterrupted rest and peace. Let us then *run with patience, the race set before us.* Heb. xii. 1. 2. And O that we could depend more upon the living God, and less upon our own wisdom and strength. Dear brother, may the God of all grace comfort your heart, and succeed your studies, and make you an instrument of good to his people in your day. This is the constant prayer of

Your affectionate brother,

DAVID BRAINERD.

To his Brother ISRAEL, *at Haddam.*

KAUNAUMEEK, January 21, 1743,4

MY DEAR BROTHER,

———THERE is but one thing, that deserves our highest care and most ardent desires; and that is, that we may answer the great end, for which we were made; viz. to glorify that God, who has given us our beings and all our comforts, and to do all the good we possibly can, to our fellow men, while we live in the world : And verily life is not worth the having, if it be not improved for this noble end and purpose. Yet, alas, how little is this thought of among mankind ! Most men seem to live to themselves, without much regard to the glory of God, or the good of their fellow creatures; they earnestly desire, and eagerly pursue after the riches, the honours, and the pleasures of life, as if they really supposed, that wealth, or greatness, or merriment, could make their immortal souls happy. But alas, what false and delusive dreams are these! And how miserable will those ere long be, who are not awaked out of them, to see that all their happiness

ness consists in living to God, and becoming *holy as he is holy!* O, may you never fall into the tempers and vanities, the sensuality and folly of the present world. You are, by Divine Providence, left as it were alone in a wide world, to act for yourself: Be sure then to remember, it is a world of temptation. You have no earthly parents to be the means of forming your youth to piety and virtue, by their pious examples, and seasonable counsels: Let this then excite you with greater diligence and fervency to look up to the Father of Mercies for grace and assistance against all the vanities of the world. And if you would glorify God, answer his just expectations from you, and make your own soul happy in this and the coming world, observe these few directions; though not from a father, yet from a brother who is touched with a tender concern for your present and future happiness. And,

First, Resolve upon, and daily endeavour to practise a life of seriousness, and strict sobriety. The wise man will tell you the great advantage of such a life, Ecclef. vii. 3. Think of the life of Christ; and when you can find that he was pleased with jesting and vain merriment, then you may indulge it in yourself.

Again, Be careful to make a good improvement of precious time. When you cease from labour, fill up your time in reading, meditation, and prayer: And while your hands are labouring, let your heart be employed, as much as possible, in divine thoughts.

Further, Take heed that you faithfully perform the business you have to do in the world, from a regard to the commands of God; and not from an ambitious desire of being esteemed better than others. We should always look upon ourselves as God's servants, placed in God's world, to do his work; and accordingly labour faithfully for him; not with a design to grow rich and great, but to glorify God, and do all the good we possibly can.

Again,

Again, Never expect any satisfaction or happiness from the world. If you hope for happiness in the world, hope for it from God, and not from the world. Do not think you shall be more happy, if you live to such or such a state of life, if you live to be for yourself, to be settled in the world, or if you should gain an estate in it: But look upon it that you shall then be happy, when you can be constantly employed for God, and not for yourself; and desire to live in this world, only to do and suffer what God allots to you. When you can be of the spirit and temper of angels, who are willing to come down into this lower world, to perform what God commands them, though their desires are heavenly, and not in the least set on earthly things, then you will be of that temper that you ought to have. Coloss. iii. 2.

Once more, Never think that you can live to God by your own power or strength; but always look to and rely on him for assistance, yea, for all strength and grace. There is no greater truth, than this, *That we can do nothing of ourselves;* John xv. 5. and 2 Cor. iii. 5. Yet nothing but our own experience can effectually teach it to us. Indeed we are a long time in learning, that all our strength and salvation is in God. This is a life, that I think no unconverted man can possibly live; and yet it is a life that every godly soul is pressing after, in some good measure. Let it then be your great concern, thus to devote yourself and your all to God.

I long to see you, that I may say much more to you than I now can, for your benefit and welfare; but I desire to commit you to, and leave you with the *Father of Mercies, and God of all grace;* praying that you may be directed safely through an evil world, to God's heavenly kingdom.

I am your affectionate loving brother,

DAVID BRAINERD.

To a Special Friend.

The Forks of Delaware, July 31, 1744.

—— CERTAINLY the greatest, the noblest pleasure of intelligent creatures must result from their acquaintance with the blessed God, and with their own rational and immortal souls. And O, how divinely sweet and entertaining is it, to look into our own souls, when we can find all our powers and passions united and engaged in pursuit after God, our whole souls longing and passionately breathing after a conformity to him, and the full enjoyment of him! Verily there are no hours pass away with so much divine pleasure, as those that are spent in communing with God and our own hearts. O, how sweet is a spirit of devotion, a spirit of seriousness and divine solemnity, a spirit of gospel simplicity, love, tenderness! O how desirable, and how profitable to the christian life, is a spirit of holy watchfulness, and godly jealousy over ourselves; when our souls are afraid of nothing so much as that we shall grieve and offend the blessed God, whom at such times we apprehend, or at least hope, to be a father and friend; whom we then love and long to please, rather than to be happy ourselves; or at least we delight to derive our happiness from pleasing and glorifying him! Surely this is a pious temper, worthy of the highest ambition and closest pursuit of intelligent creatures and holy christians. O how vastly superior is the pleasure, peace, and satisfaction derived from these divine frames, to that which we, alas, sometimes pursue in things impertinent and trifling! Our own bitter experience teaches us, that *in the midst of such laughter the heart is sorrowful*, and there is no true satisfaction but in God. But, alas! How shall we obtain and retain this sweet spirit of religion and devotion? Let us follow the apostle's direction, Phil.

ii. 12. and labour upon the encouragement he there mentions, verse 13. For it is God only can afford us this favour; and he will be sought to, and it is fit we should wait upon him for so rich a mercy. O, may the God of all grace afford us the grace and influences of his Divine Spirit; and help us that we may from our hearts esteem it our greatest liberty and happiness, that *whether we live, we may live to the Lord, or whether we die, we may die to the Lord;* that in life and death we may be his.

I am in a very poor state of health; I think, scarce ever poorer: But through divine goodness, I am not discontented under my weakness, and confinement to this wilderness: I bless God for this retirement. I never was more thankful for any thing, than I have been of late for the necessity I am under of self denial in many respects. I love to be a pilgrim and stranger in this wilderness: It seems most fit for such a poor, ignorant, worthless, despised creature as I. I would not change my present mission for any other business in the whole world. I may tell you freely, without vanity and ostentation, God has of late given me great freedom and fervency in prayer, when I have been so weak and feeble, my nature seemed as if it would speedily dissolve. I feel as if my all was lost, and I was undone for this world, if the poor heathen may not be converted. I feel in general, different from what I did when I saw you last; at least, more crucified to all the enjoyments of life. It would be very refreshing to me, to see you here in this desert; especially in my weak disconsolate hours: But, I think I could be content never to see you, or any of my friends again in this world, if God would bless my labours here to the conversion of the poor Indians.

I have much that I could willingly communicate to you, which I must omit, until Providence

gives us leave to see each other. In the mean time,
I rest,
Your obliged friend and servant,
DAVID BRAINERD.

To a SPECIAL FRIEND, *a Minister of the Gospel in
New-Jersey.*

The FORKS of DELAWARE, December 24, 1744.

REV. AND DEAR BROTHER,

——I HAVE little to say to you, about spiritual joys, and those blessed refreshments, and divine consolations, with which I have been much favoured in times past: But this I can tell you, that if I gain experience in no other point, yet I am sure I do in this, viz. that the present world has nothing in it to satisfy an immortal soul; and hence, that it is not to be desired for itself, but only because God may be seen and served in it: And I wish I could be more patient and willing to live in it for this end, than I can usually find myself to be. It is no virtue, I know, to desire death, only to be freed from the miseries of life: But I want that divine hope, which you observed, when I saw you last, was the very sinews of vital religion. Earth can do us no good, and if there be no hope of our doing good on earth, How can we desire to live in it? And yet we ought to desire, or at least to be resigned to tarry in it; because it is the will of our allwise Sovereign. But perhaps these thoughts will appear melancholy and gloomy, and consequently will be very undesirable to you; and therefore I forbear to add. I wish you may not read them in the same circumstances in which I write them. I have a little more to do and suffer in a dark disconsolate world; and then I hope to be as happy as you are. I should ask you to pray
for

for me, were I worth your concern. May the Lord enable us both to *endure hardness as good soldiers of Jesus Christ*; and may we *obtain mercy of God to be faithful, to the death*, in the discharge of our respective trusts.

I am your very unworthy brother,
And humble servant,
DAVID BRAINERD.

To his Brother JOHN, *at College.*

CROSWEEKSUNG, in *New-Jersey*, December 28, 1745.

VERY DEAR BROTHER,

———I AM in one continued, perpetual, and uninterrupted hurry; and Divine Providence throws so much upon me, that I do not see it will ever be otherwise. May I *obtain mercy of God to be faithful, to the death.* I cannot say, I am weary of my hurry; I only want strength and grace to do more for God, than I have ever yet done.

My dear brother, the Lord of heaven, that has carried me through many trials, bless you; bless you for time, and eternity; and fit you to do service for him in his church below, and to enjoy his blissful presence in his church triumphant. My brother, the time is short: O, let us fill it up for God: Let us count *the sufferings of this present time* as nothing, if we can but *run our race,* and *finish our course with joy.* O let us strive to live to God. I bless the Lord, I have nothing to do with earth, but only to labour honestly in it for God, until I shall *accomplish as an hireling my day.* I think I do not desire to live one minute for any thing that earth can afford. O that I could live for none but God, until my dying moment.

I am your affectionate brother,
DAVID BRAINERD.

To his Brother ISRAEL, *then a Student at Yale-College, in New-Haven.*

ELIZABETH-TOWN, *New-Jersey,* November 24, 1746.

DEAR BROTHER,

I HAD determined to make you and my other friends in New-England a visit, this fall; partly from an earnest desire I had to see you and them, and partly with a view to the recovery of my health; which has, for more than three months past, been much impaired. And in order to prosecute this design, I set out from my own people about three weeks ago, and came as far as to this place; where, my disorder greatly increasing, I have been obliged to keep house ever since, until the day before yesterday; at which time I was able to ride about half a mile, but found myself much tired with the journey. I have now no hopes of prosecuting my journey into New-England this winter, supposing my present state of health will by no means admit of it. Although I am, through divine goodness, much better than I was some days ago, yet I have not strength now to ride more than ten miles a day, if the season were warm, and fit for me to travel in. My disorder has been attended with several symptoms of a consumption; and I have been at times apprehensive, that my great change was at hand: Yet, blessed be God, I have never been affrighted; but on the contrary, at some times much delighted with a view of its approach. O the blessedness of being delivered from the clogs of flesh and sense, from a body of sin and spiritual death! O, the unspeakable sweetness of being translated into a state of complete purity and perfection! Believe me, my brother, a lively view and hope of these things will make the king of terrors himself appear agreeable. Dear brother, er, let me entreat you to keep eternity in your view, and behave yourself as becomes one that must shortly *give an account of all things done in the body.* That God may be your God, and prepare you for his service here, and his kingdom of glory hereafter, is the desire and daily prayer of

   Your affectionate loving brother,
     DAVID BRAINERD.

To his Brother ISRAEL, *at College; written in the time of his extreme illness in Boston, a few months before his death.*

       BOSTON, June 30, 1747.

MY DEAR BROTHER,

IT is from the sides of eternity I now address you. I am heartily sorry, that I have so little strength to write what I long so much to communicate to you. But let me tell you, my brother, eternity is another thing than we ordinarily take it to be in a healthful state. O how vast and boundless! O how fixed and unalterable! O, of what infinite importance is it, that we be prepared for eternity! I have been just a dying, now for more than a week; and all around me have thought me so: But in this time I have had clear views of eternity; have seen the blessedness of the godly, in some measure; and have longed to share their happy state; as well as been comfortably satisfied, that, through grace, I shall do so: But O, what anguish is raised in my mind, to think of an eternity for those who are christless, for those who are mistaken, and who bring their false hopes to the grave with them! The sight was so dreadful, I could by no means bear it: My thoughts recoiled, and I said, but under a more affecting sense than ever before, *Who can dwell with everlasting burnings!*

burnings! O, methought, that I could now see my friends, that I might warn them, to see to it, they lay their foundation for eternity sure. And you my dear brother, I have been particularly concerned for; and have wondered I so much neglected conversing with you about your spiritual state at our last meeting. O, my brother, let me then beseech you now to examine, whether you are indeed a new creature? Whether you have ever acted above self? Whether the glory of God has ever been the sweetest highest concern with you? Whether you have ever been reconciled to all the perfections of God? In a word, whether God has been your portion, and a holy conformity to him your chief delight? If you cannot answer positively, consider seriously the frequent breathings of your soul: But do not however put yourself off with a slight answer. If you have reason to think you are graceless, O give yourself and the throne of grace no rest, until God arise and save. But if the case should be otherwise, bless God for his grace, and press after holiness.

My soul longs, that you should be fitted for, and in due time go into the work of the ministry. I cannot bear to think of your going into any other business in life. Do not be discouraged, because you see your elder brothers in the ministry die early, one after another: I declare now I am dying, I would not have spent my life otherwise for the whole world. But I must leave this with God.

If this line should come to your hands soon after the date, I should be almost desirous you should set out on a journey to me: It may be, you may see me alive; which I should much rejoice in. But if you cannot come, I must commit you to the grace of God, where you are. May he be your guide and counsellor, your sanctifier, and eternal portion.

O my dear brother, flee fleshly lusts, and the enchanting amusements, as well as corrupt doctrines, of the present day; and strive to live to God.

Take this as the last line from
  Your affectionate dying brother,
    DAVID BRAINERD.

———————

To a young Gentleman, a Candidate for the Work of the Ministry, for whom he had a special friendship; also written at the same time of his great illness and nearness to death in Boston.

 VERY DEAR SIR,

HOW amazing it is, that the living, who know they must die, should notwithstanding *put far away the evil day*, in a season of health and prosperity; and live at such an awful distance from a familiarity with the grave, and the great concerns beyond it! And especially it may justly fill us with surprise, that any whose minds have been divinely enlightened, to behold the important things of eternity as they are, I say, that such should live in this manner. And yet sir, how frequently is this the case! How rare are the instances of those who live and act from day to day, as on the verge of eternity; striving to fill up all their remaining moments, in the service, and to the honour of their great Master! We insensibly trifle away time, while we seem to have enough of it; and are so strangely amused, as in a great measure to lose a sense of the holiness and blessed qualifications necessary to prepare us to be inhabitants of the heavenly paradise. But O, dear sir, a dying bed, if we enjoy our reason clearly, will give another view of things. I have now, for more than three weeks, lain under the greatest degree of weakness; the greater part of the time, expecting daily and hourly

hourly to enter into the eternal world : Sometimes have been so far gone, as to be wholly speechless, for some hours together. And O, of what vast importance has a holy spiritual life appeared to me, to be in this season! I have long'd to call upon all my friends, to make it their business to live to God; and especially all that are designed for, or engaged in the service of the sanctuary. O, dear sir, do not think it enough, to live at the rate of common Christians. Alas, to how little purpose do they often converse, when they meet together! The visits even of those who are called christians indeed, are frequently extreme barren: And conscience cannot but condemn us for the misimprovement of time, while we have been conversant with them. But the way to enjoy the divine presence, and be fitted for distinguishing service for God, is to live a life of great devotion and constant self dedication to him; observing the motions and dispositions of our own hearts, whence we may learn the corruptions that lodge there, and our constant need of help from God for the performance of the least duty. And O, dear sir, let me beseech you frequently to attend the great and precious duties of secret fasting and prayer.

I have a secret thought, from some things I have observed, that God may perhaps design you for some singular service in the world. O then labour to be prepared and qualified to do much for God. Read Mr. Edwards' piece on the affections, again and again; and labour to distinguish clearly upon experiences and affections in religion, that you may make a difference between the gold and the shining dross; I say, labour here, as ever you would be an useful minister of Christ: For nothing has put such a stop to the work of God in the late day as the false religion, the wild affections that attended it. Suffer me therefore, finally to entreat you earnestly to give yourself to prayer, to reading, and meditation on divine truths: Strive to penetrate to the bottom of them, and never be content with a superficial knowledge. By this means, your thoughts will gradually grow weighty and judicious; and you hereby will be possessed of a valuable treasure, out of which you may produce *things new and old*, to the glory of God.

And now I commend you to the grace of God; earnestly desiring, that a plentiful portion of the Divine Spirit may rest upon you; that you may live to God in every capacity of life, and do abundant service for him in publick, if it be his will; and that you may be richly qualified for the *inheritance of the saints in light.*

I scarce expect to see your face any more in the body; and therefore entreat you to accept this as the last token of love, from

Your sincerely affectionate dying friend,

DAVID BRAINERD.

P. S. I am now, at the dating of this letter, considerably recovered from what I was when I wrote it; it having lain by me some time, for want of an opportunity of conveyance: It was written in Boston. I am now able to ride a little, and so am removed into the country: But I have no more expectation of recovering, than when I wrote, though I am a little better for the present; and therefore I still subscribe myself,

Your dying friend, &c.

D. B.

AN

APPENDIX,

Containing some REFLECTIONS *and* OBSERVATIONS *on the preceding* MEMOIRS *of Mr.* BRAINERD.

I. WE have here an opportunity, as I apprehend, in a very lively inſtance, to ſee the nature of true religion; and the manner of its operation, when exemplified in a high degree and powerful exerciſe. Particularly it may be worthy to be obſerved,

1. How greatly Mr. Brainerd's religion differed from that of ſome pretenders to the experience of a clear work of ſaving converſion wrought on their hearts; who, depending and living on that, ſettle in a cold, careleſs and carnal frame of mind, and in a neglect of thorough, earneſt religion, in the ſtated practice of it. Although his convictions and converſion were in all reſpects exceeding clear and very remarkable; yet how far was he from acting as though he thought he had got through his work, when once he had obtained comfort, and ſatisfaction of his intereſt in Chriſt, and title to heaven. On the contrary, that work on his heart, by which he was brought to this, was with him evidently but the beginning of his work, his firſt entering on the great buſineſs of religion and the ſervice of God, his firſt ſetting out in his race. His work was not finiſhed, nor his race ended, until life was ended; agreeable to frequent ſcripture repreſentations of the chriſtian life. He continued preſſing forward in a conſtant

constant manner, forgetting the things that were behind, and reaching forth towards the things that were before. His pains and earnestness in the business of religion were rather increased, than diminished, after he had received comfort and satisfaction concerning the safety of his state. Those divine principles, which after this he was actuated by, of love to God, and longings and thirstings after holiness, seem to be more effectual to engage him to pains and activity in religion, than fear of hell had been before.

And as his conversion was not the end of his work, or of the course of his diligence and strivings in religion ; so neither was it the end of the work of the Spirit of God on his heart : But on the contrary, the beginning of that work ; the beginning of his spiritual discoveries, and holy views ; the first dawning of the light, which thenceforward increased more and more ; the beginning of his holy affections, his sorrow for sin, his love to God, his rejoicing in Christ Jesus, his longings after holiness. And the powerful operations of the Spirit of God in these things, were carried on, from the day of his conversion, in a continued course, to his dying day. His religious experiences, his admiration, his joy and praise, and flowing affections, did not only hold up to a considerable height for a few days, weeks or months, at first, while hope and comfort were new things with him ; and then gradually dwindle and die away, until they came to almost nothing, and so leave him without any sensible or remarkable experience of spiritual discoveries, or holy and divine affections, for months together ; as it is with many, who, after the newness of things is over, soon come to that pass, that it is again with them very much as it used to be before their supposed conversion, with respect to any present views of God's glory, of

Christ's

Christ's excellency, or of the beauty of divine things; and with respect to any present thirstings for God, or ardent outgoings of their souls after divine objects: But only now and then, they have a comfortable reflection on things they have met with in times past, and are something affected with them; and so rest easy, thinking all things are well; they have had a good clear work, and their state is safe, and they doubt not but they shall go to heaven when they die. How far otherwise was it with Mr. Brainerd, than it is with such persons! His experiences, instead of dying away, were evidently of an increasing nature. His first love and other holy affections, even at the beginning, were very great; but after months and years, became much greater, and more remarkable; and the spiritual exercises of his mind continued exceeding great, though not equally so at all times, yet usually so, without indulged remissness, and without habitual dwindling and dying away, even until his decease. They began in a time of general deadness all over the land, and were greatly increased in a time of general reviving of religion. And when religion decayed again, and a general deadness returned, his experiences were still kept up in their height, and his holy exercises maintained in their life and vigour; and so continued to be, in a general course, wherever he was, and whatever his circumstances were, among English and Indians, in company and alone, in towns and cities, and in the howling wilderness, in sickness and in health, living and dying. This is agreeable to scripture descriptions of true and right religion, and of the christian life. The change that was wrought in him at his conversion, was agreeable to scripture representations of that change which is wrought in true conversion; a great change, and an abiding change, rendering him a new man, a new creature: Not only a change as

to

to hope and comfort, and an apprehension of his own good estate; and a transient change, consisting in high flights of passing affections; but a change of nature, a change of the abiding habit and temper of his mind. Nor a partial change, merely in point of opinion, or outward reformation; much less a change from one error to another, or from one sin to another; but an universal change, both internal and external; as from corrupt and dangerous principles in religion, unto the belief of the truth, so from both the habits and ways of sin, unto universal holiness of heart and practice; from the power and service of Satan, unto God.

2. His religion did apparently and greatly differ from that of many high pretenders to religion, who are frequently actuated by vehement emotions of mind, and are carried on in a course of sudden and strong impressions, and supposed high illuminations and immediate discoveries, and at the same time are persons of a virulent zeal, *not according to knowledge.*

His convictions, preceding his conversion, did not arise from any frightful impressions on his imagination, or any external images and ideas of fire and brimstone, a sword of vengeance drawn, a dark pit open, devils in terrible shapes, &c. strongly fixed in his mind. His sight of his own sinfulness did not consist in any imagination of a heap of loathsome material filthiness within him; nor did his sense of the hardness of his heart consist in any bodily feeling in his breast something hard and heavy like a stone, nor in any imaginations whatever of such a nature.

His first discovery of God or Christ, at his conversion, was not any strong idea of any external glory or brightness, or majesty and beauty of countenance, or pleasant voice; nor was it any supposed
immediate

immediate manifeftation of God's love to him in particular; nor any imagination of Chrift's fmiling face, arms open, or words immediately fpoken to him, as by name, revealing Chrift's love to him; either words of fcripture, or any other: But a manifeftation of God's glory, and the beauty of his nature, as fupremely excellent in itfelf; powerfully drawing, and fweetly captivating his heart; bringing him to a hearty defire to exalt God, fet him on the throne, and give him fupreme honour and glory, as the king and fovereign of the univerfe; and alfo a new fenfe of the infinite wifdom, fuitablenefs and excellency of the way of falvation by Chrift; powerfully engaging his whole foul to embrace this way of falvation, and to delight in it. His firft faith did not confift in believing that Chrift loved him, and died for him, in particular. His firft comfort was not from any fecret fuggeftion of God's eternal love to him, or that God was reconciled to him, or intended great mercy for him; by any fuch texts as thefe, *Son, be of good cheer, thy fins are forgiven thee. Fear not, I am thy God,* &c. or in any fuch way. On the contrary, when God's glory was firft difcovered to him, it was without any thought of falvation as his own. His firft experience of the fanctifying and comforting power of God's Spirit did not begin in fome bodily fenfation, any pleafant warm feeling in his breaft, that he, as fome others, called the feeling the love of Chrift in him, and being full of the fpirit. How exceeding far were his experiences at his firft converfion from things of fuch a nature!

And if we look through the whole feries of his experiences, from his converfion to his death, we fhall find none of this kind.

Mr. Brainerd's religion was not felfifh and mercenary: His love to God was primarily and principally

cipally for the supreme excellency of his own nature; and not built on a preconceived notion that God loved him, had received him into favour, and had done great things for him, or promised great things to him: So his joy was joy in God, and not in himself. We see by his Diary how, from time to time, through the course of his life, his soul was filled with ineffable sweetness and comfort. But what was the spring of this strong and abiding consolation? Not so much the consideration of the sure grounds he had to think that his state was good, that God had delivered him from hell, and that heaven was his; or any thoughts concerning his own distinguished happy and exalted circumstances, as a high favourite of heaven: But the sweet meditations and entertaining views he had of divine things without himself; the affecting considerations and lively ideas of God's infinite glory, his unchangeable blessedness, his sovereignty and universal dominion; together with the sweet exercises of love to God, giving himself up to him, abasing himself before him, denying himself for him, depending upon him, acting for his glory, diligently serving him; and the pleasing prospects or hopes he had of a future advancement of the kingdom of Christ, &c.

It appears plainly and abundantly all along, from his conversion to his death, that that beauty, that sort of good, which was the great object of the new sense of his mind, the new relish and appetite given him in conversion, and thenceforward maintained and increased in his heart, was holiness, conformity to God, living to God, and glorifying him. This was what drew his heart; this was the centre of his soul; this was the ocean to which all the streams of his religious affections tended; this was the object that engaged his eager thirsting desires and earnest

pursuits:

pursuits: He knew no true excellency or happiness but this: This was what he longed for most vehemently and constantly on earth; and this was with him the beauty and blessedness of heaven; which made him so much and so often to long for that world of glory; it was to be perfectly holy, and perfectly exercised in the holy employments of heaven; thus to glorify God and enjoy him forever.

His religious illuminations, affections and comfort seemed to a great degree, to be attended with evangelical humiliation; consisting in a sense of his own utter insufficiency, despicableness and odiousness; with an answerable disposition and frame of heart. How deeply affected was he almost continually with his great defects in religion; with his vast distance from that spirituality and holy frame of mind that became him; with his ignorance, pride, deadness, unsteadiness, barrenness! He was not only affected with the remembrance of his former sinfulness, before his conversion, but with the sense of his present vileness and pollution. He was not only disposed to think meanly of himself as before God, and in comparison of him; but amongst men, and as compared with them: He was apt to think other saints better than he; yea, to look on himself as the meanest and least of saints; yea, very often, as the vilest and worst of mankind. And notwithstanding his great attainments in spiritual knowledge, yet we find there is scarce any thing that he is more frequently affected and abased with a sense of, than his ignorance.

How eminently did he appear to be of a meek and quiet spirit, resembling the lamblike, dovelike spirit of Jesus Christ! How full of love, meekness, quietness, forgiveness and mercy! His love was not merely a fondness and zeal for a party, but an universal benevolence; very often exercised in the most
sensible

sensible and ardent love to his greatest opposers and enemies. His love and meekness were not a meer pretence, and outward profession and shew; but they were effectual things, manifested in expensive and painful deeds of love and kindness; and in a meek behaviour; readily confessing faults under the greatest trials, and humbling himself even at the feet of those from whom he supposed he had suffered most; and from time to time, very frequently praying for his enemies, abhorring the thoughts of bitterness or resentment towards them. I scarcely know where to look for any parallel instance of self denial, in these respects, in the present age. He was a person of great zeal; but how did he abhor a bitter zeal, and lament it where he saw it! And though he was once drawn into some degrees of it, by the force of prevailing example, as it were in his childhood; yet how did he go about with his heart bruised and broken in pieces for it all his life after!

Of how soft and tender a spirit was he! How far were his experiences, hopes, and joys from a tendency finally to stupify and harden him, to lessen convictions and tenderness of conscience, to cause him to be less affected with present and past sins, and less conscientious with respect to future sins, more easy in the neglect of duties that are troublesome and inconvenient, more slow and partial in complying with difficult commands, less apt to be alarmed at the appearance of his own defects and transgressions, more easily induced to a compliance with carnal appetites! On the contrary, how tender was his conscience! How apt was his heart to smite him! How easily and greatly was he alarmed at the appearance of moral evil! How great and constant was his jealousy over his own heart! How strict his care and watchfulness against sin! How
deep

deep and sensible were the wounds that sin made in his conscience! Those evils that are generally accounted small, were almost an insupportable burden to him; such as his inward deficiencies, his having no more love to God, finding within himself any slackness or dulness in religion, any unsteadiness, or wandering frame of mind, &c. How did the consideration of such things as these oppress and abase him, and fill him with inward shame and confusion! His love, and hope, though they were such as cast out a servile fear of hell, yet they were such as were attended with, and abundantly cherished and promoted a reverential filial fear of God, a dread of sin, and of God's holy displeasure. His joy seemed truly to be a rejoicing with trembling. His assurance and comfort differed greatly from a false enthusiastick confidence and joy, in that it promoted and maintained mourning for sin. Holy mourning, with him, was not only the work of an hour or a day, at his first conversion; but sorrow for sin was like a wound constantly running: He was a mourner for sin all his days. He did not, after he received comfort and full satisfaction of the forgiveness of all his sins, and the safety of his state, forget his past sins, the sins of his youth, that were committed before his conversion; but the remembrance of them, from time to time, revived in his heart, with renewed grief. That in Ezek. xvi. 63. was evidently fulfilled in him, *That thou mayest remember, and be confounded, and never open thy mouth any more, because of thy shame; when I am pacified toward thee for all that thou hast done.* And how lastingly did the sins that he committed after his conversion, affect and break his heart! If he did any thing whereby he thought he had in any respect dishonoured God, and wounded the interest of religion, he had never done with calling it to mind with sorrow and bitterness;

ness; though he was assured that God had forgiven it, yet he never forgave himself: His past sorrows and fears made no satisfaction, with him; but still the wound renews and bleeds afresh, again and again. And his present sins, that he daily found in himself, were an occasion of daily sensible and deep sorrow of heart.

His religious affections and joys were not like those of some, who have rapture and mighty emotions from time to time in company; but have very little affection in retirement and secret places. Though he was of a very sociable temper, and loved the company of saints, and delighted very much in religious conversation and in social worship; yet his warmest affections, and their greatest effects on animal nature, and his sweetest joys, were in his closet devotions, and solitary transactions between God and his own soul; as is very observable through his whole course, from his conversion to his death. He delighted greatly in sacred retirements; and loved to get quite away from all the world, to converse with God alone, in secret duties.

Mr. Brainerd's experiences and comforts were very far from being like those of some persons, which are attended with a spiritual satiety, and put an end to their religious desires and longings, at least to the edge and ardency of them; resting satisfied in their own attainments and comforts, as having obtained their chief end, which is to extinguish their fears of hell, and give them confidence of the favour of God. How far were his religious affections, refreshments, and satisfactions, from such an operation and influence as this! On the contrary, how were they always attended with longings and thirstings after greater degrees of conformity to God! And the greater and sweeter his comforts were, the more vehement were his desires after holiness. For it is to be

observed,

observed, that his longings were not so much after joyful discoveries of God's love, and clear views of his title to future advancement and eternal honours in heaven; as after more of present holiness, greater spirituality, an heart more engaged for God, to love and exalt and depend on him, an ability better to serve him, to do more for his glory, and to do all that he did with more of a regard to Christ as his righteousness and strength; and after the enlargement and advancement of Christ's kingdom in the earth. And his desires were not idle wishings and wouldings, but such as were powerful and effectual, to animate him to the earnest, eager pursuit of these things, with utmost diligence, and unfainting labour and self denial. His comforts never put an end to his seeking after God, and striving to obtain his grace; but on the contrary, greatly engaged and enlarged him therein.

His religion did not consist only in experience, without practice. All his inward illuminations, affections and comforts seemed to have a direct tendency to practice, and to issue in it; and this, not merely a practice negatively good, free from gross acts of irreligion and immorality: But a practice positively holy and christian, in a serious, devout, humble, meek, merciful, charitable, and beneficent conversation; making the service of God, and our Lord Jesus Christ, the great business of life, which he was devoted to, and pursued with the greatest earnestness and diligence to the end of his days, through all trials. In him was to be seen the right way of being lively in religion. His liveliness in religion did not consist merely or mainly in his being lively with the tongue, but in deed; not in being forward in profession and outward shew, and abundant in declaring his own experiences; but chiefly in being active and abundant in the labours and duties of religion; not slothful in business, but fervent in spirit, serving the Lord, and serving his generation, according to the will of God.

It cannot be pretended, that the reason why he so much abhorred and condemned the notions and experiences of those whose first faith consists in believing that Christ is theirs, and that Christ died for them; without any previous experience of union of heart to him, for his excellency, as he is in himself, and not for his supposed love to them; and who judge of their interest in Christ, their justification, and God's love to them, not by their sanctification and the exercises and fruits of grace, but by a supposed immediate witness of the Spirit by inward suggestion; I say, it cannot be pretended, that the reason why he so much detested and condemned such opinions and experiences, was, that he was of a too legal spirit; either that he never was dead to the law, never experienced a thorough work of conviction, was never fully brought off from his own righteousness, and weaned from the old covenant, by a thorough legal humiliation; or that afterwards, he had no great degree of evangelical humiliation, not living in a deep sense of his own emptiness, wretchedness, poverty, and absolute dependence on the mere grace of God through Christ. For his convictions of sin, preceding his first consolations in Christ, were exceeding deep and thorough; his trouble and exercise of mind, by a sense of sin and misery, very great and long continued; and the light let into his mind at his conversion and in progressive sanctification, appears to have had its genuine humbling influence upon him, to have kept him low in his own eyes, not confiding in himself, but in Christ, *living by the faith of the Son of God,* and *looking for the mercy of the Lord Jesus to eternal life.*

Nor

Nor can it be pretended, that the reason why he condemned those, and other things, which this sort of people call the very height of vital religion, and the power of godliness, was, that he was a dead christian, and lived in the dark (as they express themselves) that his experiences, though they might be true, were not great; that he did not live near to God, had but a small acquaintance with him, and had but a dim sight of spiritual things. If any, after they have read the preceding account of Mr. Brainerd's life, will venture to pretend thus, they will only shew that they themselves are in the dark, and do indeed *put darkness for light, and light for darkness*.

II. The foregoing account of Mr. Brainerd's life may afford matter of conviction, that there is indeed such a thing as true experimental religion, arising from immediate divine influences, supernaturally enlightening and convincing the mind, and powerfully impressing, quickening, sanctifying, and governing the heart; which religion is indeed an amiable thing, of happy tendency, and of no hurtful consequence to human society; notwithstanding there having been so many pretences and appearances of what is called experimental vital religion, that have proved to be nothing but vain, pernicious enthusiasm.

If any insist, that Mr. Brainerd's religion was enthusiasm, and nothing but a strange heat, and blind fervour of mind, arising from the strong fancies and dreams of a notional whimsical brain; I would ask, if it be so, that such things as these are the fruits of enthusiasm, viz. a great degree of honesty and simplicity, sincere and earnest desires and endeavours to know and do whatever is right, and to avoid every thing that is wrong; an high degree of love to God, delight in the perfections of his nature, placing the

happiness of life in him; not only in contemplating him, but in being active in pleasing and serving him; a firm and undoubting belief in the Messiah, as the saviour of the world, the great prophet of God, and king of God's church; together with great love to him, delight and complacence in the way of salvation by him, and longing for the enlargement of his kingdom; earnest desires that God may be glorified, and the Messiah's kingdom advanced, whatever instruments are made use of; uncommon resignation to the will of God, and that under vast trials; great and universal benevolence to mankind, reaching all sorts of persons without distinction, manifested in sweetness of speech and behaviour, kind treatment, mercy, liberality, and earnest seeking the good of the souls and bodies of men; attended with extraordinary humility, meekness, forgiveness of injuries, and love to enemies; and a great abhorrence of a contrary spirit and practice; not only as appearing in others, but whereinsoever it had appeared in himself; causing the most bitter repentance, and brokenness of heart on account of any past instances of such a conduct: A modest, discreet and decent deportment, among superiours, inferiours and equals; a most diligent improvement of time, and earnest care to lose no part of it; great watchfulness against all sorts of sin, of heart, speech and action: And this example and these endeavours attended with most happy fruits, and blessed effects on others, in humanizing, civilizing, and wonderfully reforming and transforming some of the most brutish savages; idle, immoral, drunkards, murderers, gross idolaters, and wizards; bringing them to permanent sobriety, diligence, devotion, honesty, conscientiousness, and charity: And the foregoing amiable virtues and successful labours all ending at last in a marvellous peace, unmovable stability, calmness, and
resignation,

resignation, in the sensible approaches of death; with longing for the heavenly state; not only for the honours and circumstantial advantages of it, but above all for the moral perfections, and holy and blessed employments of it: And these things in a person indisputably of a good understanding and judgment: I say, if all these things are the fruits of enthusiasm, why should not enthusiasm be thought a desirable and excellent thing? For what can true religion, what can the best philosophy do more? If vapours and whimsey will bring men to the most thorough virtue, to the most benign and fruitful morality; and will maintain it through a course of life, attended with many trials, without affectation or self exaltation, and with an earnest constant bearing testimony against the wildness, the extravagances, the bitter zeal, assuming behaviour, and separating spirit of enthusiasts; and will do all this more effectually, than any thing else has ever done in any plain known instance that can be produced; if it be so, I say, what cause then has the world to prize and pray for this blessed whimsicalness, and these benign sort of vapours!

III. The preceding history serves to confirm those doctrines usually called the doctrines of grace. For if it be allowed that there is truth, substance, or value in the main of Mr. Brainerd's religion, it will undoubtedly follow, that those doctrines are divine: Since it is evident, that the whole of it, from beginning to end, is according to that scheme of things; all built on those apprehensions, notions, and views, that are produced and established in the mind by those doctrines. He was brought by doctrines of this kind to his awakening, and deep concern about things of a spiritual and eternal nature; and by these doctrines his convictions were maintained and carried on; and his conversion was evidently altogether agreeable

agreeable to this fcheme, but by no means agreeing with the contrary; and utterly inconfiftent with the Arminian notion of converfion or repentance. His converfion was plainly founded in a clear ftrong conviction, and undoubting perfuafion of the truth of thofe things appertaining to thefe doctrines, which Arminians moft object againft, and which his own mind had contended moft about. And his converfion was no confirming and perfecting of moral principles and habits, by ufe and practice, and his own labour in an induftrious difciplining himfelf, together with the concurring fuggeftions and confpiring aids of God's Spirit: But entirely a fupernatural work, at once turning him from darknefs to marvellous light, and from the power of fin to the dominion of divine and holy principles; an effect, in no regard produced by his ftrength or labour, or obtained by his virtue; and not accomplifhed until he was firft brought to a full conviction that all his own virtue, ftrength, labours and endeavours could never avail any thing to the producing or procuring this effect.

A very little while before, his mind was full of the fame cavils againft the doctrines of God's fovereign grace, which are made by Arminians; and his heart full even of a raging oppofition to them. And God was pleafed to perform this good work in him juft after a full end had been put to this cavilling and oppofition; after he was entirely convinced, that he was dead in fin, and was in the hands of God, as the abfolutely fovereign, unobliged, fole difpofer and author of true holinefs. God's fhewing him mercy at fuch a time, is a confirmation, that this was a preparation for mercy; and confequently, that thefe things which he was convinced of, were true: While he oppofed thefe things, he was the fubject of no fuch mercy; though he fo earneftly earneſtly ſought it, and prayed for it with ſo much painfulneſs, care and ſtrictneſs in religion: But when once his oppoſition is fully ſubdued, and he is brought to ſubmit to the truths, which he before had oppoſed, with full conviction, then the mercy he ſought for is granted, with abundant light, great evidence, and exceeding joy, and he reaps the ſweet fruits of it all his life after, and in the *valley of the ſhadow of death.*

In his converſion, he was brought to ſee the glory of that way of ſalvation by Chriſt, that is taught in what are called the doctrines of grace; and thenceforward, with unſpeakable joy and complacence, to embrace and acquieſce in that way of ſalvation. He was in his converſion, in all reſpects, brought to thoſe views, and that ſtate of mind, which theſe doctrines ſhew to be neceſſary. And if his converſion was any real converſion, or any thing beſides a mere whim, and if the religion of his life was any thing elſe but a ſeries of freaks of a whimſical mind, then this one grand principle, on which depends the whole difference between Calviniſts and Arminians, is undeniable, viz. that the grace or virtue of truly good men, not only differs from the virtue of others in degree, but even in nature and kind. If ever Mr. Brainerd was truly turned from ſin to God at all, or ever became truly religious, none can reaſonably doubt but that his converſion was at the time when he ſuppoſed it to be. The change he then experienced, was evidently the greateſt moral change that ever he paſſed under; and he was then apparently firſt brought to that kind of religion, that remarkable new habit and temper of mind, which he held all his life after. The narration ſhews it to be different, in nature and kind, from all that ever he was the ſubject of before. It was evidently wrought at once, without fitting and preparing his mind, by gradually convincing it more and more of the same truths, and bringing it nearer and nearer to such a temper: For it was soon after his mind had been remarkably full of blasphemy, and a vehement exercise of sensible enmity against God, and great opposition to those truths, which he was now brought with his whole soul to embrace, and rest in, as divine and glorious, and to place his happiness in the contemplation and improvement of. And he himself (who was surely best able to judge) declares, that the dispositions and affections, which were then given him, and thenceforward maintained in him, were most sensibly and certainly, perfectly different, in their nature, from all that ever he was the subject of before, or that he ever had any conception of. This he ever stood to and was peremptory in (as what he certainly knew) even to his death. He must be looked upon as capable of judging; he had opportunity to know: He had practised a great deal of religion before, was exceeding strict and conscientious, and had continued so for a long time; had various religious affections, with which he often flattered himself, and sometimes pleased himself as being now in a good estate. And after he had those new experiences, that began in his conversion, they were continued to the end of his life; long enough for him thoroughly to observe their nature, and compare them with what had been before. Doubtless he was *compos mentis*; and was at least one of so good an understanding and judgment, as to be pretty well capable of discerning and comparing the things that passed in his own mind.

It is further observable, that his religion all along operated in such a manner as tended to confirm his mind in the doctrines of God's absolute sovereignty, man's universal and entire dependence on God's power and grace, &c. The more his religion prevailed in his heart, and the fuller he was of divine love,

love, and of clear and delightful views of spiritual things, and the more his heart was engaged in God's service; the more sensible he was of the certainty and the excellency and importance of these truths, and the more he was affected with them, and rejoiced in them. And he declares particularly, that when he lay for a long while on the verge of the eternal world, often expecting to be in that world in a few minutes, yet at the same time enjoying great serenity of mind, and clearness of thought, and being most apparently in a peculiar manner at a distance from an enthusiastical frame, he at that time saw clearly the truth of those great doctrines of the gospel, which are justly stiled the doctrines of grace, and never felt himself so capable of demonstrating the truth of them.

So that it is very evident, Mr. Brainerd's religion was wholly correspondent to what is called the Calvinistical scheme, and was the effect of those doctrines applied to his heart: And certainly it cannot be denied, that the effect was good, unless we turn Atheists, or Deists. I would ask, whether there be any such thing in reality, as christian devotion? If there be, What is it? What is its nature? And what its just measure? Should it not be in a great degree? We read abundantly in scripture—of loving God with all the heart, with all the soul, with all the mind, and with all the strength, of delighting in God, of rejoicing in the Lord, rejoicing with joy unspeakable and full of glory, the soul's magnifying the Lord, thirsting for God, hungering and thirsting after righteousness, the soul's breaking for the longing it hath to God's judgments, praying to God with groanings that cannot be uttered, mourning for sin with a broken heart and contrite spirit, &c. How full is the book of Psalms, and other parts of scripture, of such things as these! Now wherein do these
things,

things, as expressed by, and appearing in Mr. Brainerd, either the things themselves, or their effects and fruits, differ from the scripture representations? These things he was brought to by that strange and wonderful transformation of the man, which he called his conversion. And does not this well agree with what is so often said, in Old Testament and New, concerning the giving of a new heart, creating a right spirit, a being renewed in the spirit of the mind, a being sanctified throughout, becoming a new creature, &c? Now where is there to be found an Arminian conversion or repentance, consisting in so great and admirable a change? Can the Arminians produce an instance, within this age, and so plainly within our reach and view, of such a reformation, such a transformation of a man, to scirptural devotion, heavenly mindedness, and true christian morality, in one that before lived without these things, on the foot of their principles, and through the influence of their doctrines?

And here is worthy to be considered, not only the effect of Calvinistical doctrines, as they are called, on Mr. Brainerd himself, but also the effect of the same doctrines, as taught and inculcated by him, on others. It is abundantly pretended and asserted of late, that these doctrines tend to undermine the very foundations of all religion and morality, and to enervate and vacate all reasonable motives to the exercise and practice of them, and lay invincible stumbling blocks before infidels, to hinder their embracing christianity; and that the contrary doctrines are the fruitful principles of virtue and goodness, set religion on its right basis, represent it in an amiable light, give its motives their full force, and recommend it to the reason and common sense of mankind. But where can they find an instance of so great and signal an effect of their doctrines, in bring-

ing

ing infidels, who were at such a distance from all that is civil, human, sober, rational, and christian, and so full of inveterate prejudices against these things, to such a degree of humanity, civility, exercise of reason, self denial, and christian virtue? Arminians place religion in morality: Let them bring an instance of their doctrines producing such a transformation of a people in point of morality. It is strange, if the allwise God so orders things in his providence, that reasonable and proper means, and his own means, which he himself has appointed, should in no known remarkable instance be instrumental to produce so good an effect; an effect so agreeable to his own word and mind, and that very effect for which he appointed these excellent means; that they should not be so successful as those means which are not his own, but very contrary to them, and of a contrary tendency; means that are in themselves very absurd, and tend to root all religion and virtue out of the world, to promote and establish infidelity, and to lay an insuperable stumbling block before pagans, to hinder their embracing the gospel: I say, if this be the true state of the case, it is certainly pretty wonderful, and an event worthy of some attention.

I know, that many will be ready to say, it is too soon yet to glory in the work, that has been wrought among Mr. Brainerd's Indians; it is best to wait and see the final event; it may be, all will come to nothing by and by: To which I answer, not to insist that it will not follow, according to Arminian principles, they are not now true christians, really pious and godly, though they should fall away and come to nothing, that I never supposed, every one of those Indians, who in profession renounced their heathenism and visibly embraced christianity, and have had some appearances of piety, will finally prove true converts:

converts: If two thirds, or indeed one half of them, as great a proportion as there is in the parable of the ten virgins, should perfevere; it will be fufficient to shew the work wrought among them, to have been truly admirable and glorious. But fo much of permanence of their religion has already appeared, as shews it to be fomething elfe befides an Indian humour or good mood, or any tranfient effect in the conceits, notions, and affections of thefe ignorant people, excited at a particular turn, by artful management. For it is now more than three years ago, that this work began among them, and a remarkable change appeared in many of them; fince which time the number of vifible converts has greatly increafed: And by repeated accounts, from feveral hands, they ftill generally perfevere in diligent religion and ftrict virtue. I think worthy to be here inferted, a letter from a young gentleman, a candidate for the miniftry, one of thofe appointed by the honourable Commiffioners in Bofton, as Miffionaries to the heathen of the Six Nations, fo called; who, by their order, dwelt with Mr. John Brainerd, among thefe chriftian Indians, in order to their being prepared for the bufinefs of their miffion. The letter was written from thence to his parents here in Northampton, and is as follows.

BETHEL, in *New-Jerfey*, January 14, 1747,8.

HONOURED AND DEAR PARENTS,

AFTER a long and uncomfortable journey, by reafon of bad weather, I arrived at Mr. Brainerd's the fixth of this inftant; where I defign to ftay this winter: And as yet, upon many accounts, am well fatisfied with my coming hither. The ftate and circumftances of the Indians, fpiritual and temporal, much exceed what I expected. I have endeavoured to acquaint myfelf with the ftate of the

Indians in general, with particular perfons, and with the fchool, as much as the fhort time I have been here would admit of. And notwithftanding my expectations were very much raifed, from Mr. David Brainerd's Journal, and from particular informations from him; yet I muft confefs, that in many refpects, they were not equal to that which now appears to me to be true, concerning the glorious work of divine grace amongft the Indians.

The evening after I came to town, I had opportunity to fee the Indians together, whilft the Rev. Mr. Arthur preached to them: At which time there appeared a very general and uncommon ferioufnefs and folemnity in the congregation: And this appeared to me to be the effect of an inward fenfe of the importance of divine truths, and not becaufe they were hearing a ftranger: Which was abundantly confirmed to me the next Sabbath, when there was the fame devout attendance on divine fervice, and a furprifing folemnity appearing in the performance of each part of divine worfhip. And fome, who are hopefully true chriftians, appear to have been at that time much enlivened and comforted; not from any obfervable commotions then, but from converfation afterwards: And others feemed to be under prefling concern for their fouls. I have endeavoured to acquaint myfelf with particular perfons; many of whom feem to be very humble and growing chriftians; although fome of them, as I am informed, were before their converfion moft monftroufly wicked.

Religious converfation feems to be very pleafing and delightful to many, and efpecially that which relates to the exercifes of the heart. And many here do not feem to be real chriftians only, but growing chriftians alfo; as well in doctrinal, as experimental knowledge. Befides my converfation with particular

ticular persons, I have had opportunity to attend upon one of Mr. Brainerd's catechetical lectures; where I was surprised at their readiness in answering questions which they had not been used to; although Mr. Brainerd complained much of their uncommon deficiency. It is surprising, to see this people, who, not long since were led captive by Satan at his will, and living in the practice of all manner of abominations, without the least sense even of moral honesty, yet now living soberly and regularly, and not seeking every man his own, but every man, in some sense, his neighbour's good; and to see those, who but a little while past, knew nothing of the true God, now worshipping him in a solemn and devout manner; not only in publick, but in their families and in secret; which is manifestly the case; it being a difficult thing to walk out in the woods in the morning, without disturbing persons at their secret devotion. And it seems wonderful, that this should be the case, not only with adult persons, but with children also. It is observable here, that many children; if not the children in general, retire into secret places to pray. And as far as at present I can judge, this is not the effect of custom and fashion, but of real seriousness and thoughtfulness about their souls.

I have frequently gone into the school, and have spent considerable time there amongst the children; and have been surprised to see, not only their diligent attendance upon the business of the school, but also the proficiency they have made in it, in reading and writing, and in their catechisms of divers sorts. It seems to be as pleasing and as natural to these children to have their books in their hands, as it does for many others to be at play. I have gone into an house where there has been a number of children accidentally gathered together; and observed, that
every

every one had his book in his hand, and was diligently studying of it. There is to the number of about thirty of these children, who can answer to all the questions in the assembly's catechism; and the bigger part of them are able to do it with the proofs to the fourth commandment. I wish there were many such schools: I confess, that I never was acquainted with such an one, in many respects. O that what God has done here, may prove to be the beginning of a far more glorious and extensive work of grace among the heathen.

I am your obedient and dutiful son,

JOB STRONG.

P. S. Since the date of this, I have had opportunity to attend upon another of Mr. Brainerd's catechetical lectures; and truly I was convinced, that Mr. Brainerd did not complain before of his people's defects in answering to questions proposed, without reason: For although their answers at that time exceeded my expectations very much; yet their performances at this lecture very much exceeded them.

IV. Is there not much in the preceding Memoirs of Mr. Brainerd to teach, and excite to duty, us who are called to the work of the ministry, and all that are candidates for that great work? What a deep sense did he seem to have of the greatness and importance of that work, and with what weight did it lie on his mind! How sensible was he of his own insufficiency for this work; and how great was his dependence on God's sufficiency! How solicitous, that he might be fitted for it! And to this end, how much time did he spend in prayer and fasting, as well as reading and meditation; giving himself to these things! How did he dedicate his whole life, all his powers and talents to God; and forsake and renounce the world, with all its pleasing and ensnaring enjoyments, that he might be wholly at liberty, to serve Christ in this work; and to please him who had chosen him to be a soldier, under the *Captain of our salvation !* With what solicitude, solemnity, and diligence did he devote himself to God our Saviour, and seek his presence and blessing in secret, at the time of his ordination ! And how did his whole heart appear to be constantly engaged, his whole time employed, and his whole strength spent in the business he then solemnly undertook, and was publickly set apart to ! And his history shews us the right way to success in the work of the ministry. He sought it, as a resolute soldier seeks victory, in a siege or battle; or as a man that runs a race, for a great prize. Animated with love to Christ and souls, how did he labour always fervently, not only in word and doctrine, in publick and private, but in prayers day and night, wrestling with God in secret, and travailing in birth, with unutterable groans and agonies, until Christ were formed in the hearts of the people to whom he was sent ! How did he thirst for a blessing on his ministry; and *watch for souls, as one that must give account !* How did he *go forth in the strength of the Lord God*; seeking and depending on a special influence of the Spirit to assist and succeed him ! And what was the happy fruit at last, though after long waiting, and many dark and discouraging appearances ! Like a true son of Jacob, he persevered in wrestling, through all the darkness of the night, until the breaking of the day.

And his example of labouring, praying, denying himself, and enduring hardness, with unfainting resolution and patience, and his faithful, vigilant, and prudent conduct in many other respects, which it would be too long now particularly to recite, may afford instruction to missionaries in particular.

V.

V. The foregoing account of Mr. Brainerd's life may afford inftruction to chriftians in general; as it fhews, in many refpects, the right way of practifing religion, in order to obtain the ends of it, and receive the benefits of it; or how chriftians fhould *run the race fet before them*, if they would not run in vain, or run as uncertainly, but would honour God in the world, adorn their profeffion, be ferviceable to mankind, have the comforts of religion while they live, be free from difquieting doubts and dark apprehenfions about the ftate of their fouls; enjoy peace in the approaches of death, and *finifh their courfe with joy*. In general, he much recommended, for this purpofe, the redemption of time, great diligence in the bufinefs of the chriftian life, watchfulnefs, &c. And he very remarkably exemplified thefe things.

But particularly, his example and fuccefs with regard to one duty in fpecial, may be of great ufe to both minifters and private chriftians; I mean the duty of fecret fafting. The reader has feen, how much Mr. Brainerd recommends this duty, and how frequently he exercifed himfelf in it; nor can it well have efcaped obfervation, how much he was owned and bleffed in it, and of what great benefit it evidently was to his foul. Among all the many days he fpent in fecret fafting and prayer, that he gives an account of in his Diary, there is fcarce an inftance of one, but what was either attended or foon followed with apparent fuccefs, and a remarkable bleffing, in fpecial incomes and confolations of God's Spirit; and very often, before the day was ended. But it muft be obferved, that when he fet about this duty, he did it in good earneft; ftirring up himfelf to take hold of God, and continuing *inftant in prayer*, with much of the fpirit of Jacob, who faid to the angel, *I will not let thee go, except thou blefs me*.

VI. There

VI. There is much in the preceding account to excite and encourage God's people to earneſt prayers and endeavours for the advancement and enlargement of the kingdom of Chriſt in the world. Mr. Brainerd ſat us an excellent example in this reſpect. He ſought the proſperity of Zion with all his might. He preferred Jeruſalem above his chief joy. How did his ſoul long for it, and pant after it! And how earneſtly and often did he wreſtle with God for it! And how far did he, in theſe deſires and prayers, ſeem to be carried beyond all private and ſelfiſh views! Being animated by a pure love to Chriſt, an earneſt deſire of his glory, and a diſintereſted affection to the ſouls of mankind.

As there is much in Mr. Brainerd's life to encourage chriſtians to ſeek the advancement of Chriſt's kingdom, in general; ſo there is, in particular, to pray for the converſion of the Indians on this continent, and to exert themſelves in the uſe of proper means for its accompliſhment. For it appears, that he in his unutterable longings and wreſtlings of ſoul for the flouriſhing of religion, had his mind peculiarly intent on the converſion and ſalvation of theſe people, and his heart more eſpecially engaged in prayer for them. And if we conſider the degree and manner in which he, from time to time, ſought and hoped for an extenſive work of grace among them, I think we have reaſon to hope, that the wonderful things, which God wrought among them by him, are but a forerunner of ſomething yet much more glorious and extenſive of that kind; and this may juſtly be an encouragement, to well diſpoſed charitable perſons, to *honour the Lord with their ſubſtance*, by contributing, as they are able, to promote the ſpreading of the goſpel among them; and this alſo may incite and encourage gentlemen who are incorporated, and intruſted with the care and diſpoſal of

thoſe

those liberal benefactions, which have already been made by pious persons, to that end; and likewise the missionaries themselves, that are or may be employed; and it may be of direction unto both, as to the proper qualifications of missionaries, and the proper measures to be taken in order to their success.

One thing in particular, I would take occasion from the foregoing history to mention and propose to the consideration of such as have the care of providing and sending missionaries among savages; viz. Whether it would not ordinarily be best to send two together? It is pretty manifest, that Mr. Brainerd's going, as he did, alone into the howling wilderness, was one great occasion of such a prevailing of melancholy on his mind; which was his greatest disadvantage. He was much in speaking of it himself, when he was here in his dying state; and expressed himself, to this purpose, that none could conceive of the disadvantage a missionary in such circumstances was under, by being alone; especially as it exposed him to discouragement and melancholy: And spoke of the wisdom of Christ in sending forth his disciples by two and two; and left it as his dying advice to his brother, never to go to Susquehannah, to travel about in that remote wilderness, to preach to the Indians there, as he had often done, without the company of a fellow missionary.

VII. One thing more may not be unprofitably observed in the preceding account of Mr. Brainerd; and that is the special and remarkable disposal of Divine Providence, with regard to the circumstances of his last sickness and death.

Though he had been long infirm, his constitution being much broken by his fatigues and hardships; and though he was often brought very low by illness, before he left Kaunaumeek, and also while he lived at the Forks of Delaware; yet his life was preserved

until he had seen that which he had so long and
greatly defired and fought; a glorious work of grace
among the Indians, and had received the wifhed for
bleffing of God on his labours. Though as it were
in deaths oft, yet he lived to behold the happy fruits
of the long continued travail of his foul and labour
of his body, in the wonderful converfion of many of
the heathen, and the happy effect of it in the great
change of their converfation, with many circumftances which afforded a fair profpect of the continuance
of God's bleffing upon them : Thus he did not depart, *until his eyes had seen God's salvation*.

Though in that winter that he lay fick at Mr.
Dickinfon's in Elizabeth-Town, he continued for a
long time in an extremely low ftate, fo that his life
was almoft defpaired of, and his ftate was fometimes fuch that it was hardly expected he would
live a day to an end; yet his life was fpared a while
longer ; he lived to fee his brother arrived in New-
Jerfey, being come to fucceed him in the care of his
Indians ; and he himfelf had opportunity to affift in
his examination and introduction into his bufinefs ;
and to commit the conduct of his dear people to one
whom he well knew, and could put confidence in, and
ufe freedom with in giving him particular inftructions
and charges, and under whofe care he could leave
his congregation with great cheerfulnefs.

The providence of God was remarkable in fo ordering of it, that before his death he fhould take a
journey into New-England, and go to Bofton :
Which was, in many refpects, of very great and
happy confequence to the intereft of religion, and
efpecially among his own people. By this means,
as has been obferved, he was brought into acquaintance with many perfons of note and influence, minifters and others, belonging both to the town and various parts of the country ; and had opportunity,

under

under the best advantages, to bear a testimony for God and true religion, and against those false appearances of it that have proved most pernicious to the interests of Christ's kingdom in the land. And the providence of God is particularly observable in this circumstance of the testimony he there bore for true religion, viz. That he there was brought so near the grave, and continued for so long a time on the very brink of eternity; and from time to time looked on himself, and was looked on by others, as just leaving the world; and that in these circumstances he should be so particularly directed and assisted in his thoughts and views of religion, to distinguish between the true and the false, with such clearness and evidence; and that after this he should be unexpectedly and surprisingly restored and strengthened, so far as to be able to converse freely; and have such opportunity, and special occasions to declare the sentiments he had in these, which were, to human apprehension, his dying circumstances; and to bear his testimony concerning the nature of true religion, and concerning the mischievous tendency of its most prevalent counterfeits and false appearances; as things he had a special, clear, distinct view of at that time, when he expected in a few minutes to be in eternity; and the certainty and importance of which were then, in a peculiar manner, impressed on his mind.

Among the happy consequences of his going to Boston, were those liberal benefactions that have been mentioned, which were made by pious disposed persons, for the maintaining and promoting the interest of religion among his people: And also the meeting of a number of gentlemen in Boston, of note and ability, to consult upon measures for that purpose; who were excited, by their acquaintance and conversation with Mr. Brainerd, and by the account of the great things God had wrought by his miniftry, to unite themfelves, that by their joint endeavours and contributions they might promote the kingdom of Chrift, and the fpiritual good of their fellow creatures, among the Indians in New-Jerfey, and elfewhere.

The providence of God was obfervable in his going to Bofton at a time when not only the honourable Commiffioners were feeking miffionaries to the Six Nations; but juft after his Journal, which gives an account of his labours and fuccefs among the Indians, had been received and fpread in Bofton: Whereby his name was known, and the minds of ferious people were well prepared to receive his perfon, and the teftimony he there gave for God; to exert themfelves for the upholding and promoting the intereft of religion in his congregation, and amongft the Indians elfewhere; and to regard his judgment concerning the qualifications of miffionaries, &c. If he had gone there the fall before, when he had intended to have made his journey into New-England, but was prevented by a fudden great increafe of his illnefs, it would not have been likely to have been in any meafure to fo good effect: And alfo if he had not been unexpectedly detained in Bofton: For when he went from my houfe, he intended to make but a very fhort ftay there: But Divine Providence, by his being brought fo low there, detained him long; thereby to make way for the fulfilling its own gracious defigns.

The providence of God was remarkable in fo ordering, that although he was brought fo very near the grave in Bofton, that it was not in the leaft expected he would ever come alive out of his chamber; yet he wonderfully revived, and was preferved feveral months longer: So that he had opportunity to fee, and fully to converfe with both his younger brethren

On the preceding Memoirs.

ren before he died; which was a thing he greatly defired; and efpecially to fee his brother John, with whom was left the care of his congregation; that he might by him be fully informed of their ftate, and might leave with him fuch inftructions and directions as were requifite in order to their fpiritual welfare, and to fend to them his dying charges and counfels. And he had alfo an opportunity, by means of this fufpenfion of his death, to find and recommend a couple of perfons fit to be employed as miffionaries to the Six Nations, as had been defired of him.

Although it was the pleafure of a fovereign God, that he fhould be taken away from his congregation, the people that he had begotten through the gofpel, who were fo dear to him; yet it was granted to him, that before he died he fhould fee them well provided for, every way.: He faw them provided for with one to inftruct them, and take care of their fouls; his own brother, whom he could confide in: He faw a good foundation laid for the fupport of the fchool among them; thofe things that before were wanting in order to it, being fupplied: And he had the profpect of a charitable fociety being eftablifhed, of able and well difpofed perfons, who feem to make the fpiritual intereft of his congregation their own; whereby he had a comfortable view of their being well provided for, for the future: And he had alfo opportunity to leave all his dying charges with his fucceffor in the paftoral care of his people, and by him to fend his dying counfels to them. Thus God granted him to fee all things happily fettled, or in a hopeful way of being fo; before his death, with refpect to his dear people. And whereas not only his own congregation, but the fouls of the Indians in North-America in general, were very dear to him, and he had greatly fet his heart on the propagating and extending the kingdom of Chrift among them ; God was pleafed to grant to him, however it was his will that he fhould be taken away, and fo fhould not be the immediate inftrument of their inftruction and converfion, yet that before his death, he fhould fee unexpected extraordinary provifion made for this alfo. And it is remarkable, that God not only allowed him to fee fuch provifion made for the maintaining the intereft of religion among his own people, and the propagation of it elfewhere ; but honoured him by making him the means or occafion of it. So that it is very probable, however Mr. Brainerd, during the laft four months of his life, was ordinarily in an extremely weak and low ftate, very often fcarcely able to fpeak ; yet that he was made the inftrument or means of much more good in that fpace of time, than he would have been if he had been well, and in full ftrength of body. Thus God's power was manifefted in his weaknefs, and the life of Chrift was manifefted in his mortal flefh.

Another thing wherein appears the merciful difpofal of Providence with refpect to his death, was, that he did not die in the wildernefs, among the favages, at Kaunaumeek, or the Forks of Delaware, or at Sufquehannah ; but in a place where his dying behaviour and fpeeches might be obferved and remembered, and fome account given of them for the benefit of furvivors ; and alfo where care might be taken of him in his ficknefs, and proper honours done him at his death.

The providence of God is alfo worthy of remark, in fo overruling and ordering the matter, that he did not finally leave abfolute orders for the entire fuppreffing of his private papers ; as he had intended and fully refolved, infomuch that all the importunity of his friends could fcarce reftrain him from doing

ing it, when fick at Bofton. And one thing relating to this is peculiarly remarkable, viz. that his brother, a little before his death, fhould come from the Jerfeys unexpected, and bring his Diary to him, though he had received no fuch order. So that he had opportunity of accefs to thefe his referved papers, and for reviewing the fame; without which, it appears, he would at laft have ordered them to be wholly fuppreffed: But after this, he the more readily yielded to the defires of his friends, and was willing to leave them in their hands, to be difpofed of as they thought might be moft for God's glory: By which means, *he being dead, yet fpeaketh*, in thefe Memoirs of his life, taken from thofe private writings: Whereby it is to be hoped he may ftill be as it were the inftrument of much promoting the intereft of religion in this world; the advancement of which he fo much defired, and hoped would be accomplifhed after his death.

If thefe circumftances of Mr. Brainerd's death be duly confidered, I doubt not but they will be acknowledged as a notable inftance of God's fatherly care, and covenant faithfulnefs towards them that are devoted to him, and faithfully ferve him while they live; whereby he never fails nor forfakes them, but is with them living and dying; fo that *whether they live, they live to the Lord; or whether they die, they die to the Lord;* and both in life and death they are owned and taken care of as his. Mr. Brainerd himfelf, as was before obferved, was much in taking notice, when near his end, of the merciful circumftances of his death; and faid, from time to time, that God had granted him all his defire.

And I would not conclude my obfervations on the merciful circumftances of Mr. Brainerd's death, without acknowledging with thankfulnefs, the gracious difpenfation of Providence to me and my family, in so ordering, that he (though the ordinary place of his abode was more than two hundred miles distant) should be cast hither, to my house, in his last sickness, and should die here: So that we had opportunity for much acquaintance and conversation with him, and to shew him kindness in such circumstances, and to see his dying behaviour, to hear his dying speeches, to receive his dying counsels, and to have the benefit of his dying prayers. May God in infinite mercy grant that we may ever retain a proper remembrance of these things, and make a due improvement of the advantages we have had in these respects! The Lord grant also, that the foregoing account of Mr. Brainerd's life and death may be for the great spiritual benefit of all that shall read it, and prove a happy means of promoting the revival of true religion in these parts of the world.

AMEN.

Mirabilia Dei inter Indicos,

OR THE

RISE AND PROGRESS

OF A REMARKABLE

WORK OF GRACE

AMONG A NUMBER OF THE

INDIANS,

IN THE PROVINCES OF NEW-JERSEY AND PENNSYLVANIA,

JUSTLY REPRESENTED IN A

JOURNAL

KEPT BY ORDER OF THE HONOURABLE SOCIETY, IN SCOTLAND, FOR PROPAGATING CHRISTIAN KNOWLEDGE.

WITH SOME GENERAL REMARKS.

By DAVID BRAINERD,

MINISTER OF THE GOSPEL, AND MISSIONARY FROM THE SAID SOCIETY.

PUBLISHED, AT THE FIRST, BY THE REVEREND AND WORTHY CORRESPONDENTS OF THE SAID SOCIETY.

NOW REPUBLISHED, WITH SOME DIMINUTION WHERE THE MATTER WAS LESS INTERESTING, BY THE EDITOR.

Instead of the thorn, shall come up the fir tree ; and instead of the brier, shall come up the myrtle tree : And it shall be to the Lord for a name, for an everlasting sign that shall not be cut off. *Isaiah* lv. 13.

I am sought of them that asked not for me : I am found of them that sought me not : I said, Behold me, behold me, to a nation that was not called by my name. *Isaiah* lxv. 1.

All thy works shall praise thee, O Lord, and thy saints shall bless thee ; they shall speak of the glory of thy kingdom, and talk of thy power. *Psalm* cxlv. 10, 11.

PRINTED AT *WORCESTER*, MASSACHUSETTS,

By LEONARD WORCESTER.

MDCCXCIII.

THE

RISE and PROGRESS, &c.

CROSWEEKSUNG, *in* New-Jerſey, *June* 19, 1745.

HAVING ſpent moſt of my time for more than a year paſt, amongſt the Indians in the Forks of Delaware in Pennſylvania ; and having in that time made two journeys to Suſquehannah river, far back in that province, in order to treat with the Indians there, reſpecting chriſtianity ; and not having had any conſiderable appearance of ſpecial ſucceſs in either of thoſe places, which damped my ſpirits, and was not a little diſcouraging to me ; upon hearing that there was a number of Indians in and about a place called (by the Indians) Croſweekſung, in New-Jerſey, near fourſcore miles ſoutheaſt-ward from the Forks of Delaware, I determined to make them a viſit, and ſee what might be done towards the chriſtianizing of them ; and accordingly arrived among them this day.

I found very few perſons at the place I viſited, and perceived the Indians in theſe parts were very much ſcattered, there being not more than two or three families in a place, and theſe ſmall ſettlements ſix, ten, fifteen, twenty and thirty miles, and ſome more, from the place I was then at : However, I preached to thoſe few I found, who appeared well

diſpoſed

difposed, and not inclined to object and cavil, as the Indians had frequently done otherwhere.

When I had concluded my difcourfe, I informed them (there being none but a few women and children) that I would willingly vifit them again the next day. Whereupon they readily fet out and travelled ten or fifteen miles, in order to give notice to fome of their friends at that diftance. Thefe women, like the woman of Samaria, feemed defirous that others might *fee the man that told them what they had done* in their lives paft, and the mifery that attended their idolatrous ways.

June 20.—Vifited and preached to the Indians again as I propofed. Numbers more were gathered at the invitations of their friends, who heard me the day before. Thefe alfo appeared as attentive, orderly and well difpofed as the others. And none made any objection, as Indians in other places have ufually done.

June 22.—Preached to the Indians again. Their number, which at firft confifted of about feven or eight perfons, was now increafed to near thirty.

There was not only a folemn attention among them, but fome confiderable impreffions (it was apparent) were made upon their minds by divine truths. Some began to feel their mifery and perifhing ftate, and appeared concerned for a deliverance from it.

Lord's Day, June 23.—Preached to the Indians, and fpent the day with them. Their number ftill increafed; and all, with one confent, feemed to rejoice in my coming among them. Not a word of oppofition was heard from any of them againft chriftianity, although in times paft, they had been as oppofite to any thing of that nature, as any Indians whatfoever. And fome of them, not many months before, were enraged with my interpreter

becaufe

because he attempted to teach them something of christianity.

June 24.—Preached to the Indians at their desire, and upon their own motion. To see poor pagans desirous of hearing the gospel of Christ, animated me to discourse to them, although I was now very weakly, and my spirits much exhausted. They attended with the greatest seriousness and diligence; and there was some concern for their souls' salvation, apparent among them.

June 27.—Visited and preached to the Indians again. Their number now amounted to about forty persons. Their solemnity and attention still continued; and a considerable concern for their souls became very apparent among sundry of them.

June 28.—The Indians being now gathered a considerable number of them, from their several and distant habitations, requested me to preach twice a day to them, being desirous to hear as much as they possibly could while I was with them. I cheerfully complied with their motion, and could not but admire the goodness of God, who, I was persuaded, had inclined them thus to inquire after the way of salvation.

June 29.—Preached again twice to the Indians. Saw, as I thought, the hand of God very evidently, and in a manner somewhat remarkable, making provision for their subsistence together, in order to their being instructed in divine things. For this day and the day before, with only walking a little way from the place of our daily meeting, they killed three deer, which were a seasonable supply for their wants, and without which, it seems, they could not have subsisted together in order to attend the means of grace.

Lord's Day, June 30.—Preached twice this day also. Observed yet more concern and affection among the poor heathens than ever: So that they

even

even conftrained me to tarry yet longer with them ; although my conftitution was exceedingly worn out, and my health much impaired by my late fatigues and labours, and efpecially by my late journey to Sufquehannah in May laft, in which I lodged on the ground for feveral weeks together.

July 1.—Preached again, twice, to a very ferious and attentive affembly of Indians, they having now learned to attend the worfhip of God, with chriftian decency in all refpects.

There were now between forty and fifty perfons of them prefent, old and young.

I fpent fome confiderable time in difcourfing with them in a more private way, inquiring of them what they remembered of the great truths that had been taught them from day to day ; and may juftly fay it was amazing to fee how they had received and retained the inftructions given them, and what a meafure of knowledge fome of them had acquired in a few days.

July 2.—Was obliged to leave thefe Indians at Crofweekfung, thinking it my duty, as foon as health would admit, again to vifit thofe at the Forks of Delaware. When I came to take leave of them, and fpoke fomething particularly to each of them, they all earneftly inquired when I would come again, and expreffed a great defire of being further inftructed. And of their own accord agreed, that when I fhould come again, they would all meet and live together during my continuance with them. And that they would do their utmoft endeavours to gather all the other Indians in thefe parts that were yet further remote. And when I parted, one told me with many tears, fhe wifhed God would change her heart ! Another that fhe wanted to find Chrift ! And an old man that had been one of their chiefs, wept bitterly with concern for his foul. I then promifed promised them to return as speedily as my health and business elsewhere would admit, and felt not a little concerned at parting, lest the good impressions then apparent upon numbers of them, might decline and wear off, when the means came to cease; and yet could not but hope that he who, I trusted, had begun a good work among them, and who I knew did not stand in need of means to carry it on, would maintain and promote it in the absence of them; although at the same time I must confess, that I had so often seen such encouraging appearances among the Indians otherwhere prove wholly abortive, and it appeared the favour would be so great, if God should now, after I had passed through so considerable a series of almost fruitless labours and fatigues, and after my rising hopes had been so often frustrated among these poor pagans, give me any special success in my labours with them, that I could not believe, and scarce dared to hope that the event would be so happy, and scarce ever found myself more suspended between hope and fear, in any affair, or at any time, than this.

This encouraging disposition and readiness to receive instruction, now apparent among these Indians, seems to have been the happy effect of the conviction that one or two of them met with some time since at the Forks of Delaware, who have since endeavoured to shew their friends the evil of idolatry, &c. And although the other Indians seemed but little to regard, but rather to deride them, yet this, perhaps has put them into a thinking posture of mind, or at least, given them some thoughts about christianity, and excited in some of them a curiosity to hear, and so made way for the present encouraging attention. An apprehension that this might be the case here, has given me encouragement that God may in such a manner bless the means I have used with Indians in other places, where there is as yet no appearance of it. If so, may his name have the glory of it; for I have learned by experience that he only can open the ear, engage the attention, and incline the heart of poor benighted prejudiced pagans to recieve instruction.

FORKS *of* DELAWARE, *in* Pennsylvania, 1745.

Lord's Day, July 14.—Discoursed to the Indians twice, several of whom appeared concerned, and were, I have reason to think, in some measure convinced by the Divine Spirit, of their sin and misery: So that they wept much the whole time of divine service.

Afterwards discoursed to a number of white people then present.

July 18.—Preached to my people, who attended diligently, beyond what had been common among these Indians: And some of them appeared concerned for their souls.

Lord's Day, July 21.—Preached to the Indians first, then to a number of white people present, and in the afternoon to the Indians again. Divine truths seemed to make very confiderable impressions upon several of them, and caused the tears to flow freely.

Afterwards I baptized my interpreter and his wife, who were the first I baptized among the Indians.

They are both persons of some experimental knowledge in religion; have both been awakened to a solemn concern for their souls; have, to appearance, been brought to a sense of their misery and undoneness in themselves; have both appeared to be comforted with divine consolations; and it is apparent both have passed a great, and I cannot but hope a saving change.

July

July 23.—Preached to the Indians, but had few hearers: Those who are constantly at home seem of late to be under some serious impressions of a religious nature.

July 26.—Preached to my people, and, afterwards, baptized my interpreter's children.

Lord's Day, July 28.—Preached again, and perceived my people, at least some of them, more thoughtful than ever about their souls' concerns. I was told by some, that seeing my interpreter and others baptized made them more concerned than any thing they had ever seen or heard before. There was indeed a considerable appearance of divine power amongst them at the time that ordinance was administered. May that divine influence spread and increase more abundantly.

July 30.—Discoursed to a number of my people, and gave them some particular advice and direction, being now about to leave them for the present, in order to renew my visit to the Indians in New-Jersey. They were very attentive to my discourse, and earnestly desirous to know when I designed to return to them again.

CROSWEEKSUNG, *in* New-Jersey, 1745.

August 3.—Having visited the Indians in these parts in June last, and tarried with them some considerable time, preaching almost daily; at which season God was pleased to pour upon them a spirit of awakening and concern for their souls, and surprisingly to engage their attention to divine truths. I now found them serious, and a number of them under deep concern for an interest in Christ: Their convictions of their sinful and perishing state having, in my absence from them, been much promoted by the labours and endeavours of the Rev. Mr. William

am Tennent, to whom I had advised them to apply for direction, and whose house they frequented much while I was gone. I preached to them this day with some view to Rev. xxii. 17. *And whosoever will, let him take the water of life freely:* Though I could not pretend to handle the subject methodically among them.

The Lord, I am persuaded, enabled me, in a manner somewhat uncommon, to set before them the Lord Jesus Christ as a kind and compassionate Saviour, inviting distressed and perishing sinners to accept everlasting mercy. And a surprising concern soon became apparant among them. There were about twenty adult persons together, (many of the Indians at remote places not having as yet had time to come since my return hither) and not above two that I could see with dry eyes.

Lord's Day, August 4.—Being invited by a neighbouring minister to assist in the administration of the Lord's supper, I complied with his request, and took the Indians along with me, not only those that were together the day before, but many more that were coming to hear me, so that there were near fifty in all, old and young.

They attended the several discourses of the day, and some of them that could understand English, were much affected, and all seemed to have their concern in some measure raised.

Now a change in their manners began to appear very visible. In the evening when they came to sup together, they would not taste a morsel until they had sent to me to come and ask a blessing on their food, at which time sundry of them wept, especially when I minded them how they had in times past eat their feasts in honour to devils, and neglected to thank God for them.

August

August 5.—After a sermon had been preached by another minister, I preached, and concluded the publick work of the solemnity from John vii. 37. And in my discourse addressed the Indians in particular, who sat by themselves in a part of the house; at which time one or two of them were struck with deep concern, as they afterwards told me, who had been little affected before: Others had their concern increased to a considerable degree. In the evening (the greater part of them being at the house where I lodged) I discoursed to them, and found them universally engaged about their souls' concern, inquiring *what they should do to be saved!* And all their conversation among themselves turned upon religious matters, in which they were much assisted by my interpreter, who was with them day and night.

This day, there was one woman, that had been much concerned for her soul, ever since she first heard me preach in June last, who obtained comfort, I trust, solid and well grounded: She seemed to be filled with love to Christ, at the same time behaved humbly and tenderly, and appeared afraid of nothing so much as of grieving and offending him whom her soul loved.

August 6.—In the morning I discoursed to the Indians at the house where we lodged: Many of them were then much affected, and appeared surprisingly tender, so that a few words about their souls' concerns would cause the tears to flow freely, and produce many sobs and groans.

In the afternoon, they being returned to the place where I have usually preached amongst them, I again discoursed to them there. There were about fifty five persons in all, about forty that were capable of attending divine service with understanding: I insisted upon 1 John iv. 10. *Herein is love,* &c.

They feemed eager of hearing; but there appeared nothing very remarkable, except their attention, until near the clofe of my difcourfe, and then divine truths were attended with a furprifing influence, and produced a great concern among them. There was fcarce three in forty that could refrain from tears and bitter cries. They all, as one, feemed in an agony of foul to obtain an intereft in Chrift; and the more I difcourfed of the love and compaffion of God in fending his Son to fuffer for the fins of men; and the more I invited them to come and partake of his love, the more their diftrefs was aggravated, becaufe they felt themfelves unable to come.

It was furprifing to fee how their hearts feemed to be pierced with the tender and melting invitations of the gofpel, when there was not a word of terror fpoken to them.

There were this day two perfons that obtained relief and comfort, which (when I came to difcourfe with them particularly) appeared folid, rational and fcriptural. After I had inquired into the grounds of their comfort, and faid many things I thought proper to them, I afked them what they wanted God to do further for them. They replied, they wanted Chrift fhould wipe their hearts quite clean, &c.

Surprifing were now the doings of the Lord, that I can fay no lefs of this day, and I need fay no more of it, than that the *arm of the Lord* was powerfully and marvelloufly *revealed* in it.

Auguft 8.—In the afternoon I preached to the Indians; their number was now about fixty five perfons, men, women, and children: I difcourfed from Luke xiv. 16.—23. and was favoured with uncommon freedom in my difcourfe.

There was much vifible concern among them while I was difcourfing publickly; but afterwards, when

when I spoke to one and another more particularly, whom I percieved under much concern, the power of God seemed to descend upon the assembly *like a rushing mighty wind,* and with an astonishing energy bore down all before it.

I stood amazed at the influence that seized the audience almost universally, and could compare it to nothing more aptly, than the irresistible force of a mighty torrent, or swelling deluge, that with its insupportable weight and pressure, bears down and sweeps before it whatever is in its way! Almost all persons of all ages were bowed down with concern together, and scarce one was able to withstand the shock of this surprising operation! Old men and women, who had been drunken wretches for many years, and some little children, not more than six or seven years of age, appeared in distress for their souls, as well as persons of middle age. And it was apparent these children (some of them at least) were not merely frighted with seeing the general concern; but were made sensible of their danger, the badness of their hearts, and their misery without Christ, as some of them expressed it. The most stubborn hearts were now obliged to bow. A principal man among the Indians, who before was most secure and self righteous, and thought his state good because he knew more than the generality of the Indians had formerly done, and who with a great degree of confidence the day before, told me, he had been a christian more then ten years, was now brought under solemn concern for his soul, and wept bitterly. Another man considerable in years, who had been a murderer, a *powwow,* (or cunjurer) and a notorious drunkard, was likewise brought now to cry for mercy with many tears, and to complain much that he could be no more concerned when he saw his danger so very great.

Y 4 They

They were almoſt univerſally praying and crying for mercy in every part of the houſe, and many out of doors, and numbers could neither go nor ſtand: Their concern was ſo great, each one for himſelf, that none ſeemed to take any notice of thoſe about them, but each prayed as freely for themſelves, and (I am apt to think) were, to their own apprehenſion, as much retired as if they had been every one by themſelves in the thickeſt deſert: Or, I believe rather that they thought nothing about any but themſelves, and their own ſtates, and ſo were every one praying apart, although all together.

It ſeemed to me there was now an exact fulfilment of that propheſy, Zech. xii. 10. 11. 12. for there was now *a great mourning, like the mourning of Hadadrimmon*. And each ſeemed to *mourn apart*. Methought this had a near reſemblance to the day of God's power, mentioned Joſh. x. 14. for I muſt ſay, I never ſaw *any day like it* in all reſpects: It was a day wherein, I am perſuaded, the Lord did much to deſtroy the kingdom of darkneſs among this people.

This concern in general was moſt rational and juſt. Thoſe who had been awakened any conſiderable time, complained more eſpecially of the badneſs of their hearts; and thoſe newly awakened of the badneſs of their lives and actions paſt; and all were afraid of the anger of God, and of everlaſting miſery as the deſert of their ſins.

Some of the white people, who came out of curioſity to hear what this babbler would ſay, to the poor ignorant Indians, were much awakened, and ſome appeared to be wounded with a view of their periſhing ſtate.

Thoſe who had lately obtained relief, were filled with comfort at this ſeaſon; they appeared calm and compoſed, and ſeemed to rejoice in Chriſt Jeſus: And ſome of them took their diſtreſſed friends by
the

the hand, telling them of the goodnefs of Chrift, and the comfort that is to be enjoyed in him, and thence invited them to come and give up their hearts to him. And I could obferve fome of them in the moft honeft and unaffected manner (without any defign of being taken notice of) lifting up their eyes to heaven as if crying for mercy, while they faw the diftrefs of the poor fouls around them.

There was one remarkable inftance of awakening this day, that I cannot but take particular notice of here. A young Indian woman, who, I believe, never knew before that fhe had a foul, nor ever thought of any fuch thing, hearing that there was fomething ftrange among the Indians, came, it feems, to fee what was the matter: She in her way to the Indians, called at my lodgings, and when I told her I defigned prefently to preach to the Indians, laughed and feemed to mock; but went however to them. I had not proceeded far in my publick difcourfe before fhe felt effectually that fhe had a foul, and before I had concluded my difcourfe, was fo convinced of her fin and mifery, and fo diftreffed with concern for her foul's falvation, that fhe feemed like one pierced through with a dart, and cried out inceffantly. She could neither go nor ftand, nor fit on her feat without being held up. After publick fervice was over, fhe lay flat on the ground, praying earneftly, and would take no notice of, nor give any anfwer to any that fpoke to her. I hearkened to hear what fhe faid, and perceived the burden of her prayer to be, *Guttummaukalummeh wechaumeh kmeleh Ndah*, i.e. *Have mercy on me, and help me to give you my heart.* And thus fhe continued praying inceffantly for many hours together.

This was indeed a furprifing day of God's power, and feemed enough to convince an atheift of the truth, importance and power of God's word.

Auguſt

August 9.—Spent almost the whole day with the Indians, the former part of it in discoursing to many of them privately, and especially to some who had lately received comfort, and endeavouring to inquire into the grounds of it, as well as to give them some proper instructions, cautions and directions.

In the afternoon discoursed to them publickly. There were now present about seventy persons, old and young. I opened and applied the parable of the sower, Matth. xiii. Was enabled to discourse with much plainness, and found afterwards that this discourse was very instructive to them. There were many tears among them while I was discoursing publickly, but no considerable cry: Yet some were much affected with a few words spoken from Matth. xi. 28. with which I concluded my discourse. But while I was discoursing near night to two or three of the awakened persons, a divine influence seemed to attend what was spoken to them in a powerful manner, which caused the persons to cry out in anguish of soul, although I spoke not a word of terror, but on the contrary, set before them the fulness and allsufficiency of Christ's merits, and his willingness to save all that came to him; and thereupon pressed them to come without delay.

The cry of these was soon heard by others, who, though scattered before, immediately gathered round. I then proceeded in the same strain of gospel invitation, until they were all melted into tears and cries, except two or three; and seemed in the greatest distress to find and secure an interest in the great Redeemer. Some who had but little more than a ruffle made in their passions the day before, seemed now to be deeply affected and wounded at heart: And the concern in general appeared near as prevalent as it was the day before. There was indeed a very great mourning among them, and yet every one
seemed

seemed to mourn apart. For so great was their concern, that almost every one was praying and crying for himself, as if none had been near, *Guttummaukalummeh, guttummaukalummeh* : i. e. *Have mercy upon me, have mercy upon me,* was the common cry.

It was very affecting to see the poor Indians, who the other day were hollowing and yelling in their idolatrous feasts and drunken frolicks, now crying to God with such importunity for an interest in his dear Son.

Lord's Day, August 11.—Discoursed in the forenoon from the parable of the prodigal son, Luke xv. Observed no such remarkable effect of the word upon the assembly as in days past. There were numbers of careless spectators of the white people; some Quakers and others.

In the afternoon I discoursed upon a part of St. Peter's sermon, Acts ii. And at the close of my discourse to the Indians, made an address to the white people, and divine truths seemed then to be attended with power both to English and Indians. Several of the white heathen were awakened, and could not longer be idle spectators, but found they had souls to save or lose as well as the Indians, and a great concern spread through the whole assembly, so that this also appeared to be a day of God's power, especially towards the conclusion of it, as well as several of the former, although the influence attending the word seemed scarce so powerful now, as in some days past.

The number of the Indians, old and young, was now upwards of seventy, and one or two were newly awakened this day, who never had appeared to be moved with concern for their souls before.

Those that had obtained relief and comfort, and had given hopeful evidences of having passed a saving

ing change, appeared humble and devout, and behaved in an agreeable and chriftian manner. I was refrefhed to fee the tendernefs of confcience manifeft in fome of them; one inftance of which I cannot but take notice of. Perceiving one of them very forrowful in the morning, I inquired into the caufe of her forrow, and found the difficulty was, fhe had been angry with her child the evening before, and was now exercifed with fears, left her anger had been inordinate and finful, which fo grieved her that fhe waked and began to fob before daylight, and continued weeping for feveral hours together.

Auguft 14.—Spent the day with the Indians. There was one of them who had fome time fince put away his wife, as is common among them, and taken another woman, and being now brought under fome ferious impreffions, was much concerned about that affair in particular, and feemed fully convinced of the wickednefs of that practice, and earneftly defirous to know what God would have him do in his prefent circumftances. When the law of God refpecting marriage had been opened to them, and the caufe of his leaving his wife inquired into; and when it appeared fhe had given him no juft occafion by unchaftity to defert her, and that fhe was willing to forgive his paft mifconduct, and to live peaceably with him for the future, and that fhe moreover infifted on it as her right to enjoy him; he was then told, that it was his indifpenfable duty to renounce the woman he had laft taken, and receive the other who was his proper wife, and live peaceably with her during life; with which he readily and cheerfully complied, and thereupon publickly renounced the woman he had laft taken, and publickly promifed to live with and be kind to his wife during life, fhe alfo promifing the fame to him. And here appeared a clear demonftration of the
power

power of God's word upon their hearts. I suppose a few weeks before the whole world could not have persuaded this man to a compliance with christian rules in this affair.

August 16.—Spent considerable time in conversing privately with sundry of the Indians. Found one that had got relief and comfort, after pressing concern, and could not but hope, when I came to discourse particularly with her, that her comfort was of the right kind.

In the afternoon preached to them from John vi. 26.—34. Toward the close of my discourse, divine truths were attended with considerable power upon the audience, and more especially after publick service was over, when I particularly addressed sundry distressed persons.

There was a great concern for their souls spread pretty generally among them : But especially there were two persons newly awakened to a sense of their sin and misery, one of whom was lately come, and the other had all along been very attentive, and desirous of being awakened, but could never before have any lively view of her perishing state. But now her concern and spiritual distress was such, that I thought, I had never seen any more pressing. Sundry old men were also in distress for their souls ; so that they could not refrain from weeping and crying out aloud, and their bitter groans were the most convincing as well as affecting evidence of the reality and depth of their inward anguish. God is powerfully at work among them ! True and genuine convictions of sin are daily promoted in many instances, and some are newly awakened from time to time; although some few, who felt a commotion in their passions in days past, seem now to discover that their hearts were never duly affected. I never saw the work of God appear so independent of means as at this time. I difcourfed to the people, and fpoke what I fuppofe had a proper tendency to promote convictions, and God's manner of working upon them appeared fo entirely fupernatural, and above means, that I could fcarce believe he ufed me as an inftrument, or what I fpake as means of carrying on his work: For it feemed, as I thought, to have no connexion with, or dependence upon means in any refpect. And although I could not but continue to ufe the means I thought proper for the promotion of the work, yet God feemed, as I apprehended, to work entirely without them: So that I feemed to do nothing, and indeed to have nothing to do, but to *ftand ftill and fee the falvation of God*, and found myfelf obliged and delighted to fay, *Not unto us*, not unto inftruments and means, *but to thy name be glory*. God appeared to work entirely alone, and I faw no room to attribute any part of this work to any created arm.

Lord's Day, Auguft 25.—Preached in the forenoon from Luke xv. 3.—7. There being a multitude of white people prefent, I made an addrefs to them at the clofe of my difcourfe to the Indians: But could not fo much as keep them orderly; for fcores of them kept walking and gazing about, and behaved more indecently than any Indians I ever addreffed; and a view of their abufive conduct fo funk my fpirits, that I could fcarce go on with my work.

In the afternoon difcourfed from Rev. iii. 20. At which time the Indians behaved ferioufly, though many others were vain.

Afterwards baptized twenty five perfons of the Indians, fifteen adults and ten children. Moft of the adults I have comfortable reafon to hope are renewed perfons, and there was not one of them but what I entertained fome hopes of in that refpect,
though

though the case of two or three of them appeared more doubtful.

After the crowd of spectators was gone, I called the baptized persons together, and discoursed to them in particular, at the same time inviting others to attend, minded them of the solemn obligations they were now under to live to God, warned them of the evil and dreadful consequences of careless living, especially after this publick profession of christianity; gave them directions for their future conduct, and encouraged them to watchfulness and devotion, by setting before them the comfort and happy conclusion of a religious life. This was a desirable and sweet season indeed! Their hearts were engaged and cheerful in duty, and they rejoiced that they had in a publick and solemn manner dedicated themselves to God. Love seemed to reign among them! They took each other by the hand with tenderness and affection, as if their hearts were knit together, while I was discoursing to them: And all their deportment toward each other was such, that a serious spectator might justly be excited to cry out with admiration, Behold how they love one another! Sundry of the other Indians at seeing and hearing these things, were much affected and wept bitterly, longing to be partakers of the same joy and comfort that these discovered by their very countenances as well as conduct.

August 26.—Preached to my people from John vi. 51.—55. After I had discoursed some time, I addressed those in particular who entertained hopes that they were *passed from death to life*. Opened to them the persevering nature of those consolations Christ gives his people, and which I trusted he had bestowed upon some in that assembly, shewed them that such have already the *beginnings of eternal life*, verse 54. and that their heaven shall speedily be completed, &c.

I no sooner began to discourse in this strain, but the dear christians in the congregation began to be melted with affection to, and desire of the enjoyment of Christ, and of a state of perfect purity. They wept affectionately and yet joyfully, and their tears and sobs discovered brokenness of heart, and yet were attended with real comfort and sweetness, so that this was a tender, affectionate, humble, delightful melting, and appeared to be the genuine effect of a spirit of adoption, and very far from that spirit of bondage that they not long since laboured under. The influence seemed to spread from these through the whole assembly, and there quickly appeared a wonderful concern among them. Many who had not yet found Christ as an allsufficient Saviour, were surprisingly engaged in seeking after him. It was indeed a lovely and very desirable assembly. Their number was now about ninety five persons, old and young, and almost all affected either with joy in Christ Jesus, or with utmost concern to obtain an interest in him.

Being fully convinced it was now my duty to take a journey far back to the Indians on Susquehannah river, it being now a proper season of the year to find them generally at home, after having spent some hours in publick and private discourses with my people, I told them that I must now leave them for the present, and go to their brethren far remote and preach to them: That I wanted the Spirit of God should go with me, without whom nothing could be done to any good purpose among the Indians, as they themselves had had opportunity to see and observe by the barrenness of our meetings at some times, when there was much pains taken to effect and awaken sinners, and yet to little or no purpose: And asked them if they could not be willing to spend the remainder of the day in prayer for me, that God would

would go with me, and fucceed my endeavours, for the converfion of thofe poor fouls. They cheerfully complied with the motion, and foon after I left them, the fun being then about an hour and half high at night, they began, and continued praying all night, until break of day, or very near, never miftrufting, they tell me, until they went out and viewed the ftars, and faw the morning ftar a confiderable height, that it was later than common bed time. Thus eager and unwearied were they in their devotions! A remarkable night it was, attended, as my interpreter tells me, with a powerful influence upon thofe who were yet under concern, as well as thofe that had received comfort.

There were, I truft, this day, two diftreffed fouls brought to the enjoyment of folid comfort in him, in whom the weary find reft.

It was likewife remarkable that, this day, an old Indian, who has all his days been an obftinate idolater, was brought to give up his rattles, which they ufe for mufick in their idolatrous feafts and dances, to the other Indians, who quickly deftroyed them, and this without any attempt of mine, in the affair, I having faid nothing to him about it; fo that it feemed it was nothing but juft the power of God's word, without any particular application to this fin, that produced this effect. Thus God has begun, thus he has hitherto furprifingly carried on, a work of grace amongft thefe Indians. May the glory be afcribed to him, who is the fole author of it.

FORKS of DELAWARE, *in* Pennfylvania, 1745.

September 19.—Vifited an Indian town called Juneauta, fituate on an ifland in Sufquehannah. Was much difcouraged with the temper and behaviour of the Indians here, although they appeared friendly when I was with them the last spring, and then gave me encouragement to come and see them again: But they now seemed resolved to retain their pagan notions, and persist in their idolatrous practices.

September 20.—Visited the Indians again at Juneauta Island, and found them almost universally very busy in making preparations for a great sacrifice and dance. Had no opportunity to get them together in order to discourse with them about christianity, by reason of their being so much engaged about their sacrifice. My spirits were much sunk with a prospect so very discouraging, and especially seeing I had now no interpreter but a pagan, who was as much attached to idolatry as any of them, (my own interpreter having left me the day before, being obliged to attend upon some important business otherwhere, and knowing that he could neither speak nor understand the language of these Indians) so that I was under the greatest disadvantages imaginable; however, I attempted to discourse privately with some of them, but without any appearance of success: Notwithstanding, I still tarried with them.

In the evening they met together, near a hundred of them, and danced round a large fire, having prepared ten fat deer for the sacrifice; the fat of whose inwards they burned in the fire, while they were dancing, and sometimes raised the flame to a prodigious height, at the same time yelling and shouting in such a manner, that they might easily have been heard two miles or more.

They continued their sacred dance all night, or near the matter; after which they ate the flesh of the sacrifice, and so retired each one to his lodging.

I enjoyed little satisfaction this night, being entirely alone on the island, as to any christian company, and in the midst of this idolatrous revel; and having walked to and fro until body and mind were
pained

pained and much oppressed, I at length crept into a little crib made for corn, and there slept on the poles.

Lord's Day, September 21.—Spent the day with the Indians on the island. As soon as they were well up in the morning, I attempted to instruct them, and laboured for that purpose to get them together, but quickly found they had something else to do; for near noon they gathered together all their powwows, or conjurers, and set about half a dozen of them to playing their juggling tricks, and acting their frantick distracted postures, in order to find out why they were then so sickly upon the island, numbers of them being at that time disordered with a fever and bloody flux. In this exercise they were engaged for several hours, making all the wild, ridiculous and distracted motions imaginable; sometimes singing, sometimes howling, sometimes extending their hands to the utmost stretch, spreading all their fingers, and seemed to push with them, as if they designed to fright something away, or, at least, keep it off at arm's end; sometimes stroking their faces with their hands, then spurting water as fine as mist; sometimes setting flat on the earth, then bowing down, their faces to the ground; wringing their sides as if in pain and anguish; twisting their faces, turning up their eyes, grunting, puffing, &c.

Their monstrous actions tended to excite ideas of horror, and seemed to have something in them, as I thought, peculiarly suited to raise the devil, if he could be raised by any thing odd, ridiculous and frightful. Some of them I could observe were much more fervent and devout in the business than others, and seemed to chant, peep and mutter with a great degree of warmth and vigour, as if determined to awaken and engage the powers below. I sat at a small distance, not more than thirty feet from them, though undiscovered, with my Bible in my hand, resolving if possible to spoil their sport, and prevent their receiving any answers from the infernal world, and there viewed the whole scene. They continued their hideous charms and incantations for more than three hours, until they had all wearied themselves out, although they had in that space of time taken sundry intervals of rest, and at length broke up, I apprehended, without receiving any answer at all.

After they had done powwowing, I attempted to discourse with them about christianity; but they soon scattered, and gave me no opportunity for any thing of that nature.

CROSWEEKSUNG, *in* New-Jersey, 1745.

Preached to my people from John xiv. 1.—6. The divine presence seemed to be in the assembly. Numbers were affected with divine truths, and it was a season of comfort to some in particular.

O! what a difference is there between these and the Indians I had lately treated with upon Susquehannah! To be with those seemed like being banished from God and all his people; to be with these like being admitted into his family, and to the enjoyment of his divine presence! How great is the change lately made upon numbers of these Indians, who not many months ago were many of them as thoughtless, and averse to christianity, as those upon Susquehannah! And how astonishing is that grace that has made this change!

Lord's Day, *October 6.*—Preached in the forenoon from John x. 7.—11. There was a considerable melting among my people, the dear young christians were refreshed, comforted and strengthened, and one or two persons newly awakened.

In the afternoon I discoursed on the story of the jailor, Acts xvi. and in the evening expounded Acts xx.

xx. 1.—12. There was at this time a very agreeable melting spread through the whole assembly. I think I scarce ever saw a more desirable affection in any number of people in my life. There was scarce a dry eye to be seen among them, and yet nothing boisterous or unseemly, nothing that tended to disturb the publick worship; but rather to encourage and excite a christian ardour and spirit of devotion.

Those, who I have reason to hope were savingly renewed, were first affected, and seemed to rejoice much, but with brokenness of spirit and godly fear; their exercises were much the same with those mentioned in my Journal of August 26, evidently appearing to be the genuine effect of a spirit of adoption.

After publick service was over I withdrew, being much tired with the labours of the day, and the Indians continued praying among themselves for near two hours together, which continued exercises appeared to be attended with a blessed quickening influence from on high.

I could not but earnestly wish that numbers of God's people had been present at this season, to see and hear these things, which I am sure must refresh the heart of every true lover of Zion's interest. To see those, who very lately were savage pagans and idolaters, having no hope, *and without God in the world*, now filled with a sense of divine love and grace, and worshipping the *Father in spirit and in truth*, as numbers here appeared to do, was not a little affecting; and especially to see them appear so tender and humble, as well as lively, fervent and devout in the divine service.

October 24.—Discoursed from John iv. 13. 14. There was a great attention, a desirable affection, and an unaffected melting in the assembly. It is surprising to see how eager they are of hearing the word

word of God. I have oftentimes thought they would cheerfully and diligently attend divine worship twenty four hours together, had they an opportunity so to do.

October 25.—Discoursed to my people respecting the resurrection, from Luke xx. 27.—36. And when I came to mention the blessedness the godly shall enjoy at that season, their final freedom from death, sin and sorrow; their equality to the angels in regard of their nearness to and enjoyment of Christ; some imperfect degree of which they are favoured with in the present life, from whence springs their sweetest comfort; and their being the children of God, openly acknowledged by him as such: I say, when I mentioned these things, numbers of them were much affected, and melted with a view of this blessed state.

October 28.—Discoursed from Matth. xxii. 1.—13. I was enabled to open the scripture, and adapt my discourse and expressions to the capacities of my people I know not how, in a plain, easy, and familiar manner, beyond all that I could have done by the utmost study: And this, without any special difficulty, with as much freedom as if I had been addressing a common audience, who had been instructed in the doctrine of christianity all their days.

The word of God at this time seemed to fall upon the assembly with a divine power and influence, especially toward the close of my discourse: There was both a sweet melting and bitter mourning in the audience. The dear christians were refreshed and comforted, convictions revived in others, and sundry persons newly awakened who had never been with us before; and so much of the divine presence appeared in the assembly, that it seemed, *this was none other than the house of God, and the gate of heaven.* And all that had any favour and relish of divine things

things were even conftrained by the fweetnefs of that feafon to fay, *Lord, it is good for us to be here.* If ever there was amongft my people an appearance of the New-Jerufalem, *as a bride adorned for her hufband,* there was much of it at this time ; and fo agreeable was the entertainment where fuch tokens of the divine prefence were, that I could fcarce be willing in the evening to leave the place, and repair to my lodgings. I was refrefhed with a view of the continuance of this bleffed work of grace among them, and its influence upon ftrangers of the Indians that had of late, from time to time, providentially fallen into thefe parts.

Lord's Day, November 3.—Preached to my people from Luke xvi. 17. more efpecially for the fake of feveral lately brought under deep concern for their fouls. There was fome apparent concern and affection in the affembly, though far lefs than has been ufual of late.

Afterwards I baptized fourteen perfons of the Indians, fix adults and eight children : One of thefe was near fourfcore years of age, and I have reafon to hope God has brought her favingly home to himfelf : Two of the others were men of fifty years old, who had been fingular and remarkable, even among the Indians, for their wickednefs. One of them had been a murderer, and both notorious drunkards as well as exceffive quarrelfome ; but now I cannot but hope both are become fubjects of God's fpecial grace, efpecially the worft of them. I deferred their baptifm for many weeks after they had given evidences of having paffed a great change, that I might have more opportunities to obferve the fruits of thofe impreffions they had been under, and apprehended the way was now clear : And there was not one of the adults I baptized, but what had given me fome comfortable grounds to hope, that God had wrought a work of special grace in their hearts; although I could not have the same degree of satisfaction respecting one or two of them, as the rest.

November 4.—Discoursed from John xi. briefly explaining most of the chapter. Divine truths made deep impressions upon many in the assembly; numbers were affected with a view of the power of Christ, manifested in his raising the dead, and especially when this instance of his power was improved to shew his power and ability to raise dead souls, such as many of them then felt themselves to be, to a spiritual life: As also to raise the dead at the last day, and dispense to them due rewards and punishments.

There were sundry of the persons lately come here from remote places, that were now brought under deep and pressing concern for their souls, particularly one, who not long since came half drunk, and railed on us, and attempted by all means to disturb us while engaged in the divine worship, was now so concerned and distressed for her soul, that she seemed unable to get any ease without an interest in Christ. There were many tears and affectionate sobs, and groans in the assembly in general, some weeping for themselves, others for their friends. And although persons are doubtless much easier affected now, than they were in the beginning of this religious concern, when tears and cries for their souls were things unheard of among them, yet I must say, their affection in general appeared genuine and unfeigned; and especially this appeared very conspicuous in those newly awakened. So that true and genuine convictions of sin, seem still to be begun and promoted in many instances.

Baptized a child this day, and perceived sundry of the baptized persons affected with the administration of this ordinance, as being thereby minded of their own solemn engagements.

I have now baptized in all forty seven perfons of the Indians, twenty three adults, and twenty four children. Thirty five of them belonging to thefe parts, and the reft to the Forks of Delaware: And, through rich grace, they have none of them as yet been left to difgrace their profeffion of chriftianity by any fcandalous or unbecoming behaviour.

Lord's Day, November 24.—Preached both parts of the day from the ftory of Zaccheus, Luke xix. 1.—9. In the latter exercife, when I opened and infifted upon the falvation that comes to the finner, upon his becoming a fon of Abraham, or a true believer, the word feemed to be attended with divine power to the hearts of the hearers. Numbers were much affected with divine truths. Former convictions were revived. One or two perfons newly awakened. And a moft affectionate engagement in divine fervice appeared among them univerfally.

The impreffions they were under appeared to be the genuine effect of God's word brought home to their hearts, by the power and influence of the Divine Spirit.

November 26.—After having fpent fome time in private conferences with my people, I difcourfed publickly among them, from John v. 19. I was favoured with fome fpecial freedom and fervency in my difcourfe, and a powerful energy accompanied divine truths. Many wept and fobbed affectionately, and fcarce any appeared unconcerned in the whole affembly. The influence that feized the audience appeared gentle, and yet pungent and efficacious. It produced no boifterous commotion of the paffions, but feemed deeply to affect the heart; and excited in the perfons under convictions of their loft ftate, heavy groans and tears. And in others who
had

had obtained comfort, a sweet and humble melting. It seemed like the gentle but steady showers that effectually water the earth, without violently beating upon the surface.

November 30.—Preached near night, after having spent some hours in private conference with some of my people about their souls' concerns. Explained and insisted upon the story of the rich man and Lazarus, Luke xvi. 19.—26. The word made powerful impressions upon many in the assembly, especially while I discoursed of the blessedness of Lazarus in Abraham's bosom.

Lord's Day, December 1.—Discoursed to my people, in the forenoon, from Luke xvi. 27.—31. There appeared an unfeigned affection in divers persons, and some seemed deeply impressed with divine truths.

Lord's Day, December 8.—Discoursed on the story of the blind man, John ix. There appeared no remarkable effect of the word upon the assembly at this time. The persons who have lately been much concerned for their souls, seemed now not so affected nor solicitous to obtain an interest in Christ as has been usual; although they attended divine service with seriousness and diligence.

Such have been the doings of the Lord here, in awakening sinners, and affecting the hearts of those who are brought to solid comfort, with a fresh sense of divine things from time to time, that it is now strange to see the assembly sit with dry eyes, and without sobs and groans!

Lord's Day, December 15.—Preached to the Indians from Luke xiii. 24.—28. Divine truths fell with weight and power upon the audience, and seemed to reach the hearts of many. Near night discoursed to them again from Matth. xxv. 31.—46. At which season also, the word appeared to be accompanied

companied with a divine influence, and made powerful impreſſions upon the aſſembly in general, as well as upon divers perſons in a very ſpecial and particular manner. This was an amazing ſeaſon of grace! *The word of the Lord, this day, was quick and powerful, ſharper than a two edged ſword,* and *pierced* to the hearts of many. The aſſembly was greatly affected, and deeply wrought upon; yet without ſo much apparent commotion of the paſſions, as was uſual in the beginning of this work of grace. The impreſſions made by the word of God upon the audience, appeared ſolid, rational and deep, worthy of the ſolemn truths by means of which they were produced, and far from being the effects of any ſudden fright or groundleſs perturbation of mind.

O, how did the hearts of the hearers ſeem to bow under the weight of divine truths! And how evident did it now appear that they received and felt them, not as the word of man but as the word of God! None can frame a juſt idea of the appearance of our aſſembly at this time, but thoſe who have ſeen a congregation ſolemnly awed, and deeply impreſſed by the ſpecial power and influence of divine truths delivered to them in the name of God!

December 16.—Diſcourſed to my people in the evening from Luke xi. 1.—13. There was much affection and concern in the aſſembly; and eſpecially one woman appeared in great diſtreſs for her ſoul. She was brought to ſuch an agony in ſeeking after Chriſt, that the ſweat ran off her face for a conſiderable time together, although the evening was very cold; and her bitter cries were the moſt affecting indication of the inward anguiſh of her heart.

Lord's Day, December 22.—Diſcourſed upon the ſtory of the young man in the goſpel, Matth. ix. 16.—22.

16—22. God made it a seasonable word, I am persuaded, to some souls.

There were sundry persons of the Indians newly come here, who had frequently lived among Quakers, and being more civilized and conformed to English manners than the generality of Indians, they had imbibed some of the Quakers' errors; especially this fundamental one, viz. That if men will but live soberly and honestly, according to the dictates of their own consciences (or the light within) there is then no danger or doubt of their salvation, &c. These persons I found much worse to deal with than those who are wholly under pagan darkness, who make no pretences to knowledge in christianity at all, nor have any self righteous foundation to stand upon. However, they all, except one, appeared now convinced, that this sober honest life of itself, was not sufficient to salvation; since Christ himself had declared it so in the case of the young man. And seemed, in some measure, concerned to obtain that change of heart which I had been labouring to shew them the necessity of.

This was likewise a season of comfort to some souls, and in particular to one (the same mentioned in my journal of the 16th instant) who never before obtained any settled comfort, though I have abundant reason to think she had passed a saving change some days before.

She now appeared in a heavenly frame of mind, composed and delighted with the divine will. When I came to discourse particularly with her, and to inquire of her, how she got relief and deliverance from the spiritual distresses she had lately been under, she answered in broken English, Me try, me try, save myself, last my strength be all gone, (meaning her ability to save herself) coud'nt me stir bit further. Den last, me forc'd let Jesus Christ alone, send me hell

hell if he pleafe*. I faid, But you was not willing to go to hell, was you? She replied, Could not me help it. My heart he would wicked for all. Could not me make him good†, (meaning fhe faw it was right fhe fhould go to hell, becaufe her heart was wicked, and would be fo after all fhe could do to mend it.) I afked her, how fhe got out of this cafe. She anfwered ftill in the fame broken language, By by my heart be grad defperately. I afked her, why her heart was glad. She replied, Grad my heart Jefus Chrift do what he pleafe with me. Den me tink, grad my heart Jefus Chrift fend me hell. Did'nt me care where he put me, me lobe him for all‡, &c.

And fhe could not readily be convinced, but that fhe was willing to go to hell, if Chrift was pleafed to fend her there. Though the truth evidently was, her will was fo fwallowed up in the divine will, that fhe could not frame any hell in her imagination that would be dreadful or undefirable, provided it was but the will of God to fend her to it.

Towards night difcourfed to them again in the catechetical method I entered upon the evening before. And when I came to improve the truths I had explained to them, and to anfwer that queftion, But how fhall I know whether God hath chofen me to everlafting life? by preffing them to come and give up their hearts to Chrift, and thereby to make their election fure, they then appeared much affected: And the perfons under concern were afrefh engaged in feeking after an intereft in him; while fome others, who had obtained comfort before, were refrefhed

---

* In proper Englifh, thus, I tried and tried to fave myfelf, until at laft my ftrength was all gone, and I could not ftir any further. Then, at laft, I was forced to let Jefus Chrift alone to fend me to hell if he pleafed.

† In plain Englifh, thus, I could not help it. My heart would be wicked for all what I could do. I could not make it good.

‡ By and by my heart was exceeding glad. My heart was glad that Jefus Chrift would do with me what he pleafed. Then I thought my heart would be glad although Chrift fhould fend me to hell. I did not care where he put me, I fhould love him for all, i. e. do what he would with me.

refreshed to find that love to God in themselves, which was an evidence of his electing love to them.

December 25.—The Indians having been used upon Christmas days to drink and revel among some of the white people in these parts, I thought it proper this day to call them together and discourse to them upon divine things; which I accordingly did from the parable of the barren fig tree, Luke xiii. 6.—9. A divine influence, I am persuaded, accompanied the word at this season. The power of God appeared in the assembly, not by producing any remarkable cries, but by shocking and rousing at heart, (as it seemed) several stupid creatures, that were scarce ever moved with any concern before. The power attending divine truths, seemed to have the influence of the earthquake rather than the whirlwind upon them. Their passions were not so much alarmed as has been common here, in times past; but their judgments appeared to be powerfully convinced by the masterly and conquering influence of divine truths. The impressions made upon the assembly in general, seemed not superficial, but deep and heart affecting. O how ready did they now appear universally to embrace and comply with every thing they heard and were convinced was duty! God was in the midst of us of a truth, bowing and melting stubborn hearts! How many tears and sobs were then to be seen and heard among us! What liveliness and strict attention! What eagerness and intenseness of mind appeared in the whole assembly in the time of divine service! They seemed to watch and wait for the dropping of God's word, as the thirsty earth for the *former and latter rain*.

December 28.—Discoursed to my people in the catechetical method I lately entered upon. And in the improvement of my discourse, wherein I was comparing man's present with his primitive state;
and

and shewing what he had fallen from, and the miseries he is now involved in, and expofed to in his natural eftate; and preffing finners to take a view of their deplorable circumftances without Chrift; as alfo to ftrive that they might obtain an intereft in him; the Lord, I truft, granted a remarkable influence of his bleffed Spirit to accompany what was fpoken, and there was a great concern appeared in the affembly: Many were melted into tears and fobs, and the impreffions made upon them, feemed deep and heart affecting.

Lord's Day, December 29.—Preached from John iii. 1.—5. A number of white people were prefent as is ufual upon the Sabbath. The difcourfe was accompanied with power, and feemed to have a filent, but deep and piercing influence upon the audience. Many wept and fobbed affectionately. And there were fome tears among the white people as well as the Indians. Some could not refrain from crying out, though there were not many fo exercifed. But the impreffions made upon their hearts, appeared chiefly by the extraordinary earneftnefs of their attention, and their heavy fighs and tears.

After publick worfhip was over, I went to my houfe, propofing to preach again after a fhort feafon of intermiffion. But they foon came in one after another, with tears in their eyes, to know what they fhould do to be faved. And the Divine Spirit in fuch a manner fet home upon their hearts what I fpoke to them, that the houfe was foon filled with cries, and groans. They all flocked together upon this occafion, and thofe whom I had reafon to think in a chriftlefs ftate, were almoft univerfally feized with concern for their fouls.

It was an amazing feafon of power among them, and feemed as if God had *bowed the heavens and come down.* So aftonifhingly prevalent was the operation

eration upon old as well as young, that it seemed as if none would be left in a secure and natural state, but that God was now about to convert all the world. And I was ready to think then, that I should never again despair of the conversion of any man or woman living, be they who or what they would.

It is impossible to give a just and lively description of the appearance of things at this season, at least, such as to convey a bright and adequate idea of the effects of this influence! A number might now be seen rejoicing that God had not taken away the powerful influence of his blessed Spirit from this place; refreshed to see so many striving *to enter in at the strait gate*; and animated with such concern for them, that they wanted to push them forward, as some of them expressed it. At the same time numbers, both of men and women, old and young, might be seen in tears, and some in anguish of spirit, appearing in their very countenances like condemned malefactors, bound towards the place of execution, with a heavy solicitude sitting in their faces; so that there seemed here, as I thought, a lively emblem of the solemn day of accounts! A mixture of heaven and hell, of joy unspeakable, and anguish inexpressible!

The concern and religious affection was such, that I could not pretend to have any formal religious exercise among them; but spent the time in discoursing to one and another, as I thought most proper, and seasonable for each, and some times addressed them all together, and finally concluded with prayer. Such were their circumstances at this season, that I could scarce have half an hour's rest from speaking, from about half an hour before twelve o'clock (at which time I began publick worship) until past seven at night.

There

There appeared to be four or five persons newly awakened this day, and the evening before, some of whom but very lately came among us.

December 30.—Was visited by four or five young persons under concern for their souls, most of whom were very lately awakened. They wept much while I discoursed to them, and endeavoured to press upon them the necessity of flying to Christ, without delay, for salvation.

December 31.—Spent some hours this day in visiting my people from house to house, and conversing with them about their spiritual concerns; endeavouring to press upon christless souls the necessity of a renovation of heart: And scarce left a house, without leaving some or other of its inhabitants in tears, appearing solicitously engaged to obtain an interest in Christ.

The Indians are now gathered together from all quarters to this place, and have built them little cottages, so that more than twenty families live within a quarter of a mile of me. A very convenient situation in regard both of publick and private instruction.

January 1, 1745,6.—Spent some considerable time in visiting my people again. Found scarce one but what was under some serious impressions respecting their spiritual concerns.

January 2.—Visited some persons newly come among us, who had scarce ever heard any thing of christianity (except the empty name) before. Endeavoured to instruct them particularly in the first principles of religion, in the most easy and familiar manner I could.

There are strangers from remote parts almost continually dropping in among us, so that I have occasion repeatedly to open and inculcate the first principles of christianity.

January 4.—Profecuted my catechetical method of inftructing. Found my people able to anfwer queftions with propriety, beyond what could have been expected from perfons fo lately brought out of heathenifh darknefs.

Lord's Day, January 5.—Difcourfed from Matth. xii. 10.—13. There appeared not fo much livelinefs and affection in divine fervice as ufual. The fame truths that have often produced many tears and fobs in the affembly, feemed now to have no fpecial influence upon any in it.

Near night I propofed to have proceeded in my ufual method of catechifing. But while we were engaged in the firft prayer, the power of God feemed to defcend upon the affembly in fuch a remarkable manner, and fo many appeared under preffing concern for their fouls, that I thought it much more expedient to infift upon the plentiful provifion made by divine grace for the redemption of perifhing finners, and to prefs them to a fpeedy acceptance of the great falvation, than to afk them queftions about doctrinal points. What was moft practical, feemed moft feafonable to be infifted upon, while numbers appeared fo extraordinarily folicitous to obtain an intereft in the great Redeemer.

Baptized two perfons this day; one adult (the woman particularly mentioned in my Journal of December 22,) and one child.

This woman has difcovered a very fweet and heavenly frame of mind, from time to time, fince her firft reception of comfort. One morning in particular fhe came to fee me, difcovering an unufual joy and fatisfaction in her countenance; and when I inquired into the reafon of it, fhe replied, that God had made her feel that it was right for him to do what he pleafed with all things; and that it would be right if he fhould 'caft her hufband and fon both

into

into hell; and she saw it was so right for God to do what he pleased with them, that she could not but rejoice if God should send them into hell. Though it was apparent she loved them dearly. She, moreover, inquired whether I was not sent to preach to the Indians, by some good people a great way off. I replied, Yes, by the good people in Scotland. She answered, that her heart loved those good people so, the evening before, that she could scarce help praying for them all night, her heart would go to God for them, &c. so that the blessing of those ready to perish is like to come upon those pious persons who have communicated of their substance to the propagation of the gospel.

January 11.—Discoursed in a catechetical method, as usual of late. And having opened our first parent's primitive apostasy, from God, and our fall in him, I proceeded to improve my discourse, by shewing the necessity we stood in of an almighty Redeemer, and the absolute need every sinner has of an interest in his merits and mediation. There was some tenderness and affectionate concern appeared in the assembly.

Lord's Day, January 12.—Preached from Isaiah lv. 6. The word of God seemed to fall upon the audience, with a divine weight and influence, and evidently appeared to be not the word of man. The blessed Spirit, I am persuaded, accompanied what was spoken to the hearts of many. So that there was a powerful revival of conviction in numbers who were under spiritual exercise before.

January 13.—Was visited by divers persons under deep concern for their souls: One of whom was newly awakened. It is a most agreeable work to treat with souls who are solicitously inquiring *what they shall do to be saved.* And as we are never to be *weary in well doing,* so the obligation seems to be

peculiarly

peculiarly strong when the work is so very desirable. And yet I must say, my health is so much impaired, and my spirits so wasted with my labours and solitary manner of living (there being no human creature in the house with me) that their repeated and almost incessant applications to me for help and direction, are sometimes exceeding burdensome, and so exhaust my spirits, that I become fit for nothing at all, entirely unable to prosecute any business sometimes for days together.

January 14.—Spent some time in private conferences with my people, and found some disposed to take comfort, as I thought, upon slighty grounds. They are now generally awakened, and it is become so disgraceful, as well as terrifying to the conscience, to be destitute of religion, that they are in eminent danger of taking up with any appearances of grace, rather than to live under the fear and disgrace of an unregenerate state.

Lord's Day, January 19.—Discoursed to my people from Isaiah lv. 7. Towards night catechized in my ordinary method. And this appeared to be a powerful season of grace among us. Numbers were much affected. Convictions powerfully revived. Divers of the christians refreshed and strengthened. And one weary *heavy laden* soul, I have abundant reason to hope, brought to true rest and solid comfort in Christ, who afterwards gave me such an account of God's dealing with his soul as was abundantly satisfying as well as refreshing to me.

He told me, he had often heard me say, that persons must see and feel themselves utterly helpless and undone, that they must be emptied of a dependence upon themselves, and of all hope of saving themselves by their own doings in order to their coming to Christ for salvation. And he had long been striving after this view of things; supposing this would
be

be an excellent frame of mind to be thus emptied of a dependence upon his own goodneſs: That God would have reſpect to this frame; would then be well pleaſed with him, and beſtow eternal life upon him. But when he came to feel himſelf in this helpleſs undone condition, he found it quite contrary to all his thoughts and expectations; ſo that it was not the ſame nor indeed any thing like the frame he had been ſeeking after. Inſtead of its being a good frame of mind, he now found nothing but badneſs in himſelf, and ſaw it was forever impoſſible for him to make himſelf any better. He wondered, he ſaid, that he had ever hoped to mend his own heart. He was amazed he had never before ſeen it was utterly impoſſible for him, by all his contrivances and endeavours, to do any thing that way, ſince the matter now appeared to him in ſo clear a light.

Inſtead of imagining now, that God would be pleaſed with him for the ſake of this frame of mind, and this view of his undone eſtate, he ſaw clearly, and felt it would be juſt with God to ſend him to eternal miſery; and that there was no goodneſs in what he then felt; for he could not help ſeeing, that he was naked, ſinful and miſerable, and there was nothing in ſuch a ſight to deſerve God's love or pity.

He ſaw theſe things in a manner ſo clear and convincing, that it ſeemed to him, he ſaid, he could convince every body of their utter inability ever to help themſelves, and their unworthineſs of any help from God.

In this frame of mind he came to publick worſhip, this evening, and while I was inviting ſinners to come to Chriſt naked and empty, without any goodneſs of their own to recommend them to his acceptance, then he thought with himſelf, that he had often tried to come and give up his heart to Christ, and he used to hope that some time or other he should be able to do so. But now he was convinced he could not, and it seemed utterly vain for him ever to try any more: And he could not, he said, find a heart to make any further attempt, because he saw it would signify nothing at all: Nor did he now hope for a better opportunity, or more ability hereafter, as he had formerly done, because he saw, and was fully convinced, his own strength would forever fail.

While he was musing in this manner, he saw, he said, with his heart (which is a common phrase among them) something that was unspeakably good and lovely, and what he had never seen before; and this stole away his heart whether he would or no. He did not, he said, know what it was he saw. He did not say, this is Jesus Christ, but it was such glory and beauty as he never saw before. He did not now give away his heart so as he had formerly intended and attempted to do, but it went away of itself after that glory he then discovered. He used to try to make a bargain with Christ, to give up his heart to him, that he might have eternal life for it. But now he thought nothing about himself, or what would become of him hereafter. But was pleased, and his mind was wholly taken up with the unspeakable excellency of what he then beheld.

After some time he was wonderfully pleased with the way of salvation by Christ; so that it seemed unspeakably better to be saved altogether by the mere free grace of God in Christ, than to have any hand in saving himself. And the consequence of this exercise is, that he appears to retain a sense and relish of divine things, and to maintain a life of seriousness and true religion.

February 8.—Spent a considerable part of the day in visiting my people from house to house, and conversing

versing with them about their souls' concerns. Divers persons wept while I discoursed to them, and appeared concerned for nothing so much as for an interest in the great Redeemer.

Lord's Day, February 9.—Discoursed to my people from the story of the blind man, Matth. x. 46.--52. The word of God seemed weighty and powerful upon the assembly at this time, and made considerable impressions upon many. Divers in particular who have generally been remarkably stupid and careless under the means of grace, were now awakened, and wept affectionately. And the most earnest attention, as well as tenderness and affection, appeared in the audience universally.

Baptized three persons, two adults and one child. The adults, I have reason to hope, were both truly pious. There was a considerable melting in the assembly, while I was discoursing particuliarly to the persons, and administering the ordinance.

March 1.—Catechised in my ordinary method. Was pleased and refreshed to see them answer the questions proposed to them, with such remarkable readiness, discretion and knowledge.

Towards the close of my discourse, divine truths made considerable impressions upon the audience, and produced tears and sobs in some under concern; and more especially a sweet and humble melting in sundry that, I have reason to hope, were truly gracious.

Lord's Day, March 2.—Preached from John xv. 1.—6. The assembly appeared not so lively in their attention as usual, nor so much affected with divine truths in general as has been common.

Some of my people who went up to the Forks of Delaware with me, being now returned, were accompanied by two of the Indians belonging to the Forks,

Forks, who had promised me a speedy visit. May the Lord meet with them here. They can scarce go into a house now, but they will meet with christian conversation, whereby, it is hopeful, they may be both instructed and awakened.

Discoursed to the Indians again in the afternoon, and observed among them some liveliness and engagement in divine service, though not equal to what has often appeared here.

I know of no assembly of christians, where there seems to be so much of the presence of God, where brotherly love so much prevails, and where I should take so much delight in the publick worship of God, in the general, as in my own congregation. Although not more than nine months ago, they were worshipping devils and dumb idols, under the power of pagan darkness and superstition! Amazing change this! effected by nothing less than divine power and grace! *This is the doing of the Lord, and it is* justly *marvellous in our eyes!*

Lord's Day, March 9.—Preached from Luke x. 38.—42. The word of God was attended with power and energy upon the audience. Numbers were affected and concerned to obtain the *one thing needful*. And sundry that have given good evidences of their being truly gracious, were much affected with a sense of their want of spirituality; and saw the need they stood in of growing in grace. And most that had been under any impressions of divine things in times past, seemed now to have those impressions revived.

In the afternoon proposed to have catechized in my usual method. But while we were engaged in the first prayer in the Indian language, as usual, a great part of the assembly was so much moved and affected with divine things, that I thought it seasonable and proper to omit the proposing of questions
for

for that time, and infift upon the moft practical truths. And accordingly did fo : Making a further improvement of the paffage of fcripture I difcourfed upon in the former part of the day.

There appeared to be a powerful divine influence in the congregation. Sundry that I have reafon to think are truly pious, were fo deeply affected with a fenfe of their own barrennefs, and their unworthy treatment of the bleffed Redeemer, that they *looked on him as pierced* by themfelves, *and mourned*, yea fome of them were *in bitternefs as for a firft born*. Some poor awakened finners alfo appeared to be in anguifh of foul to obtain an intereft in Chrift. So that there was a great mourning in the affembly : Many heavy groans, fobs and tears ! And one or two perfons newly come among us, were confiderably awakened.

Methinks it would have refrefhed the heart of any who truly love Zion's intereft, to have been in the midft of this divine influence, and feen the effects of it upon faints and finners. The place of divine worfhip appeared both folemn and fweet ! And was fo endeared by a difplay of the divine prefence and grace, that thofe who had any relifh of divine things, could not but cry, *How amiable are thy tabernacles, O Lord of Hofts !*

After publick worfhip was over, numbers came to my houfe, where we fang and difcourfed of divine things ; and the prefence of God feemed here alfo to be in the midft of us.

While we were finging there was one woman, who, I may venture to fay, if I may be allowed to fay fo much of any perfon I ever faw, was filled *with joy unfpeakable and full of glory*, and could not but burft forth in prayer and praifes to God before us all, with many tears, crying, fometimes in Englifh and fometimes in Indian, O bleffed Lord, do

come,

come, do come! O do take me away, do let me die and go to Jesus Christ! I am afraid if I live I shall sin again! O do let me die now! O dear Jesus, do come! I cannot stay, I cannot stay! O how can I live in this world! Do take my soul away from this sinful place! O let me never sin any more! O what shall I do, what shall I do! Dear Jesus, O dear Jesus, &c. In this ecstasy she continued some time, uttering these and such like expressions incessantly. And the grand argument she used with God to take her away immediately, was, that if she lived she should sin against him.

When she had a little recovered herself, I asked her, if Christ was not now sweet to her soul: Whereupon, turning to me with tears in her eyes, and with all the tokens of deep humility I ever saw in any person, she said, I have many times heard you speak of the goodness and the sweetness of Christ, that he was better than all the world. But O! I knew nothing what you meant, I never believed you! I never believed you; but now I know it is true. Or words to that effect. I answered, And do you see enough in Christ for the greatest of sinners? She replied, O, enough, enough for all the sinners in the world if they would but come. And when I asked her, if she could not tell them of the goodness of Christ; turning herself about to some poor christless souls who stood by, and were much affected, she said, O, there is enough in Christ for you, if you would but come! O strive, strive to give up your hearts to him, &c. And upon hearing something of the glory of heaven mentioned, that there was no sin in that world, &c. she again fell into the same ecstasy of joy, and desire of Christ's coming; repeating her former expressions, O dear Lord, do let me go! O what shall I do, what shall I do! I want to go to Christ! I cannot live! O do let me die, &c.

She

She continued in this sweet frame for more than two hours, before she was well able to get home.

I am very sensible there may be great joys, arising even to an ecstasy, where there is still no substantial evidence of their being well grounded. But in the present case there seemed to be no evidence wanting in order to prove this joy to be divine, either in regard of its preparatives, attendants, or consequents.

Of all the persons I have seen under spiritual exercise, I scarce ever saw one appear more bowed and broken under convictions of sin and misery, (or what is usually called a preparatory work,) than this woman. Nor scarce any who seemed to have a greater acquaintance with her own heart than she had. She would frequently complain to me of the hardness and rebellion of her heart. Would tell me her heart rose and quarrelled with God, when she thought he would do with her as he pleased, and send her to hell, notwithstanding her prayers, good frames, &c. That her heart was not willing to come to Christ for salvation, but tried every where else for help.

And as she seemed to be remarkably sensible of her stubbornness and contrariety to God, under conviction, so she appeared to be no less remarkably bowed and reconciled to divine sovereignty before she obtained any relief or comfort. Something of which I have before noticed in my Journal of February 9. Since which time she has seemed constantly to breath the spirit and temper of the new creature; crying after Christ, not through fear of hell as before, but with strong desires after him as her only satisfying portion. And has many times wept and sobbed bitterly, because (as she apprehended) she did not and could not love him. When I have sometimes asked her, why she appeared so sorrowful, and whether it was because she was afraid of hell; she

would

would anfwer, No, I ben't diftreffed about that; but my heart is fo wicked I cannot love Chrift; and thereupon burft out into tears. But although this has been the habitual frame of her mind for feveral weeks together, fo that the exercife of grace appeared evident to others, yet fhe feemed wholly infenfible of it herfelf, and never had any remarkable comfort, and fenfible fatisfaction until this evening.

This fweet and furprifing ecftafy, appeared to fpring from a true fpiritual difcovery of the glory, ravifhing beauty and excellency of Chrift: And not from any grofs imaginary notions of his human nature; fuch as that of feeing him in fuch a place or pofture, as hanging on the crofs, as bleeding, dying, as gently fmiling, and the like; which delufions fome have been carried away with. Nor did it rife from a fordid felfifh apprehenfion of her having any benefit whatfoever conferred on her, but from a view of his perfonal excellency, and tranfcendent lovelinefs, which drew forth thofe vehement defires of enjoying him fhe now manifefted, and made her long *to be abfent from the body, that fhe might be prefent with the Lord.*

The attendants of this ravifhing comfort, were fuch as abundantly difcovered its fpring to be divine, and that it was truly a *joy in the Holy Ghoft.* Now fhe viewed divine truths as living realities; and could fay, I know thefe thing are fo, I feel they are true! Now her foul was refigned to the divine will in the moft tender points; fo that when I faid to her, What if God fhould take away your* hufband from you, (who was then very fick) how do you think you could bear that? She replied, He belongs to God, and not me; he may do with him juft what he pleafes! Now fhe had the moft tender fenfe of the evil of fin, and difcovered the utmoft averfion

to

---

* The man particularly mentioned in my Journal of January 19.

to it; longing to die that she might be delivered from it. Now she could freely trust her all with God for time and eternity. And when I queried with her, how she could be willing to die and leave her little infant, and what she thought would become of it in case she should; she answered, God will take care of it. It belongs to him, he will take care of it.

Now she appeared to have the most humbling sense of her own meanness and unworthiness, her weakness and inability to preserve herself from sin, and to persevere in the way of holiness, crying, If I live I shall sin. And I then thought I had never seen such an appearance of ecstasy and humility meeting in any one person in all my life before.

The consequents of this joy are no less desirable and satisfactory than its attendants. She since appears to be a most tender, broken hearted, affectionate, devout, and humble christian, as exemplary in life and conversation as any person in my congregation. May she still *grow in grace and in the knowledge of Christ*.

March 10.—Toward night the Indians met together of their own accord and sang, prayed, and discoursed of divine things among themselves. At which time there was much affection among them. Some, who are hopefully gracious, appeared to be melted with divine things. And some others seemed much concerned for their souls. Perceiving their engagement, and affection in religious exercises, I went among them, and prayed and gave a word of exhortation; and observed two or three somewhat affected and concerned, who scarce ever appeared to be under any religious impressions before. It seemed to be a day and evening of divine power. Numbers retained the warm impressions of divine things that had been made upon their minds the day before.

March

March 14.—Was visited by a considerable number of my people, and spent some time in religious exercises with them.

March 24.—Numbered the Indians, to see how many souls God had gathered together here, since my coming into these parts, and found there was now about an hundred and thirty persons together, old and young. Sundry of those that are my stated hearers, perhaps to the number of fifteen or twenty, were absent at this season. So that if all had been together, the number would now have been very considerable; especially considering how few were together at my first coming into these parts, the whole number not amounting to ten persons at that time.

My people going out this day upon the design of clearing some of their lands above fifteen miles distant from this settlement, in order to their settling there in a compact form, where they might be under advantages of attending the publick worship of God, of having their children schooled, and at the same time have a conveniency for planting, &c. their land in the place of our present residence being of little or no value for that purpose. And the design of their settling thus in a body, and cultivating their lands, (which they have done very little at in their pagan state) being of such necessity and importance to their religious interest, as well as worldly comfort, I thought it proper to call them together, and shew them the duty of labouring with faithfulness and industry; and that they must not now *be slothful in business*, as they had ever been, in their pagan state. And endeavoured to press the importance of their being laborious, diligent and vigorous in the prosecution of their business, especially at the present juncture, (the season of planting being now near) in order to their being in a capacity of living together,

together, and enjoying the means of grace and instruction. And having given them directions for their work (which they very much wanted) as well as for their behaviour in divers respects, I explained, sang, and endeavoured to inculcate upon them, Psalm cxxviith, common metre, Dr. Watts's version. And having recommended them, and the design of their going forth, to God, by prayer with them, I dismissed them to their business.

In the evening read and expounded to my people, (those of them who were yet at home, and the strangers newly come,) the substance of the third chapter of the Acts. Numbers seemed to melt under the word, especially while I was discoursing upon verse 19. Sundry of the strangers also were affected. When I asked them afterwards, whether they did not now feel that their hearts were wicked, as I had taught them; one replied, Yes, she felt it now. Although before she came here (upon hearing that I taught the Indians their hearts were all bad by nature, and needed to be changed and made good by the power of God) she had said, her heart was not wicked, and she never had done any thing that was bad in her life. And this indeed seems to be the case with them, I think universally, in their pagan state.

They seem to have no consciousness of sin and guilt, unless they can charge themselves with some gross acts of sin contrary to the commands of the second table.

March 29.—In the evening catechised as usual upon Saturday. Treated upon the benefits which *believers receive from Christ at death*. The questions were answered with great readiness and propriety. And those who I have reason to think, are the dear people of God, were sweetly melted almost in general. There appeared such a liveliness and vigour in their attendance upon the word of God, and such eagerness to be made partakers of the benefits then mentioned, that they seemed to be not only *looking for*, but *hastening to the coming of the day of God*. Divine truths seemed to distil upon the audience with a gentle, but melting efficacy, as the refreshing showers upon the new mown grass. The assembly in general, as well as those who appear truly religious, were affected with some brief account of the blessedness of the godly at death: And most then discovered an affectionate inclination to cry, *Let me die the death of the righteous*, &c. Although many were not duly engaged to obtain the change of heart that is necessary in order to that blessed end.

March 31.—Called my people together, as I had done the Monday morning before, and discoursed to them again on the necessity and importance of their labouring industriously, in order to their living together and enjoying the means of grace, &c. And having engaged in solemn prayer to God among them, for a blessing upon their attempts, I dismissed them to their work.

Numbers of them, both men and women, seemed to offer themselves willingly to this service; and some appeared affectionately concerned that God might go with them, and begin their little town for them; that by his blessing it might be a place comfortable for them and theirs, in regard both of procuring the necessaries of life, and of attending the worship of God.

After publick worship, a number of those I have reason to think are truly religious, came to my house and seemed eager of some further entertainment upon divine things. And while I was conversing with them about their spiritual exercises, observing to them, that God's work in the hearts of all his children, was, for substance, the same; and that their

trials

trials and temptations were alfo alike; and fhewing the obligations fuch were under to love one another in a peculiar manner, they feemed to be melted into tendernefs and affection toward each other: And I thought that particular token of their being the difciples of Chrift, viz. of their having *love one toward another*, had fcarce ever appeared more evident than at this time.

April 25.—Having of late apprehended that a number of perfons in my congregation, were proper fubjects of the ordinance of the Lord's fupper, and that it might be feafonable fpeedily to adminifter it to them: And having taken advice of fome of the reverend Correfpondents in this folemn affair; and accordingly having propofed and appointed the next Lord's Day, with the leave of Divine Providence, for the adminiftration of this ordinance, this day, as preparatory thereto, was fet apart for folemn fafting and prayer, to implore the bleffing of God upon our defign of renewing covenant with him, and with one another, to walk together in the fear of God, in love and chriftian fellowfhip; and to entreat that his divine prefence might be with us in our defigned approach to his table; as well as to humble ourfelves before God on account of the apparent withdrawment, (at leaft in a meafure,) of that bleffed influence that has been fo prevalent upon perfons of all ages among us: As alfo on account of the rifing appearance of careleffnefs, vanity and vice among fome, who, fometime fince, appeared to be touched and affected with divine truths, and brought to fome fenfibility of their miferable and perifhing ftate by nature. And that we might alfo importunately pray for the peaceable fettlement of the Indians together in a body, that they might be a commodious congregation for the worfhip of God; and that God would blaſt and defeat all the attempts that were or might be made againſt that pious deſign*.

The ſolemnity was obſerved and ſeriouſly attended, not only by thoſe who propoſed to communicate at the Lord's table, but by the whole congregation univerſally. In the former part of the day, I endeavoured to open to my people the nature and deſign of a faſt, as I had attempted more briefly to do before, and to inſtruct them in the duties of ſuch a ſolemnity. In the afternoon, I inſiſted upon the ſpecial reaſons there were for our engaging in theſe ſolemn exerciſes at this time ; both in regard of the need we ſtood in of divine aſſiſtance, in order to a due preparation for that ſacred ordinance we were ſome of us propoſing (with the leave of Divine Providence) ſpeedily to attend upon : And alſo in reſpect of the manifeſt decline of God's work here, as to the effectual conviction and converſion of ſinners, there having been few of late deeply awakened out of a ſtate of ſecurity.

The worſhip of God was attended with great ſolemnity and reverence, with much tenderneſs and many tears, by thoſe who appear to be truly religious : And there was ſome appearance of divine power upon thoſe who had been awakened ſome time before, and who were ſtill under concern.

After repeated prayer and attendance upon the word of God, I propoſed to the religious people, with as much brevity and plainneſs as I could, the ſubſtance of the doctrine of the chriſtian faith, as I had formerly done, previous to their baptiſm, and had their renewed cheerful aſſent to it. I then led them

---

* There being at this time a terrible clamour raiſed againſt the Indians in various places in the country, and inſinuations as though I was training them up to cut people's throats. Numbers wiſhing to have them baniſhed out of theſe parts, and ſome giving out great words in order to fright and deter them from ſettling upon the beſt and moſt convenient tract of their own lands, threatening to moleſt and trouble them in the law, pretending a claim to theſe lands themſelves, although never purchaſed of the Indians.

them to a solemn renewal of their baptismal covenant, wherein they had explicitly and publickly given up themselves to God, the Father, Son and Holy Ghost, avouching him to be their God; and at the same time renouncing their heathenish vanities, their idolatrous and superstitious practices, and solemnly engaging to take the word of God, so far as it was, or might be made known to them, for the rule of their lives, promising to walk together in love, to watch over themselves, and one another; to lead lives of seriousness and devotion, and to discharge the relative duties incumbent upon them respectively, &c.

This solemn transaction was attended with much gravity and seriousness: And at the same time with utmost readiness, freedom, and cheerfulness; and a religious union and harmony of soul, seemed to crown the whole solemnity. I could not but think in the evening, that there had been manifest tokens of the divine presence with us in all the several services of the day; though it was also manifest there was not that concern among christless souls that has often appeared here.

April 26.—Toward noon prayed with a dying child, and gave a word of exhortation to the bystanders to prepare for death, which seemed to take effect upon some.

In the afternoon discoursed to my people from Matth. xxvi. 26.—30. of the author, the nature and design of the Lord's supper; and endeavoured to point out the worthy receivers of that ordinance.

The religious people were affected and even melted with divine truths, with a view of the dying love of Christ. Sundry others who had been for some months under convictions of their perishing state appeared now to be much moved with concern, and afresh engaged in seeking after an interest in Christ;
although

although I cannot fay the word of God appeared *fo quick and powerful*, fo fharp and piercing to the affembly, as it had fometimes formerly done.

Lord's Day, April 27.—Preached from Tit. ii. 14. *Who gave himfelf for us*, &c. The word of God at this time was attended with fome appearance of divine power upon the affembly; fo that the attention and gravity of the audience was remarkable; and efpecially towards the conclufion of the exercife, divers perfons were much affected.

Adminiftered the facrament of the Lord's fupper to twenty three perfons of the Indians, (the number of men and women being nearly equal) divers others, to the number of five or fix, being now abfent at the Forks of Delaware, who would otherwife have communicated with us.

The ordinance was attended with great folemnity, and with a moft defirable tendernefs and affection. And it was remarkable that in the feafon of the performance of the facramental actions, efpecially in the diftribution of the bread, they feemed to be affected in a moft lively manner, as if Chrift had been really crucified before them. And the words of the inftitution when repeated and enlarged upon in the feafon of the adminiftration, feemed to meet with the fame reception, to be entertained with the fame full and firm belief and affectionate engagement of foul, as if the Lord Jefus Chrift himfelf had been prefent, and had perfonally fpoken to them.

The affections of the communicants, although confiderably raifed, were notwithftanding agreeably regulated, and kept within proper bounds. So that there was a fweet, gentle and affectionate melting, without any indecent or boifterous commotion of the paffions.

Having refted fome time after the adminiftration of the facrament, (being extremely tired with the neceffary neceſſary prolixity of the work,) I walked from house to house, and conversed particularly with most of the communicants, and found they had been almost universally refreshed at the Lord's table, as with new wine. And never did I see such an appearance of christian love among any people in all my life. It was so remarkable, that one might well have cried with an agreeable surprise, Behold how they love one another! I think there could be no greater tokens of mutual affection among the people of God in the early days of christianity, than what now appeared here. The sight was so desirable, and so well becoming the gospel, that nothing less could be said of it, than that it was *the doing of the Lord*, the genuine operations of him *who is love!*

Toward night discoursed again on the forementioned Tit. ii. 14. and insisted on the immediate end and design of Christ's death, viz. *That he might redeem his people from all iniquity*, &c.

This appeared to be a season of divine power among us. The religious people were much refreshed, and seemed remarkably tender and affectionate, full of love, joy, peace, and desires of being completely *redeemed from all iniquity;* so that some of them afterwards told me, they had never felt the like before. Convictions also appeared to be revived in many instances; and divers persons were awakened whom I had never observed under any religious impressions before.

Such was the influence that attended our assembly, and so unspeakably desirable the frame of mind that many enjoyed in the divine service, that it seemed almost grievous to conclude the publick worship. And the congregation, when dismissed, although it was then almost dark, appeared loth to leave the place and employments that had been rendered so dear to them

them by the benefits enjoyed, while a blessed quickening influence distilled upon them.

And upon the whole, I must say, I had great satisfaction with relation to the administration of this ordinance in divers respects. I have abundant reason to think, that those who came to the Lord's table, had a good degree of doctrinal knowledge of the nature and design of the ordinance; and that they acted understandingly in what they did.

In the preparatory services I found (I may justly say) uncommon freedom in opening to their understandings and capacities, the covenant of grace, and in shewing them the nature of this ordinance as a seal of that covenant: Although many of them knew of no such thing as a seal before my coming among them, or at least of the use and design of it in the common affairs of life. They were likewise thoroughly sensible that it was no more than a seal or sign, and not the real body and blood of Christ. That it was designed for the refreshment and edification of the soul, and not for the feasting of the body. They were also acquainted with the end of the ordinance, that they were therein called to commemorate the dying love of Christ, &c.

And this competency of doctrinal knowledge, together with their grave and decent attendance upon the ordinance; their affectionate melting under it; and the sweet and christian frame of mind they discovered consequent upon it, gave me great satisfaction respecting my administration of it to them.

And O what a sweet and blessed season was this! God himself, I am persuaded, was in the midst of his people, attending his own ordinances: And I doubt not but many, in the conclusion of the day, could say with their whole hearts, Verily, *a day thus spent in God's house, is better than a thousand* elsewhere. There seemed to be but one heart among
the

the pious people! The sweet union, harmony, and endearing love and tenderness subsisting among them, was, I thought, the most lively emblem of the heavenly world, I had ever seen.

April 28.—Concluded the sacramental solemnity with a discourse upon John xiv. 15. *If ye love me, keep my commandments.* At which time there appeared a very agreeable tenderness in the audience in general, but especially in the communicants. O how free, how engaged and affectionate did these appear in the service of God: They seemed willing to have their *ears bored to the door posts of God's house,* and to be his servants forever.

Observing numbers in this excellent frame, and the assembly in general affected, and that by a divine influence, I thought it proper to improve this advantageous season, as Hezekiah did the desirable season of his great passover, 2 Chron xxxi. in order to promote the blessed reformation begun among them; and to engage those that appeared serious and religious, to persevere therein; and accordingly proposed to them, that they should renewedly enter into covenant before God, that they would watch over themselves and one another, lest they should dishonour the name of Christ by falling into sinful and unbecoming practices. And especially that they would watch against the sin of drunkenness, *the sin that easily besets them,* and the temptations leading thereto; as well as the appearance of evil in that respect. They cheerfully complied with the proposal, and explicitly joined in that covenant. Whereupon I proceeded in the most solemn manner I was capable of, to call God to witness respecting their sacred engagement; and minded them of the greatness of the guilt they would contract to themselves in the violation of it; as well as observed to them, that God would be a terrible witness against those who should presume to do so, in the *great and notable day of the Lord*.

It was a season of amazing solemnity! And a divine awe appeared upon the face of the whole assembly in this transaction! Affectionate sobs, sighs and tears were now frequent in the audience: And I doubt not but that many silent cries were then sent up to the Fountain of grace, for supplies of grace sufficient for the fulfilment of these solemn engagements.

Baptized six children this day.

Lord's Day, May 4.—My people being now removed to their lands, mentioned in my Journal of March 24, where they were then, and have since been making provision for a compact settlement, in order to their more convenient enjoyment of the gospel, and other means of instruction, as well as the comforts of life: I this day visited them (being now obliged to board with an English family at some distance from them,) and preached to them in the forenoon from Mark iv. 5. Endeavoured to shew them the reason there was to fear left many promising appearances and hopeful beginnings in religion, might prove abortive, like the *seed dropped upon stony places*.

May 9.—Preached from John v. 40. in the open wilderness; the Indians having as yet no house for publick worship in this place, nor scarce any shelters for themselves. Divine truths made considerable impressions upon the audience, and it was a season of solemnity, tenderness, and affection.

May 19.—Visited and preached to my people from Acts xx. 18. 19. And endeavoured to rectify their notions about religious affections: Shewing them on the one hand, the desirableness of religious affection, tenderness and fervent engagement in the worship and service of God, when such affection flows from a true spiritual discovery of divine glories; from a justly affecting sense of the transcendent excellency

excellency and perfections of the blessed God ; a view of the glory and lovelinefs of the great Redeemer : And that fuch views of divine things, will naturally excite us to *ferve the Lord with* many *tears*, with much affection and fervency, and yet with all humility of mind. And on the other hand, obferving the finfulnefs of feeking after high affections immediately, and for their own fakes, that is, of making them the object our eye and heart is nextly and principally fet upon, when the glory of God ought to be fo. Shewed them, that if the heart be directly and chiefly fixed on God, and the foul engaged to glorify him, fome degree of religious affection will be the effect and attendant of it. But to feek after affection, directly and chiefly to have the heart principally fet upon that, is to place it in the room of God and his glory. If it be fought that others may take notice of and admire us for our fpirituality and forwardnefs in religion, it is then abominable pride : If for the fake of feeling the pleafure of being affected, it is then idolatry and felf gratification. Laboured alfo to expofe the difagreeablenefs of thofe affections that are fometimes wrought up in perfons by the power of fancy and their own attempts for that purpofe, while I ftill endeavoured to recommend to them that religious affection, fervency and devotion, which ought to attend all our religious exercifes, and without which religion will be but an empty name and lifelefs carcafs.

Lord's Day, June 1, 1746.—Preached both forenoon and afternoon from Matth. xi. 27. 28. The prefence of God feemed to be in the affembly, and numbers were confiderably melted and affected under divine truths. There was a defirable appearance in the congregation in general, an earneft attention and agreeable tendernefs, and it feemed as if God defigned to vifit us with further fhowers of divine grace.

grace. I then baptized ten perfons, five adults and five children, and was not a little refreſhed with this *addition made to the church, of ſuch as* (I hope) *ſhall be ſaved.*

June 6.—Difcourfed to my people from part of Iſaiah liii. The divine prefence appeared to be amongſt us in ſome meaſure. Divers perſons were much melted and refreſhed; and one man in particular, who had long been under concern for his foul, was now brought to fee and feel in a very lively manner, the impoſſibility of doing any thing to help himfelf, or to bring him into the favour of God, by his tears, prayers and other religious performances, and found himfelf undone as to any power or goodneſs of his own, and that there was no way left him, but to leave himſelf with God to be difpofed of as he pleafed.

June 7.—Being defired by the Rev. Mr. William Tennent to be his affiſtant in the adminiſtration of the Lord's fupper: My people alfo being invited to attend the facramental folemnity, they cheerfully embraced the opportunity, and this day attended the preparatory fervices with me.

Lord's Day, June 8.—Moſt of my people, who had been communicants at the Lord's table before, being prefent at this facramental occafion, communicated, with others, in this holy ordinance, at the defire, and, I truſt, to the fatisfaction and comfort of numbers of God's people, who had longed to fee this day, and whofe hearts had rejoiced in this work of grace among the Indians, which prepared the way for what appeared fo agreeable at this time.

June 9.—A confiderable number of my people met together early in the day, in a retired place in the woods, and prayed, fang and converfed of divine things, and were feen by fome religious perfons of the white people, to be affected and engaged,

and

and divers of them in tears in thefe religious exercifes.

June 19.—Vifited my people with two of the reverend Correfpondents. Spent fome time in converfation with fome of them upon fpiritual things; and took fome care of their worldly concerns.

This day makes up a complete year from the firft time of my preaching to thefe Indians in New-Jerfey. What amazing things has God wrought in this fpace of time for thefe poor people! What a furprifing change appears in their tempers and behaviour! How are morofe and favage pagans, in this fhort fpace of time, transformed into agreeable, affectionate and humble chriftians! And their drunken and pagan howlings, turned into devout and fervent prayers and praifes to God! They *who were fometimes darknefs, are now become light in the Lord.* May they *walk as children of the light and of the day.* And *now to him that is of power to ftablifh them according to the gofpel and the preaching of Chrift ; to God only wife, be glory, through Jefus Chrift, forever and ever.* Amen.

BEFORE I conclude the prefent Journal, I would make a few general remarks upon what to me appears worthy of notice, relating to the continued work of grace among my people.

It is worthy of remark, that numbers of thefe people are brought to a ftrict compliance with the rules of morality and fobriety, and to a confcientious performance of the external duties of chriftianity, by the internal power and influence of divine truths (the peculiar doctrines of grace) upon their minds ; without their having thefe moral duties frequently repeated and inculcated upon them, and

the

the contrary vices particularly expofed and fpoken againft.

Thofe doctrines which had the moft direct tendency to humble the fallen creature; to fhew him the mifery of his natural ftate ; to bring him 'down to the foot of fovereign mercy, and to exalt the great Redeemer, difcover his tranfcendent excellency and infinite precioufnefs, and fo to recommend him to the finner's acceptance, were the fubject matter of what was delivered in publick and private to them, and from time to time repeated and inculcated upon them.

And God was pleafed to give thefe divine truths fuch a powerful influence upon the minds of thefe people, and fo to blefs them for the effectual awakening of numbers of them, that their lives were quickly reformed, without my infifting upon the precepts of morality, and fpending time in repeated harangues upon external duties.

When thefe truths were felt at heart, there was now no vice unreformed; no external duty neglected. Drunkennefs, the darling vice, was broken off from, and fcarce an inftance of it known among my hearers for months together. The abufive practice of hufbands and wives in putting away each other, and taking others in their ftead, was quickly reformed: So that there are three or four couple who have voluntarily difmiffed thofe they had wrongfully taken, and now live together again in love and peace. The fame might be faid of all other vicious practices. The reformation was general; and all fpringing from the internal influence of divine truths upon their hearts ; and not from any external reftraints, or becaufe they had heard thefe vices particularly expofed, and repeatedly fpoken againft: For fome of them I never fo much as mentioned ; particularly that of the parting of men and their wives, until fome, having their confcience awakened by God's

God's word, came, and of their own accord confeſſed themſelves guilty in that reſpect.

And as all vice was reformed upon their feeling
the power of theſe truths upon their hearts, ſo the
external duties of chriſtianity were complied with,
and conſcientiouſly performed from the ſame internal influence ; family prayer ſet up and conſtantly
maintained, unleſs among ſome few more lately
come, who had felt little of this divine influence.
This duty conſtantly performed even in ſome families where there were none but females, and ſcarce a
prayerleſs perſon to be found among near a hundred
of them. The Lord's Day ſeriouſly and religiouſly
obſerved, and care taken by parents to keep their
children orderly upon that ſacred day, &c. And
this, not becauſe I had driven them to the performance of theſe duties by a frequent inculcating
of them, but becauſe they had felt the power of
God's word upon their hearts, were made ſenſible
of their ſin and miſery, and thence could not but
pray, and comply with every thing they knew was
duty, from what they felt within themſelves.
When their hearts were touched with a ſenſe of their
eternal concernments, they could pray with great
freedom as well as fervency, without being at the
trouble firſt to learn ſet forms for that purpoſe. And
ſome of them who were ſuddenly awakened at their
firſt coming among us, were brought to pray and
cry for mercy with utmoſt importunity, without ever
being inſtructed in the duty of prayer, or ſo much
as once directed to a performance of it.

The happy effects of theſe peculiar doctrines of
grace which I have ſo much inſiſted upon with this
people, plainly diſcover, even to demonſtration, that
inſtead of their opening a door to licentiouſneſs (as
many vainly imagine, and ſlanderouſly inſinuate)
they have a direct contrary tendency : So that a cloſe
application,

application, a senfe and feeling of them, will have the moſt powerful influence towards the renovation and effectual reformation both of heart and life.

A view of the bleſſed effect of honeſt endeavours to bring home divine truths to the conſcience, and duly to affect the heart with them, has often minded me of thoſe words of our Lord, (which I have thought might be a proper exhortation for miniſters in reſpect of their treating with others, as well as for perſons in general with regard to themſelves) *Cleanſe firſt the inſide of the cup and platter, that the outſide may be clean alſo.* Cleanſe, ſays he, the inſide, that the outſide may be clean. q. d. The only effectual way to have the outſide clean, is, to begin with what is within; and if the fountain be purified, the ſtreams will naturally be pure. And moſt certain it is, if we can awaken in ſinners a lively ſenſe of their inward pollution and depravity; their need of a change of heart; and ſo engage them to ſeek after inward cleanſing, their external defilement will naturally be cleanſed; their vicious ways, of courſe, be reformed, and their converſation and behaviour become regular.

Now, although I cannot pretend that the reformation among my people, does, in every inſtance, ſpring from a ſaving change of heart, yet I may truly ſay, it flows from ſome heart affecting view and ſenſe of divine truths that all have had in a greater or leſſer degree.

I do not intend by what I have obſerved here, to repreſent the preaching of morality, and preſſing perſons to the external performance of duty, to be altogether unneceſſary and uſeleſs at any time; and eſpecially at times when there is leſs of divine power attending the means of grace: When for want of internal influences, there is need of external reſtraints. It is, doubtleſs, among the things that
ought

ought to be done, while *others are not to be left undone*. But what I principally defigned by this remark, was to difcover plain matter of fact, viz. That the reformation, the fobriety and external compliance with the rules and duties of chriftianity, appearing among my people, are not the effect of any mere doctrinal inftruction, or merely rational view of the beauty of morality, but from the internal power and influence that divine truths (the foul humbling doctrines of grace) have had upon their hearts.

It is remarkable alfo that God has fo continued and renewed the fhowers of his grace here; fo quickly fet up his vifible kingdom among thefe people; and fo fmiled upon them in relation to their acquirement of knowledge, both divine and human. It is now near a year fince the beginning of this gracious outpouring of the divine Spirit among them: And although it has often feemed to decline and abate for fome fhort fpace of time (as may be obferved by feveral paffages in my Journal, where I have endeavoured to note things juft as they appeared to me from time to time) yet the fhower has feemed to be renewed, and the work of grace revived again.

And as God has continued and renewed the fhowers of his grace among this people for fome time, fo he has with uncommon quicknefs fet up his vifible kingdom, and gathered himfelf a church in the midft of them. I have now baptized feventy feven perfons; whereof thirty eight are adults, and thirty nine children; and all within the fpace of eleven months paft. And it muft be noted that I have baptized no adults, but fuch as appeared to have a work of fpecial grace wrought in their hearts: I mean fuch who have had the experience not only of the awakening and humbling, but (in a judgment of charity) of the renewing and comforting influences of the divine Spirit.

I

I likewise administered the Lord's supper to a number of persons, who, I have abundant reason to think (as I elsewhere observed) were proper subjects of that ordinance, within the space of ten months and ten days after my first coming among these Indians in New-Jersey. And from the time that, I am informed, some of them were attending an idolatrous feast and sacrifice in honour to devils, to the time they sat down at the Lord's table (I trust) to the honour of God, was not more than a full year. Surely Christ's little flock here, so suddenly gathered from among pagans, may justly say, in the language of the church of old, *The Lord hath done great things for us, whereof we are glad.*

Much of the goodness of God has also appeared in relation to their acquirement of knowledge, both in religion and in the affairs of common life. There has been a wonderful thirst after christian knowledge prevailing among them in general, and an eager desire of being instructed in christian doctrines and manners. This has prompted them to ask many pertinent as well as important questions; the answers to which have tended much to enlighten their minds and promote their knowledge in divine things. Many of the doctrines I have delivered, they have queried with me about, in order to gain further light and insight into them; particularly the doctrine of predestination. And have from time to time manifested a good understanding of them, by the answers to the questions proposed to them in my chatechetical lectures.

They have likewise queried with me, respecting a proper method as well as proper matter of prayer, and expressions suitable to be made use of in that religious exercise; and have taken pains in order to the performance of this duty with understanding.

GENERAL REMARKS. 71

They have likewife taken pains, and appeared remarkably apt in learning to fing pfalm tunes, and are now able to fing with a good degree of decency in the worfhip of God.

They have alfo acquired a confiderable degree of ufeful knowledge in the affairs of common life: So that they now appear like rational creatures, fit for human fociety, free of that favage roughnefs and brutifh ftupidity, which rendered them very difagreeable in their pagan ftate.

And as they are defirous of inftruction, and furprifingly apt in the reception of it, fo Divine Providence has fmiled upon them in regard of proper means in order to it. The attempts made for the procurement of a fchool among them have been fucceeded, and a kind Providence has fent them a fchoolmafter, of whom I may juftly fay, *I know of no man like minded, who will naturally care for their ftate.*

He has generally thirty or thirty five children in his fchool: And when he kept an evening fchool (as he did while the length of the evenings would admit of it) he had fifteen or twenty people, married and fingle.

The children learn with furprifing readinefs; fo that their mafter tells me, he never had an Englifh fchool that learned, in general, comparably fo faft. There were not above two in thirty, although fome of them were very fmall, but what learned to know all the letters in the alphabet diftinctly, within three days after his entrance upon his bufinefs; and divers in that fpace of time learned to fpell confiderably: And fome of them fince the beginning of February laft (at which time the fchool was fet up) have learned fo much, that they are able to read in a Pfalter or Teftament without fpelling.

They are inftructed twice a week in the reverend affembly's fhorter catechifm, viz. on Wednefday and Saturday. And some of them, since the latter end of February, (at which time they began) have learned to say it pretty distinctly by heart considerably more than half through: And most of them have made some proficiency in it.

They are likewise instructed in the duty of secret prayer, and most of them constantly attend it night and morning, and are very careful to inform their master if they apprehend any of their little school mates neglect that religious exercise.

It is worthy to be noted also, to the praise of sovereign grace, that amidst so great a work of conviction, so much concern and religious affection, there has been no pravelency, nor indeed any considerable appearance of false religion, (if I may so term it) or heats of imagination, intemperate zeal, and spiritual pride; which corrupt mixtures too often attend the revival and powerful propagation of religion; and that there have been so very few instances of irregular and scandalous behaviour among those who have appeared serious.

But this work of grace has, in the main, been carried on with a surprising degree of purity, and freedom from trash and corrupt mixture. The religious concern that persons have been under has generally been rational and just; arising from a sense of their sins and exposedness to the divine displeasure on the account of them; as well as their utter inability to deliver themselves from the misery they felt and feared. And if there has been in any instances an appearance of irrational concern and perturbation of mind, when the subjects of it knew not why, yet there has been no prevalency of any such thing; and indeed I scarce know of any instance of that nature at all. And it is very remarkable, that although the concern of many persons under convictions of their perishing state has been very great

and

and preffing, yet I have never feen any thing like defperation attending it in any one inftance. They have had the moft lively fenfe of their undonenefs in themfelves; have been brought to give up all hopes of deliverance from themfelves; and their fpiritual exercifes leading hereto, have been attended with great diftrefs and anguifh of foul: And yet, in the feafons of the greateft extremity, there has been no appearance of defpair in any of them.

The comfort that perfons have obtained after their diftreffes, has likewife in general appeared folid, well grounded and fcriptural; arifing from a fpiritual and fupernatural illumination of mind, a view of divine things (in a meafure) as they are, a complacency of foul in the divine perfections, and a peculiar fatisfaction in the way of falvation, by free fovereign grace in the great Redeemer.

Their joys have feemed to rife from a variety of views and confiderations of divine things, although for fubftance the fame. Some, who under conviction feemed to have the hardeft ftruggles and heart rifings againft divine fovereignty, have feemed at the firft dawn of their comfort, to rejoice in a peculiar manner in that divine perfection, have been delighted to think that themfelves, and all things elfe, were in the hand of God, and that he would difpofe of them juft as he pleafed.

Others, who juft before their reception of comfort, have been remarkably oppreffed with a fenfe of their undonenefs and poverty, who have feen themfelves, as it were, falling down into remedilefs perdition, have been at firft more peculiarly delighted with a view of the freenefs and riches of divine grace, and the offer of falvation made to perifhing finners *without money and without price*.

Some have at firft appeared to rejoice efpecially in the wifdom of God, difcovered in the way of falvation by Chrift; it then appearing to them *a new and living way*, a way they had never thought nor had any juft conception of, until opened to them by the fpecial influence of the Divine Spirit. And fome of them, upon a lively fpiritual view of this way of falvation, have wondered at their paft folly in feeking falvation other ways, and have admired that they never faw this way of falvation before, which now appeared fo plain and eafy, as well as excellent, to them.

Others again have had a more general view of the beauty and excellency of Chrift, and have had their fouls delighted with an apprehenfion of his divine glory, as unfpeakably exceeding all they had ever conceived of before : Yet without fingling out (as it were) any one of the divine perfections in particular. So that although their comforts have feemed to arife from a variety of views and confiderations of divine glories, ftill they were fpiritual and fupernatral views of them, and not groundlefs fancies, that were the fpring of their joys and comforts.

Yet it muft be acknowledged, that when this work became fo univerfal and prevalent, and gained fuch general credit and efteem among the Indians, that Satan feemed to have little advantage of working againft it in his own proper garb; he then *transformed himfelf into an angel of light*, and made fome vigorous attempts to introduce turbulent commotions of the paffions in the room of genuine convictions of fin, imaginary and fanciful notions of Chrift, as appearing to the mental eye in a human fhape, and being in fome particular poftures, &c. in the room of fpiritual and fupernatural difcoveries of his divine glory and excellency, as well as divers other delufions. And I have reafon to think, that if thefe things had met with countenance and encouragement, there would have been a very confiderable harveft

GENERAL REMARKS.

vest of this kind of converts here. Spiritual pride also discovered itself in various instances. Some persons who had been under great affections, seemed very desirous from thence of being thought truly gracious; who, when I could not but express to them my fears respecting their spiritual states, discovered their resentments to a considerable degree upon that occasion. There also appeared in one or two of them an unbecoming ambition of being teachers of others. So that Satan has been a busy adversary here as well as elsewhere. But blessed be God, though something of this nature has appeared yet nothing of it has prevailed, nor indeed made any considerable progress at all. My people are now apprized of these things, are acquainted that Satan in such a manner *transformed himself into an angel of light* in the first season of the great outpouring of the Divine Spirit in the days of the apostles, and that something of this nature, in a greater or lesser degree, has attended almost every revival and remarkable propagation of true religion ever since. And they have learned so to distinguish between the gold and dross, that the credit of the latter is *trod down like the mire of the streets:* And it being natural for this kind of stuff to die with its credit, there is now scarce any appearance of it among them.

And as there has been no prevalency of irregular heats, imaginary notions, spiritual pride, and satanical delusions, among my people, so there has been very few instances of scandalous and irregular behaviour among those who have made a profession, or even an appearance of seriousness. I do not know of more than three or four such persons that have been guilty of any open misconduct, since their first acquaintance with christianity, and not one that persists in any thing of that nature. And perhaps the remarkable purity of this work in the latter respect, its freedom from frequent inftances of fcandal, is very much owing to its purity in the former refpect, its freedom from corrupt mixtures of fpiritual pride, wild fire and delufion, which naturally lay a foundation for fcandalous practices.

May this bleffed work in the power and purity of it prevail among the poor Indians here, as well as fpread elfewhere, until their remoteft tribes fhall *fee the falvation of God*. Amen.

ENUMERATING fome of the difficulties which obftructed his fuccefs in chriftianizing the Indians, Mr. Brainerd fays,

I have met with great difficulty in my work among thefe Indians, from the rooted averfion to chriftianity that generally prevails among them. They are not only brutifhly ftupid and ignorant of divine things, but many of them are obftinately fet againft chriftianity, and feem to abhor even the chriftian name.

This averfion to chriftianity arifes partly from the view of the immorality and vicious behaviour of many who are called chriftians. They obferve that horrid wickednefs in nominal chriftians, which the light of nature condemns in themfelves: And not having diftinguifhing views of things, are ready to look upon all the white people alike, and to condemn them alike for the abominable practices of fome. Hence, when I have attempted to treat with them about chriftianity, they have frequently objected the fcandalous practices of chriftians, and caft in my teeth all they could think of that was odious in the conduct of any of them. Have obferved to me, that the white people lie, defraud, fteal, and drink, worfe than the Indians: That

they

they have taught the Indians thefe things, efpecially the latter of them; who before the coming of the Englifh, knew of no fuch thing as ftrong drink: That the Englifh have by thefe means, made them quarrel, and kill one another, and in a word, brought them to the practice of all thofe vices that now prevail among them. So that they are now vaftly more vicious, as well as much more miferable, than they were before the coming of the white people into the country.

Thefe, and fuch like objections, they frequently make againft chriftianity, which are not eafily anfwered to their fatisfaction; many of them being facts too notoriously true.

The only way I have to take in order to furmount this difficulty, is, to diftinguifh between nominal and real chriftians, and to fhew them that the ill conduct of many of the former proceeds not from their being chriftians, but from their being chriftians only in name, not in heart, &c. To which it has fometimes been objected, that if all thofe who will cheat the Indians, are chriftians only in name, there are but few left in the country to be chriftians in heart. This, and many other of the remarks they pafs upon the white people, and their mifcarriages, I am forced to own, and cannot but grant, that many nominal chriftians are more abominably wicked than the Indians. But then I attempt to fhow them that there are fome who feel the power of chriftianity, that are not fo. And I afk them when they ever faw me guilty of the vices they complain of, and charge chriftians in general with. But ftill the great difficulty is, that the people who live back in the country neareft to them, and the traders that go among them, are generally of the moft irreligious and vicious fort, and the conduct of one or two perfons, be it never fo exemplary, is not fufficient to counterbalance the vicious behaviour of so many of the same denomination, and so to recommend christianity to pagans.

Another thing that serves to make them more averse to christianity, is a fear of being enslaved. They are, perhaps, some of the most jealous people living, and extremely averse to a state of servitude, and hence are always afraid of some design forming against them. Besides, they seem to have no sentiments of generosity, benevolence and goodness: That if any thing be proposed to them, as being for their good, they are ready rather to suspect that there is at bottom some design forming against them, than that such proposals flow from good will to them, and a desire of their welfare. And hence, when I have attempted to recommend christianity to their acceptance, they have sometimes objected, that the white people have come among them, have cheated them out of their lands, driven them back to the mountains, from the pleasant places they used to enjoy by the sea side, &c. That therefore they have no reason to think the white people are now seeking their welfare; but rather that they have sent me out to draw them together under a pretence of kindness to them, that they may have an opportunity to make slaves of them as they do of the poor negroes, or else to ship them on board their vessels, and make them fight with their enemies, &c. Thus they have oftentimes construed all the kindness I could shew them, and the hardships I have endured in order to treat with them about christianity. "He never would (say they) take all this pains to do us good; he must have some wicked design to hurt us some way or other." And to give them assurance of the contrary, is not an easy matter, while there are so many, who (agreeable to their apprehension) are only seeking their own, not the good of others.

To remove this difficulty I inform them, that I am not sent out among them by those persons in these provinces, who, they suppose, have cheated them out of their lands, but by pious people at a great distance, who never had an inch of their lands, nor ever thought of doing them any hurt, &c.

But here will arise so many frivolous and impertinent questions, that it would tire one's patience, and wear out one's spirits to hear them; such as that, "But why did not these good people send you to teach us before, while we had our lands down by the sea side, &c? If they had sent you then, we should likely have heard you and turned christians." The poor creatures still imagining that I should be much beholding to them in case they would hearken to christianity, and insinuating that this was a favour they could not now be so good as to shew me, seeing they had received so many injuries from the white people.

Another spring of aversion to christianity in the Indians, is, their strong attachment to their own religious notions, (if they may be called religious) and the early prejudices they have imbibed in favour of their own frantick and ridiculous kind of worship. What their notions of God are, in their pagan state, is hard precisely to determine. I have taken much pains to inquire of my christian people whether they, before their acquaintance with christianity, imagined there was a plurality of great invisible powers, or whether they supposed but one such being, and worshipped him in a variety of forms and shapes: But cannot learn any thing of them so distinct as to be fully satisfying upon the point. Their notions in that state were so prodigiously dark and confused, that they seemed not to know what they thought themselves. But so far as I can learn, they had a notion of a plurality of invisible deities, and paid some kind of homage to them promiscuously,

under

under a great variety of forms and shapes. And it is certain, those who yet remain pagans pay some kind of superstitious reverence to beasts, birds, fishes, and even reptiles; that is, some to one kind of animal and some to another. They do not indeed suppose a divine power essential to, or inherent in these creatures, but that some invisible beings (I cannot learn that it is always one such being only, but divers; not distinguished from each other by certain names, but only notionally) communicate to these animals a great power, either one or other of them, (just as it happens) or perhaps sometimes all of them, and so make these creatures the immediate authors of good to certain persons. Whence such a creature becomes sacred to the persons to whom he is supposed to be the immediate author of good, and through him they must worship the invisible powers, though to others he is no more than another creature. And perhaps another animal is looked upon to be the immediate author of good to another, and consequently he must worship the invisible powers in that animal. And I have known a pagan burn fine tobacco for incense, in order to appease the anger of that invisible power which he supposed presided over rattlesnakes, because one of these animals was killed by another Indian near his house.

But after the strictest inquiry respecting their notions of the Deity, I find, that in ancient times, before the coming of the white people, some supposed there were four invisible powers who presided over the four corners of the earth. Others imagined the sun to be the only deity, and that all things were made by him: Others at the same time having a confused notion of a certain body or fountain of deity, somewhat like the anima mundi, so frequently mentioned by the more learned ancient heathens, diffusing itself to various animals, and even to inanimate

mate things, making them the immediate authors of good to certain perfons, as was before obferved with refpect to various fuppofed deities. But after the coming of the white people, they feemed to fuppofe there were three deities, and three only, becaufe they faw people of three different kinds of complexion, viz. Englifh, Negroes and themfelves.

It is a notion pretty generally prevailing among them, that it was not the fame God made them who made us; but that they were made after the white people; which further fhews, that they imagine a plurality of divine powers. And I fancy they fuppofe their god gained fome fpecial fkill by feeing the white people made, and fo made them better: For it is certain they look upon themfelves and their methods of living (which, they fay, their god exprefsly prefcribed for them) vaftly preferable to the white people, and their methods. And hence will frequently fit and laugh at them, as being good for nothing elfe but to plough, and fatigue themfelves with hard labour; while they enjoy the fatisfaction of ftretching themfelves on the ground, and fleeping as much as they pleafe, and have no other trouble but now and then to chafe the deer, which is often attended with pleafure rather than pain. Hence, by the way, many of them look upon it as difgraceful for them to become chriftians, as it would be efteemed among chriftians for any to become pagans. And now although they fuppofe our religion will do well enough for us, becaufe prefcribed by our God, yet it is no ways proper for them, becaufe not of the fame make and original. This they have fometimes offered as a reafon why they did not incline to hearken to chriftianity.

They feem to have fome confufed notion about a future ftate of exiftence, and many of them imagine that

that the Chichung (i. e. The shadow) or what survives the body, will at death go southward, and in an unknown, but curious place, will enjoy some kind of happiness, such as hunting, feasting, dancing, and the like. And what they suppose will contribute much to their happiness in that state is, that they shall never be weary of those entertainments. It seems by this notion of their going southward to obtain happiness, as if they had their course into these parts of the world from some very cold climate, and found the further they went southward the more comfortable they were; and thence concluded, that perfect felicity was to be found further towards the same point.

They seem to have some faint and glimmering notion about rewards and punishments, or at least happiness and misery in a future state, that is, some that I have conversed with, though others seem to know of no such thing. Those that suppose this, seem to imagine that most will be happy, and that those who are not so, will be punished only with privation, being only excluded the walls of that good world where happy souls shall dwell.

These rewards and punishments they suppose to depend entirely upon their conduct with relation to the duties of the second table, i. e. their behaviour towards mankind, and seem, so far as I can see, not to imagine that they have any reference to their religious notions or practices, or any thing that relates to the worship of God. I remember I once consulted a very ancient, but intelligent Indian, upon this point, for my own satisfaction; asked him whether the Indians of old times had supposed there was any thing of the man that would survive the body. He replied, Yes. I asked him, where they supposed its abode would be. He replied, It would go southward. I asked him further, whether it would be happy there.

there. He answered, after a considerable pause, that the souls of good folks would be happy, and the souls of bad folks miserable. I then asked him, who he called bad folks. His answer (as I remember) was, those who lie, steal, quarrel with their neighbours, are unkind to their friends, and especially to aged parents, and in a word, such as are a plague to mankind. These were his bad folks; but not a word was said about their neglect of divine worship, and their badness in that respect.

They have indeed some kind of religious worship, are frequently offering sacrifices to some supposed invisible powers, and are very ready to impute their calamities in the present world, to the neglect of these sacrifices; but there is no appearance of reverence and devotion in the homage they pay them; and what they do of this nature, seems to be done only to appease the supposed anger of their deities, to engage them to be placable to themselves, and do them no hurt, or at most, only to invite these powers to succeed them in those enterprises they are engaged in respecting the present life. So that in offering these sacrifices, they seem to have no reference to a future state, but only to present comfort.

What further contributes to their aversion to christianity, is, the influence that their powwows (conjurers or diviners) have upon them. These are a sort of persons who are supposed to have a power of foretelling future events, of recovering the sick, at least oftentimes, and of charming, enchanting, or poisoning persons to death, by their magick divinations. And their spirit, in its various operations, seems to be a satanical imitation of the spirit of prophecy that the church in early ages was favoured with. Some of these diviners are endowed with this spirit in infancy. Others in adult age. It seems not to depend upon their own will, nor to be acquired.

ed by any endeavours of the person who is the subject of it, although it is supposed to be given to children sometimes in consequence of some means the parents use with them for that purpose: One of which is to make the child swallow a small living frog, after having performed some superstitious rites and ceremonies upon it. They are not under the influence of this spirit always alike; but it comes upon them at times. And those who are endowed with it, are accounted singularly favoured.

These things serve to fix them down in their idolatry, and to make them believe there is no safety to be expected, but by their continuing to offer such sacrifices. And the influence that these powwows have upon them, either through the esteem or fear they have of them, is no small hindrance to their embracing christianity.

F I N I S.

www.ingramcontent.com/pod-product-compliance
Lightning Source LLC
Chambersburg PA
CBHW051735300426
44115CB00007B/575